Through Different Eyes

Through Different Eyes

Black and White Perspectives on American Race Relations

Edited by
PETER I. ROSE, STANLEY ROTHMAN,
AND WILLIAM J. WILSON

Oxford University Press
London Oxford New York

OXFORD UNIVERSITY PRESS

London Oxford New York
Glasgow Toronto Melbourne Wellington
Cape Town Ibadan Nairobi Dar es Salaam Lusaka Addis Ababa
Delhi Bombay Calcutta Madras Karachi Lahore Dacca
Kuala Lumpur Singapore Hong Kong Tokyo

The following essays are reprinted by the kind permission of their original publishers:

"Black Nationalists" by J. Herman Blake, published under the title "Black Nationalism" in the Annals of the American Academy of Political and Social Science, March 1969, Volume 382.

"White Professors" by Robert Blauner, published under the title "Race and the White Professor" in *Racial Oppression in America* by Robert Blauner, copyright © 1972 by Robert Blauner. Reprinted by permission of Harper & Row, Publishers, Inc.

"Prison Personnel" by Winston E. Moore, published under the title "My Cure for Prison Riots: In-Prison Racism." Reprinted by permission of *Ebony Magazine*. Copyright 1971 by Johnson Publishing Company, Inc.

"The White Ethnics" by Paul Welks, published under the title "As the Blacks Move In, the Ethnics Move Out" in *The New York Times Magazine,* January 24, 1971. Copyright © 1971 by The New York Times Company.

"The Irish" by Andrew M. Greeley, published under the title "A Most Distressful Nation" in the October 1971 issue of *Dissent*. Copyright © 1971 by Oxford University Press, Inc.

This reprint, 1974-2

Library of Congress Catalogue Card Number: 73-82673
First published by Oxford University Press, New York, 1973
First issued as an Oxford University Press paperback, 1974
Printed in the United States of America

PREFACE

This book came about as a result of a variety of personal and professional experiences. By way of introduction it should be noted that two of us are white, one is black; one of us comes from a middle-class background, two from the working class. One of us is a city boy from Brooklyn, one from a small town in Pennsylvania, one from upstate New York. We went to very different types of undergraduate institutions: one to a city college near home, one to a small private school in the Midwest, one to a large private university. Our doctoral degrees are from Cornell, Harvard, and Washington State, and we have lived and conducted research in many different communities in this country and abroad.

We have many things in common, too. We are all social scientists (two are sociologists, one is a political scientist); each has taught and written about race relations in the United States; two of us have been directly involved in the establishment of Black Studies Departments, and all have had ambivalent feelings about certain trends that have paralleled their development. Moreover, as friends and occasional colleagues in the "Five College Area" of Western Massachusetts, we have discussed many aspects of the Civil Rights Movement, Black Power, the character of ethnic stratification in America, the debate over group rights *vs.* individual rights, and the seeming resurgence of ethnicity affecting various groups, black and brown and red and white. In a very real sense this volume is a result of our differences *and* our mutual concerns.

Several years ago we thought it would be an interesting exercise to try to gather a number of views of fellow social scientists whose own racial and social and political backgrounds were at least as diverse as our own. The idea grew into a plan.

We would select some 18 to 20 individuals, half of them black, half white, and invite them to offer assessments of the perceptions of people in different sectors of American society, for example, inner-city dwellers, white southerners, welfare workers, black immigrants, radical students, and others. Once the papers were collected and made available, readers would (hopefully) find themselves in that bewildering but critical position of the Japanese magistrate in the story of *Rashomon.* The various arguments could be studied and some sense might be made of the differing views.

The plan was spelled out in a proposal, and Oxford University Press agreed to publish the results.

A number of persons were asked to join us, all noted for their writing on one or more aspects of the general problem of race and ethnicity. Most agreed immediately and many stayed with the project. (Some of those we had wanted were unable to sign on owing to the press of other commitments; others agreed but later had to drop out because they, too, were spreading themselves too thin. On three occasions we found we had to substitute previously published essays for ones that were promised but never delivered.)

It took two years longer than we had planned to complete the gathering and editing of all papers and to get the manuscripts to the publisher and through the various stages of publication. We should have been prepared for such delays but, like some of our more punctual authors, we sometimes feared that *Through Different Eyes* would never see the light of day.

Now, at last, the book is finished. It is as varied in style and tone and "feel" as we had envisaged. It is also incomplete, for there are many voices that could have been added and many other interpretations that might have been included. Still, we think that the book is both informative and provocative and that the desire to place differing views of race in America in the late 1960's and early 1970's in juxtaposition has been at least partially realized.

That we have reached this point is in no small measure due to the contributions of our authors, the labors of our editors, and the patience of our respective families.

July 1973

PETER I. ROSE
STANLEY ROTHMAN
WILLIAM J. WILSON

CONTENTS

ON THE CAMPUS

EPILOGUE

Prologue

Through Different Eyes

PETER I. ROSE

Tocqueville was right.

One hundred and twenty-five years ago the French observer predicted that the racial situation in the United States would be a continuing source of domestic unrest. He doubted that even with the emancipation of slaves and the granting of full citizenship, whites and blacks would ever accept one another as brothers. The majority of whites would never overcome their views of the innateness of their own superiority; the majority of blacks would never lose their enmity for the humiliation and suffering they had experienced.

I

Yet so much has happened to America and the composition of her people that even saying that Tocqueville was right and that racism remains abroad in the land is to oversimplify the situation. For one thing, in Tocqueville's time most of the people here were "Anglo-Saxon" or "Negro." That is certainly not the case today. When he visited America, most people lived in small towns or on farms (and plantations) in a preindustrial world that could not even envisage the technological and social revolutions that were to come. And, of course, the American Ideal itself was of a very different nature. No center of empire, the United States was then seen as a crude, if open, frontier which only the brave or the foolish, the refugee, or the slave, would call home. It was a long way from "Columbia, the Gem . . ." to "Amerikkka," as the country was to be called by its most vociferous critics of the 1960's. Many things happened to the country and her people (some actually foreseen by Tocqueville, others unimagined). Consider the following:

The slave trade was ended. The Civil War was fought and the Union survived, although the South was never to be the same again. Emancipation freed the slaves and Radical Reconstruction gave them hope—a hope that was soon to be dashed by the steady chipping away of newly acquired privileges. Southern and Eastern European immigrants broadened the *vox populi* and added competition in the marketplace. Industrialization encouraged the first substantial northward trek of former slaves and their children, and black ghettoes began to appear alongside or, as often, in the wake of the white ones. Booker T. Washington, "the Great Compromiser," began to lose favor as his adversary, W. E. B. DuBois, helped to found the inter-racial National Association for the Advancement of Colored People, the NAACP, ushering in a new era of civil rights protest.

The Great War was fought and more blacks moved north, sometimes as strike breakers. The soldiers returned and told the "niggers" to go back home. Race riots occurred and through the years continued to be the most blatant manifestations of the intergroup tensions at flashpoint. But all was not conflict, even then.

The Jazz Age brought many avant-garde ideas—preachers, profiteers, and political awakening; Marcus Garvey and his black legions; and, above all, a cultural renaissance in Harlem. For the second time it seemed as if the American people, at least some of them, were opening their minds to the fact that blacks, too, had a cultural style and a point of view to share. But it all came crashing down in the Great Depression when everyone went on the dole and some, like Richard Wright, joined The Party.

Then there was FDR and a "New Deal" for everyone, though black people never gained what they thought they had been promised. War once again. Executive Order 8802 requiring non-discrimination in federal employment . . . and still the military (a federal force!) remained as segregated as ever.

In the postwar period the economy boomed and blacks shared, if marginally, in the prosperity. Absolute gains were tremendous; relative gains proved less so, although there was decided improvement in social and economic status. Black Americans began to look back to Africa and many hoped that the independence movement there would help to get their fellow citizens to accelerate *their* demands for *Uhuru* (or "Freedom Now!"). There was more northward migration; more westward movement; more blackening of the central cities and white flight to the suburbs. There were challenges to recalcitrant America, bitter reactions (Paul Robeson who once sang Earl Robinson's "Ballad for Americans," lost faith, became a communist sympathizer, and was denounced), and some progress—or so it seemed. A new liberalism was abroad in the land. White men in black face like Amos 'n' Andy, and black ones in white mold like Stepin' Fetchit, no longer were to be heard or seen. "Home of the Brave" and "Pinky" and "Gentleman's Agreement" substituted new stereotypes of bright, compassionate, white-washed Negroes (and emancipated Jews) for the old slouches and shylocks. (And in time the in-joke would be "Guess who's coming to dinner?"). It was all of a piece.

So, in a way, was the fact that highly educated and carefully selected Jackie Robinson was to be the first black man to play in the major leagues ("How decent we were becoming") and the late Ralph Bunche held high office in the United Nations ("Anyone can make it"). Harry S. Truman ordered the army to be integrated, too . . . but it was three years later when a reluctant President Eisenhower implemented the order. Then Brown challenged the Board of Education in Topeka, and in the civil rights case of the century the Supreme Court of the United States unanimously supported him. "Separate can never be equal." Civil rights leaders, clergymen, professional liberals believed that the millennium had arrived.

But progress was slow and the speed far from deliberate. New words became daily news copy, words like "interposition" and "nullification." CORE (the Congress of Racial Equality) increased its challenge and its Freedom Riders were beaten. The Civil Rights movement grew, new organizations emerged (like the Southern Christian Leadership Conference and the Student Non-Violent Co-ordinating Committee), and new leaders, black and white, began to assert the efficacy of nonviolent direct action. Martin Luther King became a new symbol for justice at home and peace in the world

("I have a dream"), and for the first time since the early Chicago days of the Fellowship of Reconciliation the fight to end slavery's legacy and to promote peace ("Hell, no, we won't go") were joined. New voices were added, some now but dimly remembered; H. Rapp Brown and Stokely Carmichael, the Reverend Galamison and Rhody McCoy, Julian Bond, Leroi Jones, Ron Karenga, Roy Ennis, and George Wiley. And Malcolm X. There were riots in Harlem and Rochester and Watts and Hough and Detroit and Newark—and there was backlash. There was Black Power and Black Pride; Black Panthers in the streets, Black Studies on the campus, and in every political and professional organization a Black Caucus. By 1970 it had become a time to be black (if you were ever a Negro), and a time to be white if you weren't. Indeed, by 1970 polarization seemed to reach new heights (or depths), with rising anxiety and fear and rage marking an America, one nation, deeply divided.

II

These, then, were the people and the events. At least they were the most newsworthy, publicly recounted ones; the highlights of the various episodes in the history of race relations which occurred between the Ages of Jackson and Richard Milhous Nixon. Inevitably such an abbreviated listing tends to oversimplify complex situations and relationships. As such it only tells a part of the story. For example, it does not (and cannot) tell what it meant to be a former slave in 1866—or, for that matter, what it meant to be a former slaveholder. It does not express the meaning of thinking that you had finally been assured of land and education and a voice in the running of your community by northern friends, only to have Jim Crow laws put in as they pulled out. Such notations do not give adequate representation to the views of thousands who came to America during the latter half of the nineteenth century, the new immigrants who rarely saw a Negro and whose only real connection with black people was symbolic: they shared his plight of being seen as a source of cheap labor (when times were good) or as convenient scapegoats (when times were bad). Nor do they do justice to the fact that many blacks shared in the values of the wider society and strove mightily to achieve them, often seeking to emulate the ways of whites—sometimes even their appearances (with skin whiteners and "good" hair). It does not indicate the extent to which many southern whites actually had more in common with their black neighbors than with the damnyankees up north. Nor, finally, does it relate how fickle fortune can be.

Who would have thought that Bayard Rustin, the old socialist who accused W. E. B. DuBois of conservatism, would be marked as a sellout while DuBois would become the hero of the militant Left? Who would have believed that James Farmer, the founder of the Congress of Racial Equality, would be the first black to join the administration of a Richard M. Nixon? Who would have expected a mayor of New York to attempt to obtain urban peace by a coalition of WASP patricians, upper-middle-class Jews, and minority group members, then to turn around and join the party dominated by those he had most alienated, the white working class?

One wonders what might have happened had William Styron published his *Confessions of Nat Turner* ten years earlier, at a time when he might well have been praised by black critics for making a Nat Turner a Mosaic-like figure. (He was too late—Ché was the revolutionary hero of the day, not Moses.) Daniel P. Moynihan might have been lauded instead of damned. (Kenneth Clark was praised. He said pretty much the same things, relying on many of the same sources.) But then had it not been for shifting climates Charles Evers might never have become the Mayor of Fayette, Mississippi, nor Shirley Chisholm a candidate for the Presidency nor Angela Davis the most symbolic political person indicted on a capital charge since Sacco and Vanzetti.

How does one deal with the contradictions that have long existed on the racial front? There are, after all, white people who have fought to force the nation to honor its own ideals since the early days of the Abolition Movement, who have never accepted the general view about white superiority or, for that matter, black distinctiveness, who truly believe in the colorblind brotherhood of man.

How does one relate to the thinking that goes on in the mind of Klansmen who preach hate or preachers who speak of love—in their segregated parishes? What of the ambivalent sentiments of middle-class whites who pride themselves on their tolerance but keep asking (and not rhetorically) "Why can't they be like us?" And what about the feelings of those white immigrants far removed from slaving, from slaveholding, from segregation, who skimped and saved and tried to eke out their own meager living, whose own lives were consumed with the struggle to maintain their own shaky status in a highly competitive society, who were often too poor themselves to enjoy the luxury of liberal ideology, who now feel blacks are getting favored treatment of a kind they never received? And what of those working class people just out of the ghettoes themselves, who often fear the violence which they associate with the black poor, who feel they are being used to assuage the self-righteous indignation of good liberals far removed from the problems?

And what of blacks? No monolithic category of faceless men and women as they have long been—and still are—so often portrayed. The fact is that some internalized the status they were forced to occupy and acted out the "appropriate" roles, sometimes for generations. In doing this they often played into the self-fulfilling prophecy of whites who claimed blacks were different. And what of those who turn the argument inside out, saying they are different and are tired of being stuffed into the white man's bag?

Some blacks found their niches and others lived schizophrenically in two social worlds. Some found bittersweet solace in the unpaved sections of southern towns and in tenemented ghettoes where they lived and died (and continue to live and die) within the various strata of their caste-like society. Hanging on street corners, politicking, preaching, hustling, going to the factory or the farm, going downtown to work for the Man, going uptown to be with Brothers, becoming a Tom, or a Token, or a superfunky badass somebody. Becoming a nobody . . . and knowing it.

And what about those blacks who chafe at the restraints of discrimination, who seethe behind the various psychological and social barriers erected to keep them in their places, who seek and sometimes find short-lived release in stoning cops and burning stores on the streets of Watts or Detroit or Newark, who join the Panthers and become urban guerrillas. What about them?

III

Despite the fact of marked differences of style and structure within as between the black and white communities, despite the reality of quickly shifting conventional wisdoms ("Integration is the Way;" "Look Out White Man, Black Power's Gone Get Your Momma;" "There is but one race: the Human Race;" "Black is..."), despite the difficulty of making predictions when the future is being used as a guide to the past, certain themes persist. From the days of Tocqueville to the present if one is white and conservative one blames racial tensions on "them," the minority. If one is white and liberal, one is more apt to blame oneself ("What have we wrought?"). If truly radical, the system is obviously at fault. Thus, it can be asserted that anything whites do for or with any blacks is paternalism, while inaction (whether apathy or purposeful avoidance) is prejudice. It usually follows that anything blacks do is legitimate in that they are combating a rotten society.

There are counterparts in the black communities as well though, to be sure, the words conservative, liberal, and radical have different meaning as well as coloration!

This book is an attempt to get beneath the rhetoric and the stereotyped response, to see how conservatives and liberals and radicals (black and white) as well as students and teachers, professors and politicians and policemen, northerners and southerners, integrationists and separatists, see race relations today. In a very real sense this is a *Rashomon* approach to contemporary race relations. Here a number of black writers and a number of whites present their picture of the current scene as refracted through the prisms of those for whom they were asked to write.

At the outset, however, it should be recognized that in planning the book we were faced with a twofold problem. In asking people to write from a particular vantage point we purposely tried to delimit their frame of reference. Thus, while from their previous writings we knew that Joyce Ladner, Robert Blauner, Roy Bryce-Laporte, Lawrence Rosen, and others had strong personal opinions about a number of issues related to American race relations, they were asked only to represent the view of those in their assigned category (in the above cases this meant the inner-city blacks, white students, black immigrants, and policemen, respectively). Once the papers came in we realized that even our assignment demanded a sort of detachment that few of our chosen "spokesmen" were able to maintain. Each in his or her own way proved to be a rather strong advocate for a particular point of view. And so, in a sense, what we have here is *Rashomon* at various levels.

For a variety of reasons we felt it best to divide some of the essays according to subject rather than the color of the authors (and the color of those for whom they purported to speak). In some cases an arbitrary decision was made as to where to best place a particular essay. In most instances, however, they were rather easy to categorize.

All told, we are satisfied that we do have a series of papers on race relations in America as seen through different eyes. We hope our readers will be enlightened by the commentary, stimulated by the contradictions, and challenged by the authors to attempt their own dialogue as we have done ourselves in the Epilogue.

A Spectrum of Black Views

The Urban Poor

JOYCE LADNER

It is not unusual for racial, ethnic, religious, and nationality groups to view themselves from perspectives entirely different from those used by outside groups in viewing them. Differences in experiences, socialization patterns, and life histories all contribute to the varying images that groups develop vis-à-vis one another. Thus, one observes a disparity between the views of the middle and working classes; between the Catholics and Jewish religious groups; and between native- and foreign-born groups.

The field of race relations offers a great deal of insight into the ways in which different racial, ethnic, and nationality groups regard each other. There is probably no better way of demonstrating this than by focusing on the factors that have affected the vision of low-income Afro-Americans. First, no other minority group in the United States has suffered as has this group from negative stigmatizing labels (the gamut of labels running from social and mental to biological inferiority) rendering them open to political, economic, religious, and social exploitation. Second, the Black poor, being virtually a powerless group, have for the most part been unable to reject these labels. Thus, they have suffered at the hands of other groups without being able to fully present their own views. Finally, when allowed to express themselves about other social groups, and, most important, about themselves, their statements are frequently "misquoted" and often highly distorted. The inability of Afro-Americans to prevent the misrepresentation of their attitudes only reflected the general condition of the disfranchised, poverty-stricken masses whose destinies were, until recently, determined largely by the exploiting dominant ruling class.

In order to understand the dominant group's perpetuation of distorted ideas about poor Blacks, one must also understand the impact institutional racism has made upon the interpersonal and structural relations between Blacks and whites. Since the beginning of the Afro-American's sojourn in the United States, the relationship between him and Caucasians has been determined primarily by the dictates of race and color caste. The creation of subordinate and superordinate relations based upon color has so structured relationships that the entire society has been conditioned to perceive social relations essentially in terms of race. Today, it has become commonplace for the Afro-American masses to ascribe their plight to the institutional racism of the society, racism which has penetrated the core of politics, economics, religion, and culture. Institutional racism has been defined as:

> . . . the operating policies, priorities, and functions of an on-going system of normative patterns which serve to subjugate, oppress, and force dependence of individuals or groups by: (1) establishing and sanctioning unequal goals; and (2) sanctioning inequality in status as well as to goods and services.[1]

Blacks view institutionalized racism as the major determinant of race relations.

What perceptual differential do Afro-Americans possess and use to define, respond, and relate emotively to their physical and cultural environments? What, in fact, are the "different eyes" which characterize this group?

The "Black Perspective," as it has come to be known, is that conceptual and pragmatic tool utilized by the Black masses in both perceiving and operationalizing their world. One must emphasize the fact that the masses of Afro-Americans have always possessed a sharply different view of themselves than that held by the larger society. The Black Perspective went largely unrecognized by social scientists researching various aspects of Afro-American life, and where evidence of its existence was found, it was usually dismissed as irrelevant or explained away as a deviant phenomenon. Only during the last decade has any serious attempt been made to understand the Black Perspective by placing a badge of legitimacy on it, acknowledging it as one of the many cultural aspects of this pluralistic society.

The Black Perspective has its roots in the historical experiences of Black people in the United States. It grows out of two primary influences: (1) the Africanisms or African "survivals" transplanted from the West African societies (those of the slave-trading areas) and preserved during slavery; (2) segregation and the postslavery "isolation" from the larger American society to which Afro-Americans were subjugated.

Africans brought to the New World as captive slaves came with a long history of highly developed social organization. Historians date the earliest period of complex cultures in West Africa to 500 A.D., when the Ghana Kingdom flourished, some thousand years before the discovery of America. Complex cultures had existed on other parts of the African continent as early as 400 B.C., when the Sudanese civilization flourished along the Nile River. The latter included sophisticated institutions governing politics, distribution of wealth, marriage and family life, religion, and the general social life of tribal society. Customs and laws were so entrenched in these various African societies that by the time slave-trading began in the 16th century the African people who became captives were those who had been born and reared in a highly developed social organization. When the transplantation to American soil occurred, much of this culture was carried with them and retained, despite intensive efforts by the slave-holding overlords to crush all of its elements. The close familial bonds, religious expression, music, some language, dance, and art forms survived the slave experience to a degree and were assimilated into the mainstream of Afro-American life. Even today, some of these Africanisms can be recognized in a small number of isolated areas of the rural South, particularly off the coasts of Georgia and South Carolina, and to a much greater extent in the West Indies, notably in Haiti.

The second influence in the emergence of the Black Perspective was slavery itself, and the racial segregation and discrimination following its abolition. Slavery acted to forge a distinctive culture among Blacks and create an entirely new way of life that affected every social institution. It did not simply encourage or allow the slave to emulate the culture of his master because, in spite of how hard he may have tried to do so, his resources for achieving such a way of life were always minimal. Perhaps an even more important consideration is that slaves must have found this new way of life repulsive, certainly completely alien to their own cultural traditions. For example, one reads accounts of slaves escaping into wooded areas to observe their native religious rites, speaking to each other in their tribal languages, and using herbs to cure their ailments. These do not suggest that such practices still continue, for with time much of the old civilization was forgotten and/or assimilated into new cultural forms.

A most important outgrowth of the *old* and the *new* was the fusion of two different social realities. Because Afro-Americans were continually exposed to a dominant group's culture, they were able to perceive the world, to some extent, through that group's eyes. At the same time, their own social realities varied markedly. This phenomenon has been accurately described by the prominent Afro-American historian, W. E. B. DuBois, whose concept of "double consciousness" is now widely used. According to DuBois, Afro-Americans grow up with a "double consciousness" because they are exposed to two cultures—one black and one white. In 1903, he wrote:

> . . . The Negro is a sort of seventh son, born with a veil, and gifted with second sight in this American world,—in a world which yields him no true self-consciousness, but only lets him see himself through the revelation of the other world. It is a peculiar sensation, this double consciousness, this sense of always looking at one's self through the eyes of others, of measuring one's soul by the tape of a world that looks on in amused contempt and pity. One ever feels his twoness,—an American and a Negro; two souls, two thoughts, two unreconciled strivings, two warring ideals in one dark body whose dogged strength alone keeps it from being torn asunder.[2]

This dual perception of the world by Afro-Americans often creates ambivalence toward life. It is an ambivalence that one never entirely escapes because one's very existence is intricately interwoven with both the white and the black environments. However, this is less of a problem today than in the past because increasing numbers of Afro-Americans are refusing to view themselves through the eyes of white Americans. Instead, they are demanding that the "tape" used to measure one's soul—one's existence—be indigenous to their own people. White models can no longer fulfill this purpose. The perception which poor Blacks, residing in the so-called ghettos of the United States, have of race relations provides us with a good case study.

Regardless of all the apparent concern on the part of social scientists for understanding the problems facing the population under discussion, few white writers have attempted to allow Afro-Americans to interpret from their own perspective the phenomena which affect their lives. Notable among these phenomena are their perceptions of dominant-minority group relations and the full extent of racial oppression.

A common theme found in social-scientific studies devoted to Blacks is the observation that most of this population suffer from a weak self-image, a lack of ego-strength, and a feeling of "self-hatred" which frequently precludes their functioning adequately in the dominant society. This traditional viewpoint has ignored the conception that Afro-Americans regard themselves as highly resourceful people, not only capable of being acted upon, but also entirely qualified to create and shape the environment in which they live.

The problem of "self-hatred" among Blacks has been an hypothesis expressed by both Black and white psychiatrists, psychologists, and psychoanalysts. However, instead of viewing "self-hatred" as a problem emanating from the oppressive social structure, these scientists tend to trace its origin to the individual. Frantz Fanon, the late Algerian psychoanalyst and author, dealt with the warped psyches of Blacks who encounter the "superior" dominant culture, whether it be that of Algeria or the United States. Although Fanon recognized the psychological problems Blacks would encounter as members of the oppressed class, he was able to transcend the approach which treats Black personality problems in isolation from social or structural pressure, and focus on the psychic dilemmas encountered by Blacks caught between the influences of the dominant "superior" white culture and the cultural experience of the Black subculture.[3]

It is impossible for Blacks, born into a society that makes such a strong distinction between *white* and *Black* (and even between light and dark skin shades within the race), to grow up without, at some point, entertaining feelings of inferiority because they are not members of the majority group which has attached a high premium to white skin. To some extent, all Blacks must have made comparisons between the inferior, subjected status they occupy in society and the positive value and privileges automatically attached to being *white.* Even the most emotionally stable Black can probably recall his first, painful awareness of the lifelong restrictions which would be placed on him because of his color.

While it cannot be denied that the system of racial oppression has taken a heavy toll on the psychological and physical development of Black people, we can inquire, however, whether the impact has been as severe as some scholars maintain. The level of psychological impairment that has been projected in the literature is rarely approximated in real life. There appears to be a negative correlation between findings about Black identity and the *actual* existence of the problem. One of the most forceful rebuttals to the "self-hatred" thesis is advanced in the writings of Robert Coles, child psychiatrist, who has conducted research on Black youth. Coles maintains that the involvement of Black children in racial demonstrations enhances the development of a more stable, well-integrated personality.[4]

From 1964 to 1968, I undertook a study among low-income Black females in St. Louis, Missouri, interviewing about 100 subjects ranging from preadolescents to adults (but concentrating on adolescents), in an attempt to ascertain their views of racial and economic oppression.[5] I wanted to know what they considered the major barriers to their successful assimilation into American society. Specifically, I sought to understand through observation of their everyday behavior and their verbalizations in what manner they were affected by racism and most important, what adaptations they found necessary to make to these conditions.

When I began this study, I expected three basic types of responses to my queries concerning racial identification and the effects of oppression. To some extent, I had anticipated that responses about being poor Blacks would typify some of the stereotypes regarding feelings of inadequacy, worthlessness, and self-disparagement. I also felt that some would have been influenced by the Black consciousness movement which grew out of the civil rights movement of the past decade and would articulate "Black pride" sentiments. Still others would, I expected, be proud Blacks without having come under the influence of Black pride slogans and ideology. Many of these Blacks possessed an abundance of human resourcefulness and hope for improving their life chances. And the hatred, if present at all, instead of being directed inward, was directed toward the individuals and institutions that inflicted pain upon them. I must admit, however, that a small number of females did not fit this model, but were more akin to the stereotypes that fill much of the literature. Perhaps a good explanation of such females would be that they had tried to succeed in the dominant society, and, failing to do so, had given up hope and succumbed to the personal pressures and problems they faced.

A fairly common assumption of psychologists and psychiatrists is that Black women develop a negative self-image because of their Black skin tone, kinky hair, and broad facial features. These "liabilities" cause them to feel inferior and to express a desire to be white. Thus, one of my concerns was to find out to what extent my subjects wished to be white or felt psychologically crippled because they were Black. I asked all of them what it meant to be a poor Black girl. Some of the representative responses follow:

A thirteen-year-old said:

> I'm proud of being a Negro. I mean it's not bad to be a Negro and that's why I am proud. A lot of people ask me, "Don't you wish you were white? . . ." I say no. I ask them what's wrong with being a Negro. They say they don't know but they still want to know if I want to be a white person. . . . Some white people ask me that sometimes.

A fifteen-year-old stated:

> I feel that I'm just as good as the next person. I feel that a white person or someone of any other race, if they're as good as I am, well I feel that I'm even better. . . . I don't think there should be any setback just because I'm a Negro.

A sixteen-year-old responded:

> I feel good as a Negro. I think that we have special rights as everyone else because you know Thomas Jefferson said every man was created equal and I think that just being a Negro doesn't mean we can't have the finer things of life just as the white person does.

An eighteen-year-old answered:

> I feel very proud of it [being a Negro]. Nothing can be done about it so I have to feel proud about it myself. . . . I wouldn't change it if I could.

A fourteen-year-old felt:

> I'm glad that I'm a Negro. . . . Well, some white people dislike Negroes and some Negroes dislike white people. But to me it doesn't make any difference. Some white people are poorer than Negroes.

A fifteen-year-old was very specific about her position:

> I'm very fond of being a Negro because Negroes have much talent. . . . I was kind of glad to see that we have one Negro in the White House working and they can sing and dance, and do things just as well as white people can. I don't mind being poor . . . because I'm getting along and it doesn't matter to me. . . . I think my friends feel the same because I never hear any of them say anything like "I wish I was white." . . . To me a Negro knows how to have fun.

The most politically articulate girl, a seventeen-year-old, said:

> I see myself as being *not* an "Uncle Tom." . . . [That means to] believe in the white people. Believe that Negroes can't live without them; and, too, believe that I love the white people when they do not love nor like the Negro race. . . . We are not Negroes. We are "so-called" Negroes. That's the name they gave us. Our original name is Black. . . . If you look it up in the dictionary they say the people originally came from Africa and they are the so-called American Negroes. . . .

I asked her why she felt that Blacks had allowed themselves to be called "Negroes" without protesting. Her reply was:

> Some of them try to be white. Some of them make themselves up like white people. They just don't know that the Black race is trying to

> get more and more like the white race but the white race is trying to get more and more like the Black race.

A fifteen-year-old was very expressive on the subject:

> I've always been proud of being Black because I think it is a superior color. I never thought of being . . . well, you know, white is pure and Black is dirty. I've always thought of being Black as a way, a will. If you see someone Black it's not a dirty thing. . . . Black stands out against any color.

I asked her if she could describe how things had gotten better for Blacks in recent years. She said:

> Well, we are changing. We are seeing that there is a way. We are beginning to shape up. If you put anything in a cage where it can't go out and can't see anything on the outside, it is always going to think that this is the right way and that there is no other way but this one. But if you can see out of this cage and you see that this bird is flying not only from this end to the other but up and down, the other bird will go up and down and all around. We see now that we can go to college and other places to improve ourselves and we will.

Being Black has many negative consequences, even though one still could be proud of his race. Two girls spoke on this. First, a fifteen-year-old:

> I'd rather be a Negro than be a white person . . . because they say that the "nigger" does more bad things than the white people do. Like when you walk in the store, they look at the "nigger" first while the white people are stealing. I went downtown one day with my brother and my sister. . . . The white people were just putting blouses and dresses and stuff in their pockets, while they [salespeople] were watching us.

Finally, an eighteen-year-old talked about her difficulties in being Black and poor:

> I consider it hard for me to . . . be a Negro . . . financially and the fact that I have to live here in the city being poor. And again it doesn't bother me too much because there are so many that are in this condition that it seldom crosses my mind. . . . There are a lot of things that rich people have that I don't have . . . and things that I need. Maybe someone in the family will get sick and a rich person

can go right ahead and have it taken care of whereas poor people have to wait and wait and wait and sometimes it is too late.

Clearly, these girls' statements speak for themselves. There is a wide range of views on what it means to be *poor* and *Black* in the city today. A very small number of girls did not speak favorably of being Black, but none wished to be white. The overwhelming majority of them seemed proud of their race and accepted it as a factor of life which, although problematic at times, was still real and did not need to be changed. Thus, no evidence was found of low self-esteem and severely damaged psyches among these young women. They did not seem to experience feelings of inadequacy and lack of popularity because of their racial status. As a whole, they were widely accepted by their peers, boyfriends, and other reference groups. They saw themselves as desirable love objects, mothers, jobholders, valued friends, and individuals with a great deal of resourcefulness. Not a single girl expressed disdain for her physical features or skin color. In other words, *none desired to be white.* Perhaps they felt *Black and proud* long before the slogan came into being.

When asked to comment on the problem of being Black in American society, most of these young women did not speak directly on the volatile issues now being raised by young Black people in communities throughout the country. Although the civil rights movement which once concentrated in the South had moved north, most of the subjects had experienced very little direct contact with racial demonstrations and other forms of organized protest activity. Much of this can be explained in terms of the geographical and political climate of the city in which they lived. As a conservative midwestern city, St. Louis has never been known for having a "liberal" atmosphere that would encourage the growth of Black radical groups and activities. Another equally important factor, however, is that a very large segment of the Black urban population rarely, if ever, come into direct contact with activities designed to transform the society which oppresses them. Therefore, it is not surprising that these girls did not often comment on the issues of Black consciousness, Black nationalism, and Black revolution. This does not imply that they were unaware of the effects of being Black in American society. They were strongly aware! It is only that their awareness was manifested in statements directly tied to their *own* experiences with racial oppression.

In a variety of ways, all these young women were clear about what the negative consequences of being Black and poor meant. The best description of this realization and the preparation for its consequences came from a fifteen-year-old girl, Ruth, whose parents had migrated to the North from Mississippi before she was born. At the time of the study, both her parents were unemployed and close to retirement age. In a conversation with Ruth, I asked her what it meant to be a poor Black.

> My family is actually real poor. No one in my family has a job and I intend to go through school and help my mother and father after I get out because I know I will be unable to go to college. . . . After I finish high school, I will get a job and *support* my mother and father. . . . We really do have a hard time. Our parents don't have jobs. . . . There are some that do have jobs, and others who just finished high school and can't get the actual good jobs they really deserve. . . . I hope things change because the Negroes really do need jobs. I thought it was nothing to it. Then I sat down and watched my mother and father and how hard it was for them. My mother didn't go to school and my father didn't either. My real father doesn't know how to read. . . . When I just looked at my mother and my stepfather it made me feel kind of ashamed of myself because I felt that I was the only one left to go to school and make something of myself. Negroes just need help. If girls and boys would just finish high school I think we would be able to make it and there would be some changes in the near future.

Implicit in the minds of all these girls is an acceptance of sharing the double burden of being Black and being poor. Few of them spoke directly to racism, except when asked a pointed question; however, all their feelings about poverty alluded to it as one of the manifestations of being Black. Somehow, there was a strong sentiment that things would not be as bad if they were not Black. This was especially evident when they spoke of racial discrimination involving themselves and poor white girls when both were applying for employment. Several girls had observed that white girls secured the jobs that they had also applied for, only to be told that no positions were available.

Ruth's thirteen-year-old niece, Hazel, spoke of the same condition when I asked her to make three wishes for the things she desired most out of life.

> First, I would wish for a new home, mostly for my grandmother and grandfather, but also for my mother too. Because they are getting older and maybe I would wish for a couple of maids, doctors, and nurses in case they get sick and someplace to take care of us in [rest home] when we get old. . . .
>
> Second, I wish that I can go all the way through school and maybe to college and come out making a nice life so I could support myself. . . . I would like to be a nurse or maybe a secretary and I would like for my life to turn out happy.

There is no difference between these two girls' conceptions of their present status and the routes they feel they must take to enhance their life chances. Education was viewed by the majority of the girls as the most viable way to improve their lives. They all expressed a desire to emulate their teachers, nurses, secretaries, and other professional people with whom they had had contact.

An eighteen-year-old who lived with various relatives and sometimes with friends expressed a desire to elevate her status above what she described as "tough, bad, and dirty" Negroes. She was the only girl in the study who expressed disdain for other Black people. She also may have been the most honest person I interviewed; others may have shared her feelings without expressing them. She said:

> I would like to be better off than I am now because I want to hurry up and get my education so I can be on my own. I don't like to depend on people to take care of me. . . . My grandfather takes care of me now because my mother gets a welfare check for my younger sister but not for me. I'm not on welfare. My grandfather gives me money and he used to buy my clothes when he was staying here. But now that he has moved back home [to the country] he sends me money every now and then. That's why I want a job, so I can buy my own things and don't have to depend on anyone.

Although Miriam was prone to express dislike for Black people and to blame their condition on their "laziness," she also understood that the three generations of abject poverty which her family had experienced in the city resulted from racial as much as class factors. The strong attitude she held about the hard life and the difficulty involved in succeeding was reflected in the seriousness with which she approached her schoolwork. She rarely missed school, because she saw education as the means to her goal—to overcome the impoverished environment in which she had always lived. On at least two occasions she spoke of her own difficulty in finding summer employment with the full knowledge that white girls her age found it less difficult.

The manner in which the girls described their environment was also a measure of racial identification. It was very common for them to perceive their environs as a downtrodden, dilapidated, faceless community. Edith, an eighteen-year-old, described her neighborhood in the following way:

> I would say that I live in one of the slum areas of St. Louis. . . . There is nothing to do around here. I like to write poetry because . . . there is nothing else to do around here. People around here think you are "jive" [square] if you tell them you like to write poetry.

For Miriam, the description was even more precise:

> If I could change my neighborhood I would get a bomb and blow up the liquor store on the corner, because there are too many wine heads there. Then I would fix up the houses. I would tear them down and build them over completely because some of them aren't any good. But I would fix up those that are pretty good.

Anna, a very intelligent eighth-grader, expressed her feelings this way:

> If I could change my neighborhood I would tear every house down. . . . I wish we would move. . . . I would have a two-story house and then a one-story house throughout the neighborhood. There would be a drugstore at one corner and a grocery store at the other. . . . At the other end of the street, I would have an apartment house of five stories with about four rooms.

Melba, an eighteen-year-old high school dropout, made the following observations:

> If I could change my neighborhood I would make some of the people move out or try to straighten themselves out. The ones that

> are loud and the others that stay up all night with a lot of noise disturbing people are the ones I am talking about. . . . As far as the houses are concerned I would just try to make it look a little better for the people who come through the neighborhood so that it would look like a nice neighborhood.

This strong concern with improving the physical and human quality of their surroundings symbolizes their stark awareness of poverty produced by oppression. None of the girls visualized their neighborhood as a desirable place to continue to live in unless changes were made. To all of them, it represented the worst of the human condition. A few girls refused to allow their more economically stable friends to visit them in their homes because they were ashamed to do so. Josetta, a seventeen-year-old girl who described herself as having "strong perseverance," indicated that:

> I know girls at school who have their own telephones in their bedrooms. I like to go to school to watch the fashions. Some of the girls wear real fine clothes. . . . I don't like for them to come home with me because I don't want them to see how we live . . . poor and all.

She continued:

> I work for the Neighborhood Youth Corps in the dietetic department. I work four hours on Saturdays and Sundays and I make ten dollars a week. I use the money to keep my clothes clean or buy a new pair of shoes if I need them. Sometimes my brother needs some money and I loan it to him but he pays it back. . . . If only I could get away from around here, which I am in about a year from now. This neighborhood brings you down. That is what brings you down. People down here are always making a scene. If someone from out west were to come down here and look at our streets, I would be ashamed. ["Out west" is a better section of the Black community in St. Louis.]

Despite such statements, the community was not always viewed in negative terms because it did provide a certain amount of security, various forms of entertainment, and, above all else, was home.

The early formation of a distinct realization and open expression of disliking whites for the roles they played in the maintenance of the oppressive system was present among some of the girls. One of the girls had come under the influence of the Black Muslims through a sister and brother-in-law who were then members of the Nation of Islam. Janice, at age seventeen, held open contempt for whites and angrily described them as the "blue-eyed devils" who were responsible for the poverty and discrimination which afflicted all the Black people she knew. Her anger and dislike were so intense that she alluded to "secret" plots she knew of that were to be carried out by her Black male friends against white people who came into her neighborhood. The following is an excerpt from one of my conversations with Janice:

> Before the Civil Rights Bill was passed you didn't see Black men or Black women with white men and women. After the bill was passed you saw more Black men in their convertible cars with their cigar or cigarette hanging in their mouth with a white woman sitting so close to them that you just thought it was just him in the car. But the only difference is that you know it is a white woman because he is so dark or brown, and the white next to him stood out. I dislike it. . . . It looks like if a Black man is going to get him a white woman, he should get one that has character, decency, and one that looks like something and has a job. But most Black men have these women that look like they have been doing a little of everything. They've been prostituting. . . . They've been in every little hole in the city of St. Louis. . . . And when they do something bad white people look upon them as Negro. They don't count them as white. The Negroes are with tramp women.

Janice also described how the behavior between Black men and white women had, she felt, been curtailed in her neighborhood.

> In the housing project now, none of this goes on because . . . just about everyone feels they don't like white people. I had a boyfriend once. He was definitely Black but he was very light-complexioned. He looked like he was white but if you would keep looking at him, you know that he was Negro. When he first came down here and started dating me, they thought he was white and these boys in my buildings were going to jump on him because they thought he was white. We had an argument one night. This was before they found out he was Black. They were going to jump on him that night. They said, "If that white so-and-so ever hits you, we'll kill him." Well, after I got them together that he was Black, everything was okay.

Janice's friends shared her feelings toward whites and this probably accounts for her belief that "in the housing project . . . just about everyone feels they don't like white people."

To be sure, she and her male friends were in the vanguard in terms of verbalizing their feelings, for there were no others who referred to secret plots to kill whites, although a small number of girls did discuss the knowledge of planned robberies and physical attacks upon white bill-collectors and salesmen. However, because of the robbery element involved, none of these assaults appear to have taken on purely racial motives. But it would seem reasonable to assume that race, as well as robbery, could act as sufficient incentive in itself to assault whites when one considers the fact that the people of this community are among the most economically, politically, and socially oppressed classes in the nation. Sometimes robbery was probably the only motive, since occasionally Blacks were also robbed.

Racial identification and its implications for these people's lives can be measured by the kind of understanding they have about the various forces operating in their environment to perpetuate exploitative conditions. Their antipathy is directed at the bill-collectors, venal merchants, abusive police, and other whites who have economic and political interests in the community in which the girls live. Thus, there is some justification, they feel, for retaliation against these forces. It was very common to hear of young boys boasting about eluding the police, throwing bottles and other objects out of the windows at whites in the neighborhood, and stealing food from the local grocer. Various types of manipulative strategies are used against the "exploiters" to obtain certain resources. Stealing is one form of behavior that is fairly common. Although, on the one hand, most of the girls expressed an almost reflexive opposition to stealing, on the other hand they were able to rationalize it. A typical reaction to stealing came from sixteen-year-old Scarlet:

Interviewer: How much do you consider yourself to be like the kids in your neighborhood?

Scarlet: I'm not really like them but I think that some of the things they do are really all right. I wouldn't sit around and talk about them stealing. . . . It's all right and I wouldn't mind my boyfriend stealing. . . . I would be scared he might get caught and put in jail, but stealing is just a way of getting some money.

Interviewer: Do you think it's necessary for some people to steal? And, if so, under what conditions?

Scarlet: I think it is all right to steal when they can't get a job and don't want to join the Army and get sent to Vietnam or something like that. They steal to get some money.

Interviewer: Have you ever gotten any clothes or other things that were stolen?

Scarlet: Yes. I buy them all the time.

Interviewer: Does your mother care if you buy them?

Scarlet: She'll buy them.

Scarlet's justification of stealing can be considered a form of defiance against what, she probably feels, is an illegitimate system. Her reference to unemployment and opposition to serving in the Vietnam War directly relates to her feeling that things would be better if these problems did not exist.

The general attitude toward stealing among these girls is one whereby they feel a "right" to do so. It is not strictly perceived in terms of "stealing" but rather of "taking": she feels entitled to "take" the object she wants. This sentiment seems to have its formation in early childhood and continues throughout adolescence. Thus, although a five-year-old girl does not have the necessary monetary resources with which to purchase a candy bar, she will take one from a store because she feels she has a right to have it. These girls are forced to deal with the fact that others possess and enjoy objects which seldom filter down to their world; while others have access to such objects, they probably never will. It is difficult, if not impossible, to explain to a five-year-old the ethics involved in "taking" things when he is constantly deprived of them, sees no possibility of being able to acquire them in the near future, and yet is aware of their existence and of the fact that they are positively valued by others. Therefore, when I asked eight-year-old Sharon and twelve-year-old Connie why they stole "goodies" from a small candy store, the only reply was:

Connie: Because I wanted them. I don't have any money so I just took them.

Interviewer: Did you think it was wrong?

> *Sharon*: I don't know, maybe, I don't know. I just wanted them but I couldn't buy them.

This behavior may be carried out by some children throughout the stages of adolescence. Connie told me:

> I stole the baby clothes from the rummage sale for Alice's baby [Alice is her sixteen-year-old sister]. They were pretty little clothes. I wish you could have seen them but Mama made me take them back. . . . I got in the shop through the broken window.

As some of the girls who stole grew older, a gradual change took place in the type and relative worth of objects stolen. There is a progression from stealing a candy bar; to stealing from the rummage sale shop; to stealing from downtown department stores; to stealing, signing, and cashing welfare checks.

There were two peer groups of about fifteen girls who often obtained their clothing via stealing. One of these, a fifteen-year-old, discussed her activities with me:

> Well, I need clothes and things like that that my mama can't buy me. I remember when I first started stealing, the children at school and around the project had things that were much better than mine. I didn't have any shoes or any kind of good clothes and I started hearing children talking about stealing so I said, "Now I care about what they say about me when I start doing this but how do I know they haven't stolen what they have on? They might have stolen their clothes too." So I started stealing then.

Thus she is able to rationalize her activities both on the basis of sheer need and because she has been socialized into this activity by others in her environment, thus becoming "just like everyone else."

The point I am trying to make is that stealing items has a high functional value for these girls because of their impoverished circumstances. They are able to rationalize their activities because they serve a highly utilitarian purpose. A girl will have money to buy food; will have adequate clothes to wear; will be able to share some of life's necessities which would otherwise be unavailable to her. Again, the risk of getting caught is often not seen as being as important as the valued object itself: the valued object is worth the risk involved in getting caught, and when one is caught the consequences are somehow manageable.

Concern with providing the essentials for oneself by whatever available means is forthrightly expressed in the girls' feelings. It is important to understand that they are operating within two value contexts—one which condones stealing because it is functional and another which condemns it for ethical reasons. The moralistic attitude traditionally taken toward stealing does not apply within this context because it is dysfunctional. This is perhaps one of the most blatant symbols of the inequities of the society in their minds; for when one is forced to steal food and clothing because they are otherwise unavailable, one has the necessary proof that the social system can and should be violated. It is in this sense that their awareness of racial subjugation can be most clearly observed. The indirect and/or subtle manifestions of the violation of the oppressive system clearly shows their antagonism toward it because the poverty they must endure, or devise coping strategies to deal with, is a product of that system.

Another theme related to their conceptions of oppression is their attitude toward the police. The police are regarded, most often, as antagonistic forces whose duties are to punish rather than to protect the community. Children learn to fear and avoid the police at a very early age. They learn to conceptualize the community's response to the police. The early internalization of this fear occurs because they observe the various confrontations and conflicts which take place between the police and their relatives, friends, and other members of their community. They have witnessed the beatings, jailings, shootings, and various other types of violence carried out by the police. Thus, the stereotyped image of the policeman as the protector who guides young children and old ladies across the street is alien to their notion of his functions. Rather, he is the person they try to evade when necessary. Although they may occasionally seek his aid because of his granted official right to use force and violence against them, he is generally viewed as being a hostile agent. Too often, they have seen him use repressive actions against people they know, people who usually are unable to strike back.

The theme of violence and its consequences was an ever-present symbol in the lives of these girls. Since violence is such a frequent occurrence in their community, it was often discussed. Therefore, the police, who are usually called on to deal with this violence, must necessarily be a preoccupation. A fourteen-year-old said:

> The cops come down in our neighborhood and beat people up if they want to. You don't have to be doing anything for them to do it. I have seen them beating boys over the head with their clubs when they were just standing around in a group talking.

For another girl (sixteen years old), the police were necessary, although she viewed them in a hostile manner:

> This man and his wife were fighting and she called the police and they arrested him. The man was beating her so they should have taken him away, but they didn't have to beat him up.

Thus, the policeman is viewed negatively because he has the power to incarcerate, punish, and therefore oppress. Yet, he was, on occasion, vital for his ability to provide aid in time of trouble. It is this ambivalent attitude that many of the girls were groping with.

It is probably this confusion and highly troubled environment that encourage them to desire a more orderly and less troubled world. It is very important to note that they have not yet succumbed to the pressures of their day-to-day lives and given up all hope for a better world. While there were a few girls who expressed little hope for a better life in the future, the overwhelming majority felt there was a great deal for them. Indeed, some were able to extend their aspirations beyond clearing up the chaos and problematic situation of their immediate environments to hope for a "better world" in the universal sense. They see their world as one involving a conflict between the rich and the poor, and they envision the day when this conflict will be resolved. A fifteen-year-old girl spoke about the inequities that were involved in her projections for her own life.

> *Interviewer*: When you grow up what kind of life would you like to live?
>
> *Respondent*: I wouldn't want to be rich at all. I don't think it's fair for anyone to be rich and not help people because if they think back they will realize that deep down inside they could have been the people that they now see walking the streets looking like tramps. I just want to

> be the average person like I am now, have a good job to support my mother and father or my own family.

A "better world" also involves a desire for peace; for a world that is free from the strife of war. Conflict on the international scale was perceived by some as a greater problem than strife within their immediate environment. They spoke of the problems that the Vietnam War presented. Fifteen-year-old Karen tells it as she sees it:

> If I could wish for anything in the world, I'd like for there not to be so much war. . . . I wish the war in Vietnam would stop because what they are fighting for doesn't seem right. Most people—like relatives—they go over there and get shot and it causes a whole lot of crying. There shouldn't be a war over something that doesn't hardly make sense. It could be solved if they actually wanted to solve it. . . . Most of the people I know who went to war live down here in the housing project. . . . If the President had a little get-together and actually talked about things, then there wouldn't be too much fighting. Actually, everyone should be satisfied with what they've got. . . . Maybe the land is not big enough for food for the people the Vietnamese government has or something like that. People always want more than they have when they are greedy.

Melanie, a fifteen-year-old, also spoke out against the war.

> As long as they are sending men to fight in Vietnam, we won't have any peace here. If I could wish for something, I would want peace for everybody. I am tired of all the confusion that is going on. . . . People need to get together and talk about how they are going to stop killing each other.

This concern with justice, elimination of war, and oppression speaks to the various manifestations of what it means to be Black today. The subjects' statements show, in a variety of ways, perceptions of their environment and their strong feeling that changes must be forthcoming to eliminate the problems of which they speak.

When one closely views the girls' responses concerning the effects of unemployment, the role of the police, and their rationalizations for stealing, it is soon apparent that, rather than blaming themselves for their predicament, they usually place the burden of blame upon the root causes; i.e., racial oppression. Their clear understanding of the "whys" and "hows" of their conditions is phenomenal. Thus, their ability to cope with, and to find some means of eradicating, these conditions is a decided advantage they have over white middle-class children whose adaptability to poverty and racism would be more difficult to manage were they suddenly confronted with one or the other. In this context, self-hatred becomes meaningless and invalid because it does not apply.

The Black Perspective on race relations which these young women held is not dissimilar to that viewpoint expressed by many Blacks throughout the United States. Their perception of a positive racial identification, economic exploitation, police brutality, the consequences of the Vietnam War, and numerous other oppressive environmental conditions not only represents the way in which they define their present subordinate status in the white dominant society, but also provide us with some clues on how they think these problems may be resolved.

Although this analysis has been limited to a female sample located in a particular low-income urban environment, I feel that this case study does offer a comprehension of the dynamics operative in race relations in these urban communities and the various coping strategies which Blacks have devised to deal with them.

The Black Bourgeoisie

JOHNNETTA B. COLE

I. Introduction

I will focus on that group within Black America variously labeled as "the black bourgeoisie," "the black middle class," or "the black Anglo-Saxons." However, certain difficulties arise when applying terms such as "bourgeoisie" and "middle class" to Black Americans. A bourgeoisie, in the sense of a clearly recognizable class of individuals as owners of capital, has not developed among blacks in the United States (nor in Africa or the Caribbean). Rather, an élite exists in the sense of an intelligentsia of professionals, white-collar workers, civil servants, and skilled workers. The term "middle class" is questionable because the black upper class (in terms of income and status) is negligible. We must ask, therefore, middle-class with respect to whom? Characteristics associated with the term "middle class" tend to be based on the white middle class: the "*black* middle class" shares some, but not all, of these characteristics. In particular, even though some white middle-class individuals may maintain an ethnic identification, their world is never burdened by the racism that haunts so-called middle-class blacks. Blacks fall far short of the white American middle class in terms of income for comparable educational training and skills. Therefore, despite their widespread usage the terms "black bourgeoisie" and black "middle class" will not be used here.

Following the anthropological custom of using the term used by the people themselves, we refer to them as the "bougies." The only disadvantage in using the term "bougie" is the fact that for some blacks it has an inevitable negative connotation; however, for most it is always exclusively descriptive, though occasionally invoked in a derogatory sense. Two major advantages arise from employing this term. First, it comes out of the folk system: that is, the way this group is conceptualized by blacks. Second, it brings under a single term all those individuals perceived as distinct and separate from the majority, an important dichotomy in any society particularly significant among an oppressed people. Distinctions between "middle-" and "upper-" class blacks are sometimes made by Black Americans—but with considerably less frequency than that made between those who are and those who are not bougie.[1]

This essay is based on a review of published literature on both the "black bourgeoisie" and the Black Power movement, and also on what anthropologists call the ethnography of experience—in this case, data from my own experiences in bougie communities and as a participant in the movement for black liberation. Although data from the ethnography of experience are often more haphazard and casual than those which come from a carefully designed research project, they may have the advantages of greater intimacy of detail and breadth of exposure. The experiences on which I draw come from residence of at least two years each in bougie communities in southern, midwestern, far western, and eastern towns. Further, it is based on more than fifteen years of continuous participation in a movement which has changed its name from Civil Rights to Black Power and its tactics from sit-ins to experiments in alternative institutions.

II. **Bougie Status and the Colonial Condition**

The assumption that the plight of blacks in America is that of a colonized people, an assumption on which this essay is based, leads to the conclusion that the bougie class is an outgrowth of an institutional system founded on economic exploitation and its handmaid racism. Thus, little understanding results from viewing the behavior patterns, attitudes, and values of this group of blacks as a peculiar, idiosyncratic reaction to a unique situation in the United States. Using the notion of domestic colonialism, as early as 1962, Harold Cruse explained:

> From the beginning, the American Negro has existed as a colonial being. His enslavement coincided with the colonial expansion of European powers and was nothing more or less than a condition of domestic colonialism. . . . The only factor which differentiates the Negro's status from that of a pure colonial status is that his position is maintained in the "home" country in close proximity to the dominant racial group.[2]

Several years later, J. H. O'Dell picked up this theme of domestic colonialism when he wrote:

> A people may be colonized on the very territory in which they have lived for generations *or* they may be forcibly uprooted by the colonial power from their traditional territory and colonized in a new territorial environment so that the very environment itself is "alien" to them. *In defining the colonial problem it is the role of the institutional mechanisms of colonial domination which are decisive.* Territory is merely the stage upon which these historically developed mechanisms of super-exploitation are organized into a system of oppression.[3]

What, then, are the major characteristics of a colonial relationship? Politically, it means the systematic subjugation of one group to the power of another, whether in terms of European control of the parliaments and governments of India and Pakistan, or the absence of black political power commensurate with black people's numbers in the United States. Further, it means a legal framework and militia to buttress the political institutions and *mores.* Economically, colonialism means the establishment of trade, investment, and profit apparatus on the basis of securing cheap land, cheap labor, and cheap resources—whether on the plantations or in the cities of Latin America and the Caribbean, or on the land and resources of the native American Indian, or on the sweat of black slaves and workers in the United States. Indeed, the impetus for the transportation of African peoples to American soil was economic.

Socially, colonialism leads to class divisions among the colonized. In his book *Black Awakening in Capitalist America,* Robert Allen observes:

> In fact, colonial rule is predicated upon an alliance between the occupying power and indigenous forces of conservatism and tradi-

> tion. Thus, the colonial power played tribes off against each other and used traditional tribal chiefs as puppets and fronts for the colonial administration. In return, the rajahs, princes, sheikhs, and chiefs who collaborated with the colonial powers were rewarded with favors and impressive-sounding but usually meaningless posts.[4]

The situation in the United States differed to the extent that the importation of African slaves ironically created an egalitarian situation, whereby all slaves were equal, without rights and status. However, the very system which initiated that classlessness brought on divisions among the slaves themselves—the crucial distinction being between "field" and "house niggers," the lasting effect clearly being discernible in the social divisions found among blacks today.

Psychologically, colonialism everywhere brings the identity conflicts and illusionary worlds so pointedly described by Fanon in *Black Skins, White Masks.* Oppressed peoples share what might be called "the denial urge"—the rejection of one's physical characteristics and culture in an attempt to reject one's second-class status. This denial urge is what led black Americans to bleach their skin and straighten their hair, Chicanos to Anglicize their names, Asian women to undergo surgery to reduce the slant of their eyes. It is also the basis of Black Americans' rejection of African culture for that of white America, and Africans' rejection of their own traditional way of life for that of their European colonizers.

Finally, we note two other institutional and structural supports for colonialism. In the colonization of a people, organized religion initially plays a key role in opening the path to economic and political exploitation and domination, as in the case of Africa and the New World. A subsequent function of the church is to maintain peace through advocacy of other-worldly rewards and the elevation to sainthood of nonviolent figures.[5] As Fanon puts it, "The colonialist bourgeoisie is helped in its work of calming down the natives by the inevitable religion. All those who have turned the other cheek, who have forgiven trespasses against them, and who have been spat on and insulted without shrinking are studied and held up as examples."[6] In the United States, Latin America, Asia, Australia, and throughout Africa, there is factual reality to the African saying: "When you [Europeans] came we had the land, you had the Bible. Now we have the Bible and you have the land." The partitioning of territory into what Fanon calls opposing zones occurs in all colonized areas:

> The settler's town is a well-fed town, an easygoing town; its belly is always full of good things. The settler's town is a town of white people, of foreigners. [By contrast,] the town belonging to the colonized people, or at least the native town, the negro village, the medina, the reservation is a place of ill fame, peopled by men of evil repute. . . . It is a world without spaciousness; men live there on top of each other, and their huts are built one on top of the other. The native town is a hungry town, starved of bread, of meat, of shoes, of coat, of light. The native town is a crouching village, a town on its knees, a town wallowing in the mire. It is a town of niggers and dirty Arabs.[7]

Of even greater significance is Fanon's conclusion concerning the consequences of this zoned world:

> The look that the native turns on the settler's town is a look of lust, a look of envy; it expresses his dreams of possession—all manner of possession: to sit at the settler's table, to sleep in the settler's bed, with his wife if possible. The colonized man is an envious man. And this the settler knows very well; when their glances meet he ascertains bitterly, always on the defensive, "They want to take our place." It is true, for there is no native who does not dream at least once a day of settling himself up in the settler's place.[8]

The aspirations, the behavior, the values of the so-called black bourgeoisie are a predictable set of responses to the oppressive conditions of racism, economic exploitation, and political subjugation.

This discussion of "bourgeoisie" groups as an inevitable consequence of a colonized (albeit domestic) society is not offered as an excuse for or justification of the behavior and values of bougies. However, it is an attempt to balance the underlying assumption of most studies—that "this is just the way they are." For even though scholars speak of the conditions of racism and exploitation under which bougies struggle, one rarely senses a causal connection between these conditions and bougie life-style. Descriptions of the make-believe world of cocktail parties, football games, and Greek-letter organizations are rarely contrasted with the drabness and boredom of severe poverty. The illusory sense of influencing white opinion and creating changes is rarely juxtaposed to the real sense of powerlessness which most blacks experience. Accounts of the opulence of expensive cars, elaborately decorated homes, and fashionable clothes are not followed by detailed reports of the paucity of material goods accruing to a family in which each individual must supply *all* his needs on $1.15 a day. The pretentiousness of fancy words and long titles is seldom seen as a relief from the indignity of being called "boy" and waiting in welfare lines.

Prior to the Black Power era, bougie status represented the most obvious avenue to an improved condition for blacks. (As one of my colleagues put it, "I don't particularly want to live among white folks, but, then, I refuse to live with rats.") This point, made in passing in the works of Hare, Frazier, and others, rarely receives proper emphasis, for any accurate critique of the black middle class must clearly expose the racism and oppression against which bougie values and behavior are a reaction. The way of life of bougies, like the culture of any people, is a coping device, a means of dealing with one's environment; for black folks, the most pervasive aspect of the environment is racism. But, while bougie status may serve as an individual's means of dealing with racism, it is not an instrument for the total destruction of racism.

We will later discuss in some detail the attitudes and behavior of bougies as an expression of a neo-colonialist situation. At this point, we need simply outline the contours. The assumption here is that black America is being transformed from a colonized nation into a neo-colonial society, a process operative in many countries of Africa, Asia, and Latin and South America. Neo-colonialism provides formal political independence (as in the case of African countries) or increased political rights and economic benefits (as in the case of black America), while the colonized people remain subject to a more subtle form of economic, political, social, and psychological control. It is what Julius Nyerere refers to as "flag independence." The middle classes play an essential role in promoting this illusory sense of equality and self-determination. Robert Allen has argued convincingly that the United States is currently engaged in such a program of domestic neo-colonialism. It is instructive to quote Allen at length on this point:

> In the United States today a program of *domestic colonialism* is rapidly advancing. It was designed to counter the potentially revolutionary thrust of the recent black rebellions in major cities across the country. This program was formulated by America's corporate elite—the major owners, managers, and directors of the giant corporations, banks, and foundations which increasingly dominate the economy and society as a whole—because they believe that the urban revolts pose a serious threat to economic and social stability. . . .
>
> In this task the white corporate elite has found an ally in the black bourgeoisie, the new, militant black middle class which became a significant force following World War II. . . . In effect, this new elite told the power structure: "Give us a piece of the action and we will run the black communities and keep them quiet for you." . . . The white corporatists accepted this implicit invitation and encouraged the development of "constructive" black power. They endorsed the new black elite as their tacit agents in the black community, and black self-determination has come to mean control of the black community by a "native" elite which is beholden to the white power structure.[9]

III. Attributes of Bougie Status

Few systematic analyses of the bougie life-style have been made. It is of interest, however, that two of these works are by black sociologists: *Black Bourgeoisie* by E. Franklin Frazier and *The Black Anglo-Saxons* by Nathan Hare.[10] Frazier saw the origins of this group of black Americans in the slavery and plantation system of the rural South. In response to the demands of plantation economy and *mores*, blacks were stratified into three categories: field hands, artisans and craftsmen, and household servants. In addition, there were the "free" blacks, those who had won their freedom or purchased it. Sexual exploitation of black women by white men produced the mulatto group which formed the majority of the household servants. Thus, occupation, color, and proximity to whites became early indicators of status. In tracing the recent history of the "black bourgeoisie," Frazier saw the Negro college as an important institution. These colleges not only provided an avenue to the professions and white-collar positions that are a badge of this class, but they also inculcated the values which allowed the black bourgeoisie to view themselves as distinct from the larger black population. On the whole, however, as Frazier stated, the black bourgeoisie was made up not of "captains of industries nor even the managers of large corporations," but the wage-earners and salaried professionals. Nonetheless, Frazier was more concerned with the make-believe world of debutante balls, fancy cars, and society-page news of these blacks than with their occupations as schoolteachers, preachers, lawyers, doctors, post office clerks, and foremen. In short, Frazier, at various points in his analysis, identified the following as important indicators of bourgeoisie status: color, occupation, income, education, values, proximity to whites.

Acknowledging his debt to Frazier's work, Nathan Hare combined anecdotes, material from the mass media, and his experiences with sociological concepts to form the basis of his ". . . exposé—a double exposure, if you will—of black Anglo-Saxons on the one hand, on the other, the white norms they so blindly and eagerly ape. . . ."[11] Hare categorized black Anglo-Saxons into twelve types (note the term "types," not "mutually exclusive categories"). He argued that while the black Anglo-Saxons are most often middle class by occupation and income, they are not exclusively so. Above all, they are identifiable by their denial of their blackness and by their relentless drive to own and display the badges of white American society. In an epilogue to a recent edition of his work, Hare identifies a new group of black Anglo-Saxons, the "Nouveau blacks." He notes that, while conforming to the current fashion of blackness (natural hair styles and dashikis), they continue to hold onto the orientation and values of the old black Anglo-Saxons, such as acquisitiveness, Greek-letter organizations, and cocktail parties.

Although occupation, education, and income are examined, the crucial elements in the analyses by Frazier and Hare are these: a group of blacks (a) reject identification with blacks and their traditional culture and strive to be accepted by whites (by trying to appear as physically white as possible and imitating acquisitive white society), and (b) while serving as spokesmen for black people (spokesmen self-appointed and hand-picked by whites), they exploit the black masses as ruthlessly as whites do.

It is suggested here that while the Frazier and Hare analyses appear to lack precision—switching back and forth among income, values, and education as indices of bougie status—nonetheless it is an accurate picture of the perception of many black folks. That is, being bougie is on a sliding scale rather than on a fixed point; it is a term applied to a number of traits but also to a complex of those traits. Whereas an individual may consider himself and/or be considered by others to be bougie solely on the basis of income, or solely on a given level of education, or solely on occupation, or solely on a set of social values, or solely on his influence with the power structure, or on a combination of any of these characteristics, the archetype of the bougie is the individual who possesses all of these characteristics. We turn now to a brief discussion of each of these attributes of the bougie life-style.

Education-Occupation as the Basis of Bougie Status

The occupations associated with bougie status run a wide gamut, from those of professionals to those of blue-collar wage-earners. Thus, we would include the following diverse occupations reflecting educational attainments that range from primary education to specialized professional schools: doctors, lawyers, insurance men, beauticians, mechanics, railroad porters, postal clerks, teachers. What these occupations have in common is that they provide an *income* which supports one in a style beyond that of the poor and "the working class." However, the designation of bougie can be, and often is, applied to some individuals who do not have this level of income or associated values. Students at the university stage, even if their income is subsistence level (as based on scholarship funds) and their orientation is that of the street life-style, may be called bougie by old friends who didn't go to college. Thus, students who grew up in black communities speak of the difficulties of relating to their neighbors and friends when only a few months separate them from their former status.

Income as the Basis of Bougie Status

Although the designation of bougie is most often applied to individuals with a "good" income, advanced education, and either a white-collar or professional job (doctors, lawyers, teachers), persons who have income in the absence of a certain educational and occupational level may be similarly labeled, for example, beauticians, seamstresses, racketeers, Pullman car porters, and industrial plant workers. In the final analysis, bougie status is associated with the material possessions that accrue from a "comfortable" income, not from the notion of an income in the abstract.

Values as the Basis of Bougie Status

In their study of Bronzeville, Drake and Clayton profiled an upper-, middle-, and lower-class way of life. They note the importance of occupation and income in determining middle-class status, but argue that in the final analysis neither of these is the decisive measuring rod.

> . . . The middle class is marked off from the lower class by a pattern of behavior expressed in stable family and associational relationships, in great concern with "front" and "respectability," and in a drive for "getting ahead." All this finds an objective measure in standard of living—the way people spend their money, and in *public behavior.*[12]

Influence on the Power Structure as the Basis of Bougie Status

Although the cases are no doubt rare, it is possible for individuals who have an influence on the power structure but lack the "proper" income, education, occupation, and values to be labeled bougie. To cite an example, during a period when members of an urban "street gang" were working with a neighborhood church group and an antipoverty organization, a member of another gang indicated to me that their rivals had "gone bougie." Of all of the characteristics of bougie status, this is perhaps the most difficult to isolate as a sole basis of status because in some sense it is the ultimate badge. It signals that a black individual has altered his status sufficiently to exercise an impact on the very power structure which defines and controls that status. This attribute is shared by a relatively small number of blacks, in comparison with the other attributes of income, education, and values. Those black Americans who do have influence in the power structure in addition to the other attributes of a particular education, occupation, income, and set of values, will be referred to as "power brokers." In an article, Allison Davis singled out "catering to whites" as a particularly negative characteristic of a group which at times he referred to as the upper class and at other times as the bourgeoisie.

> The most discouraging aspect of this *bourgeoisie,* then, is its loss of courage, its readiness to sell its racial heritage for a private mess of pottage at any time. Of course, for most upper-class Negroes this selling-out to the white man is not so melodramatic as the bare statement sounds. In practice, it usually means only that these Negroes are constantly on the alert for favors from the white world and that they have no scruple of race loyalty to prevent acceptance of such soups.[13]

In the remaining pages of this article, I will concentrate on this subgroup of bougies, the "power brokers," by examining their former modus operandi of vacillation, and their current strategies in response to the demands of Black Power.

IV. Vacillation: The Policy of Power Brokers

In the works of Frazier and Hare, power-broker bougies are characterized as being obsessed with the need to deny their blackness while at the same time viewing themselves as the leaders of black folks. These two concerns (to deny their blackness and yet to lead blacks) involve a conflict: how to be the spokesmen for a people from whom they claim to differ. Thus, bougies could not actually deny their blackness and adopt the white way but, rather, they developed a policy of vacillation between the black and white worlds of the United States.[14] Pursuing such a policy of vacillation has a number of disadvantages—those of insecurity and tension experienced by any "middle man." However, there are substantial advantages to be gained. First, and most importantly, vacillation was the very basis of their role as "race leaders." Because of their caste, it was assumed that bougies could understand, counsel, and, to some extent, control the black masses. In bringing information, concerns, and demands from the black masses to the power structure, it was assumed that the bougies—if anyone could—would gain favorable responses for black folks. The legitimization of their role as "Negro leaders" required that the bougies move between the powerful and the powerless. At the very least, they had to be with and among black folks enough to avoid being publicly disowned by them.

Second, black professionals and skilled workers, who are also power brokers, maximize their own status by vacillating between the black and the white worlds. Although its members usually earn less than their white counterparts, the black community offers greater respect for their occupations. Thus, although a black physician over a lifetime may receive 60 per cent less income than his white counterpart, he may enjoy considerably more status as a "leader of his race," an influential member of the community, a man of prestige.

Third, those of bougie status are forced to vacillate because of prejudice and discrimination by whites. For example, many blacks continue to live in black ghetto areas because of the difficulties of "integrating" the suburbs. Regardless, therefore, of the strength of any desire to assimilate, the overwhelming majority of bougies work in black settings, live in black neighborhoods, send their children to predominantly black schools, receive services in black-operated (but seldom black-owned) businesses, and socialize with black folks.

Finally, many power broker bougies continue to swing between a traditional black culture and that of mainstream America, because they prefer or are less ill-at-ease with certain aspects of the black way of life. There have always been two streams in Black American thought, one which echoes the notion of black inferiority, the other which proclaims the superiority of black folks.

Like all oppressed peoples, blacks have, to some extent, come to view themselves as they are viewed by the oppressors. The condemnation of one's status and, by extension, one's self led black folks to suffer considerable expense and inconvenience to look, act, and be as white as possible. Black folks, like white folks, spoke of the primitiveness of Africa and how "niggers ain't ready." But not all black people bought the myth of white superiority. In the works of "middle-class blacks" such as W. E. B. DuBois in the early 1900's, the Harlem Renaissance writers such as Claude McKay, Countee Cullen, Langston Hughes, and Sterling Brown, the myth of black inferiority was rejected and replaced with the notion of black superiority in beauty and character.[15]

Many of the in-group jokes of Black Americans (middle class as well as those of the street-life style) refer to the inadequacy of whites in a number of areas. Indeed, many Afro-Americans feel that soul and style are distinctive black characteristics, and that it is these characteristics that make blacks superior musicians, dancers, lovers, rappers, dressers, cooks, and sportsmen.

For some bougies, therefore, there is a public white way of life and a private black style: Standard American English by day, but the rap of the black idiom at night; the "refined" sounds of classical music at public concerts, but the soulful strut of Aretha Franklin and Ray Charles in one's private record collection; conservative attire at the office, but the current black fashions at parties. As one woman put it, "After fronting before white folks all day, I just want to come home, lock my door, take off my wig, turn up some sounds and grit on some neck bones."

V. **Black Power and Power Brokers**

A sense of black pride and efforts to liberate black Americans date back to the arrival of slaves in the New World. However, it is possible to document surges in these attitudes and actions, the most recent of which goes back to the late 'fifties and is subsumed under the label of the Black Power Movement.

The preceding civil rights era had emphasized integration in the sense of voting rights and expanded access to public transportation, accommodations, and educational facilities. These issues were of importance to bougie blacks, but they were not of utmost concern to poor black folks who were without jobs or adequate housing. Poor blacks were not impressed with the right to stay in expensive hotels, play golf at country clubs, or eat at Howard Johnson's. The issues which plagued the masses of black people remained largely untouched by the civil rights movement: inadequate welfare payments, unemployment, dilapidated slums, police brutality, and poor medical facilities.

Although the strategies and goals of Black Power advocates vary widely, nonetheless they agree in their rejection of integration per se, in the sense taken in the 'fifties and 'sixties, as the earmark of black liberation. It is too early to assess the ultimate effects of the Black Power Movement; however, a clear pattern is developing. Large numbers of Black Americans have acquired a positive sense of themselves, their history, and their culture. This revolution in identity is particularly noticeable among young Black Americans, but is expressed throughout the range of black society in terms of Africa-inspired hair styles, dress, and cultural patterns, and in an interest in black studies. At the same time that these psychological victories are being enjoyed by large numbers of Black Americans, substantial material gains in the form of better housing, schools, jobs, and health conditions are still limited to those in black society who have always experienced the few benefits of social change, the bougies. Following the urban revolts of the 1960's (and especially following the assassination of Martin Luther King), corporations, government agencies, colleges, and universities hired, in the words of Sam Greenlee's novel, *A Spook To Sit by the Door.* The demand for visibility of a few blacks was easily satisfied by the so-called middle-class Afro-Americans.

At the same time that these black power brokers are reaping the material fruits of the Black Power Movement, their role within black communities is being more severely challenged than ever before in history. The two dominant ideologies within the Black Power Movement (cultural and revolutionary nationalism) require that bougies choose a camp, rather than vacillate between opposing forces. Further, each of these positions questions the very style and aims of the old bougie class.

Prior to the surge in black consciousness and militancy, the black power brokers stood between the black masses and the white power structure. In this three-part system, as noted below, communications flowed only through the bougies. The ideal progression to power moved from left to right, and the chain of rewards moved from right to left.

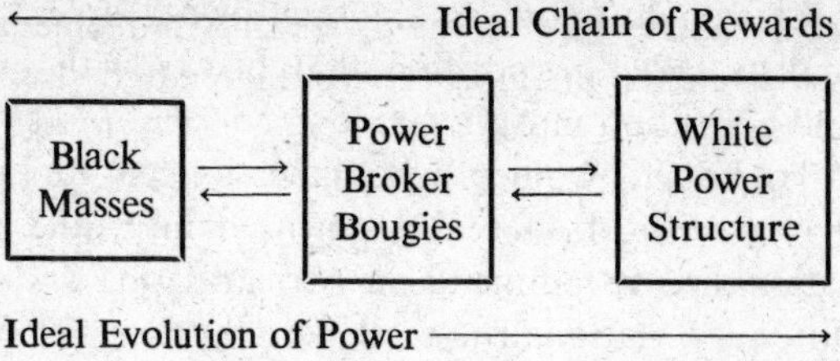

In contrast, both cultural and revolutionary nationalism demand a two-part system and the two parts are viewed as being in perpetual opposition.

Cultural nationalism seeks a change in the conditions of black life through an emphasis on the aesthetics, culture, and history of blacks and the construction of a black world—either as a separate state or as an enclave within a larger entity. The distinctiveness of black people is emphasized and celebrated and the world is viewed as a dichotomy of

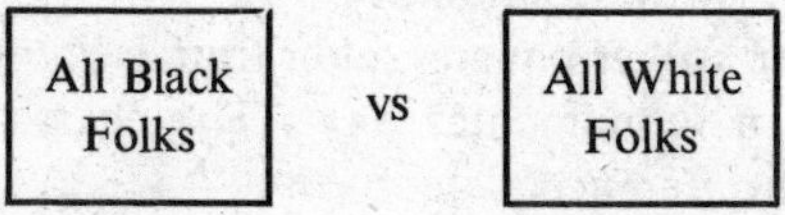

Revolutionary nationalism calls for fundamental changes in the institutions and power arrangements in American society as affording the only avenue to black liberation. The opposing forces are not viewed, however, in racial terms, but in terms of their commitment to radical change as opposed to maintenance of the present institutions of power. The dichotomy is that of

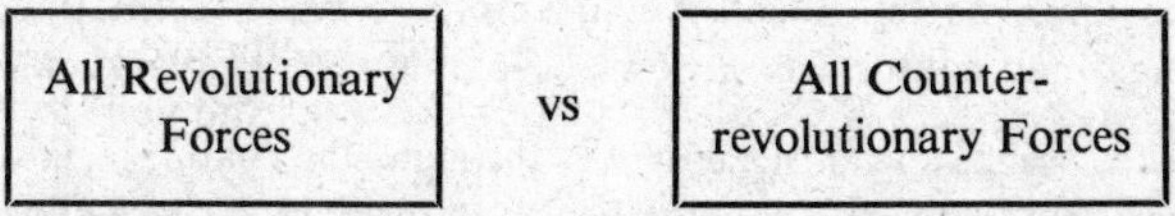

Cultural and revolutionary nationalists openly criticize the very attributes which the bougie class has struggled to acquire. To note only a few examples: Bougies have fought to move out of ghettos and into "better neighborhoods," which usually means white communities. Cultural nationalists criticize such moves, arguing that black folks ought to live among their own people. Revolutionary nationalists take the position that blacks with middle-class incomes and education must live among and learn to struggle with the poor. To bougie women who have longed for and finally succeeded in wearing fashionable gowns, minks, and jewels, the cultural nationalists recommend an African lappa and buba, and the revolutionary nationalists call for the simple dress of a revolutionary force. Nationalists reproach bougie males who have finally managed to "integrate" an all white business firm. The cultural nationalists say that blacks ought to be busy operating black-owned businesses, and the revolutionary nationalists argue that blacks must reject the very notion of capitalism. While the black bourgeoisie rejoices over new positions on faculties and staff of white colleges and universities, cultural nationalists insist that blacks ought to be at southern black schools, while revolutionary nationalists argue that black folks ought to be involved in street academies and other programs that attempt to bring the resources of the university to the community.

The old power broker bougies differ from current black nationalists, therefore, in fundamental ways. The chart below illustrates three aspects of difference.

Although cultural and revolutionary nationalists reject the style and aims of the old power brokers, the very nature of their respective views makes it easier for the black bourgeoisie to accommodate the cultural nationalists. Nathan Hare captures this point in the epilogue to *The Black Anglo-Saxons*:

> There is also a hard-core species of Nouveau Blacks who reject much of the more debonair phenomena described thus far. They are, however, no less Black Anglo-Saxons in basic orientation, though they may conform to a now acceptable style of black nationalism.
>
> They seek social acceptance through the natural hairdo ("au naturel" to them), switching back and forth, in the case of women, to the traditional process . . . with the emergence of the natural wig, they are able to retain their processed hair-styles and yet go slumming ("souling") in a "natural" at "Afro-American" affairs.
>
> Many Nouveau Blacks unconsciously overplay the process or state of *being* black and its symbols in order to avoid *doing* black.[16]

Comparison of Power Broker Bougies and Current Black Nationalists

	Power Broker Bougies	*Cultural Nationalists*	*Revolutionary Nationalists*
Style	"Bougie" Emphasis on social affairs Drive for status Conspicuous consumption	*(A) Nativistic, e.g. African dress, African cultural patterns **(B) Other-worldly	Revolutionary combination of black street-life style and an "international revolutionary life style," e.g. berets
Role re. White Power Structure	Power Brokers	(A) Use the power structure for the black state (B) Autonomy from it whenever possible	Antagonistic
Consequence if successful	Share positions in the status quo	(A) Cultural enclaves (B) Separate state	Establish socialism

*A. Organizations such as US and The United Front of Newark
**B. Nation of Islam

Of perhaps greater significance is the fact that the white power structure is the least threatened by bougie adoption of the forms of cultural nationalism.

VI. Power Brokers vs. Black Power: Patterns of Accommodation

At this point in time, it is impossible to ascertain what the responses of the black power brokers and the white power structure to the demands of black people for their liberation will be. However, a number of clear patterns are currently in operation.

The most obvious and frequent pattern is a continuation in the leadership of the old black power brokers but with the symbolism of black nationalism. Robert Allen has offered a penetrating analysis of these "bourgeoisie black nationalists," [17] the "middle-class" blacks (in terms of education, comfortable incomes, and bougie values) who speak of black control and freedom from oppression, but spearhead programs which benefit their own private class. As Allen notes, middle-class individuals and organizations are usually better organized than are militants and thus it is fairly easy for these "representatives of the privileged black bourgeoisie to take control of organizations ostensibly dedicated to militant reform, to enabling black people to assume control over their own lives." [18] Black capitalism is a prime example of this pattern. Dressing a basic American value and set of institutions in current blackness (thus, *black* capitalism), the bougies can simultaneously satisfy their own interests (for materialism and profits) and perpetuate the interest of corporate capitalism in maintaining control of the American economy, and yet speak to the black masses in nationalist terms ("own black" and "buy black").

A second pattern involves leadership by bougie individuals in programs which, although reformist, come closer to addressing the needs of black people. On the basis of casual observation, it appears that this pattern is most likely to exist when the organization or program is of recent origin, as opposed to attempts to redirect long-standing "civil rights" efforts. A few, a very few, Black Studies programs fall into this category. The leadership—the faculty and many of the students—is middle class in terms of income and education, but they examine black history and culture from the perspective of the oppressed, they attempt to bring some of the resources of universities to urban ghetto communities (urban centers, street academies), and they participate in political projects such as community organizing. The major difficulty with such programs is that even when they remain accountable to black people, they involve services (education, cultural events) which many poor blacks regard as luxuries in the face of survival needs.

The third pattern comprises leadership drawn from the folk, as opposed to the bougies, but the folk come to administer as did the old power brokers. This process occurs in many poverty programs where emphasis is placed on "maximum feasible participation by the poor" and might be labeled "the bougie embrace." The poor who are chosen (or volunteer) to administer in Office of Economic Opportunity programs are rarely the "very poor." They tend to be individuals from the upper strata of a poverty group who are willing to communicate with and work alongside middle-class individuals. The OEO staff, poverty board members, and local power structure exert a strong middle-class influence which often encompasses the "poverty leader," who consequently comes to share their values.

Finally, a very few situations actually do involve a leadership from among the masses of black people and a program which addresses the immediate survival needs of the people. The Black Panther Party breakfast program and much of the work of the National Welfare Rights Organization fit this pattern. However, the survival of such organizations is constantly in jeopardy, for their vocal opposition to the white power structure brings repeated efforts to silence them.

The dominant pattern of leadership in black America remains, therefore, in the hands of a class of power brokers. At the very least, however, growing black consciousness and direct action by increasing numbers of black people pose a challenge to what was once the monopolistic position of those of bougie status.

Black Immigrants

R. S. BRYCE-LAPORTE

The primary objective of this collection of papers is to disclose the wide and complex myriad of views on race relations represented by a range of significant constituencies of this society. The black immigrant is perhaps the least visible, even though perhaps not the least articulate and active, of these constituencies. On the one hand, as blacks, their demands and protests as a constituent group receive the same basic disregard and neglect that the larger society and its leaders display toward the efforts of native Black Americans to improve their positions in American society. While the disproportionately high number of leadership positions held by these immigrants and the significant influence they have exercised in black politics, protest, and progress distinguish them *as blacks*, their cultural impact *as foreigners* has generally been ignored or barely mentioned in American social and cultural history. The point is that they suffer double invisibility on the national level—as blacks *per se* and as black foreigners as well.

Understanding race relations or other facets of American society, as the black immigrant experiences them, must be pursued on at least two principal levels—the direct subjective level, in which the actor as individual or aggregate reports, and the indirect objective level, in which answers are derived from the study of structural relations between actors and context. We will examine both levels here.

Consider that no attention has been given to black immigrants—in historical interpretations of the innumerable waves of immigrants who entered this country in search of frontier and freedom and who contributed, by their presence and participation, to its cultural richness, political complexity, and material-technological advancement. Consider also that, in a technical sense, all races now residing in this country were originally immigrants and that blacks constituted one of the earliest immigrant groups in the Americas. But, slavery deprived early African newcomers from making maximal contributions to the society and culture of early America. White racism led to the denial and degradation of the cultural input and historical contribution of blacks, as Africans, to the more exalted levels of American life and culture. Until recently, most things African were depicted as dark—meaning backward, barbarous, and brutish. It is not surprising, therefore, that the views and experiences of more recent black immigrants have yet to be treated as intrinsically valuable historical or sociological data. In fact, such information is not even sought at present. One major aspect of American race relations, as viewed through the prism of the black immigrant, is the general disregard of his intrinsic worth or historical role. Whenever his feats do win the notice of white society, they are usually presented in comparison with the native Black American rather than with the white alien or total population of the country.

The only comprehensive sociological work devoted to black immigrants, *The Negro Immigrants*, by the late Black American sociologist Ira de Reid, was published in 1939. The works of anthropologist St. Clair Drake and social psychologist Kenneth Clark, both of West Indian parentage, are not directed specifically to the West Indian experience. West Indians Eric Williams, C. L. R. James, and Sir Arthur Lewis have given some attention to American race relations as part of their broader considerations. Greater insight into the West Indian immigrants' views and experience may be derived indirectly from other written sources—novels and poetry, polemical treatises, biographies, and journalism. The poetry and prose of the Jamaican Claude McKay is imbued with his immigrant fascination, displeasure, and impatience with America and his nostalgia for Jamaica. A less known novelist, Eric Waldrond, was moved by similar nostalgia. He wrote *Tropic Death* and an unfinished manuscript *The Big Ditch* on the lives and labor of Black Americans and West Indians during the construction of the American Canal across the Isthmus of Panama. James Weldon Johnson, who was also of West Indian ancestry, on many occasions wrote of the West Indian immigrant in New York City and the U.S. Panama Canal Zone. Recently Paule Marshall, of Barbadian parentage, has written two books on West Indian life. Her first, *Brown Girl, Brown Stones*, depicts the Barbadian immigrant in Brooklyn; her second, *The Chosen Place, The Timeless People*, deals with life in Barbados. Rosa Guy, of Trinidadian birth, and Piri Thomas, a black Puerto Rican immigrant, have written autobiographical accounts centered in Harlem; native Black Americans Claude Brown and Louise Meriwether, in similar works, brought to their readers *en passant* native Black Americans' views of their West Indian neighbors in Harlem. The American Harold Cruse and West Indians Richard Moore, Cyril Briggs, and W. A. Domingo have engaged in much polemics on the influence and contributions of West Indian immigrants to black political and racial struggles of blacks in the United States. Among the occasional journalistic treatments of the subject Vincentean Orde Coombs's "West Indians in New York Moving Beyond the Limbo Pole" (*New York Magazine*, July 1970) is most outstanding. Early issues of the *Amsterdam News, Boston Chronicle, Baltimore Afro-American*, and *Pittsburgh Courier* (at one time owned or edited by West Indians) represent rich sources of coverage of black immigrant life. Also available are studies of the writings and biographies of Marcus Garvey and Thomas Blyden, two West Indian-born nationalists who proselytized in the United States, and the analytic or programmatic statements of leading political and racial leaders of West Indian birth or ancestry such as Malcolm X, Stokely Carmichael, LeRoi Jones, Harry Belafonte, Ossie Davis, Shirley Chisolm, Constance Baker Motley, Elliot Skinner, Roy Innis, and Vincent Harding.

The African component is less in evidence at this time. Aside from Essien-Udoms's *Black Nationalism*, on the Black Muslim, and the occasional statements by the political giants of the emerging "black continent," very little has been published in terms of serious analytical or descriptive efforts by Africans on American domestic race relations. Even more, America is yet to benefit from a black overview comparable to that of Tocqueville, Bryce, Olmsted, or

Myrdal. America is yet to experience a comprehensive treatise on its national character, culture and society written with the outlook of a black African or West Indian. A book on the United States or North America as seen from the lands of origin of its blacks is glaringly missing from the shelves of Americana.

Slight references are made to West Indians and other blacks of foreign ancestry in some of the more conventional sociological studies on race relations. In these, the tendency has been to make favorable comments on blacks of non-American ancestry relative to black natives along lines of stability, academic achievement orientation, and social striving, and conventional forms of success and leadership. Such statements usually stand unaccompanied by either theoretical advances or analytical support. The black immigrant as a social phenomenon has yet to be treated analytically and profoundly, in isolation or in comparative terms, in the social sciences and by social or cultural historians. And, black immigrants are yet to benefit from "insider studies" comparable with those of Louis Wirth on the Jews, Florian Znaniecki on the Poles, Peter Munch on the Norwegians, and Paul Campisi on the Italians, to name a few. Hopefully, the forthcoming works of black scholars on the Black Diaspora will approach this goal.

If the immigration of foreign blacks were insignificant, diminishing, or a matter of the past, it would not be necessary to delve into a demographic or preliminary trend study of blacks coming into this country. However, a cursory exploration shows that of the 45,162,638 aliens who entered the United States between 1820 and 1970, 1,000,000 (2 per cent) of them were West Indians and 76,473 (0.1 per cent) of them were Africans.*

Of 373,326 incoming immigrants in the year 1970, a total of 10 percent, 38,380, came from predominantly black countries, (34,262 West Indians, 1,763 Guyanese, 496 Central Americans presumably

* Using even the American definition of black, these figures are not a perfect representation of the in-flow of black immigrants for many reasons: they may include non-black Latins and Arabs; do not include blacks from Central and South America and other parts of the world; do not include culturally marginal offsprings of immigrant parents and grandparents, and do not cover alien persons residing in the states in categories not legally defined as immigrants even though they are immigrants in a broader sense of the term. Nevertheless, these figures are important as *estimates* and conservative indications of the magnitude of the population over time.

from British Honduras and the Canal Zone, 2,120 Sub-Saharan Africans). In addition, there were 739 blacks who changed their nonimmigrant status to "permanent" residents of the United States. Jamaica, Trinidad, and Haiti together had 29,315 entrants, more than half the total number of black immigrants for the year. Beyond the category of dependents, the greater proportion of black immigrants coming from these three countries were classified occupationally as follows: craftsmen, operators, domestics, professional, and clerical in relative order. Craftsmen were more than double the number in any of the categories.

The sex ratio of black immigrants in 1970 is almost even. For the same three countries, the greatest number of immigrants are in the ten through twenty-nine age group. More than 50 per cent of the 1970 immigrants established New York State as their place of residence. Jamaicans concentrated in the New York metropolitan area, extending to cities in New Jersey and Connecticut; other concentrations are in Florida and Washington, D.C. Trinidadians went in great numbers to Boston, New York City, and Washington, D.C., metropolitan areas, while Haitians went to New York City and the Chicago and Miami areas.

The U.S. Immigration Reports show 51,596 Jamaicans reporting their addresses in 1970, with 35,509 of those reporting located in New York State and smaller concentrations in New Jersey, Connecticut, and Florida. It also shows 2,093 black aliens becoming U.S. citizens by naturalization. None of the "Big Three" has had more than 500 of its citizens naturalized as Americans since 1961 except Jamaica, which had 501 cases in 1966. The highest occupational categories of those naturalized from these three countries in 1970 were professional, clerical, and dependents. The ratio of men to women naturalized was three to two, and the highest concentration was between twenty and thirty-nine years old. The highest number of persons naturalized from the "Big Three" were those who entered in 1962 and 1963. The highest number of persons ever naturalized from these three countries entered the United States in 1962 and 1963, at least one year after the independence of Jamaica and Trinidad and at the height of François Duvalier's dictatorial regime. (The profile for 1971 had not been completed when this paper was being prepared.) However, it is to be anticipated that the economic policies now being pursued and more stringent rulings by the Labor Department and the Immigration Service, inasmuch as they are motivated by the rising unemployment situation in the United States, will probably affect adversely the admission of black immigrants.

From this brief demographic exposition it is clear that black immigrants constitute an ongoing segment of American population. They are not newcomers and cannot be isolated in any special category or location beyond the imposition due to color. Emigration figures were not as easily available, but neither emigration nor naturalization seems to be increasing significantly. Even though the birth-rate indices do not suggest a significant difference between foreigners and natives, the number of black immigrants (when defined in broad terms to include second generation) would nevertheless increase naturally. The increase is compounded by the emigration thrust from the islands, historically prevalent among West Indians. At the turn of the century, according to demographer George Roberts 146,000 Jamaicans left the island for other parts of the hemisphere. Of these 46,000 left for the United States directly, the others went to Panama, Cuba, and Central America to provide labor for American-owned enterprises.

The emigrant flow from the West Indies is real; it is neither abstract rhetoric nor romantic poetry. Davidson shows a total of 82,084 emigrants leaving the West Indies Federation for the United Kingdom from 1958 through 1960 (the period just preceding their independence and also shortly before the 1965 U.S. Immigration Act previously discussed). The 1960 figures for these emigrants (464,449) represented 290 per cent, or almost three times, the 1958 figures (15,998). Using the total emigration of West Indians to the U.K. from 1958 through 1960, Jamaica ranks first with 54,157 (66 per cent), Barbados second with 7,001 (8 per cent), and Trinidad third with 3,804 (5 per cent). Davidson, who disagreed with the notion that population density or population pressure on crop land were the explanations for emigration from the islands, gave primacy to the argument of per capita income as the principal determinant. Accordingly, the three countries with the largest out-migration flow had the lowest migration pressures as measured by per cent of population acquiring passports. The windward islands which were at the bottom of the national income scale in the Federation had the highest indices of migration pressure. Consequently, Davidson concluded with a delicate policy implication:

> Had there been no migration, every year Jamaica would have had 47,000 more people to feed. The migration has meant that only 30,000 more people each year have had to find sustenance in the island. In order to keep peace with Britain, even maintaining the existing considerable disparity in living standards, the Jamaican economy would have had to expand several times more quickly than the British economy. Jamaica's gross national product, which had the increase of 93.8 million pounds between 1955 and 1960, was impressive but in no way adequate to cope with its population explosion.

The realities of demographic pressures on the limited economic development rate in the islands would suggest increased migration pressure in the 1970's. And, given the relative unattractiveness of Africa and Asia as targets of emigration among the masses at this time, the restrictions of Australia and New Zealand and the reluctance of England, then the greatest of the flow is likely to be toward the United States and Canada. If the big North American neighbors choose to be miserly in both economic aid and immigrant admission, the political situation is likely to become acute and unsustainable by the islands, especially since white Americans and Canadians have been buying land indiscriminately in the region. Perhaps the most significant problem for the governments of the new West Indian states is to reconcile population growth and emigration orientations with rate of development and space limitations. An interesting aside is the policy being pursued by Burnham's government in Guyana inviting blacks to settle in the rural areas. This, though, is not a new idea. A similar campaign was carried out earlier in the decade without much success.

The case of the Africans is quite distinct. Aside from slavery, the movement of blacks from the old to the new world has been very limited, selective, and often temporary. Moreover, despite the economic underdevelopment, Africans are neither pressed by land shortage nor pressured by industrial or commercial economies to the point of provoking an exodus from the continent. Much of the African movement is contained within this continent, in itself one of the largest in size, and lowest populated in the world. With the exception of South Africans, at one time Biafrans, and now Asians, the movement of people of Sub-Saharan Africa to the United States and other metropolitan countries has tended to be very specified in purpose, and short-termed, in sharp distinction to that of West Indians and Latin Americans.

Until after World War II either most of the countries with large or predominantly black populations were colonies or their black population constituted a political minority. Inasmuch as the ruling component in all these societies was white and presumably of European stock and because racial membership generally corresponded with life-chances, it is simply untrue that the average black immigrant has come out of a nonracist situation. American social observers and tourists have been prone to make such a generalization largely because they either misjudge what constitutes the dividing line in the local definition of races, overlook that in particular countries other "visibles" rather than blacks may comprise the sociological minority, or fail to recognize the particular nuances of racism in such countries. In many of these countries the white or lighter-skinned élite has capitalized on the myth of no racial problem and has disseminated false ideology and images of racial egalitarianism to their advantage. Lower- and middle-class citizens of such countries come to accept this definition, which, on the one hand, is ego-inflating and perhaps self-fulfilling, but on the other, the basis of a vicious, self-defeating trap which prevents them from attacking subtle racist abuses directly or publicly less *they* be considered racist and unpatriotic. Sensitive Black American visitors to such a country often meet rebuff if they should inquire about racism and are often told they are misguided if they claim that such inequities do exist. Black immigrants from such countries often subscribe to the myth themselves once they reach America, denying the existence of color problems at home, often in the pathetic hope that they will escape the dehumanizing stigma and mistreatment directed to native Black Americans by the larger society. Many black immigrants are instructed by persons at home and in the United States to emphasize their distinctiveness by use of exotic apparel, display of heavy accents, and avoidance of contact and association with Black Americans. Ira de Reid speaks of the black Latin American who would speak Spanish louder than all his lighter friends to warn the rest of the world that he is a Latin American, not a Black American, as if in his own country his blackness did not bring him disadvantages relative to his lighter cohorts.

The point is that racism exists in most of the countries from which black immigrants come to the United States. However, it often differs categorically, manifests itself differently, and may not be of the same order of magnitude or saliency as that practiced in the United States. While almost all black immigrants have come from countries with some racist practices, the effect on them depends on the degree of institutionalization or personalization, blatancy or subtlety, permanence or transitoriness that characterized racism in the country (or the part of it) from which they came. Of equal importance is the matter of how each immigrant would have been perceived and treated within the racial categories of his native land.

In Panama (the land of my birth), for instance, both the institutionalized, blatant, and apparently permanent form of racism existed side by side, with the personalized, subtle, and apparently transitory form, and persons often shuttled from one to the other. In the American-administered Canal Zone, the first form predominated; but to the extent that blacks lived in homogeneous communities, had local institutions, could practice some forms of their own culture, and had access to a more relaxing situation in the Panamanian cities the personal levels were only felt during moments of formal unsymmetrical interaction, that is, at work, in prison, in hospitals, and so forth.

In the Republic itself racism was subtle, and so transitory that it even seemed attributable to the American presence in the Zone and within reach of gradual solution by way of assimilation and advancement of the sizeable black population. But, it was much more personalized than in the Zone. Thus, the average black Panamanian would not encounter day-to-day racial discrimination since he was usually in interaction with persons in his same socioeconomic or local stratum. Wealth, white aesthetic prejudice, and European cultural ethnocentrism (all which he often subscribed to as well) militated against his race as a group being associated with progress, purity, power, and other ultrapositive virtues in what seemed an open, competitive system. Yet, the fluidity of the society and the relative mobility and success of individuals would lead blacks from both the Zone and the Republic to accept their problems as issues of economic and (in the case of immigrant blacks) cultural assimilation. Intermarriage, racial interbreeding, and racially heterogeneous neighborhoods existed in the lower and urban lower-middle classes, where most of the blacks were likely to be found. The children of such interracial mixing especially those with above-average education or wealth would have greater options for advancement than their less-mixed black parents or their poor or uneducated white parents. At no time in the history of the young country were there not men of color in high positions and possessing wealth (even though not accepted in the inner circles of the élite families). There were role models and symbols of hope, which in a sense younger blacks could aspire to or emulate. As in the West Indies and Africa, where it was more realistic to do so, many dreamt of becoming President of the Republic. Panama already has had two black vice-presidents who occupied the presidency in the absence of the incumbent, and also justices of the Supreme Court, ministers of government, legislators, high provincial, municipal, military, and university officials, and token diplomatic and ecclesiastical officials. Yet, it seemed not even remotely possible that in open politics a black presidential candidate could be put forward, much less elected. If for some reason, however, it should happen, he was likely not to be identified as a *black* president. Similarly no black official was expected to include in his official or unofficial purview the special affairs of black citizens. On the one hand, this speaks to the notion that money or power makes you white. (In other words, you can't be black and be endowed with the virtue of wealth, and so forth—you must be white.)

On the other hand, it speaks to the emphasis of nationality and culture over race (so that every effort would be made to overlook a successful contender's race and to emphasize his background providing that the latter does not mean recognizing his African or

West Indian ancestry as a positive factor). This meant that some blacks as individuals may make it even though they may suffer subtle inequities. In the American-administered Canal Zone, however, none will make it, and one learned early that it was futile to risk battling subtleties since the system had no place for black administration at the very top, unless it had to do with local black affairs. In the Republic a black official was not free to identify overtly with his race or ethnic ancestry; in the Zone he was not free to go beyond such identity.

My Isthmian background provides a basis for another set of insights. From 1840 through 1940 the Isthmus of Panama was the target of waves of West Indian immigrants, many who have settled and whose offspring constitute a noticeable and slowly assimilating ethnic group in the urban areas. Panama was the last of the independent Spanish-speaking countries on the hemispheric mainland to gain its independence. It always has had a substantial Spanish-speaking black and mixed population with some slavery but little colonial plantation background. The confrontation between "nationalist" Panamanian "natives"—white and black and mixed—with pronounced waves of socially defined *black*, English-speaking, Protestant immigrants who came under American auspices to work in the Canal Zone and the United Fruit Company plantations on the western Caribbean coast have produced parallels to continental American intergroup relations. Some have been influenced directly by race problems and policies in the United States.

In general, however, if racism is not invisible or deniable in the countries of origin of black immigrants to the United States, it is often not as pervasive. It is a less critical issue, not a principal mode of organizing or mobilizing people, and often is obscured by the socioeconomic stagnancy or the internal or neo-colonial policies which overwhelm those countries. Most immigrants, black and white, are aware of the severity and blatancy of the race problem in the United States relative to their own. Hence, as Mills, Senior, and Golden suggested it was for this reason that many mixed-blood and marginal Puerto Rican blacks hesitated to settle in this country, and why many of the other Puerto Ricans who did settle may have tried to pass as nonblacks or even non-Puerto Ricans whenever possible.

It is equally true, however, that most immigrants, black or white, are also very aware of the widly differing economic situations in their countries of origin and in the United States. And because of this many foreign blacks have risked the probability of racial conflict and have come prepared to tolerate some of the less personal forms of racial discrimination without unduly aggravating the *status quo.* Their goal is to try their luck at improving their life-chances, creating opportunities for their loved ones, or acquiring money, experience, or knowledge to return home in success and to a higher station in life. The mass media, Americans living abroad, overoptimistic correspondence, and impressive remittances or gifts from relatives residing in "de States" often leave them with two levels of distortion—exaggeratedly negative pictures of the racial situation and exaggeratedly positive pictures of the economic opportunities in the United States. Thus, in the old push-pull vocabulary of immigration sociology, the black immigrant is pushed more by the adverse socioeconomic conditions of his country than by its subtle racism (except perhaps in South Africa), and he is pulled by the relatively open socioeconomic opportunity structure of the United States more than he is repelled by its severe and institutionalized racial practices. One could hypothesize that the black persons who immigrate to the United States are largely represented by those for whom economic advancement and social mobility have higher positive valence and saliency than the issue of racism. This is not to deny that black persons immigrate to the United States for other reasons—education, family, health, and so forth—but perhaps to suggest that some conflict or apprehension arises for those conscious of the race situation and thus influences where such immigrants are likely to choose to live. It also suggests that black immigrants' motivation for coming to this country tend to be more specific and instrumental, rather than generalized and expressive.

Aside from the unusually sophisticated few, and those who may have visited the country before, most black immigrants are likely to suffer great shock and anguish upon first reaching the United

States. In addition to the distorted hopes upon which they have based their anticipation, most black immigrants are coming from less complex societies and economies and often more traditional countries, and they are really not prepared for the size, movement, complexity, and anonymity of urban American society (even though they may have read general literature on the subject). The expectations they had are exaggerated, and what they encounter is often beyond their rustic imagination and alien worldview. However, such immigrants usually do not come to "the States" as isolated individuals; they come to settle with relative or friends. Even if they come with a contractual arrangement with a white stranger or agency, they tend to locate themselves in areas traversed by kin network or situated by a nearby ethnic enclave. It is within this context, on the first job and as wards of their ethnic elders, that they undergo the first stage of resocialization. Here they get their first lessons of reinterpretation of what America is all about, the black-white problem, and their differences from and with *Black* Americans.

What is this " 'Merica' " or, "the States" all about? It is a place of many promises but also one of many prohibitions. They are told it is a place not to trust people you believe you know, nor to be too friendly with those you do not know, nor to walk casually across the streets or in the subway trains in the rush hours of the day, nor to walk alone and carelessly at night. Not to expect kindness or assistance from people if you are in need, and not to be too eager to give or open your doors and windows in the presence of those pretending they are in need. Given the population composition of the neighborhoods these newcomers live in, the daily routes they use, and the jobs they take, their fears are directed to blacks and Puerto Rican strangers and stragglers they meet in passageways, on the sidewalks, and in the subways. Reinforcement for this attitude comes from the kinds of newspapers they read, the television programs they watch, the sermons they hear, the admonitions they get from protective relatives and compatriots. The white landlord, the white shopkeeper, the white "boss" will also tell them of their moral superiority over the American black and the distinctiveness of their accent—leaving them to believe that they are the recipients of exceptional favors, when in fact they are being exploited no less than Black Americans. In fact, in many cases the whites who make such pronouncements are immigrants or ethnics themselves and no more prepared in English and Anglo-Saxon orientation or Continental savoir faire than many of the West Indians and Africans they dare to validate, and certainly less American than the native blacks they tend to criticize.

It is a general belief that despite the same kinds of discrimination and exploitation, West Indians manage to "make out," perhaps even "make it," where Black Americans flounder and sometimes fail to be even considered. There is perhaps enough truth in the belief that it can be conceded, but the concession should not be granted without exploring the point. The claim is a complex one because the converse is also true and, moreover, the notion of *making it* (whether the emphasis be on the activity or the end being pursued) raises issues of value judgment.

Black immigrants were not born into the American system and even if born in this country of alien parents, they tend to be exposed to a socializing experience rather different from that of Black Americans. They do not take their presence in this country for granted or as a birthright but often define that presence in instrumental and purposive terms. Before coming to the United States, they may already have been very mobile persons with relatively specified objectives and role-models in their own societies. In the case of the middle class they may already have achieved important steps toward their ultimate aspirations. Their decision to try to enter the United States is often made after they conclude that it is not as possible to fulfill their capacities or aspirations at home. To come to the United States often means various preparatory steps and many efforts before passing the consular requirements, that is, obtaining affidavit of support, financial deposit, job permit, literacy and health tests, police and tax records, visa and departure permits, money for transit, and so forth, plus meeting the standards shared by the other local people themselves—new and appropriate clothing, luggage, arrangement for taking care of those left behind, and so on. Upon arriving they are eager to, and must, necessarily obtain a job quickly to meet debts as well as to establish independence from their relatives. Hence, they have little time or choice to loiter around; they are not likely to want to misrepresent their noble aspirations by "loafing around" or refusing jobs acquired for them by their sponsors. Furthermore, they would have few adequate reference points by which to assess the prestige and profitability of the jobs they "land." As foreigners, they came to this country with less inhibitory socialization either in terms of pride and confidence in themselves or previous exposure to *de facto* or *de jure* prohibitions about public conduct vis-à-vis whites. They have not been imbued with the penchant for conspicuous consumption, symbolic striving, or predilections for conning as their native brothers do. They are accustomed to unemployment without welfare, hard work, low pay, and thus relative deprivation in regard to many of the things Americans consider basic necessities. The latter may not be true of the black middle-class immigrants, who are accustomed to having maids, nurses, gardeners, and perhaps even chauffeurs, at a much lower cost than in the U.S. Their background in an agrarian-based status system often leads them to yearn to own land and other immovable properties, to dislike being kept in a perpetual state of debt, and to fear the disgrace which could come from imprisonment, deportation, or public rejection. Hence, the average black immigrant becomes an ardent practitioner of what Americans call the Protestant Ethic. He comes to believe that if he is enterprising he will have moved from his low stratum to prominence as a professional, social leader, property-owner, small businessman, or landlord within a decade or two. Local gossip and home folklore abound with these success stories. Few of the failures are taken notice of and if so with criticism rather than sympathy for those involved.

Often the black immigrant would try to exact the same sense of daring, discipline, drive, and dedication from his American-born offspring and his American-born black neighbors. Whether by conscious effort or not, he then becomes a traditionalist in favor of the status quo, convinced on the one hand that other blacks can do it too if they try, and on the other hand unable and unwilling to support any position of change which will seemingly threaten his newly acquired interest or status. After black immigrants overcome the original stereotypes and fears acquired during their first period in the country, they still tend to be critical, even if sympathetic, toward American blacks. They are appalled by the failure of native blacks to take advantage of "opportunities," their tendencies to spend money on big cars and fancy clothes rather than on homes, their predilection for conning each other rather than cooperating to do something constructive, their penchant for buying on credit rather than saving, their inclination to criticize and feel superior to other blacks' countries, their attitudes of envy and ridicule toward black foreigners rather than emulation of their serious pursuit of education and investment, their tendency to take their jobs for granted and be irresponsible rather than aggressive and competitive, their tendency to be wasteful, destructive, or disrespectful of other people's property and the law, and to engage in wild and ostentatious exercises without resources to defend themselves or to follow through.

However, the immigrants' criticisms do not take into account the difference in background and prerogative between themselves and the natives, and in some cases resemble the more generalized caricatures whites have made about blacks in justifying their colonization or enslavement all over the world. Finally, many of these comments are interesting parallels to observations white Europeans make about their American peers. Most black immigrants do little travel across the country, have had little contact or interaction with nonblacks beyond work or other business conditions, and, therefore, have a distorted vision of black and white ways of life. Thus, they often do not realize how American and generalized the traits are which they criticize in Black Americans.

The black foreigner is often said to be envied and disliked by his native-born black peers as well. The reasoning goes that black foreigners are aggressive and arrogant, aloof and insensitive to issues of domestic race relations and black solidarity; they "speak funny," and are brainwashed, "Tommish," "hick"; often choosing white association and European models over Afro-Americans, and seemingly not angry at these "white, blue-eyed devils." The complement to this reasoning goes that whites find it easier to give black foreigners the "breaks" than to deal with black natives. By so doing, whites try to divide the race, soothe their souls, improve their images, and buy favor with or keep in good graces with the governments of black countries. Like most stereotypes these charges are not altogether false or true; they are usually oversimplifications and too broad generalizations of individual cases or historical times.

Black Americans also overlook some important facts in their criticism of the alien black. Perhaps most important among these is that he is a foreigner, and his exposure to European colonialism has been much more direct and persistent than that of Americans, white and black. Notwithstanding the common African heritage, poverty, slavery, and recent agrarian and underdeveloped economic backgrounds which most blacks share, the alien black subculture, like that of contemporary Black American domestic workers, shows the consequences of the close uneven contact with their white or colonial overlords as they imitate, mimic, and realize the "high culture." In this sense the interaction of the black native and the black alien is not unlike the old immigrant versus new immigrant struggles and competition among whites. In fact, something of this took place even among the slaves.

Enough is known in sociology about immigrant versus native struggles in colonial societies, chances for mobility into insterstitial statuses that strangers and marginal people enjoy, and about the dynamics of self-fulfilling prophecies. Yet, even the recognition of the gains in status and image which black immigrants presumably enjoy relative to black natives must not be accepted wholly until sufficient statistical evidence and comparative complications are considered. But more important in view of their weak collective situation in a world still dominated by white racist systems, and which cannot differentiate among blacks without destroying one of its most entrenched ideological myths, continued divisiveness among blacks can only lead to the perpetuation of their exploitation and subjugation.

Regardless of their presumed gains and protective caution, which they may have developed concomitantly, black immigrants *are* subject to white racist discrimination, aware of their subjugation, and prone to sympathize and participate in the domestic struggle for black liberation and community development. When one considers the drive which black foreigners reputedly display (not to speak of the previous Anglo-Saxon conditioning which some underwent in the Indies, on the African mainland, and in the

British and Canadian cities) one can ask what would be their position if they had been born in the American social structure and what cultural esteem would their alien tradition have brought them if they were not perceived and treated as blacks? From this follows all the other forms of discrimination and segregation they have suffered alongside American blacks—in voting, housing, schools, jobs, and so forth. Ira de Reid illustrates the operation of this principle quite effectively in the case of a Georgia statute which redefined the term "persons of color" broadly enough so that it would include all persons "having any ascertainable trace of either Negro or African, West Indian or Asiatic Indian blood in their veins, and all descendants of any person having either Negro or African, West Indian or Asiatic Indian blood in his or her veins." Powers do not only divide and conquer, sometimes they combine to control.

Notwithstanding the powerful differences in the experience, resources, and attitudes of black immigrants vis-à-vis their native-born black peers, the overriding similarities in the trans-historical subordinate position of blacks in white-dominated societies has also nurtured a consciousness of kind among them. Not only are they sharers of a supposedly common ancestral past but they are also brothers in the struggle for black liberation (however broadly defined). In the United States, the record stands for itself insofar as the activism and involvement of black "foreigners" are concerned. An extensive litany of names could be developed just on the black immigrant and second-generation individuals who have led protests, civil rights demonstrations, and created or headed local black community institutions, organizations, or projects. The black immigrants run the political gamut from conservative to radical and include both sexes, and various age and regional groups.

Perhaps the question may be asked: Why do foreign blacks become so involved and rise so fast in nationally oriented black organizations of the United States? As the story of the black immigrants remains largely untold, the picture of American race relations continues to be truly unfinished. Neither can be fully developed without due consideration for the other.

The Integrationists

EDGAR G. EPPS

Concepts and Definitions

Much of the uncertainty about goals and strategies in the Black revolution is attributable to the emergence of what J. H. O'Dell, associate editor of the quarterly journal *Freedomways*, refers to as the "Black Syndrome."[1] The complex of behavior connoted by the term "Black Power" includes both the demand for separatism and a willingness to use violence to attain that liberation of Black Americans. It also implies the affirmation of Black values and pride in the African heritage. To some extent, Blacks are divided on such issues as "violence vs. nonviolence," "separatism vs. integration," and "Black identity vs. American identity." Some observers would even say that the basic schism is a division along the lines of "militancy vs. moderation" in strategies for achieving racial equality. James L. Farmer, former national director of CORE and now a college professor, states: "The question stripped bare is this: What is the way for Black Americans to find a meaning for their existence and to achieve dignity in the American context? Is it through assimilation? Or is it through racial cohesiveness?" [2] In his opinion, and I think he is basically correct in his observations, events today seem to support the forces of cohesion. Given this racial climate in the Black community, most individual leaders and organizations avow the concept of Black identity even if they reject separatism and the use of violence.

The "integrationist" label has been used to describe individuals and groups who differ widely in both social characteristics and political tactics. On the one hand, integrationists are perceived as persons or groups who espouse racial assimilation as a goal. On the other hand, individuals and organizations who accept the principle that Blacks and whites can work together to eliminate racial oppression within a pluralistic context are considered to be integrationists. Some Black Power advocates are also called integrationists. Part of the confusion results, obviously, from conflicting definitions of integration. These range from the idea of minimal biracial contact (such as the use of desegregated public facilities) to that of continuous interaction in intimate informal settings. An additional problem is presented by the tendency of some separatists and militants to use "integrationist" as a synonym for "Uncle Tom."

Some of the difficulty in selecting a definition for this essay can be resolved by conceptualizing "integration" and "separatism" as labels used to describe polar patterns of interracial interaction. The latter may be regarded as social behavior occurring along a continuum that runs from complete separation of racial groups (separatism) on the one hand, to complete assimilation of racial groups on the other. Anything less than complete separation implies some degree of racial integration. Therefore, an "integrationist" is defined as a person who does not believe in complete racial separation.

Since this essay is not concerned with the separatist end of the continuum, it will be sufficient for present purposes simply to delineate three types of integrationists. These "types" are described in terms of the willingness of Black Americans to interact with whites in intimate day-to-day patterns of living and their willingness to protest against racial injustice.[3] The three types of integrationists are labeled as follows: (1) accommodationist; (2) assimilationist; and (3) cultural pluralist.[4] Each type is discussed in the paragraphs that follow.

The *accommodationist* (the traditional "Uncle Tom") accepts the values of the dominant society, including the preference for only gradual approaches to the elimination of racial inequities. His stated goals are those of the white American middle class. He does not protest overtly: He believes in integration but will not fight for it. The accommodationist is the Black prototype of the "other-directed" man. He is constantly attuned to the demands and expectations of white America. He attempts to find out what white people expect of him so that he can conform to these expectations. The accommodationist differs from the assimilationist not so much in terms of goals but in his refusal to battle aggressively for equality, justice, and dignity. Accommodationists are most likely to be found among older persons, and least likely among the young. We would also expect this attitude to be more prevalent among Southerners than among Northerners, and, in the North, to be more prevalent among adults who were reared in the South than among those who grew up in the North. Consciously, or unconsciously, accommodationists accept dominant-group evaluations of Black institutions and Black people. It is among this group that one finds tacit acceptance of the notion of Black inferiority.

The *assimilationist* has faith in the promise of a society free of racial barriers, a society throughout which Black people will be randomly distributed and lose their group identity. The melting-pot ideal is, in his view, an attainable goal. The assimilationist does not question the basic value premises of American society. He believes in competition and is eager to compete with whites on an equal basis. The major problem, as seen from the perspective of the assimilationist, is the need to provide equal opportunities for competition within the American system as we know it. Some assimilationists are quite militant in pressing their demands and are willing to resort to direct protest as well as to more conventional legalistic strategies in attempting to obtain these egalitarian goals. While Dr. Martin Luther King is not a prototype of an assimilationist, a statement of his given below can be taken as an illustration of the orientation of assimilationists:

> If we are to move toward the truly integrated society, then it will be necessary for white and black Americans to realize that their destinies are tied together. Whether we like it or not, culturally, biologically, and otherwise, every white person is a little bit Negro and every Negro is a little bit white. Our language, our music, our material prosperity and even our food are an amalgam of black and white. There will be no separate black path to power and fulfillment that does not intersect white routes. There can be no separate white path to power and fulfillment short of social disaster that does not recognize the necessity of sharing that power with black aspirations

> for freedom and human dignity. In this interrelated pluralistic society we are all caught in an inescapable network of mutuality.[5]

Assimilationists are not very likely to be convinced of the importance of their African cultural heritage, but they feel very sure that Black people have made important contributions to the development of this country. Therefore, Blacks are entitled to a fair share of all that America has to offer as well as to representative and accurate portrayal in American history books. The assimilationist probably believes that European culture is superior to non-European, and he tends to see himself basically as a "cultural European" with a dark skin. Hence, he is likely to value his "American" heritage above his "African" heritage. The assimilationist is likely to feel that much of the behavior of Black Americans is actually substandard in relation to that of whites, or that it is dysfunctional for achievement in American society. Since he does not expect the society to be overthrown by revolution, he feels that realism demands that Blacks adapt to American culture and values.

Both assimilationists and accommodationists stress individual achievement. The assimilationist, however, feels much more confident about his ability to compete, while the accommodationist finds a considerable amount of comfort in those aspects of segregation which protect him from competition with whites. The accommodationist seeks to maintain his "protected" market; the assimilationist attempts to expand his area of operation to include formerly restricted markets (opportunities) which will place him in direct competition with whites. Clearly, some ambivalence is to be found in the assimilationist's mind about the ability to compete, as evidenced by Whitney Young's plea for a domestic Marshall Plan and preferential treatment of Blacks as compensation for past oppression.[6]

The *cultural pluralist,* like the assimilationist, wants his share of material prosperity, power, and human dignity. He differs from the assimilationist in the way in which he defines a pluralistic society. The cultural pluralist is willing to live among whites and to interact with them in schools and on the job, but he prefers to maintain his African heritage and develop a strong sense of identification with the Black community and peoples of African descent throughout the world. He prefers Black cultural patterns and life-styles in respect to those institutions which are most intimately involved in setting the tone of human relationships in a community (family, religion, recreation). On the level of social organization, pluralists also work to strengthen Black institutions and organizations so as to achieve both group power and group pride. Cultural pluralists view America as a society composed of a variety of different ethnic groups all striving for various goods and services. Black pluralists believe that if they are to compete on an equal basis with other ethnic groups, Blacks too must come together and build a common power base from which they can more effectively vie for a share of the wealth and power of the total society.

African dress and hair styles are often an outward expression of pluralistic attitudes, but these symbols are also adopted by Black Americans of all political leanings. The pluralist expects to achieve an ultimate integration of groups based on ethnicity. In this view, Blacks will eventually attain parity with other ethnic groups in American society. Pluralists tend to place more emphasis on *group* mobility than on *individual* mobility when they discuss strategies for improving the social and economic status of Black Americans. They are likely to advocate broad-based reforms, for example, income maintenance, Black political power, community control of schools, and Black capitalism. Operation PUSH (People United To Save Humanity), under the leadership of the Reverend Jesse Jackson, is an example of an organization with a pluralistic style. It appeals to Black pride and Black unity and encourages Black people to work toward symbolic "nationhood" within the framework of American social institutions. Separatists and revolutionary militants (a brand of integrationists not considered in this paper) would argue that a Black "nation" is inconceivable within a capitalistic racist society. We must, however, keep in mind that the cultural pluralists are reform-oriented rather than revolutionary in their goals and strategies. Thus, they urge their followers to strive for Black Power (through electoral politics) as well as for "green power" (through boycotts, rent strikes, welfare reform, Black capitalism, unionization, and hiring quotas). Like assimilationists, they see little possibility of Blacks gaining power through violent revolution.

Leaders and Organizations

While the typology of integrationists described above may be useful for analytical purposes, it would be difficult to find individual leaders or organizations that fit entirely neatly into the designated conceptual categories. To begin with, the dynamics of race relations in the United States since 1965 have been characterized by drastic shifts in both rhetoric and strategy with the result that no Black leader or organization could maintain a large following by openly advocating an accommodationist strategy. The late Congressman William Dawson of Illinois, who served from 1942 to 1970, was a good example of the political accommodationist. Today's Black politician, even when supported by a powerful political machine, must be less obvious in adhering to accommodationist policies. Accommodationist spokesmen, usually businessmen or religious leaders, find few supporters among young, politically active Blacks.

The assimilationist position is equally unpopular today. Even an avowed integrationist of the stature of Roy Wilkins is careful to point out that integration, as he defines it, is not a synonym for assimilation. He wrote, in 1970, that "The policy of integration does not mean, as so many opponents seem to contend, a melting into other peoples, the loss of color, identity and the racial heritage that 350 years of life as Americans have built into the Negro population."[7] Wilkins is convinced that integration is the most appropriate goal for Black Americans and that coalitions with white liberals are useful when they help in the attainment of that objective. He is unswerving in his support for integration, but he does not identify himself as an assimilationist.

Before the emergence of the Black Power movement, nearly all Black Americans accepted the goal of integration. Strategies were variously accommodationist or assimilationist, but (after the dissolution of the Garvey movement) little consideration was given to separatism or pluralism before 1966. The Black Muslims stood alone and represented a relatively small proportion of the Black population. All the nationally recognized civil rights organizations —CORE, NAACP, National Urban League, SCLC, and SNCC— opted for integration and actively worked to achieve this end during most of the 1960's. However, once SNCC and CORE, the most militant groups, accepted the Black Power ideology in 1966 and became advocates of racial separatism, the other civil rights organizations found it necessary to come to grips with the question of Black identity.

Since the most militant and politically alert young people were associated with SNCC and CORE, the other groups (especially SCLC) found themselves hard-pressed to maintain their credibility as leaders in the struggle for Black liberation. O'Dell has written that the major contribution of SNCC, CORE, and SCLC was their action in carrying out mass demonstrations and protests in the struggle for civil rights.[8] Of these three mass-action organizations, only SCLC survived the impact of the Black Power ideology with a substantial national following. By maintaining its emphasis on nonviolence, while at the same time focusing on the need to develop and strengthen Black institutions and organizations, SCLC solidified its position as a mass-based, but tactically moderate organization. With the Black Panthers usurping the radical militant position and SCLC holding strong in the liberal-militant slot, SNCC and CORE were left without a viable role in the Black revolution and subsequently lost most of their enthusiasts.

The NAACP and the National Urban League, both traditionally moderate organizations with a middle-class orientation, have remained moderate but have found it necessary to incorporate certain elements of Black identity in their programs. They have not become separatist, nor have they abandoned the goal of integration. They have, however, adopted some of the rhetoric of Black identity, especially the plea for unity and for the elimination of class distinctions within the movement for Black liberation. Their ideology continues to focus on the elimination of discrimination in voting, education, housing, and employment. Their recognition of the needs of poor people is illustrated by their recent concern with welfare rights and the plight of prisoners.

The Future of Integration

Survey results indicate that, as of 1968, most Black Americans still rejected separatism as an ultimate goal.[9] Strong support was evident for increasing Black pride (teaching Black history in schools) and moderate advocacy of identification with Africa. These surveys also found moderate enthusiasm for Black control of institutions in the Black community. Black respondents were more likely to endorse such middle-of-the-road leaders as Ralph Abernathy, Roy Wilkins, Carl Stokes, and Whitney Young than more militant and separatist leaders. The majority of subjects reported that they preferred nonviolent protests and demonstrations. However, "There is a clear trend for younger people, especially among men, to be more separatist in thinking . . ."[10] Since 1968, a tendency toward greater acceptance of Black consciousness can be noted, as well as a move toward greater unity among Black political and civil rights leaders. The drift seems to indicate that cultural pluralism, a relatively nonthreatening adaptation of "Black Power ideology," rather than separatism or revolution, will be the dominant mood of Blacks in the 'seventies.

The findings of the surveys reported above are supported by research in other settings. For example, a number of studies were conducted by the Division of Behavorial Science Research at Tuskegee Institute.[11] Results indicate that southern Black college students are more likely to identify with symbols of African heritage and Black pride than are Black high school students or Black adults. The college students were also more likely to question the desirability of integration as a goal and to express pessimism about the possibility of completely eliminating racial discrimination in this country. In this group, males were more likely than females to endorse aggressive protest strategies, including the use of violence. According to the Tuskegee studies, as well as the national surveys cited above, the National Association for the Advancement of Colored People received more support from respondents than did any other organization. The Southern Christian Leadership Conference and the National Urban League were endorsed by a larger proportion of respondents than were any of the more separatist organizations or those whose leaders or rhetoric appeared to call for violent protest tactics.

Tuskegee studies also indicated that the majority of young people, both high school students and college students, tended to be cultural pluralists, while older persons were more likely to be assimilationists. It is probable—although I cannot support this contention with empirical data—that the more highly educated Black Americans are those most likely to be attracted to cultural pluralism. Available data do provide limited evidence that nationalist separatism has more appeal for poverty-level respondents than for those whose incomes are above the poverty level.[12]

Youthful leaders who adopt a militant stance while at the same time stressing Black unity and Black pride seem to have the greatest potential for mass appeal in the current political climate. Julian Bond and Jesse Jackson are examples of young men who appeal to young Blacks. Other popular political figures include Carl Stokes, John Conyers, and Shirley Chisholm. While these Black leaders challenge the current power structure, they all advocate working within the framework of the American political system. They can best be described as militant reformers, not as revolutionaries.

Ambivalence is still widespread among Black Americans as to the relative efficacy of pursuing a policy of "dispersion" rather than a strategy of developing political strength through numerical superiority in Black communities (ghettos or larger areas). While advocates of both positions claim considerable support, it seems obvious that both theories are actually being practiced and that these dual approaches will continue to find support from members of the Black community. The absence of a dichotomy is to be expected, in view of the wide range of experiences that make up the collective "Black Experience."

Among the integrationists, the cultural pluralists are most aware of the pervasiveness of racism in American institutions. Accommodationists and assimilationists are more likely to be satisfied with tokenism. Cultural pluralists know that surface changes do not tangibly affect the power of whites to dominate the affairs of Blacks. But the NAACP, the National Urban League, and SCLC all include in their membership persons who might be classified as accommodationists, assimilationists, and cultural pluralists. In other words, the organizations employ multiple strategies and implement widely differing views. They will work for collective power through voter registration and increased political participation, while at the same time working for dispersal by trying to break down barriers to housing for Blacks in the suburbs; some members will work for community control of schools while others are supporting desegregation through mass busing. Each of these seemingly contradictory approaches is attuned to the reality that some Black Americans will view the attainment of each objective as progress.

I will conclude by pointing out that this essay assumes that the term "integrationist" is not a concept possessing only a single meaning. When we consider the great variety of people who can be called integrationists, it seems logical to conclude that some form of integrationism will be prominent in the Black movement for some time to come. This analysis suggests that the pluralist integrationist is more likely to emerge as a political force in the decade of the 'seventies.

Black Nationalists

J. HERMAN BLAKE

The price the immigrants paid to get in America was that they had to become Americans. The black man *cannot* become an American (unless we get a different set of *rules*) because he is black.

LEROI JONES

It is one of the bitter ironies of American history that the seeds of the contradiction which created black nationalism were sown in the colony of Jamestown in 1619. When the settlers accepted twenty captured Africans as servants—an act which eventually led to slavery—the reality of black inequality in America was established at the same time that the rhetoric of democracy was articulated.[1] Black nationalism has been a major form of protest against this contradiction since the early nineteenth century. Early nationalist protest followed several different emphases, but in the twentieth century these different strands were incorporated into a unified form of protest. The most recent trends in black nationalism reveal some unique features which have significant implications for future developments.

Black nationalist thought is a consequence of the duality of the experience of Afro-Americans, a people who are identified by racial characteristics as different from the "typical" American and denied full participation in this society for that reason, while, at the same time, they are expected to meet all the responsibilities of citizenship. It reflects the negative self-image which many black people have unconsciously developed, and the sense of hopelessness that has persisted in the Afro-American community as a consequence of being treated as inferiors.

Early Trends

The first distinctive form of black nationalism was the desire to separate from America expressed by some free blacks in the early part of the nineteenth century.[2] The proponents of this form of *political nationalism* argued for the establishment of a black nation in Africa or some other territory. Their views were based on a conviction that Afro-Americans would never receive justice in America and that the only hope was to leave the country and establish a political entity for black people. The apex of this development came at the Emigration Convention of 1854, when three men were commissioned to investigate the possibilities of emigration of blacks to Central America, the Black Republic of Haiti, or the Niger Valley in West Africa.

The apparent permanence of American slavery and the racial barriers set up against freed blacks led these men to the conviction that true justice and equality for black people would never be reached in this country, and there were other territories to which they might emigrate. Thus, those in favor of emigration argued that the only hope for the black man was to leave this country and establish a black nation in which the emigrants could live free from fear, racial prejudice, and discrimination. The Civil War and emancipation of the slaves brought black agitation for emigration to a halt, and black people devoted themselves to the task of becoming a part of the American society.

Though emancipation increased the hopes of blacks that full participation in the society was forthcoming, post-Reconstruction developments made it increasingly clear that such was not to be the case. The depressing conditions which followed the Hayes compromise led to the development of philosophies of self-help, particularly as expressed in *economic nationalism.* This emphasis called for racial solidarity and economic co-operation as the solution to the problems of the Afro-American. The growing influx of Europeans into Northern cities and factories increased the pessimism of some influential Afro-Americans and led them to look for salvation within the race. Booker T. Washington, a major proponent of economic nationalism, felt that industrial education and the perfection of agricultural skills in the rural South would lead whites to the realization that black people were worthy of equal treatment. In his famous Atlanta Exposition Address of 1895, Washington revealed that he was aware of the impact of European immigration upon American industry, and evidently felt that this trend closed the doors of opportunity in the North to blacks. Therefore, he pursued a policy of racial solidarity and economic self-sufficiency, establishing the National Negro Business League in 1900 for the purpose of stimulating business enterprise. At the 1904 convention of the League, Washington viewed the developments of black businesses through the support of black people as crucial to the removal of racial prejudice in America.[3] Unlike political nationalism, economic nationalism revealed a desire for participation in the society, but in the face of rejection by Americans, the economic emphasis worked on strengthening the internal community as part of an attack upon the racial barriers.

Cultural nationalism was another response to the denial of equality to Afro-Americans. Like economic nationalism, the emphasis was upon racial solidarity, with added attraction given to the development of racial pride and dignity. These goals were sought through the study of the history of the black man and his contribution to mankind. The essential belief of the cultural nationalists was that a scholarly analysis and study of the history of black people throughout the world, particularly in America, would show blacks and whites that Afro-Americans are descended from a proud heritage and have made outstanding contributions to human progress. It was thought that such an understanding would have two consequences: (1) It would give blacks a positive self-image and further the development of racial pride and solidarity; and (2) it would show whites that blacks were no better nor worse than any other race and that because of their contributions, they should be fully accepted into the society.

Although there were attempts to develop the study of Afro-American history before the Civil War, cultural nationalism received its greatest impetus during the latter part of the nineteenth century. The desire to give scholarly attention to the historical past of the black man resulted in the organization of the Association for the Study of Negro Life and History in 1915, and to the establishment of the *Journal of Negro History.*[4]

Political, economic, and cultural forms of black nationalism all had their roots in the social conditions confronting Afro-Americans. During the days of slavery, the desire for emigration and separation increased with the growing conviction that slavery would never be eliminated. It is noteworthy that the emigration movement among blacks reached its most significant point during the 1850's and that such interest declined with the onset of the Civil War. In the latter part of the nineteenth century, economic and cultural nationalism developed as a consequence of continued hostility and repression. The end of Reconstruction, the rise of Jim Crow, the lack of economic opportunity, and similar conditions led to the development of economic and cultural attempts to foster individual and collective strength within the black community while pursuing an attack upon the prejudiced and discriminatory behavior of the larger society. The major proponents of these various emphases came from the upper levels of the Afro-American community. Martin R. Delaney, a supporter of emigration, was a physician and Harvard graduate; Booker T. Washington was the undisputed leader of black people from 1895 until his death in 1915; and Arthur A. Schomburg, Carter G. Woodson, and W. E. B. DuBois were all highly educated and literate men. Black nationalist movements did not develop a foundation among the masses until after World War I.

Twentieth-Century Patterns

Black nationalism as a mass movement followed the creation of a ready audience and the combination of the various strands of nationalistic thought into an integral whole. When Marcus Garvey, a native of Jamaica, established the Universal Negro Improvement Association and African Communities League (UNIA) in New York City in 1917, he brought *integral nationalism* to a people who were looking for hope in what appeared to be a hopeless situation.[5]

Garvey made his strongest appeal to the many blacks who had migrated out of the South shortly before his arrival in the country, seeking employment in the industrial centers of the North. Agricultural depression and the appearance of the boll weevil in Southern cotton had made living conditions extremely difficult. At the same time, the European war had placed heavy demands on Northern industry, and the supply of European immigrant labor had been cut off. Therefore, Northern industrialists began a campaign to induce blacks to leave the South and work in Northern factories. It is estimated that in one two-year period a half-million black people moved to the North.[6]

The many blacks who made this journey found that though they were often openly recruited, they were seldom welcomed, for they were crowded into urban slums and faced a continual round of unemployment, depression, and indigence. Furthermore, they met the massive hostility of whites—many of them newly arrived in this country—who saw the black in-migrants as threats to their economic security and reacted against them with devastating riots. The continued hardships of the blacks and the intense hostility of the whites created a situation in which Garvey's appeal seemed eminently rational. They were the same conditions which led to earlier forms of nationalism, except that the blacks perceived them in a much more intensified manner than previously. Garvey's integral form of black nationalism flourished in this situation, and its significance was not only that it was the first major social movement among the black masses; it also indicated the extent to which they "entertained doubts concerning the hope for first-class citizenship in the only fatherland of which they knew." [7]

The UNIA program combined previous emphases in black nationalism. Drawing upon the Booker T. Washington philosophy of economic independence, Garvey established various commercial enterprises, among them the Black Star Line, a steamship company designed to link the black peoples of the world through trade, and the Negro Factories Corporation, designed to build and operate factories in the industrial centers of the United States, Central America, the West Indies, and Africa. In the tradition of the political nationalists, Garvey sought to have all whites expelled from Africa so that it could become a territory for black people only. He told Afro-Americans that race prejudice was such an inherent part of white civilization that it was futile to appeal to the white man's sense of justice. The only hope was to leave America and return to Africa. His vigorous promotion of racial solidarity and black consciousness was one of his most lasting successes. Exalting everything black, he renewed the assertions that Africa had a noble history and urged Afro-Americans to be proud of their ancestry. Coming when it did, his program had a profound impact upon the black masses, and even his severest critics admit that in the early 1920's, his followers numbered perhaps half a million.[8]

The Garvey movement did not show the dualism found in earlier nationalist sentiment. It was a philosophy that fully embraced blackness and vigorously rejected white America. Although the movement declined after his imprisonment in 1925, the integral form of black nationalism was to continue. In the early 1930's the Lost Found Nation of Islam in the Wilderness of North America was established in Detroit, and began to grow under the leadership of Elijah Muhammad.

After two decades of relative obscurity, the Nation of Islam experienced rapid growth during the 1950's, particularly when the brilliant and articulate ex-convict, Malcolm X, began speaking around the country in the name of the organization. Like the UNIA, the Nation of Islam is an unequivocal rejection of white America and a turn inward to the black man and the black community as the only source of hope for resolving racial problems. Unlike the UNIA, the Nation of Islam contains a strong religious component which is a major binding force in the organization. There is the Holy Koran which provides scriptural guidance, Elijah Muhammad (The Messenger) who provides everyday leadership, an eschatology, and a set of rituals which give the members a valuable shared experience.[9] The rejection of white America involves a rejection of Christianity as the religion of the black man, English as the mother tongue of the black man, and the Stars and Stripes as the flag of the black man. Muslims also refuse to use the term "Negro," their family names, and traditional Southern foods, which are all taken as remnants of the slave condition and a reaffirmation of that condition so long as they are used.

The Nation of Islam places great emphasis upon black consciousness and racial pride, claiming that a man cannot know another man until he knows himself. This search for black identity is conducted through the study of the religious teachings of Islam, as interpreted by Elijah Muhammad, and through the study of Afro-American and African history.

Muslims also follow a strong program of economic nationalism, with their emphasis upon independent black businesses. Muslim enterprises, mostly of the service variety, have been established across the country and have been quite successful. They are now opening supermarkets and supplying them with produce from Muslim-owned farms. There is also some movement now into light manufacturing.

The Muslim emphasis upon a separate territory for black people gave new emphasis to political nationalism. They have never specified whether that land should be on this continent or another, but they have consistently argued that since blacks and whites cannot live together in peace in this country, it would be better if the blacks were to leave the country and set up an independent nation. In the Muslim view, such a nation would be an Islamic theocracy. This new element of political nationalism, emphasizing land rather than Africa, emigration, or colonization, has become a significant element of contemporary black nationalist protest.

The Nation of Islam had a profound effect upon the development of contemporary trends in black nationalism. There are very few ardent black nationalists today who have not had some close contact with the Nation of Islam either through membership or through having come under the influence of one of its eloquent ministers. Even though the Nation of Islam grew rapidly there were many black people who were deeply influenced but were not persuaded by the doctrine of total separation from America or by the religious emphasis. This was particularly true of college-educated blacks. The break between Malcolm X and the Nation of Islam in early 1964 had a profound impact on current trends by spurring the development of black nationalism among countless numbers of blacks who supported the Muslim emphasis upon black consciousness and racial solidarity.

The Universal Negro Improvement Association and African Communities League under Marcus Garvey and the Lost Found Nation of Islam in the Wilderness of North America under Elijah

Muhammad have been very successful and influential forms of integral nationalism. Both the leaders and the followers came primarily from among the black masses of the urban North, whose lives had not seen the steady progress toward perfection which characterizes the myth of the American dream of success. These two movements brought the various threads of nineteenth-century black nationalism together, and wove them into a matrix out of which the more recent trends in black nationalist thought have developed. Contemporary trends, however, add some distinctive elements of their own which are shaping black nationalism and the current pattern of race relations in America.

Contemporary Developments

The development of black-nationalist-protest thought in recent years is related to the same conditions which produced such sentiment in earlier periods, as well as to some new and unique conditions. In recent years, the urbanization of the black man has proceeded at a very rapid pace. In 1960, a higher proportion of the black population (73 per cent) were residents of the cities than ever before, and this proportion exceeded that of the white population (70 per cent). Not only are blacks moving into the cities; whites are moving out, so that more of the central cities are becoming all-black enclaves. Between 1960 and 1965, the proportion of blacks in central cities increased by 23 per cent while the proportion of whites declined by 9 per cent.[10]

It is not simply that black people are now predominantly urban; in recent years, black urban residents have become new urbanites for two major reasons. Not a small proportion of the in-migrants to central cities are younger blacks who are generally better educated than those whites who remain in the cities.[11] Furthermore, a new generation of black people is coming to maturity, young people who were born and raised in the urban black communities. They do not use a previous Southern pattern of living as the framework through which they assess their current situation, but use an urban, mainstream-America framework, usually learned from the mass media rather than experienced. These youth comprise a very large proportion of the urban residents and are less enchanted by the view that, although things are bad, they are better than they used to be.[12] As such, they are very critical of attitudes of those blacks who see the situation of the black man as improving. A small but significant proportion of the new urbanites are young people who have graduated from first-rate colleges and hold white-collar positions in integrated firms. The subtle prejudices which they have encountered, along with the empty lives of the many middle-class whites whom they have met, have increased their awareness that there is a style and tone of life in the black community which gives much more satisfaction than that of the white middle class.[13] The heightened interaction of black youth as a result of urban living, the coming-of-age of a generation of post-World War II youth, and the rejection of some white middle-class values in the attempt to articulate values which grow out of the black experience[14] are some of the internal dynamics of black communities in the 1960's which are producing a new upsurge in nationalism.

The postwar independence movements around the world have also affected the thinking of black people. Earlier generations of black nationalists predicted the rise of Africa as part of the world community. They had preached about the day when "princes would come out of Ethiopia," but the present generation has witnessed that rise. Black urbanites, seeing African diplomats welcomed by American presidents and taking leading roles in the United Nations, became increasingly bitter about the limited freedom and opportunity of Afro-Americans.

While Africans and Asians were gaining independence and taking seats in the halls of world council, the gap between black and white Americans was not changing perceptibly. Since 1960, black males have not made appreciable gains on white males in income and occupation, black communities are more separated from white communities than ever before, and the education of black youth is still woefully inadequate. Even for those middle-class blacks who appear to have made many strides during the 1960's, the evidence indicates that they have made large relative gains over lower-class blacks, but have not reduced the gap between themselves and middle-class whites.[15]

There is one major positive change that has taken place in the past few years, however; a higher proportion of black youth are completing high school and college. Such youth are not following past patterns of individualistic escape from the black community—with their heightened awareness and knowledge, they are becoming more involved in black communities as residents and as activists. An important and new element in black nationalism is this union of black intellectuals and the black masses. While nationalism in the nineteenth century was notable for its lack of mass support, and for its lack of intellectual backing, in the mass movements of the twentieth century in recent years, intellectuals and the masses have combined their skills to give new impetus to nationalist movements. An excellent example is the development of the Mississippi Freedom Democratic Party.[16]

The key figure in the development of the recent trends was the late El-Hajj Malik El-Shabazz.[17] After his break with the Nation of Islam, he began to link the struggle of Afro-Americans with the struggle of oppressed peoples throughout the world, and particularly in Africa. He also emphasized *human rights* rather than *civil rights,* thereby increasing the hope that the Afro-American struggle might come before the United Nations. In this way, he internationalized the conditions of Afro-Americans and increased their awareness of the value of links with the non-Western world.[18]

Malik El-Shabazz gave new emphasis to the possibility of reform in America, an idea which was not contained in the view of either Marcus Garvey or Elijah Muhammad. In his "The Ballot or the Bullet" speech, he expressed the view that it was possible to produce a bloodless revolution in this country. His views were close to those of earlier nationalists who saw the development of the inner strengths of the black community as a first step in attacking racial barriers.

Another key contribution was his ability to appeal to both intellectuals and the masses and bring them together. El-Shabazz was very widely read, and a brilliant and articulate spokesman. His knowledge and logic impressed black intellectuals deeply. He was also an ex-convict and a man of the streets. Consequently, those who were the most deprived could identify as strongly with him as could the intellectual. His dual appeal to intellectuals and the masses, along with his emphasis upon racial solidarity, helped to bring these two elements of the black community into greater harmony.

In addition, Malik El-Shabazz spurred the development of black consciousness and black dignity. He was a living example of the positive effect of black consciousness, and there were few black people who met him who were not profoundly moved by what he was. Said one writer: "The concept of Blackness, the concept of National Consciousness, the proposal of a political (and diplomatic) form for this aggregate of Black Spirit, these are the things given to us by Garvey, through Elijah Muhammad, and finally given motion into still another area of Black Response by Malcolm X." [19] Another captures the nature of the appeal of El-Shabazz:

> It was not the Black Muslim movement itself that was so irresistibly appealing to the true believers. It was the awakening into self-consciousness of twenty million Negroes which was so compelling. Malcolm X articulated their aspirations better than any other man of our time. When he spoke under the banner of Elijah Muhammad, he was irresistible. When he spoke under his own banner, he was still irresistible. If he had become a Quaker . . . and if he had continued to give voice to the mute ambitions in the black man's soul, his message would still have been triumphant: because what was great was not Malcolm X but the truth he uttered.[20]

In the minds of present-day nationalists, El-Hajj Malik El-Shabazz was the greatest prince to come out of Ethiopia, and he is now the martyred saint of the movement.[21]

The articulation and development of the concept of Black Power continues the emphasis on an integral form of black nationalism,[22] yet with new elements. The political emphasis of Black Power renews the hope for reform in America, but with attention given to a reform of *values* as well as *behavior.* As such, it strikes more deeply at the basis of the problems separating blacks and whites. Black Power advocates also add a strong community orientation to black nationalism. They have not sought to build a unified mass movement around the country, but rather to develop programs and policies relating to the particular needs, conditions, and expressed desires of specific communities. The articulation of Black Power by a student-based organization, along with its community orientation, continued the unified approach of the intellectuals and the masses.

The development of black nationalist thought since the rise of El-Hajj Malik El-Shabazz has brought new emphasis to old issues, particularly the political and cultural forms of nationalism. The political emphasis is developing around the issues of colonization of black people, land, independence, self-determination for black communities, and the accountability of black leaders. When Malik El-Shabazz began to link black people with the Third World—a trend continued by Black Power advocates—black people became more aware that their situation in this country was very similar to that of colonized peoples throughout the world.

The large numbers of blacks in central cities, along with the presence of agencies of social control directed by forces outside of the black communities, bears a strong resemblance to a colonial situation.[23] This awareness has brought many blacks to the realization that such aggregations are similar to nations in the same way that Indian tribes saw themselves as nations, and they now occupy a territory which can be viewed as their own. LeRoi Jones puts it thus:

> What the Black Man must do now is to look down at the ground upon which he stands, and claim it as his own. It is not abstract. Look down! Pick up the earth, or jab your fingernails into the concrete. It is real and it is yours, if you want it.
>
> All the large concentrations of Black People in the West are already nations. All that is missing is the consciousness of this state of affairs.[24]

This awareness and consciousness is growing rapidly, and the emphasis upon self-determination for black communities is evidence of this fact. Indeed, if one understands this intense desire of black people to control their own communities and to determine their destinies, the urban insurrections of recent years take on another facet. If the community is seen as a colony and the social control agencies as colonial agents, then spontaneous outbursts may also be interpreted as attempts to reaffirm local rather than foreign control of the community. An altercation between a police officer and a black man is an assertion of colonial control, and the ensuing outburst, however destructive, is a reaffirmation of the view that such control does not lie exclusively with the colonial agencies.[25] Related to self-determination is the emphasis upon accountability being developed by nationalists. This view holds that those who hold positions of power which affect the black community must answer exclusively to the black community.

Colonization, land, self-determination, and accountability are the basic elements in recent developments in black nationalism, particularly the expansion of its political emphasis. Such views led one group of black militants, the Federation for Self-Determination in Detroit, to reject a grant of $100,000 from the New Detroit Committee in early 1968 on the ground that there were too many controls attached to the grant. Such views led the militant Black Panther party, based in Oakland, California, to begin to develop a political program on the grounds that black men who represent either of the major political parties cannot be held wholly accountable by the black community. Similar examples can be found in black communities across the nation, for these views are crucial aspects of the present framework of action of black nationalists today.

In recent years, black consciousness has received added impetus in terms of racial solidarity and a positive self-image. Thus, there is the new emphasis upon black as beautiful, and black youth are adopting African-style clothing and wearing African or natural hair styles.[26] They are seeking to establish black studies and black curricula on college campuses. These courses of study however, are to have a strong community and service orientation, rather than to become wholly intellectual pursuits. It is unquestionably the development of black consciousness and racial solidarity, along with the attitude of self-determination and black accountability, which has spurred the revolt of black athletes in many colleges and the attempt to obtain a black boycott of the 1968 Olympic Games. This is a new and revolutionary black consciousness, exemplified by El-Hajj Malik El-Shabazz and activated among black communities across the land.

Summary and Conclusion

Black nationalism has been one of the most militant and strident forms of Afro-American protest. It has grown out of the social conditions which have repeatedly indicated to black people that, though they are in this country, they are not a part of this country. The most recent emphases in nationalist thought are clearly developing the inner strengths of the black community through cultural nationalism, and expanding the concept of political nationalism. It may well be that black people will find that after all other barriers between the races have been eliminated, the barrier of color will prove to be ineradicable. Such a realization will give new and revolutionary impetus to black nationalism.

> Some of us have been, and some still are, interested in learning whether it is *ultimately* possible to live in the same territory with people who seem so disagreeable to live with; still others want to get as far away from ofays as possible.
>
> ELDRIDGE CLEAVER

Some White Perspectives

White Southerners

LEWIS M. KILLIAN

No group of people in the United States has acquired a worse reputation for prejudice and discrimination against blacks than have white Southerners, yet no group has been more vociferous in proclaiming its love for black people. Neither the stereotype of the vicious bigot nor the self-portrayal of the benign master accurately reflects the actual range and complexity of white Southerners' attitudes toward blacks. Blacks in the South have long differentiated between different types of whites, even while keeping in mind that the "love" of white Southerners for them has been qualified by the concept of "the Negro's place." Blacks have also known better than many whites that American racism has never been confined to the South—it appears elsewhere in different guises in different regions.

To conceive of the white southern viewpoint toward blacks primarily in terms of the hatred and cruelty of the frustrated "redneck" is to overlook the subtle but pervasive controls of a racial order which holds even the kindest, best-adjusted men in bondage and blinds them to the intrinsic cruelty of their way of life. A simplistic conception may also reinforce the erroneous conclusion that individual prejudice is the fundamental cause of collective discrimination. On the contrary, institutional racism constitutes the milieu in which benign but insulting paternalism becomes normal and hateful persecution is permitted. As white people in every section of the United States attempt to establish a modus vivendi with blacks living amongst them instead of only those in the South, they may learn much from the experience of Southerners, white and black.

It is possible to describe a specific white southern viewpoint towards blacks, shared by most white Southerners, which arose during slavery, yet still lingers long after freedom. This viewpoint has influenced the attitudes of countless individuals differing greatly from one another in their sympathy for, and behavior toward, blacks. It is the concept of the "color line" or "the Negro's place," which, as Herbert Blumer has observed, "has grown up as a primary basis for the organization of southern life." Yet, the notion of how this "place" is to be defined has undergone historical changes and is still in the process of evolution. Blumer suggests, "The color line is not appropriately represented by a single, sharply drawn line but appears rather as a series of ramparts, like the 'Maginot Line,' extending from outer breastworks to inner bastions." [1] A color line or racial order, as found in the South or in any other society, reflects and prescribes a hierarchical arrangement of groups in terms of power and status. It also demarcates the boundaries of groups whose members inhabit separate social worlds.

Not until structural and identificational assimilation, as characterized by the sociologist Milton M. Gordon, have taken place, do these boundaries disappear.[2] The behavior which maintains and symbolizes the dominance and the exclusion which are the prerogatives of the group high in the racial order may change, but the color line may still persist. Thus, Blumer says of the South,

> the color line was carried over from the old situations to the new situations—from the plantation to the factory, from the rural area to the city, from the old institutional settings to the new institutional settings. The Negro was subjected to essentially the same subordination and exclusion. . . . The color line persisted with vigor, changing in form as it adapted to new conditions such as the use of the automobile, but preserving essentially intact the social positions of the two racial groups.[3]

Although white supremacy has been the paramount theme of the racial order in the South, variations on it may be noted. Just as there have been successive reincarnations of the extreme of white southern bigotry symbolized by the Ku Klux Klan, there have existed successive generations of white liberals who have questioned the justice of the color line. The white southern liberal of each generation has found himself debating the issues which, in his day and time, were regarded as most salient by the majority of whites and blacks. Other pertinent issues he ignored as minor or explained away as false; he often did this with the issue of intermarriage. As a result, the liberals of one generation often appear incredibly naïve and conservative to their successors.

The spiritual ancestor of all white southern liberals, George Washington Cable, was cursed by a vision far too advanced for his time. Writing and speaking in the period of transition from white supremacy based on slavery to a new system of second-class citizenship for blacks, Cable foresaw that no equality could be effected with separation of the races. So, in the 1880's, he argued against the trend toward segregation of blacks in the schools, in public transportation, and in places of public accommodation. He pleaded for the need to guarantee the right of blacks to vote if democracy were to be a reality in the South. In vain, he called for the "Silent South" to speak out in agreement with him. Even when Cable felt that the battle was lost, he retained his faith in the existence, somewhere, of a significant number of liberal white Southerners. He believed that they had been intimidated into silence by unscrupulous politicians and were left without outside support as northern enthusiasm for civil rights diminished.

Thomas E. Watson of Georgia was the Vice-Presidential candidate of the Populist party in 1896, but he later became a race-baiting Democratic Senator. In his Populist period, he sounded the last loud cry from the white South for first-class citizenship for blacks before disenfranchisement and segregation made white supremacy virtually unassailable. Already, however, Watson saw the issues in narrower terms than had Cable. His major concern was the economic exploitation of small farmers and laborers by eastern financial interests. He regarded a political alliance between lower-class whites and black freedmen as a necessity in the struggle against forces which would use the race issue to exploit all workers and small farmers. Watson's Populism has been described as "the most promising experiment in interracial politics in the history of the South," but some analysts feel that his subsequent reversal to virulent racism signified that his concern for blacks had always been secondary to his passion for the welfare of lower-class whites.[4]

In 1896, the Supreme Court of the United States gave constitutional sanction to racial segregation by enunciating the "separate-but-equal" principle. Throughout the South, segregation became the law of the land and the taken-for-granted framework of the white Southerner's way of life. For half a century, the main thrust of white southern liberalism was to be aimed at equality of the races within this framework. White liberals may have privately disapproved of segregation, but by and large, they remained part of the "Silent South" regarding this issue. They concentrated on improving the conditions of life for blacks behind the wall of segregation. One of their first targets was the crime of lynching, valiantly attacked by the Association of Southern Women for the Prevention of Lynching. White southern liberals deplored the crass exploitation of black workers under the sharecropping system. They condemned the violence of the Ku Klux Klan and the unequal treatment of black defendants in the courts. Many white Southerners gave of their wealth to help improve the separate colleges for blacks which abounded in the region; some quietly subsidized the attendance of talented black youth at northern colleges.

In the 1940s, extending the right to vote in primary elections to blacks and providing equal financial subsidies for black public schools became "hot" issues. They were hot, for to be praised as a "friend of the Negro" or to be attacked as a "nigger lover" before 1954 did not require that the white Southerner go so far as to attack segregation itself. In 1946, Ellis Arnall, acclaimed nationally as a liberal governor of Georgia after he had dethroned Eugene Talmadge, published a book-length treatment of white southern liberalism,[5] in which he condemned the Ku Klux Klan, the poll tax, the white primary, and economic abuse of blacks. Of segregation, he said gingerly, "Where segregation exists, equivalent facilities must be afforded. Segregation must not be a device for robbing the Negro, as it has become in the instance of some classes of public transportation."[6]

When the Southern Regional Council was formed in 1944, neither the white liberals nor the blacks in its leadership felt compelled to put the issue of segregation at the top of their agenda. While noting the efforts of the National Association for the Advancement of Colored People to obtain a reversal of the separate-but-equal rule, the Council itself concentrated on attacking inequalities within the system. It took a strong public stand condemning the resurgence of antiblack violence which followed World War II, and it denounced the revival of the Ku Klux Klan. It lobbied with city councils and state legislatures to urge the employment of black policemen. The Council also launched a special project to monitor services offered to veterans, particularly black veterans, by federal and state agencies. These were not popular activities in the South at the time, and members of the Council and its local affiliates made themselves more unpopular by meeting and working interracially, even though they did not formally challenge the legality of segregation.

With the forces of regional law and custom arrayed against even these changes that would make separate more nearly equal, and with the United States Supreme Court repeatedly avoiding the constitutional question of the separate-but-equal principle established in *Plessy vs. Ferguson*, the task of overthrowing segregation seemed formidable, indeed. A few white southern voices were heard demanding its rapid erasure. In 1946, Lillian Smith, already ostracized because of her novel, *Strange Fruit*, openly proclaimed her belief that segregation dehumanized both blacks and whites. She expressed her disapproval of the gradualism characteristic of white southern liberalism: "I cannot endure the idea so many liberals hold that segregation must change slowly. I believe it can change as rapidly as each of us can change his own heart." In words reminiscent of the pleas of George W. Cable she declared, "We must say why segregation is unendurable to the human spirit. We must somehow find the courage to say it aloud. For, however we rationalize our silence, it is fear that is holding our tongues today." [7]

Whatever the issues on which they have taken their stands, white southern liberals have always found themselves opposed by enemies standing at the other end of the scale of white southern attitudes. While Cable was appealing to the Silent South to speak out against segregation, disenfranchisement, and exploitation, "Pitchfork Ben" Tillman, governor of South Carolina and later senator of that state, was preaching the innate inferiority of the black man and terrorizing his audiences with descriptions of black bestiality. His spiritual descendants defended lynching as necessary for the protection of white womanhood. Later generations of race-baiters argued that giving blacks the right to vote, equal education, and equal pay would lead to black domination of the South and to the ultimate evils, intermarriage and "mongrelization."

Yet, always a range of attitudes has been openly expressed. Neither the attacks of white liberals on discrimination in its various forms nor the defense of the most vicious forms of persecution by the bigots precisely mirrors the complex, ambivalent perception of blacks and of race relations held by the majority of white southerners. Each extreme represents a variation on the central theme of the color line. Describing this common concept as "a line which separates whites and Negroes, assigning to each a different position in the social order and attaching to each position a differential set of rights, privileges and arenas of action," Herbert Blumer has identified three important features:

> First, it represents a positioning of whites and Negroes as abstract or generalized groups; it comes into play when members of the two races meet each other not on an individual basis but as representatives of their respective groups. . . . Second, the color line is a collective definition of social position and not a mere expression of individual feelings and beliefs. Whites may have, and do have, a wide and variable range of feelings toward Negroes, from profound hostility to deep kindness and sympathy, yet adhere to the color line when and where the social code requires its application. . . . Third, as a metaphor, the color line is not appropriately represented as a single sharply drawn line, but appears rather as a series of ramparts. . . ."[8]

For the white South, the popular expression of the proper attitude towards blacks has been, "The Negro is all right in his place," not, "We hate Negroes." Moreover, the color line has existed and still exists outside the South without de jure segregation. Blumer observes of the North and West:

> Historically in these sections Negroes were barred, by tacit agreement if not by law, from equal access to many parts of the public arena; they were restricted predominantly to the lower levels of industrial occupation; they were scarcely ever allowed to enter the arena of white management; they were subjected to strong residential separation; and they were excluded generally from private circles of white association.[9]

In the South, however, the color line was never invisible like this. Instead of tacit "gentlemen's agreements," nonexplicit employment policies, and restrictive covenants in real estate deeds, segregation and an elaborate "etiquette of race relations" developed, supported by a vast and explicit structure of law and custom. Why the difference between the regions, if the end result in both instances was to keep blacks down and out?

Until recent decades, the number and proportion of blacks in the population of nonsouthern regions had been relatively small. More important, patterns of racial exclusion and subordination evolved in the North during an era when black workers occupied a peripheral position in its economy as compared with foreign immigrants. Blacks constituted only a minor threat to the superior position of whites and they could easily be ignored. As recently as 1962, James Baldwin said of the northern white, "He never sees Negroes. Southerners see them all the time. Northerners never think about them whereas Southerners are never really thinking of anything else." [10]

In the South during the years of transition following the Civil War, blacks constituted almost forty per cent of the population. They were scarcely invisible or hidden in small islands within large cities as in the North. They were everywhere. Except in atypical mountain areas, into which slavery had not penetrated, the white Southerner came in daily contact with them. This was particularly true in the world of work, for blacks, even as freedmen, were to remain an important sector of the labor force, particularly in agriculture and service. Reliance on black workers to fill positions as bellboys, janitors, cooks, nursemaids, and cleaning women maximized physical contact between the races. Whites had been accustomed to such intimacy with blacks who were slaves, but not with blacks who were free men and citizens. The poorer whites who could not afford slaves had, during the existence of the "Peculiar Institution," been able to console themselves with the thought that they were superior to the blacks because they were, at least, "free, white, and twenty-one." Emancipation and citizenship, along with the illiteracy and poverty which afflicted large numbers of whites and blacks alike, threatened to destroy the variety of white supremacy which made the poorest white superior to any black. During Reconstruction, the activities of northern reformers seemed to endanger the color line itself.

When northern ardor for reform of the South flagged, the most threatened classes of white Southerners, the impoverished small farmers, set about to restore white supremacy—political, economic, and social. Yet, blacks could not be entirely banished from the society; there were too many of them and they were too important as a source of cheap labor. Disenfranchisement, the growth of southern industry utilizing white labor, and the formalization of the etiquette of race relations provided the answer as to how to live with blacks who were no longer slaves.

The etiquette, symbolizing through its complicated ritual the constant inferiority of the black, no matter how closely he might associate with the white, made clear what the Negro's place was to be and served to keep him in it. Bertram Doyle, a black sociologist, has shown that much of the protocol was adopted from the rituals which white masters and black slaves had observed in plantation society.[11] Robert E. Park, a sociologist of the Chicago school and for many years the foremost student of race relations in the United States, observed that the development of a castelike pattern of segregation after Reconstruction resulted in "the emancipation of the poor white man. . . . It gave him an equality with the planter aristocracy he had never had under the old regime." [12]

Park captured the essence of the color line, southern-style, and of the traditional white southern view of the black man when he wrote:

> People not reared in the southern tradition have sometimes assumed that southern people's insistence on racial segregation is evidence

> that they cherish some deep, instinctive antipathy for the Negro race. Anyone who accepts that conception of the matter is likely to be somewhat mystified when he learns that the Negro is quite all right in his place.[13]

This, indeed, has been the normal, modal perception of the Black American for white Southerners. Catered to by courteous, patient domestics; seeing their floors swept and their garbage removed by strong, black arms shining with sweat; entertained by the singing and laughter of happy, childlike "Sambos"—how could they help but love a people who made life so charming for them? The faithful black servant or helper could be the recipient of the same sort of genuine affection that a parent lavishes on a child—or a master on his dog. All that was required was that the beneficiary show that he knew his place. Even the black who was above menial labor—the teacher, the preacher, the postal employee—could be viewed as that object of respect and liking as long as he adhered to the intricacies of the etiquette. It was not that blacks were ever so willing, so loving, or so happy as white Southerners believed them to be. Yet, much of the time they were careful not to shatter the illusion—they lived up to what Sarah Patton Boyle, a Virginia aristocrat converted from southern orthodoxy, has called "the Good Negro image." She has written:

> The Good Negro is full of music and rhythm, wit and good humor; he is philosophic and possessed of sweet faith; he is temperamentally cheerful and even in privation and ill-fortune, filled with deep contentment and exuberance of spirit. Sympathetic, understanding, swift to forgive, he is so responsive and outgoing that he feels abiding gratitude for the smallest kindness.[14]

Boyle exposes the fundamental ambivalence implied by the notion of "the Negro's place" by describing "the Bad Negro image" held by the same white Southerners—"a repulsive, dangerous, sub-human creature with no feeling or standards of decency." [15] The conviction with which both attitudes were held resulted in the inconsistency of behavior which so many non-Southerners have found difficult to comprehend:

> When a segregationist affirms that he loves Negroes, then goes out and deliberately insults or abuses one, he is not, as many people

> think, posing in the first instance, expressing his true feeling in the second. He's reacting first to the Good Negro image, then to the Bad. Something has called his Bad Negro image out.[16]

Yet, the treatment of blacks by white Southerners has been essentially cruel, whether the latter were responding to the Good Negro image or the Bad. Varieties of cruelty were practiced, some intentional and some unwitting.

The very paternalism stemming from the white Southerner's traditional conception of "the Negro's place" was often benign but it was inescapably and inherently cruel. Most of its monstrousness could not be traced back to some basic quantum of hatred for the black that had been trained into white Southerners, as some theories of prejudice imply. It was, instead, an unintended and even unrecognized consequence of the observance of the color line.

In short, many of the slights and insults which whites inflicted on blacks according to prevailing racial protocol resulted from a combination of unthinking conformity and patterned ignorance. The study, "The Transmission of Racial Attitudes Among White Southerners," by the sociologist Olive Westbrook Quinn, is unsurpassed as a portrayal of the depth of indoctrination which was normal for white Southerners.[17] Her observation, "Learning that one is white is part of the process of learning the identity of the self and the symbols and expectations appropriate to the position of that self," applies to white people throughout the United States. The symbols and expectations were simply more elaborate and formal in the South under segregation. The process of learning them was so subtle and yet so pervasive that the etiquette of race relations seemed natural to the "normal" white Southerner. Quinn says of this process:

> For the most part the South does not teach attitudes to its white children. Such teaching is not necessary; in establishing practices, by precept, by example, and by law, which separate the races and make distinctions between interracial and intraracial behavior, the South has established a way of life which can have but one meaning for those who diligently practice it. And to escape such practice has, until very recent times, been extremely difficult, for racial etiquette has been woven into the entire institutional fabric of southern culture.[18]

Thus, it simply did not occur to the white Southerner that calling adult blacks by their first names, sending them to the back of the bus, assigning their children to separate schools, and paying them wages defined by local norms as "good money for a nigger" were actions perceived by blacks as barbarously insulting and unjust. Worse yet, the power differential which segregation symbolized prevented whites from realizing how blacks felt. The worst indignity inflicted on black Southerners was that they were forced to act as accomplices in preserving the indifference of their oppressors. It demanded rare courage of a black to tell his white employer how he really felt about their relationship. It was safer simply to quit the job than to appear "uppity." Thus, the social distance which segregation established was paralleled by a wall of ignorance. The forthright critiques of southern racial customs which came from outside the region could not penetrate this wall, for the white Southerner could always point to "his" seemingly happy blacks to refute the criticisms of "outsiders." No one knows how many long-suffering domestic servants were coerced by white housewives, speaking in saccharine tones, into confirming that "those things" some Yankee had written were not true.

A second source of cruelty was what was perceived as the normal mode of enforcement of the color line—"keeping the Negro in his place." As Boyle pointed out, when a black person—particularly a man—violated the expectations reflected in the etiquette, the white Southerner felt threatened; the Bad Negro image was evoked. Again, the assumption that the black is menacing when he "gets out of place" is not peculiar to the southern variety of racism. In *Seize the Time*, Bobby Seale graphically portrays the anger and, more significantly, the bewilderment of white policemen in California when Black Panthers failed to cringe before them but asserted their constitutional rights. He describes one episode in which a group of Oakland policemen demanded that Huey Newton let them see a pistol which was lying on the seat of his car. Newton refused to hand it to them and ordered them away from the vehicle. The confusion of the police is described by Seale:

> "Well, I can ask *him* [Seale] if I want to see his pistol or not," the pig says. So I said, "Well, you can't see the pistol!" The motherfuckers

> try to get indignant. They were blabbing and oinking to each other about who in the hell we thought we were and, "Constitution, my ass. They're just turning it around." Then a pig said to Huey, "Who in the hell you think you are?" [19]

In the South in which blacks normally "stayed in their place," it was not only the police who assumed that they could punish on the spot any black who violated the convention. Any white person felt that he could do so. In fact, if a white permitted a challenge to the racial order to go unpunished, he himself might be enjoined by other whites. It was the fear of appearing "soft" that inhibited many whites who would not participate themselves from openly opposing lynchings and the Klan. The excesses of lynch mobs and of the hooded order were always justified as "keeping the Negro in his place," and anyone who criticized them might find himself accused of attacking the principle as well as the deed. Often the reproof directed at the black was merely verbal, but nevertheless harsh. Sometimes it was physical—a cuff on the head or a kick. If the black retaliated in kind, he knew he would be in "big trouble." He became a "bad nigger" in the eyes of whites and, as such, had no defense before the white man's law.

Despite the inherent severity of the system, conformity to white southern *mores* did not require that the white person hate the black and purposefully hurt him. Indeed, senseless, deliberate cruelty violated the norms. Yet, the very nature of the system which rendered the black community powerless made possible the third, most vicious form of inhumanity. This was the intentional, yet frivolous, tormenting of blacks by "mean" white men with a reputation among both whites and blacks for "hating niggers."

While emphasizing the normality of prejudice and discrimination in a "Herrenvolk democracy" such as that of the United States, Pierre van den Berghe, a sociologist who has studied race relations in many societies, points to the existence of pathological racism which goes beyond mere conformity:

> . . . There is unquestionably a psychopathology of racism, but in racist societies most racists are not "sick." They simply conform to social norms without "internalizing" their prejudices at any depth. Racism for some people is a symptom of deeply rooted psychologi-

> cal problems, but for most people living in racist societies racial prejudice is merely a special kind of convenient rationalization for rewarding behavior.[20]

The white South, like any other society, has contained individuals who, because of psychological problems having nothing to do with the racial order, derive personal satisfaction from attacking beings more defenseless than themselves. In some parts of the United States, Jews have been the butts of such people. During World War I, German-Americans were prime targets; during World War II, Japanese-Americans; today, long-haired youth are among their prey. But, members of no other group in the United States have been so vulnerable to the mindless attacks of pathological racists for so long as have been black Southerners. The fact that "nigger chaser" is a colloquialism for firecracker in the South symbolizes the casualness of the persecution of blacks "just for the hell of it." Such persecution ranged from malicious teasing to raping black women or murdering black men on the slightest pretext. The record of the differential in court sentences by race shows that felonious attacks by whites against blacks were hardly ever severely punished.

Lacking power, black communities could defend themselves against such depredation only at great risk. Bitter experience had taught black Southerners to keep little faith in the white police, yet, to take up arms in self-defense was a desperate measure—as it is today in the ghettos of New York, Chicago, and California.

If the "conforming prejudice" of white Southerners required "being kind to good colored folks," why did not the majority of whites restrain the pathological racists amongst them? Again, as in the case of lynchings, showing too much concern about the mistreatment of a black by a white exposed even the most highly-placed white to the danger of being branded a "nigger lover." Excessive cruelty was often deplored, but rarely challenged. The exceptional case in which a black could expect a white to take his side against another white only served to confirm the subordinate position of the blacks. The only black who could anticipate that a white who mistreated him would encounter proportionate retribution was one who had strong sponsorship in the white community. If a powerful white man regarded him as "his nigger," any other white who harmed him might incur the anger of the white sponsor. An unfortunate but valid comparison must be made: To torment one of "Mr. Charley's niggers" was like throwing rocks at his dog. Both affection for a highly regarded pet and a sense of threat to the master's status were brought into play in either case.

Ignorance of the effect on the black of the etiquette of race relations, defense of the traditional superiority of the white man, and the permissive attitude toward deviant acts of willful barbarity combined to constitute a system of oppression whose harshness could be fully known only to its victims. Most white Southerners did not conceive of themselves as being unkind to blacks, and they regarded instances of gross mistreatment as rare and aberrant. When critics characterized such excesses as typical southern behavior, the average white Southerner became angry and defensive. The veil of ignorance which blinded most white Southerners to the cruelty of the color line remained essentially intact until the voice of the United States Supreme Court emboldened blacks to rip it apart.

The two years following the Supreme Court's school desegregation decision of 1954 was the most traumatic period for white Southerners since Reconstruction. Even though the day the decision was handed down was characterized as "Black Monday," segregationists could at first cling to their illusion that "their colored people" were happy. It was only blacks from outside the South, from NAACP headquarters in New York, who really wanted a radical revision of the racial order, they thought. Soon, however, it became evident that an unheard of number of black Southerners wanted the decision implemented in their communities. Then, when thousands of blacks took to the streets in the Montgomery bus protest, the patterned ignorance of the past was dispelled. White Southerners began to say, "I always thought I knew our colored people, but now I wonder if I ever understood them." Not even the polite assurances of "Mandy" that she didn't want her children going to white schools were enough to make "Miss Annie" feel as secure as she once had. Moreover, under the pressure of federal law and nonviolent demonstrations, white

Southerners saw many of the symbols of "the Negro's place" destroyed.

As Blumer predicted it would, the color line shifted before the onslaught of the civil rights movement and federal laws. The most dramatic change came in the protocol of race relations, particularly in public contacts. While local islands of resistance still persist, today blacks eat in "white" restaurants, stay in the best motels, and sit in the front of buses; whites do not appear to care. The token desegregation of schools—the presence of a minority of black students in a previously all-white school—has, for the most part, been accepted as inevitable. In many cases, whites have made the best of a development which they once bitterly fought; many high school football coaches now prize their black stars. Even the election of some blacks to state legislatures, city commissions, and school boards has come to be taken as "normal." So many of the visible signs of the "Negro's place" in the South have disappeared that the change seems miraculous.

It would be a gross error to misinterpret these changes as signifying any serious weakening of the color line. No longer enforceable except at great cost to whites, many of the ritual acts of the etiquette have simply lost their symbolic value. That Black Americans, even black Southerners, are challenging the traditional definition of the Negro's place is a truth that can no longer be hidden by the ritual; hence, there is no point in following the old patterns. The fact that so many white Southerners seem unperturbed by violations of the latter does not signify that they have abandoned their assumptions of white superiority. Instead, they defend the racial order in different ways and at other points.

Tokenism has become acceptable, but any signs of real black equality or, even more, of black dominance, are vigorously resisted. Sending white children to a school historically identified as "Negro" or one in which black pupils and teachers outnumber whites is perceived as one such sign. Such a school is still regarded as a "Negro school" and as inferior. If whites cannot prevent school desegregation from reaching the stage where they must send their children to "black schools," those who can afford it send them to a private school—one of the more than three hundred "segregation academies" that have been established.

The election of enough black officials to give blacks real power, not just an improved bargaining position, remains intolerable to the average white Southerner, as it does to the average white American. It is only by the logic of the color line, the premise that America is a white man's society, that government by a minority of whites in a community with a black majority has been regarded as "natural" while the reverse is abhorrent. The same reluctance to regard white and black as interchangeable in a democracy applies in the world of work. For whites to bow to the necessity of accepting blacks as fellow workers is one thing; to accept them as supervisors arouses the old defensiveness. To admit black workers as members of unions has gradually become acceptable. To have them control unions, combining black power and union power, evokes resistance from employers and white workers alike.

In another respect, the color line has "changed" while remaining intact. Permitting blacks to enjoy access to places of public accommodation without challenge does not signify personal intimacy. In fact, a decrease in intimacy between whites and blacks can be observed in the South today. Under the protection of the old conventions of race relations, blacks and whites lived in separate social worlds but they talked to each other, albeit in a limited and restrained fashion. With the protocol of deference lacking, they talk to each other less and less. It becomes dangerous to talk too much when the black person may not feel constrained to preserve the white's illusions. At the same time, the declining prevalence of domestic servants reduces one of the major areas of personal contact. Even when the white housewife employs a black domestic, the chances are that the white woman is away at work, recreation, or club meetings while the servant is in the house.

While this sector of face-to-face interaction diminishes in significance, the realm of private, leisure-time association remains almost totally separate. The private club and the family swimming pool have become not only more important but more available to affluent white Americans. For the less affluent, the clubhouses of fraternal orders and the "education buildings" of churches remain important refuges in a world in which the bastions of public segregation have been overrun. Except among Catholics, the church remains the most segregated public institution in the South today.

White Southerners were frightened and offended by the threat of integration. Yet, after vigorously, but vainly, defending the outer bulwarks of the color line, they learned how to isolate and suppress the black man without the aid of the law, as whites in other regions had long done. Now they find themselves confronted with the enigma of black power and black nationalism. Despite the abrasiveness of the rhetoric of black power, white Southerners gain some solace from it. They interpret the demands of some blacks for strong, separate black institutions as confirmation of their own argument that blacks never did really want to "mix" with whites. At the same time, they are angered and upset by the verbal and sometimes physical aggression of the new-style black radicals. The image of the Bad Negro in its most bestial form is evoked. The old spirit of the lynch mob is revived, but expressed in the slogan "Law and Order." Newspaper accounts and television pictures of armed blacks in northern cities lend credence to the fear that the racial order is about to be overthrown in the whole nation, not by integration, but by brutal, black force.

No segment of white southern society has been more threatened by shifts in the color line and in black demands than the minority of nonconformists identified as white southern liberals. As deviants who were always reinforcing black militants in their attacks on successive ramparts of the color line, their position was never comfortable. In the 1940's, Myrdal characterized white southern liberals as virtually powerless and as committed only to a limited approach. He wrote:

> For the same reason—lack of expectation to be in power—the Southern liberal, in an extraordinary way, has become inclined to stress the need for patience and to exalt the cautious approach, the slow change, the organic nature of social growth. . . . In their activities Southern liberals have developed the tactics of evading principles; of being very indirect in attacking problems; of cajoling, coaxing and luring the public into giving in on minor issues.[21]

Lacking significant power in white society, white southern liberals were convinced of the sins of discrimination and, eventually, of segregation. They were never satisfied with their efforts to obliterate these evils, however, and they reacted to their inadequacy in a variety of ways.

One such reaction has been for the white liberal to take the guilt of the whole white South upon his own shoulders. No one can be more critical of the South than a guilt-ridden liberal who feels that to have been born a Southerner was an innate misfortune. That whites in other regions might be equally racist in their own way is difficult for such people to recognize. This masochistic attitude has often been accompanied by a glorification of the black, an inability to view him as a real human being possessing faults like other men. For such a person, trying desperately to atone for the sins of his forefathers and his contemporaries, association with blacks in defiance of custom brings a spiritual elation far out of proportion to the benefits derived by the blacks. Often the self-righteousness so obviously enjoyed by the white is as offensive to the black recipient of his liberality as is the crude prejudice of the orthodox segregationist.

A corollary of the glorification of the black as the pure and redeeming victim is an ill-concealed hatred of the "typical" white Southerner, particularly the representative of the lower classes. In retrospect, Will Campbell, the courageous white southern liberal now working as an independent minister to lower-class whites as well as blacks, observed:

> We white liberals romanticized the racial problem and sought to identify with the Negro movement by either ignoring the poor white or seeing his movement which manifests itself most often in such groups as the Ku Klux Klan as only a police problem.[22]

Myrdal had noted earlier that "the general public of the South is often spoken of by southern liberals as hopelessly backward. . . ." [23] These were marginal men, moving only occasionally and tentatively into the world of black Southerners but remaining ill-at-ease in white society. It may be postulated that the liberalism of some white Southerners has been motivated more by resentment of some form of rejection by other white Southerners than by a sincere sympathy for blacks. The question may be raised as to whether some of them were not marginal men before they became liberals, rather than having become marginal as a consequence of their deviant racial attitudes. Charles Levy, a northern white who taught in a black college in the South, notes the marginality of even northern whites who entered into "voluntary servitude" in the Negro movement, saying, "The dependence of the White [on blacks] largely results from a rejection of the White world and, in its place, an acceptance of the Negro world." [24] He suggests that as the civil rights movement shifted from a "lost" to a "won" cause, white recruits became increasingly less marginal.

The most mature and realistic form of white southern liberalism was—and is—to be found in the attitudes of white Southerners who, like James McBride Dabbs, former president of the Southern Regional Council, have viewed both white and black Southerners as coinheritors of a tragic history and fellow victims of a system which oppressed them both.[25] Another such liberal, the late Ralph McGill, former editor of the Atlanta *Constitution*, suffered much for his defense of the rights of black Southerners but never lost his deep love of all the people of the region, even those whites who denounced him. While seeing clearly the sickness inherent in southern racism, such men have also been able to perceive that racism was an American, not merely a southern, problem.

All white southern liberals, even such realists as these, found their dilemma intensified by the series of desegregation decisions handed down by the Supreme Court beginning in 1954. With the "separate-but-equal" principle nullified by the highest court in the nation, the issue of segregation could no longer be avoided in words or in deeds. Liberals could not plead, as they had in the past, that the question of "social equality" was a false point of contention interjected by bigots into debates about economic and political justice. Desegregated schools represented the very sort of intimacy that segregationists had always invoked as a vision of doom. Now the liberal had to affirm his willingness to accept and defend this sort of intimacy or give up his claim to being a southern liberal. Some of the widely acclaimed liberals of the New Deal era, such as John Temple Graves and Virginius Dabney, were shaken out of the ranks by this issue.

Even more disturbing was the fact that actions which had once been clearly illegal became legal, but not popular. A new breed of blacks—"protest leaders"—began to test the willingness of white Americans to abide by the laws handed down by their own courts. In doing so, they defied local laws of dubious constitutionality and regional customs long deemed sacred. When they did so, they did not ask for the acquiescence or the support of white liberals; they took the initiative, but severely judged those whites who failed to rally to their support when the forces of repression came into action. So, the very same blacks whom the white liberals so desperately wanted to love and to help became, in one aspect, threatening figures.

Blacks in the civil rights movement sensed this ambivalence. They kept insisting that they wanted white people to do things with them, not for them. It was well-nigh impossible, however, for even the most liberal, sympathetic white to abandon his accustomed posture of leadership. Having matched wits with conservative whites on behalf of the black man for so long, he was reluctant to surrender his role as strategist. Even white liberals from the North who went south to join the struggle could not divest themselves of their missionary, "uplift" attitudes. So, white liberals, southern and northern, found themselves confronted by the distrust and rejection symbolized in the slogan, "Black Power."

This latest dilemma of the southern white liberal is worse than any he has ever encountered before. The enemy of black liberation has ceased to be simply the segregationist. A spokesman for the Southern Regional Council put it this way in 1970:

> In the beginning our adversary was simply the recalcitrant white South, large in numbers, capable of swift, violent resistance, holding all of the power. When we took on the white segregationists we did so with great relish and moral fervor. And when the surface battles were won and the civil rights acts passed we found that many young blacks, casualties of the long disheartening struggle, were talking their own brand of separatism. Now as the school desegregation controversy has moved north a new adversary, whom we once called friend, has developed—the accommodating northern liberal.[26]

The adversary was not just disillusioned blacks and accommodating northern liberals, however. It was the cherished ideals of the white southern liberal himself; the enemy was within.

First, the white southern liberal had firmly believed that the Constitution of the United States, if interpreted in the spirit of the Declaration of Independence, was adequate to guarantee racial equality. Segregation and racial discrimination were viewed as perversions of the true values of American society. These values were believed to be embodied in the American creed as described by Gunnar Myrdal. Thus, Frank P. Graham, a leading white southern liberal, declared:

> The southern youth movement had its origin not in Moscow but in Greensboro, N.C. Its deeper sources are in the idealism declared in Carpenters' Hall, Philadelphia, on July 4, 1776. Its distant headwaters are in the Judean Hills where the carpenter's son preached the gospel of equal freedom and sacred dignity of all persons as children of one God and brothers of all people. This youth movement is a contemporary expression of the unfulfilled idealism of the American Revolution and is a local expression of the on-rolling revolution of colonial colored and exploited people of the earth.[27]

A second article of the liberal's faith was affirmation of the rule of law and rejection of extralegal violence. For either black or white dissenters to resist violently what they regarded as evil laws had always been regarded by them as both immoral and dangerous. Violence had been the traditional weapon of the Ku Klux Klan. The highly moralistic white liberal could not lose faith in the conventional adage that "two wrongs don't make a right." The nonviolent strategy of the civil rights movement appealed to him because, even though it was dangerous, it was redeeming in its morality.

Implicit in both these tenets was a third, the ideal of love. The white southern liberal's definition of the southern tragedy was that blacks had, beyond all reason, bestowed on whites an unrequited love. The answer seemed to be for whites to prove that they did, indeed, love their black brothers and sisters, even if to do so demanded a dangerous affront to the tradition of segregation. The exhilaration which interracial meetings provided derived primarily from the fact that in their course liberal whites defiantly manifested their love for blacks rather than from any appreciable effect of the programs on the social order. They were love-feasts. Though white liberals might wince at the hatred that lay behind the epithet, they took some pride in being called "nigger lovers." Indeed, they would often reply, "We love all God's children."

Finally, when the Brown decision made the issue of segregation central to the national debate over race relations, white southern liberals committed themselves absolutely to the absolute value of integration. Sanctioned by the highest court, portrayed as the heavenly vision in Martin Luther King, Jr.'s, "I Have a Dream" address, it incorporated and implemented the liberals' other convictions. As integration progressed, the Constitution would truly become color-blind; the violence of the state would be exercised only against those who sought to keep the races in an unnatural state of separation; whites and blacks would learn to love one another from childhood. In the South during the active years of the civil rights movement, to call for "respect for law" meant to demand that integration be allowed to progress without hindrance. White southern liberals rejoiced in every token step which brought blacks and whites together. Even though they might recognize the long-range inadequacy of these small beginnings, they took comfort from the maxim that "the longest journey begins with the first step."

Then, beginning with the ascendance of Stokely Carmichael and the Black Power movement, the signals from blacks became contradictory and confusing. Notions of "compensatory treatment" and "reparations" arose to conflict with the ideal of a law which would be color-blind and based solely on respect for individual, not group, rights. Blacks made clear their basic distrust of the white man's police and his courts, even at the federal level. Faith in the efficacy of nonviolent action diminished among black people, and the Deacons and the Panthers took up arms in self-defense. Even moderate black leaders informed whites that it was not love but justice that they required from them. To achieve justice, some also demanded power—black power, not white liberal or coalition power. Worst of all, some of the loudest black voices bespoke a new kind of separation—black culture, black studies, black control of black institutions, and black communities.

Even though not all blacks, perhaps not even most, seemed thus to be turning away from the goal of integration, for any of them to do so was profoundly disturbing for the white southern liberal. He had traditionally suffered abuse and ostracism if he had merely spoken out for integration, for respect for law, for the loving community. He may have been beaten or jailed if he had gone beyond words. Whereas the new black leaders of the civil rights movement had simply threatened him with their demands for unqualified support, the newer leaders of the black power movement appeared to actually betray him, to deliver him into the hands of his old enemy, the segregationist.

The present situation of the white southern liberal causes him anguish for several reasons. He is torn by the discrepancy between procedures and results, the age-old conflict between means and ends. Leslie Dunbar, formerly director of the Southern Regional Council, observes:

> The liberal faith has been in procedures, in following the rules of the game, and in accepting the outcome of fairly reached decisions. To say that liberalism must learn to value good results as highly, or even more highly, than good procedures is to arouse apprehension of authoritarian elites. Yet I think this is the dilemma of contemporary liberalism.[28]

He goes on to say:

> The Bill of Rights is no longer a sufficient cause. I say this to liberals. We have to affect the conditions of life. We shall not make the old rights real unless we relate them to life. Liberals will not like my formulation, but our task is to make the Bill of Rights worthwhile, and that means coming to helpful terms with the cause of those making a revolution.[29]

Further, the white southern liberal is unlikely to share the disillusionment with tokenism which so many blacks experience so profoundly. The changes that have come to the South since 1954 truly have been so great that it is hard for the white liberal not to perceive them as signs of genuine progress and as stimuli to greater efforts in behalf of integration. If he accepts the verdict of some blacks that whites are not going to allow real integration to come about, where can he turn? He has rejected the world of the white segregationists and he cannot inhabit the new world where black is beautiful. Even if he can intellectually grasp the disillusionment of blacks with tokenism, he cannot really experience "black rage." Although he may hate some whites, he can never be tempted as are many blacks to hate all of them.

The worst aspect of the white southern liberal's predicament, however, is one which reveals that even he cannot escape the taint of racism in a racist society. The most drastic challenge that the Black American can pose for the white American is to demand the right of self-determination. For the white liberal, committed to integration and the loving community, this demand requires that the black be free to choose to continue the struggle for integration now, to postpone his reconciliation with the white man until he feels that he has become reconciled with himself, or to elect the path of separatism. To the white liberal struggling to make blacks first-class citizens, what could be more shocking than the assertion by leaders of the now defunct black separatist organization, Republic of New Africa, that blacks were never asked whether they wanted to be citizens at all—that citizenship was simply conferred on them? The illusion which is most difficult for the white liberal to dismiss is the essentially racist belief that he has the right and the competence to judge what is best for the black man. As more and more blacks deny him the right to make such a judgment, no matter how good his intentions, the more isolated from both blacks and other whites he feels. It is his turn to admit that not even he ever understood "*his* colored folks."

While the white liberal grows increasingly bewildered and forlorn, the white southern segregationist, moderate or radical, finds his image of the Bad Negro confirmed and strengthened. College students and television performers with "Afros" and dashikis; appeals for black studies departments and black dormitories; demands for recognition of black student organizations; Black Panthers in shoot-outs with the police—all combine to assure him that he was right all along. Blacks really prefer to stay with "their own kind," he asserts anew. Furthermore, given a taste of power and freedom, they do run wild, as he has always said they would. Adjusted to the shifts in the color line, token integration now appears reasonable to him; he and his children have learned to live with a few qualified Negroes. The tension and turmoil of northern cities confirm his predication that letting blacks "get out of place" will lead to national disaster. Although the nature of the color line may have changed, the belief of the average white Southerner that America must remain a white man's society is stronger than ever. He is heartened, however, by the growing number of whites throughout the rest of the land who seem to agree with him.

The Silent Majority

NORBERT WILEY

The main point I want to make is that the people most to blame for American racism are the rich, the powerful, and the famous. They have the greatest control over the major sources of racism and they gain the most from it. In contrast to this élite, the silent majority or broad mass of prejudiced people are relatively blameless, for, even though they often have the worst of intentions, they just don't have the power to do much of the harm. Their individual acts of discrimination function as a smokescreen to obscure the deeper sources of the problem, and this makes them a front line of defense for racist institutions. But, in reality, they should be pitied, for the same racist institutions that the average white defends hurt him as well as the blacks. The diagnosis of Tom Watson, the populist American congressman, spoken some six decades ago to the ordinary black and white, is still basically true:

> You are kept apart so that you may be separately fleeced of your earnings. You are made to hate each other because upon that hatred is rested the keystone of the arch of financial despotism which enslaves you both. You are deceived and blinded that you may not see how this race antagonism perpetuates a monetary system which beggars you both.[1]

If Watson's words sound exaggerated today, it is because they make it sound as if somebody "up there" is planning the whole thing, and that some gigantic capitalistic plot is in operation to divide and conquer. Unfortunately, there is no such plot. If there were, the task of straightening out this most kinky of American problems would be a lot easier. Just find the mastermind conspirators and stop their game! In fact, though, the roots of racism are now impersonal, "built-in," institutional, and all intertwined with nonracist elements. The relation of these roots to the people responsible for them is indirect and veiled. Half the job of acting on this problem is in just getting a fix on what's happening, and the whole apparatus of smokescreens, blind alleys, vicious circles, and self-disguising practices—all of which defy clear analysis—is one of the main obstacles to intelligent action.

The purpose of this essay, therefore, is to try to locate the major strands of racism, to get some idea of cause and effect, and, in particular, to distinguish the role of the silent majority of bigoted Americans from the role of the master institutions and the élite which stands behind them. To do this, I will first contrast individual and institutional racism, then show how individual racism is interwoven with institutional racism, and, finally, say a little about changing things. None of this will be particularly new. Most of it has been said before by critical economists and sociologists, but it is basically correct and worth attempting to elaborate upon a little further.

Individual and Institutional Racism

When a white person holds a prejudicial attitude or executes some harmful act toward a Black, this form of racism and the moral responsibility for it can be attributed to that specific individual. This is individual racism, and its severity ranges from harmless fantasies and minor insults to the extremes of house-burnings and murders. Individual racism is highly visible and dramatic; it captures the imagination and makes good newspaper copy. The Black man who was beaten to death when he stopped to change a tire in Chicago's stockyards neighborhood a few years ago is remembered with greater outrage than are the thousands who die unnecessarily in childbirth, from preventable disease, or in the front lines of Asian wars. Even though individual racism, particularly lynching, has declined a great deal in recent decades, it still plays an important role, and it will be helpful to list the main explanations for it.

Since individual racism is strongest among the white working class, especially the poor, it is not surprising that one major theory for this racism is that it is basically economic, taking its origin from competition over the limited supply of jobs, housing, and other material goods. It is unfair competition, of course, but if Blacks can be kept from better-paid manual jobs, better-quality housing, and more comfortable schools, there is all the more for the whites to enjoy. This "fighting over crumbs," as a Negro congressman recently called it, is hardly a sensible economic strategy for poor whites, and there is some question whether whites make even short-run gains from it, but it still may be an important part of the motivation for individual racism.

A second and related theory, which is noneconomic, is that individual discrimination comes from competition over status, with some whites feeling that they make status gains from Black subordination. No matter how poor and lowly the white, he can always say, "At least I'm not a nigger," and that keeps him from ever hitting rock bottom. According to this view, status fears hit middle-level people, too, if they don't feel secure in their situation. If a middle-level person, such as a farmer, small businessman, or skilled tradesman, sees a slow slipping-away of his position, this insecurity may lead him to attack Blacks just as readily as a white of lower but more secure status.

Sometimes the theory of status competition is embedded in a broader theory of authoritarianism, according to which some people have a syndrome of personality qualities that are highly autocratic and military, along with an excessive concern for status and dislike of presumed status inferiors. But this theory does not add much to the simple notion of status competition, mainly because it is fuzzy and not well-proved, and it need not detain us here.

The third, and most popular, theory of individual racism is that of scapegoating or "displaced hostility." This view argues that prejudice and discrimination are often a way of ventilating anger that would more properly be directed at some other target—one's boss, spouse, or whoever was the cause of the original frustration. Poor people are especially prone to this mechanism because they have more material frustrations and have little power to fight the real source of their frustrations. They take it out on a group even lower and more powerless than themselves and get at least a false sense of satisfaction in that way. There is a fair amount of evidence for this interpretation, but I find this theory too individualistic in flavor and will later give a more political and social version of it.

Competition, status rivalry, and scapegoating all seem to be involved in individual racism, and it is no big problem understanding the racism of individual whites, but these processes do not operate in a vacuum. They have their origins in institutional pressures on the whites themselves and result not in lessening, but in strengthening, the very pressures they are designed to alleviate. But before discussing that we must look more closely at institutional racism.

Racism, along with all the main forms of injustice in the United States, is built into the nation's central institutions. The situation of the poor, of Blacks and other minority ethnics, of women, of the aged, and so on, is a result of the normal, legal workings-out of life. These injustices are technically just, and any serious attempt to rectify them bumps into some solid part of the established order: the laws, the government, the sanctity of private property, the sacred teachings of the churches, and other features of settled American life. White racism, especially, has its roots in the core institutions, and this is why the race problem is so intractable. Resolving it would require tampering with the whole institutional fabric, an authentic "new deal" (Did you ever wonder why Harry Truman felt the need to call for a "Fair Deal" after FDR had just completed his "New Deal?"), and, in the short run, would hurt many powerful and unwilling interests.

The term "institutional racism" can be used in at least three senses: that the harmful action be customary or patterned rather than individually thought out and deliberately done, that it be done by collective or corporate entities rather than by individuals, and that it be not morally attributable to actual individual persons. Correspondingly, there seem to be three major sources of institutional racism: cultural systems, bureaucracies, and economic markets. Such cultural systems as language, beauty standards, moral codes, and legal systems are complex patterns, standing over and above everyday activity and giving shape to social action, both individual and corporate. The large-scale organizations we call bureaucracies are the major corporate entities in America, and their power and pervasiveness are now far greater than that of private individuals. Economic markets, with their formulation of wages and salaries, interest rates, and commodity prices, operate at a level beyond morality. No specific individuals, or so it would seem, set up the high rents, low wages, or high prices in the ghetto. Blame it on the market.

Of these three sources, markets and bureaucracies stand in the foreground, and cultural systems, acting more as effects than causes, stand in the background as legitimizing devices. If the racism of markets and bureaucracies were eliminated, cultural standards would change, too, in due course. One of the best discussions of market and bureaucratic racism in the mid-1960's is in the writings of Harold Baron,[2] who made an analysis of institutional racism in Chicago, a city which, for our purposes, can stand for the rest of American cities.

There is a separate Negro market in Chicago for loans, housing, buying of all kinds, and, to a great extent, for employment. In every case, the workings of supply and demand—limited as this may be in a large-corporation economy—and the sanctity of private property are protected, just as in the larger white market, but the separateness in each case gives the Blacks less economic power. The dual set of markets establishes artificial scarcities and forces Blacks to compete less successfully than whites do in white markets. Therefore, housing is more expensive, loans come at greater interest, work pays less, and ordinary shopping items cost more. If Blacks could compete equally in the larger white markets, they would be at whatever economic level they could reach, still subject to the institutional exploitation that capitalism inflicts on all of its have-not groupings, but at least not victimized by that extra exploitation that comes from institutional racism.

In addition, there is a dual set of public bureaucracies in Chicago in the areas of schools, political institutions, welfare agencies, police districts, and the like. These bureaucracies develop somewhat different standards and informal procedures from their counterparts in white neighborhoods and this results in inferior, but basically quite legal, service, just as the separate submarkets result in higher prices and lower wages. Baron calls these sets of subinstitutions a web, like a spider web, and sees their racist strength in their joint effects and mutual support, not in the strength of any single one of them.

Baron also points out that these separate institutions, while they operate in a relatively automatic way now, had to be high-pressured into existence when Blacks came north in the early twentieth century. This took quite a bit of legal skullduggery, trade union cooperation, financial collusion, a few bloody race riots, and a militant northern Ku Klux Klan.

Up to now, we have discussed the difference between individual and institutional discrimination, the two major forms of racism, and pointed out that, even though institutional racism is not a great deal more severe than the exploitation that touches the lower white groups, its severity is enough to place blacks in a permanently bottom-dog status.

Relation of Individual to Institutional Racism

While individual and institutional racism are distinct, they also bear a relationship to each other, and any attempt to alleviate racism must avoid the mistakes of the past and take account of that relationship.

Until the 1960's, attempts to do something about racism, especially white attempts, focused mainly on individual racism. The main weapon was to be white education, both formal and informal, and, on the assumption that low education somehow causes racism, it was assumed that educating the population generally would make it less bigoted. This weapon, since it took no account of institutional racism, proved to be a very blunt one, and the idea of education as the antidote to racism has basically been a failure.

More recent attempts have been aimed directly at institutional racism, via legal action, mass demonstrations, political pressures, and various forms of violence. In this way, it was hoped, the major institutional forms would be changed and the racism of individuals could be bypassed. Eventually, individuals would come into line with the new institutional realities. This strategy, while more successful than education, has not worked well, either, largely because the silent majorities of voters and counter-demonstrators have limited the effectiveness of direct attacks on institutions and intimidated those few authorities that might otherwise have been willing to support limited institutional changes.

Clearly, individual and institutional racism are mutually supportive and a successful attack on racism will have to hit on both levels, as well as at the connection between them. This connection is a complex one, but I think the key to it is in the way the class and race systems interlock in this country. Class domination, as such, is purely economic and has no necessary implications for ethnic or racial relations. Race domination, as such, is noneconomic and involves the oppression of a physically distinct group on purely biological grounds. But the two forms of domination, class and race, are concretely connected and, in the United States, this relationship gives a strength to each that neither would have on its own.

The link between class and race can be seen if we look again at the scapegoating process, this time as a socially structured and not as an individualistic process. The racism of the white under and working class is largely a result of the frustrations they meet in their own class subordination. Low income, employment insecurity, inadequate education, a feeling that things are not improving, all these economic and social weaknesses are grist for the mill of scapegoating. The reason why the poorest and lowest-educated whites are often the worst bigots is simply that they are poor and have meagre educations and cannot do anything about it. In sociological terms, they are the victims of blocked opportunity, caught in the bind between an attraction for material success, on the one hand, and the lack of means to success, on the other.

A more rational response to blocked opportunity is to join a workingman's political party and push for the laws that would increase equality of opportunity and equality of life in the United States. But no such political party exists, and the two major parties that do exist offer no way of rectifying the basic injustices that many white Americans are subject to. In the absence of a rational means for fighting back against the system that hurts them, the lower-class white takes out his frustrations on Blacks and on other available targets.

This scapegoating, itself an indirect result of economic oppression, has the effect of solidifying the very oppression that causes it, for it divides the poor, Black and white, into two hostile groupings and prevents them from uniting politically to fight their common enemies. Tom Watson was right on this. And, ironically enough, one reason the white worker has no viable avenue of fighting back is that the racial cleavage destroys the class solidarity on which a workingman's party would have to be based.

When Blacks attempt to change institutions by themselves, with their own protest organizations and without the help of the lower-class whites, they find themselves weighted down by these whites in several ways. (1) Lower-class whites are partly responsible for the present Black condition through the scapegoating process already described. (2) But when Blacks frame broad reform programs, they find they would have to change the whole class system, not just the racist part of it, because to make the economic and other institutional changes that Blacks need, they would have to make them for whites also. Thus, Blacks must fight the battle for the (absent) whites as well as the one for themselves. (3) And, to add insult to injury, these same whites whose cause is being advanced by Blacks are doing their darndest to block the efforts of Blacks to change the system. Thus, the Blacks bump into the poor whites both coming and going, as, with a stupidity beyond words, the whites hurt their own cause.

The importance of individual racism, then, is not in its direct harm for the life chances of Blacks. Institutions get the main blame for that. The importance, instead, is in creating a political climate which supports institutional oppression of all kinds, racist and otherwise, and in preventing the interracial alliances that a thoroughgoing social reform would require. That is why neither individual nor institutional racism can be fought separately; they support each other and form a vicious circle.

The relation between individual and institutional racism operates at the bottom levels of society much as we have described it, but, in another way, it operates at the top of society. It is possible, for example, to be an extremely tolerant person, both in attitudes and behavior, yet work for a basically racist corporation. This is a general pattern. The people with the greatest power over large corporate entities, business and nonbusiness alike, are usually college graduates, frequently from the liberal Ivy League universities, who pride themselves on being above the bigotry of the uneducated. Yet these people function, conscience-free, in racist institutions. How does this moral blindfold work? Let us first look at the market.

The idea of the market, developed by the British economists in the late eighteenth and early nineteenth centuries, is that economic life operates according to natural principles, much like the stars or tides, and that man's conscious actions have no effect on economic life. The market is never moral or immoral; it's amoral. This notion of the market has long been known, especially by people at the bottom, to be somewhat of an exaggeration, but it held sway as a general definition of things and was supported by the idea that no single buyer or seller was big enough to influence the price of anything. Prices were determined by the joint influence of many buyers and sellers, each pursuing his individual profit.

The importance of this market notion is that it divorced economic life from individual moral responsibility. If the market hurt someone, caused great inequalities in wealth, caused high prices for those least able to afford them, became implicated in race discrimination, no one could be blamed. It was just an economic law, like any other natural law. And if anyone tried to inject morality into the economy, by passing a law or imposing some kind of community control, *this* was considered immoral and was labeled as that most vicious of modern sins, socialism.

Actually, many economic laws have been passed in this country in the last few decades, and many community controls imposed on the economy, but most of them are superficial and for show. Perhaps the major law has been the Wagner Act of 1935, which supported the unionization of large manufacturing industries. But this has primarily benefited the middle third of the work force, overwhelmingly white. The bottom third, working in workplaces that are small and difficult to unionize, has benefited little. Most Blacks, coincidentally, are in that bottom third.

The moral immunity of the market, which leaves people conscience-free to participate in an oppressive system without feeling any guilt, is one of the main pillars of institutional racism, and all attempts to alleviate the worst excesses of the market have had little effect on the Black situation.

In the case of bureaucracy, the moral blindfold again involves organization and anonymity, but in a different way. Bureaucracies are hierarchical organizations with a machinelike internal structure based on a strict division of labor, impersonality, and a clear set of rules. On the face of it, bureaucracy is the exact opposite of the market. Bureaucracy is centralized rather than dispersed, based on direct policy-making rather than on the blind interplay of many forces, and the like. But, for our purposes, there are important similarities, deriving mainly from their moral climate. Bureaucracies are self-defined as purely technical instruments, operating solely in the pursuit of efficiency and neutral toward all moral issues. This is made explicit in the role-prescriptions of underlings. One obeys orders, indeed makes a fetish of doing so, regardless of their moral character.

At the top, at the policy-making level, policy is made in pursuit of bureaucratic objectives, usually the maximization of profit. The policy-makers are understood to be acting in the role of policy-makers and not as real people. One shelves his private conscience for the organization. This fiction, that it is not people but bureaucrats acting and, therefore, morality is irrelevant, goes even deeper into the very identity of the organization. Organizations are legally conceived as persons. The Fourteenth Amendment of the Constitution, originally framed to protect the rights of Blacks, was interpreted to mean that corporations, too, were persons, and their rights as persons, quite generously conceived, could not be abridged except by "due process." Thus, an amendment framed to help Blacks was twisted around to give corporations the legal-moral position which made it ever easier for them to exploit Blacks. The corporation itself is a person, while the people in corporations are nonpersons. They are merely "incumbents," and their actions are morally attributable to the corporation itself, not to these people personally.

In this way, the real people, especially the powerful ones, are taken off the moral hook and an abstract organization is made to carry their sins. With clean hands and pure hearts, the top dogs run a racist society, placing the blame for the latter on the markets and bureaucracies that make them rich.

So, the bottom people, who are personally the most racist, can do little harm except in supporting the institutional structure. The top people, who own and control that structure, are morally insulated from it. Scapegoating, on the one hand, and the amorality of markets and bureaucracies, on the other, are the two links between individual and institutional racism. Any program for change must break those two links.

Possibilities for Change

No one can talk about improving the race situation without feeling pessimistic. All indications are that American institutions are something of a dinosaur, too overdeveloped for change. And, since World War II, none of our basic problems, foreign or domestic, are even being honestly examined, let alone solved. But it is possible that this institutional freeze will thaw a bit in the next few years as internal and foreign pressures mount, and it is extremely important that such an opening be used well.

Everything I have said so far argues that the race problem cannot be solved in isolation from other problems. If race is mixed with class, then the race problem must be resolved along with changes in the class system. If racism is embedded in institutions, then it must be eliminated as part of a more elaborate restructuring of institutions. At the present time, there are no clear pictures of what a restructured United States might look like. There are no maps for how to get there. Existing ideologies were evolved with less-developed societies in mind, and since there has been no revolution yet in a developed society, it is anybody's guess whether, when, where, and how it might come. But some general guidelines can be given for the present United States.

Automatic reform, especially in race relations, just does not seem likely. Nothing in American history indicates that this is a self-reforming country. Historically, whatever angry group one looks at—farmers, labor, minorities, women, the poor—the story is one of false reform, based on tokenism, symbolic concessions, divide-and-conquer, or whatever tactic was necessary to outlast the reform momentum. The basically unchanging distribution of income in the twentieth century tells the real story of reform. A business-as-usual strategy could produce only that, business as usual.

At the other extreme, placing total emphasis on a violent revolutionary strategy is also an obvious loser. Even though many Americans have far more justification for revolution than the colonists did in 1775, there are not enough of them powerful enough to bring it off.

Between the two extremes, many tactics are operating now—but no clear strategies—and the general feeling on the Left seems to be to try everything at once, since no one approach has any clear superiority over any other and no master strategy can dictate tactics. To this I can only add that organization of the deprived must, at some point, cross racial lines and reverse the Black-versus-white, divide-and-conquer process that is maintaining the present stalemate. Perhaps an initial organization of the dark minorities into separate groupings of Chicanos, Blacks, Indians, Puerto Ricans, and so on is just what the poor whites need to encourage themselves to get organized and into alliances with the groups they now scapegoat. Such a process will take many years and will be constantly imperiled by the blandishments of false reform that the system will offer to leaders. But false reform rises from the present system of bureaucracies and markets that is central to our social problems. If the deprived groups identify the institutional sources of their oppression and move toward a more humane set of institutions, false reform may be avoided, and the United States may yet have a chance to heal itself.

The Irish

ANDREW M. GREELEY

"As a pilgrim father that miss th' first boats, I must raise me claryon voice again' th' invasion iv this fair land be th' paupers and arnychist iv effete Europe. Ye bet I must—because I'm here first. . . . As I told ye I come a little late. Th' Rosenfelts an' th' Lodges bate me be at last a boat lenth, an' be th' time I got here they were stern an' rock bound thimsilves. So I got a gloryous rayciption as soon as I was towed off th' rocks. Th' stars an' sthripes whispered a welcome in th' breeze an' a shovel was thrust into me hand an' I was pushed into a sthreet excyvatin' as though I'd been born here."

MR. DOOLEY, FINLEY PETER DUNNE

"The whole race . . . is madly fond of war, high-spirited and quick to battle, but otherwise straightforward and not of evil character. And so when they are stirred up they assemble in their bands for battle, quite openly and without forethought, so that they are easily handled by those who desire to outwit them; for at any time or place and on whatever pretext you stir them up, you will have them ready to face danger, even if they have nothing on their side but their own strength and courage. On the other hand if won over by gentle persuasion they willingly devote their energies to useful pursuits and even take to a literary education. Their strength depends both on their mighty bodies, and on their numbers. And because of this frank and straightforward element in their character they assemble in large numbers on slight provocation, being ever ready to sympathize with the anger of a neighbor who thinks he has been wronged."

STRABO, SPEAKING OF PRE-CHRISTIAN CELTS
Quoted by Myles Dillion and Nora Chadwick
in *The Celtic Realms* (New York:
New American Library, 1967), p. 7.

The most obvious thing one can say about the American Irish is that every accusation made against more recent immigrant groups to the large cities was made against the Irish first. They were lazy, shiftless, dirty, savage (as early as the Revolutionary War there were considerable doubts as to whether you could trust an Irish soldier).

> . . . The Irish soldiers abounded in our armies, and have fought in some of our battles; but sir, they have only fought as they were commanded, they have never led in any skirmish that I know of, and if they had known how to do anything but fight, they would never have been commanded to fight some of the battles that are the glory of our annals. It is vain for them or their friends to say anything of their patriotism and love of their adopted country—they needed the bounty and the pay and risked their lives for that.[1]

Irish convents were burned, Irish citizens were killed, an occasional Irish priest was martyred, and while they were tolerated on the American shore, the Irish certainly were not welcomed. In the words of the Reverend William Alger:

> When this naked mass of unkept and priest-ridden degradation, bruised with abuse, festering with ignorance, inflamed with rancors, elated with blind expectations has sprung upon this continent . . . shall we . . . give this monstrous multitude instantaneous possession of every political prerogative, letting it storm our ballot-boxes with its drift of mad votes, and fill our offices with its unnaturalized fanatics? [2]

Nor did things improve as the nineteenth century went on and "Paddy" became a familiar cartoon figure, more gorilla than man, with a stovepipe hat, a jug of beer in one hand and a shillelagh in the other. *Harper's* magazine took particular delight in publishing the ape cartoons and was fond of pointing out how criminal the Irish were:

> "They [the Irish] have so behaved themselves that nearly 75% of our criminals are Irish, that fully 75% of the crimes of violence committed among us are the work of Irishmen, that the system of universal suffrage in large cities has fallen into discredit through the incapacity of the Irish for self-government. . . ." The editor added that the Irish made terrible soldiers anyway, and he rebuked them harshly for not parading to honor the Prince.[3]

Irish revolutionary organizations such as the Finnians (bent on freeing Ireland) and the Mollie Maguires (bent on seizing control of the coal fields) were cited as evidence of the inhuman savagery of the Irish. Everyone knew, of course, that the Irish couldn't hold their liquor, and that the Irish "athletic clubs," such as the notorious Regan Colts in Chicago, had at least as bad a press as did their successors in Chicago, the Blackstone Rangers (recently renamed the Black P. Stone Nation).

Table 1

Retardation Rates Among Children in Public Schools in 30 American Cities in 1910 by Ethnicity and Generation

	*Per cent retarded**
Native-born	
White	28
Negro	67
Indian	48
Foreign-born	
English	27
Irish	29
German	32
Hebrew German	32
Hebrew Russian	42
Italian-Northern	42
Italian-Southern	63
Polish	58

* Two years or more older than normal for their grade. Adapted from Table 15, page 31, Reports of *The Immigration Commission: The Children of Immigrants in Schools. Vol. 1*, Washington: U.S. Government Printing Office, 1911.

The "Five Points" district in New York was not a safe place to walk through at night, or even, for that matter, in the middle of the day. The Irish volunteer fire associations usually spent more time fighting each other than putting out fires, and the bloody, vicious draft riots during the Civil War in New York City (which dwarf all urban violence since then) fundamentally represented a revolt of the Irish rabble.

Table 2

Annual Income of Males 18 Years and Older in 1910 by Ethnicity and Generation*

Native-born of native parents

White	$666
Negro	445

	Native-born of foreign-born parents	*Foreign-born*
English	586	$673
Irish	612	636
Italian-Northern	402	480
Italian-Southern	408	396
Polish	537	428
German	619	579
Hebrew	492	513

* *Ibid.*, Table 54, page 407.

Daniel Patrick Moynihan has pointed out that, while the Irish may not have been the largest immigrant group to American society, their numbers constituted the largest proportion of any nation's population to emigrate. It would appear that between one-third and one-half of the Irish who were not buried by the British government in the potato famine of 1849 left the country to come to Canada or the United States. The conditions under which they migrated were perhaps better than those of the Middle Passage, but the circumstances under which they had to live in the mid-nineteenth-century metropolises in America were infinitely worse than what virtually any American has to endure today. And little came in the way of support from the élite classes in the country for the plight of the Irish immigrant; there was no sympathy at all for "Irish power," but the Irish took it anyway.

Much of the past has been forgotten. The present-day respectable, upper-middle-class Irish professionals may casually iterate of others the same stereotypes once used to vilify their parents and grandparents (substituting, perhaps, drugs for alcohol in their allegations). The intellectual élites in the country, in their eagerness to charge white ethnics with bigotry, forget the bigotry against the forebears of the white ethnics. And some of the New Poor are quite unaware that there were others who in bygone years were also oppressed by American society.

From the point of view of the present writer, however, the most unfortunate part of it all is that the American Irish have lost the memory of the Finnians and the Mollie Maguires, the Regan Colts, the Five Points, the draft riots, the ape with the booze and shillelagh, and even, and God forgive them for it, Mr. Dooley.

However difficult the transition to American life proved to be for the Irish, and however much they were resented by their Anglo-Saxon predecessors on American shores, the Irish still came with two immense advantages over any other ethnic immigrant group: they spoke the language and they understood the political style. Indeed, from the point of view of the Protestant Ascendency, they understood the political style all too well, because in many large American cities the Irish promptly seized political control and have, in some instances, maintained it ever since.

Two tables adapted from the report of the Dillingham Commission give some evidence of what this advantage meant to the Irish. The Irish were, first of all, at no greater educational disadvantage than English immigrants or, indeed, native-born whites, and in terms of annual income they did almost as well as native-born whites and better than English immigrants. The Dillingham Report, of course, was not based on the sophisticated probability sampling methodology that is available to us today, so one cannot put absolute confidence in the materials presented in Tables 1 and 2. Nevertheless, the tables do illustrate the initial advantages the Irish enjoyed.

Nor has that initial advantage been lost. According to data collected in the middle of the 1960's, fifty years after the Dillingham Commission Report, the Irish still enjoyed a substantial lead in education, occupational prestige, and family income over the other three principal Catholic immigrant groups. Nor is the Irish advantage merely the result of the fact that they came earlier and have had more opportunities for education than the other immigrant groups. For example, we observe in Table 4 that when generation and father's occupation and education are held constant, the gross differences in occupational prestige between the Irish and the other three Catholic immigrant groups are only modified somewhat. When not only father's occupation and education and generation are held constant, but also one's own educational achievement, the differences between the Irish and the Germans and the differences between the Irish and the Italians and the Poles decline, but differences do remain. The point of this observation is not that the Irish enjoy any kind of cultural or biological superiority over the Germans, the Italians, and the Poles, but rather to stress that the advantage of being familiar with the language and the political system has apparently persisted many long years after the immigrant experience was over.

A number of observers of the American Irish, such as William Shannon and Daniel Patrick Moynihan, have lamented the fact that the Irish have not made more of this advantage, that they have not in fact become financially successful. Indeed, Moynihan has even suggested that the decision of the Irish to concentrate their energies on political power may have prevented them from achieving financial and social success in American society. If this observation means that no more than a handful of the Irish (such as the Kennedy clan) have achieved fabulous wealth then the observation is valid—but then neither has any other American immigrant group. If the observation is meant to indicate that the Irish have not even achieved the very high level of financial success which characterized American Jews (and one suspects that Jews are the norm for comparison in Moynihan's observations) then the observation is also valid. However, if the implication is that the American Irish are, on the average, less successful economically than the typical white Anglo-Saxon Protestant living in the same cities as the Irish do, then the observation is quite invalid. Research carried on over a decade at the National Opinion Research Center reveals that holding region of the country and city size constant, the Irish are not merely on the average as financially successful as the WASP, but perhaps a trifle more so. They may not be numbered among the very rich, nor among the very poor. They may not have been quite as successful as the Jews, but the notion that the Irish have somehow or other failed financially in American society is complete myth.

Table 3

Differences Among Certain American Males

*Ethnic groups**	*Irish*	*German*	*Italian*	*Poles*
Mean years at school	12.98	11.60	11.20	11.25
Mean occupational prestige (1–100)	44.2	36.2	34.8	32.2
Mean family income	$8,530	$8,059	$8,159	$8,219
(Numbers of persons interviewed)	(138)	(153)	(182)	(80)

* Father's main ethnic background.

Table 4

Differences in Occupational Prestige Between Irish and Other Ethnic Groups

	German	*Italian*	*Poles*
Gross differences in prestige scores	8.0	9.4	12.2
Net differences when father's occupation and education and generation are taken into account	6.4	8.6	13.8
Net differences when father's occupation and education, generation and own education are taken into account	– .2	3.9	6.9

It is also commonly assumed among the Irish self-critics that even though the Irish have been overwhelmingly loyal to the Democratic party, it is still a "conservative" style of democracy.

The words "conservative" and "liberal" are obscure in their meaning. If research on political attitudes demonstrates anything, it is that there is not a high correlation, save among ideologues of the Left or the Right, between a conservative position on one set of issues and a conservative position on other sets of issues. Thus, many members of the working class can be quite "liberal" on economic issues and still rather "conservative" on racial issues. Nonetheless, the data available to us at the National Opinion Research Center's ethnic program, fail to substantiate the myth of Irish conservatism. Indeed, on the two critical issues of racism and anti-Semitism, the Irish are the most enlightened of the Catholic immigrant groups, as Table 5 indicates.

Nor is this more enlightened attitude merely the result of the superior occupational or educational achievement of the Irish. As Table 6 demonstrates, the basic difference between the Irish and the other three principal Catholic ethnic groups on the anti-Semitism score diminishes only slightly even when father's education and occupation and own education and occupation and family income are held constant. At this point in our understanding of the differences among American ethnic groups, no attempt can be made to explain the phenomenon reported in Table 6 beyond saying that perhaps the long-standing political alliance between the Irish and Jews in the Democratic Party might possibly account to some extent for the phenomenon.

Thus far, we have only been able to compare the Irish with other Catholic immigrant groups. However, data obtained from NORC's study of 1961 college alumni indicate that on a scale measuring sympathy for student and black militancy, the Irish have a higher score than all other American groups save the Jews. Furthermore, this difference does not change even with a control for the number of years of graduate school attendance by the 1961 graduates.

Much more research will be required of course to put to rest the myth of the Irish political reactionary masquerading under the Democratic label. However, the NORC data not only do not confirm this myth but also call into very serious question whether the myth can ever possibly be confirmed.

And yet the myth persists, bandied about both by the Irish self-critics and by those academic liberals who bitterly resent the

Table 5

Differences Among Certain American Males

*Ethnic groups**	*Irish*	*German*	*Italian*	*Poles*
Mean score on racism scale (0–5)	2.42	2.45	2.60	2.61
Mean score on anti-Semitism scale (0–2)	.84	1.23	1.11	1.71
(Numbers of persons interviewed)	(138)	(153)	(182)	(80)

* Father's main ethnic background.

Table 6

Differences in Anti-Semitism Scores

	German	*Italian*	*Poles*
Mean	.394	.273	.871
Father's education and occupation	.403	.370	.783
Father's education and occupation and own education	.322	.256	.667
Father's education and occupation and own education and occupation	.280	.238	.704
Father's education and occupation and own education and occupation and 1963 family income	.271	.235	.698

persistence of Irish political control in many cities and states. It is legitimate then to ask the reason for the persistence of the myth because the answer may give us some hint as to the peculiar and ambivalent role of the Irish in American life.

Not the least important explanation is the latent self-hatred of the Irish. As one Jewish colleague of mine observed, "The fundamental difference between the Irish and the Jews is that we know that we have a problem of self-hatred and you don't. The advantage of knowing about it is that you can take it into account and, indeed, turn it to a profit. You people haven't been able to do either."

In reading the revised edition of *Beyond the Melting Pot*, one detects a note of both dismay and glee in the authors' account of the Jews' rout of the Irish in the political life of New York City. Similarly, many of the official lay intelligentsia of the American Catholic Church (which often means exseminarians who have failed their Ph.D. exams in major American universities) seem to have a vested interest in denouncing Irish Catholicism because it enables them to pen the blame for the so-called failure of the so-called conservatism of the Irish on the hated institutional Church. Any myth which can play such an important function is not likely to die easily.

Furthermore, there is some reason to question whether nativist antagonism to the Irish has been completely purged from the American body politic. No one has paid much attention to the subject in recent years (although the fact that nativist bigotry came within 110,000 votes to denying the presidency to John F. Kennedy but a decade ago would suggest that anti-Catholicism is still a factor in American society).[4] There is no American Irish Committee to correspond to the American Jewish Committee, nor is there an Irish Anti-Defamation League which could sponsor research on anti-Irish or anti-Catholic sentiment. It might be difficult for any but the most sophisticated research to discover such sentiment, since those who are most likely to hold it probably know all about the authoritarian personality. And yet one can legitimately raise the question of whether the intense hatred for Mayor Daley to be found among Jewish and Protestant academic intellectuals does not have something to do with the fact that he is not merely a politician but an *Irish* politician. Anyone who thinks that the treatment accorded the administration of Chicago's mayor in the official liberal journals bears any relation to what actually happens in Chicago politics is quite unfamiliar with the realities of Chicago life. It is surely not the intention of the present author to defend the mayor and his administration but it is merely to argue that the bias against him is so great as to raise serious questions as to its origin. When one points out that Daley has been elected and re-elected repeatedly with the overwhelming support of both the black and

Polish populations of the city, one is told that that is merely a manifestation of "ethnic politics," as though this were an answer and not a mere restatement of the question.

In the mind of the present writer the issue of whether anti-Catholic, and in particular, anti-Irish nativism has vanished from American society is still a very open one.

Table 7

Score on Scale Measuring Sympathy for Political Militancy
(June 1961, College Graduates Responding in 1968)
(Scale: 0–18)

All	9.5	(4,324)
Jews	11.9	(100)
Catholics		
Irish	10.6	(269)
German	9.2	(280)
Polish	10.5	(54)
Italian	8.3	(168)

A closely related phenomenon is the profound suspicion in Jewish and WASP circles of the Irish political style. Writers such as Edward Levine and James Q. Wilson have pointed out that the Irish political style is both pragmatic and informal. The Irish politician is much more interested in winning elections than in taking the politically "pure" position and he also much prefers informal, off-the-record solutions to difficult problems than neat, orderly, and formal solutions. He is much more at home in the world of implicit compromise than in the world of explicit confrontation, and above all else he prizes the loyalty of his colleagues. As one young Irish political leader put it to me, "A man who will not be loyal to his friends will never be loyal to an idea."

These facets of the Irish political style can be seen clearly in the careers of John and Robert Kennedy—that is, the real Kennedys and not the Kennedys of liberal myth-makers. It is interesting that the myth-makers have completely forgotten how suspicious they were of both the Kennedy brothers when they were still alive. Thus, the editors of the *Nation*, one presumes, have conveniently forgotten how at the time of the steel price increase crisis they exulted in Kennedy's embarrassment by announcing in a lead sentence of their editorial that the steel crisis was Kennedy's domestic Bay of Pigs. The fact that the editorial appeared on the streets the day after Kennedy had routed Roger Blough and R. Conrad Cooper did not at all induce the editors of *Nation* to admit that they had been wrong or to apologize. Quite the contrary, they rather testily seemed willing to accept credit for what turned out to be anything but a Bay of Pigs. Similarly, the liberal myth-makers would have us believe that the Kennedys underwent a conversion to the cause of racial justice during the 1960's. The thought has occurred to rather few of them that both Kennedys might have very well believed in racial justice before 1960 but decided to do something about their convictions only when changing political pressures and attitudes made such action politically practical. The Irish politician is prepared to believe that certain ideal goals must be postponed until they become feasible. Indeed, he is quite incapable of understanding why so many American liberals seem bent on going down to defeat for causes which are splendid but unwinnable, while the American liberal, on his side, is shocked by what he thinks is the Irishman's almost unholy desire for victory, especially when victory seems to necessitate compromise. One can, of course, explain the Irish inclination to pragmatism, informality, and compromise in terms of the experiences of the penal times under British rule; but still, as long as an Irishman wants so desperately to win, his liberal credentials must be called seriously into question.

Unfortunately, it has been very difficult for scholars to understand Irish politics "from the inside." The Banfield and Wilson school has described in great detail—and not without considerable admiration—the performance of Irish politicians. And Edward Levine, in a book which must be described as a fascinating preliminary study, has come closer than anyone to understanding what makes an Irish politician tick. But, as someone who does experience the Irish politician "from the inside" on the instinctual level, the present writer must assert that he does not believe American scholarship has even begun to comprehend the baffling phenomenon of Irish politics. It may be that the novelists will do it before the social scientists, though even here one must say that however colorful it was *The Last Hurrah* was not, in the final analysis, a successful description of the Irish politician (and there are very considerable numbers of young Irish lawyers who are not at all ready to accept the idea that the hurrah was the last one).

Another aspect of the puzzle of the difference between the Irish myth and the Irish reality is the tendency of both the American Irish and their critics to use the Jews as a reference group. Clearly, Jews have been more successful in the United States than the Irish economically and educationally. The Jewish involvement in, and contribution to, the cultural and intellectual life in America has been far greater than that of the Irish. The Irish have provided some first-rate writers of fiction, some entertainers, and some topflight athletes but, compared to that of the Jews, Irish scholarship is almost infinitesimal, and Irish involvement in the fine and popular arts is almost invisible. On the other hand, the same comment could be made of every other immigrant group. If Irish Catholics are compared, for example, with German Lutherans—a comparison which historically and culturally would make much more sense—then their success in American life would not look at all small. However, there may be some realism in the comparison for, after all, the Irish and the Jews do tend to be concentrated in the same cities and frequently have engaged in a contest for political power in these cities. That Irish intellectuals would feel inferior is quite understandable because by intellectual standards they have every reason to feel inferior, and that Jews would feel superior is also understandable because, by any measure other than political control (and now in New York even in that) the Jews have every reason to feel superior. Such comparisons, of course, are foolish because they overlook the very different background experiences of the two immigrant groups, but because they are foolish does not mean that they are not made, and certainly does not mean that they do not create a very difficult relationship between the two groups.

On the other side of things, the Irish are also under serious fire from other Catholic ethnic groups who bitterly resent the domination of Catholic life in the United States by the Irish. To some extent, this domination was inevitable for the Irish did come with both the language and the political skills, and they also did develop an immensely successful ideology for their control by emphasizing the need of the immigrant group to become "Americanized" which often for the other Catholic groups meant becoming Hibernicized. The Irish ecclesiastical leaders, however, have consistently displayed much less imagination and skill at playing the game of ethnic politics than did their brothers and cousins in the world of secular politics. While there are some German bishops in the American Church, a handful of Slavic bishops, and one or two Italian bishops (and recently a Portuguese-American was named archbishop of Boston), the Irish domination of the hierarchy is still almost complete. In addition to Boston, only Philadelphia and Brooklyn, of the major sees, are presided over by southern or eastern European bishops.

Antagonism toward the Irish has never really been hidden in these groups but as some of their members begin to move out into the mainstream of American intellectual and journalistic life, the resentment comes into the open. The Irish position, then, is extremely awkward. To the extent that any nativist bigotry survives, WASPs would resent the Irish as the most "pushy" of the Catholics. The Irish and the Jews are locked in combat for political control of a number of cities with the Irish tending to feel a cultural inferiority in relation to the Jews. And, on the other side, the more recent Catholic immigrant groups strongly resent Irish power. To make the picture complete, the Irish personality had never much been marked by self-confidence (save perhaps when under the influence of John Barleycorn—and the Irish alcoholism rate, according to studies done at the Yale Alcoholic Center, is twenty-five times higher than that of the national population). Under such circumstances, just about everyone has a vested interest in suggesting that the Irish are political reactionaries who have failed in American society.

It has been the purpose of the first section of the present paper to call into serious question the myth. Let there be no mistake about it, the questioning is done by a member of the Irish group who has his own biases against the myth. But this is not to argue that the writer intends a panegyric for Irish ethnics. There have been serious failures, indeed, on occasion, tragic failures among the

American Irish. It is not my intention to argue that the Irish should not be criticized but rather to argue that they ought to be criticized for the things they have really failed at.

It seems to me that the fundamental tragedy of the American Irish is that they have not been precisely those things which everybody says they are. In political affairs they have not been pragmatic enough. In religious affairs they have not been Americanized enough. In cultural affairs they have not been creative madmen, nor the half-intoxicated mystic of the stereotype so often portrayed.

With the background that has already been established it is now possible to say some tentative things about the relationships between the American Irish and the American blacks.

1. As the data we presented earlier would indicate, the Irish are less likely to be antiblack than any other ethnic immigrant group, and, indeed, this difference seems to persist even when most relevant background variables are held constant. The Irish are not unprejudiced; they are simply less prejudiced, if our data are to be believed, than the other groups. Much further research will be necessary to explain this phenomenon before one could tentatively hypothesize that their mastery of the language and their political success have given the Irish a stronger base of security from which to view other immigrants to American cities. Again, let me repeat, I am not asserting that the Irish are not prejudiced. Anyone who has lived his life in the Irish American community knows that they are. They are simply less prejudiced than other groups (even when educational and occupational variants are held constant).

2. Many of the myths about the Irish attitudes toward the blacks must certainly be called into question in view of the data presented at the beginning of this article. Thus, the notion that the Irish attitudes toward blacks by a competition between the Irish immigrants and freed slaves in the occupational market in the 1860's and 1870's remains to be proven. There is no doubt that there was some such competition and that it was involved in the horrendous New York race riots of 1863 (which had to be put down by troops summoned from the Battle of Gettysburg). Nevertheless, antiblack sentiment seems stronger among other ethnic groups which do not have the Civil War experience.

3. Apparently the Irish long since left behind the tendency to fight or to riot when the neighborhoods were threatened with black immigration. The last Irish race riot was the 1919 riot in Chicago (though there was a minor reprise of it in the 1950 Peoria Street riot in that same city). While the southern and eastern European groups stubbornly resist, occasionally with violence, black immigration, the Irish tendency is to shrug shoulders and move to another neighborhood.

4. The Irish are also not very likely to engage in obviously racist behavior or to join in obviously racist organizations. The various antiblack militant groups in northern American cities lack Irish leadership and, generally speaking, Irish membership. One very militant community organization on the southwest side of Chicago is presided over by a suspended Irish priest but the membership strength is eastern and southern European rather than Celtic.

5. Among Catholics, and particularly among the Catholic clergy, the most enthusiastic "inter-racialists" are Irish, even though they may not speak for a majority of their colleagues. Slavic and Latin names are virtually invisible in the ranks of the Catholic leadership enthusiastically sympathetic to the cause of blacks.

6. In some cities the Irish political leadership has actively supported the development of black political leadership. Although it is true that the fall from power of the Irish in New York City can in part be explained by the failure of the Irish to respond sympathetically to the problems of the blacks, New York is not typical in this respect. As one moderately militant black leader in Chicago said to me, "I'm sticking with the Organization because for all its faults I don't see any other system likely to get as much for us as the Organization can. They don't get for everybody everything that they want but they do get enough to keep most groups happy most of the time, and that's the only way we're going to move ahead in this city."

In other words, this black leader saw progress inside the system as largely a matter of cooperation between blacks and the Irish minority that acts as a power broker between the blacks and other ethnic populations in the city. One may disagree with his conclusion and argue that blacks should wreck the system or at least work outside it; however, at this point in the city about which he was talking, it is clear that the vast majority of blacks are willing to bet on working within the system instead of outside it. With two Congressional seats and as many as fifteen aldermen, to say nothing of a host of other elected and appointed jobs, blacks have something to display for their efforts.[5] The willingness to slate black candidates in something resembling their proportion in the total population is characteristic of Irish political pragmatism. Some observers from the inside of Irish politics claim that there is a good deal more sympathy toward blacks than might commonly be supposed. They contend that it is necessary to understand the rhetoric and the vocabulary, particularly of the old-time political leaders, to understand that while they may not use the approved categories of liberal ideology, their substantive positions are rather more problack than antiblack.

There may be some validity in this assertion though one would need to know much more of the mysterious internal world of Irish politics to be sure. Yet, I remember talking to one grizzled and tough—and very wealthy—general contractor about the pressure that he was receiving from his well-to-do friends to provide summer employment for their sons on college vacation. Quoth the contractor, "There aren't that many jobs this summer and if I hired all those kids I'd have to lay off some of my regular people who have families. You can't fire a family man even if he happens to be a nigger."

Young priest that I was at the time, I was horrified by what I thought was an obviously racist comment, but upon reflection, I'm not so sure. The man had employed black laborers in an industry which at that time was not conspicuous for its eagerness to provide jobs for blacks and, while his choice of language left something to be desired, he made it clear that he was not going to discriminate against his black employees even if he was under pressure from his close friends to do so. His categories of expression may have been inadequate but his behavior could not be faulted.

This is the positive side of the balance sheet. It is stated first precisely so that the judgments implied in the negative side which is to follow will not be seen as one-sided condemnations.

1. Despite all of the qualifications listed in the previous paragraphs, it still must be said that the Irish, with a splendid and

ancient revolutionary tradition of their own, have not been nearly as sympathetic with the black cause as one might have expected. Those who produced the Regan Colts ought to be able to understand the Blackstone Rangers. Those who produced the Mollie Maguires ought to be able to understand the Black Panthers. Those whose forebears were in the thick of the New York riots of 1863 and the Chicago riots of 1919 ought to understand the forces at the root of urban violence. And those even today who honor Bernadette Devlin ought to sympathize with Julian Bond. Perhaps the problem is that the respectable well-to-do American Irish have forgotten their own past. This is convenient for them but from any moral point of view quite unacceptable.

2. The Irish political leadership, for all its pragmatic skills—even in Chicago where its pragmatic skills are most skillful and most pragmatic—still does not seem to be able to understand the new black militancy. Even if that militancy's public manifestations is limited to a small handful of TV spokesmen, it still represents the smoldering sentiments of one part of the personality of the many, many blacks and particularly the younger blacks. A pragmatic political leadership ought to be able to do more to respond to the restlessness of the young blacks than the Irish political leadership in the American cities has been able to do. To give them their credit, they have not necessarily discriminated against blacks in this respect because they don't seem to be able to understand the restlessness of the young whites including their own offspring either. I cannot escape the impression that in both cases the older, and even the middle-aged Irish political leadership, is not trying very hard. By their own standards of pragmatism, this lack of effort to understand the new restlessness is a grave mistake.

3. By permitting the deterioration of their creative talents, the Irish have deprived the rest of the society of the poets, the philosophers, story tellers, and the visionaries who might have created a dream of the good life in an urban setting, in which white and black alike would exist in an atmosphere of relative peace and trust, enjoying the variety and diversity of urban ethnic groups instead of being threatened by such variety and diversity. As the first of the non-Anglo-Saxon groups, it is the one, with the possible exception of the Jews, that has been most successful in adjusting to

the American environment, and it would seem that the Irish ought to have been uniquely able to dream visions of what American cities could have become, but they have been too busy with their golf and their cocktails at the country club.

4. When all is said and done, there is, in my judgment no way to escape the fact that there is a powerful strain of dislike of the blacks in the Irish personality. It may not rear its head as overt prejudice, it may not lead to political or occupational discrimination, it may coexist with a commitment to equality in American life, but it's still there.

If my argument about Irish self-hatred is correct, this prejudice may be seen as a result of the fact that the black is a convenient inkblot into which the Irishman may project his dissatisfactions with himself. Furthermore, while the blacks are not so much a threat to the Irish as they are to the more recent immigrant groups, it still may be that the Irish are not yet secure enough in the upper middle-class status not to be afraid of those who are still much farther down the ladder. It is also possible that what we are here dealing with is the residual suspicion and distrust most of us have for those who are different from us, and that the Irish feeling toward blacks may not be substantially different from the way many WASPs still feel about the Irish.

Finally, with their own past record of shrewd and pragmatic political and social advancement, the Irish may be quite intolerant toward other groups whose cultural background does not equip them quite so well for the competitive struggle in American society.

And yet it is my impression that all these explanations taken together do not fully explain the distrust, fear, and dislike for blacks which is latent in many Irish personalities. If I were a black I would be ill at ease in dealing with an Irishman. He's not going to hit me; he's not going to insult me; he's not going to cheat me. He's very likely to approve of my desire for better housing, education and occupation; he may even be willing to vote for me in an election (at least more willing than other American ethnics) and yet, deep down inside, I'm willing to bet that he doesn't like me and is afraid of me, but I can't quite understand why.

Perhaps he can't either.

Finally, contrary to those who say that the Irish have not been successful enough in American society, I would be inclined to argue that they have been far too successful.

If the Irish had really been political pragmatists they would have responded much more quickly to the aspirations and needs of blacks and Spanish-speaking groups in the large cities. The fundamental reasons the Jews replaced the Irish in political power in New York City was not, as Moynihan and Glazer imply, the cultural superiority of the Jews, but rather that the Jews were able—through their WASP figurehead, John Lindsay—to communicate a sense of responsiveness to the nonwhite groups in New York, something at which the Irish failed miserably. Real political pragmatists would not have failed to recognize and respond to this challenge. In Chicago, the Irish have been much more successful in holding their coalition of Slavic and black supporters together and arriving at a much better modus vivendi with the Poles than the New York Irish have been able to do with the Italians. While some of the success of the Chicago coalition can be attributed to the astuteness of the Irish leadership, an astuteness which seems to be much superior to that of the Irish in New York, perhaps a more basic reason for the success of the Chicago Irish is that they have much smaller Jewish and WASP populations to contend with. Furthermore, in the Church, pragmatic leadership would have long ago recognized the legitimate complaints of the non-Irish ethnic groups. Furthermore, pragmatic leadership—to say nothing of religiously committed leadership—would have been far more aware of the necessity of identifying with the aspirations of the poor, the oppressed in the core of the city. In other words, to state the matter more generally, the Irish, themselves the victims of long centuries of oppression, and heirs of an ancient revolutionary tradition, ought to have been pragmatic enough to know how to respond to other men's sense of oppression and to other men's struggle for freedom. Their failure to do so represents a failure to honor the best of their own principles. Comparison with most other ethnic groups is false but one can legitimately criticize them for not being radical enough when compared with their own ancestors. Nor does there seem much left of Irish creativity as they become part of the country club society. The Farrells, the Fitzgeralds, the O'Haras, the O'Connors, and the Powers seems to be the last of the breed. There are many young men and women with Irish names diligently working on doctoral dissertations or beginning their academic careers but if there is any flair or mysticism in their personalities, they keep these characteristics discreetly hidden. I was once asked by an editor of a Catholic literary magazine to write an article on the descendants of Studs Lonigan (assuming that Studs's child was given a chance to come into the world). To my shame, be it said, it was the first time I had read Farrell's *Trilogy.* To the editor's question as to how the Irish had changed since they moved from Fifty-seventh and Indiana to Ninety-third and Hoyne, I was forced to respond, "Not one damned bit." But on reflection, I think there was one major change. If Jimmy Farrell had been born at Ninety-third and Hoyne he never would have set a word on paper. His family would never have let him.

Farrell described Lonigan's story as a "tale of defeat endured in an atmosphere of spiritual poverty." Physical poverty was a very real thing for Studs Lonigan; indeed, he died of pneumonia contracted while seeking a job. For his descendants in the country club set physical poverty is no longer a very serious possibility. But the spiritual poverty persists and grows worse. If there are no Jimmy Farrells arising at Ninety-third and Hoyne it is not because there are not gifted and creative young people among the Chicago Irish. On the contrary, there are an incredibly large number of them but the paralyzing Irish quest for respectability combined with the American success ethic has succeeded in putting the creativity and the vision of the fourth-generation Irish Americans in chains they will never be able to break, and this is a tragedy of immense consequences both for the Irish and the rest of American society.

I am not suggesting that the Irish become "failures" in American society. Quite the contrary, they are likely to be ever more successful and they are also likely to break out of the narrow parochialism the descendants of Studs Lonigan brought from Fifty-seventh and Indiana to Ninety-third and Hoyne. The most basic tragedy of the American Irish is that the WASPs will finally have won and the grandchildren and the great grandchildren of the immigrants will cease to be Irish in any meaningful way. They will have lost their flair for political leadership and their knack of telling stories. The WASPs will be happy, the Catholic liberals will be happy, and, of course, the Irish mothers will be happy.

For, if the Jewish mother says to her children, "Eat more of your chicken soup; it's good for you," the Irish mother says to hers, "There is not enough chicken soup to go around, and if you're not good and do what mother tells you to do, you won't get any chicken soup at all." Studs Lonigan was an Irish Portnoy.

There are some of us, however, who will feel that something has been lost, but we can always go back to the peat bogs and stare at the mists and dream of what might have been. We can think, for example, of men like John England, the first bishop of Charleston, who was sent to the United States at the age of thirty-four because he was too much of an Irish radical for the Church in Ireland. More than a century and a quarter before the Vatican Council he turned over the governance of his diocese to an elected board of five priests and ten laymen, and a few weeks after he became an American citizen he stood before the Congress of the United States and lectured that august body—with telling effect—on the virtues of being American. Yes, indeed, we can sit on the side of the peat bog, our clay pipe in our mouth, the rain soaking through to our skin and dream of all the splendid things that might have been.

We Irish are very good at dreaming of the splendid things that might have been.[6]

The Jews

MURRAY FRIEDMAN

With the exception, perhaps, of the Quakers, no group in American life has been more firmly identified with the black man's struggle for equal rights than have been Jews. It is a relationship stretching back to the colonial and pre-Civil War period when Jews held few slaves, participated disproportionately in their liberation, and were numbered among the earliest members of the first abolitionist society.[1] It includes support by Sears philanthropist Julius Rosenwald of the work of Booker T. Washington and other black causes, assistance in the founding and early battles of the NAACP by Joel and Arthur Spingarn (who served as presidents for many years), the legal efforts of Louis Marshall and other Jewish leaders early in the century, drafting and lobbying for civil rights legislation by Jewish community relations agencies in the 1950's, the role of young activists in Freedom Rides and voter registration drives in the South in the 1960's, and involvement of large numbers of Jews currently in legal, financial, and other assistance to neighborhood groups and even extremist black movements.

Yet there is no mistaking the severe strains that have arisen in this alliance climaxed by the black-Jewish confrontation during the public-school strikes in New York City in 1968 and 1969 and the controversy over the introduction of low-cost housing in Forest Hills in Queens in 1972. Summing up the deterioration of the alliance in a report released early in 1969, the Anti-Defamation League concluded, "Raw, undisguised anti-Semitism is at a crisis level in New York City where, unchecked by public authority, it has been building for more than two years."[2]

No longer can Jewish support for issues or positions espoused by Negroes be taken for granted. In the New York City civilian review board referendum in November 1966, only 40 per cent of the Jewish voters in Brooklyn supported it; 55 per cent were opposed.[3] Jewish civil rights groups have called attention increasingly to the threat from black militants and the dangers of widespread use of quotas to integrate blacks. While the Jewish "backlash" has been less than that of other groups—Irish and Italians, for example—its existence may seem surprising, given the historical relationship of blacks and Jews and Jewish liberalism. Some have feared a growing trend to the right among Jews. A majority of Jews voted against John Lindsay, who had identified himself with school decentralization and civilian review, and supported his conservative opponents, John Marchi and Mario Procaccino, in the 1969 New York City mayoralty election. In Philadelphia, an estimated 50 per cent of the Jewish vote was cast for hard-line Police Commissioner Frank Rizzo in his successful race for mayor against a liberal Republican opponent in 1971. (Blacks opposed him 3 to 1.)[4]

The heart of the matter is that today Negroes and Jews are meeting each other in head-on collisions for the first time. Heretofore they have dealt with one another as images rather than in terms of the respective positions they occupy in and the special set of values and experiences they bring to American life. For blacks, recognition that they faced in common with Jews a hostile white Christian world created the not unreasonable belief that they are natural allies. The course Jews had pursued from biblical slavery to freedom and even affluence was the "glory road" they sought to follow, and they looked for Jewish leadership and support. Even the Jewish "style"—family solidarity, racial pride and identification, emphasis on education and training—has been seen by black leaders from Booker T. Washington to Martin Luther King and Malcolm X as worthy of emulation.

For Jews, the plight of the black man has had special poignancy and appeal. In the 1930's and 1940's this stemmed from the common experience of discrimination and disadvantages, but as the Jewish position improved economically and socially in the '50's and early '60's, identification with the black cause was assumed to be a part of Jewish liberalism and the prophetic concern for social justice. Even secularists like Andrew Goodman and Michael Schwerner might be said to have been wearing their yarmulkas as they went into the South where they met their martyrdom. Lenora E. Berson has pointed out, also, in a penetrating insight that the Jewish relationship with the black man has been tied in somehow with Jewish uneasiness with success. Some Jews, she argues, tend to look back almost with nostalgia to past poverty, discrimination, and radicalism so that "the black man has become a stand-in for himself." [5]

It is true, of course, that even during an earlier era of good feeling, the relationship was more complex. Many Jews, like other Americans, saw the Negro as, essentially, an inferior person. And much as they admired and sought to emulate Jews, some black leaders were aware of areas of conflict and expressed, at times, anti-Jewish sentiments. "Do you know the reason why a Jew moves into a colored neighborhood?" Booker T. Washington asked in 1902. It was because colored people were not acting intelligently, he said. If a Negro "doesn't stop and use your own brain and think for yourself, somebody else will use it for you and take advantage of you." [6]

Group relations in our society are not a product simply of healthy or unhealthy attitudes. Nor are they improved, necessarily, by getting to know one another or by the passage of time. As I have suggested elsewhere, we are a nation of groups as well as of individuals, and as groups we enjoy or lack political, economic, and social privileges.[7] To some degree, American life is a process of ethnic succession in which "ethnics ins," "outs," and "in-betweens" jockey with one another to gain entry and move up or seek to preserve the superior positions and way of life they enjoy. Our society is built upon a series of ethnic or racial struggles for power and accommodations, which Jews and blacks have tended to ignore heretofore.

By the 1960's, the positions of many blacks and Jews in American life had changed significantly and their special interests, values, and even styles drew them apart. It was in this decade that a movement had gotten under way among black intelligentsia and masses alike of greater group awareness and for more radical change than that sought by sympathetic white allies. In a group sense, Negroes were now getting themselves together and beginning to make their own bid for full entry into American life.

As the emerging black bourgeoisie took their first steps up the ladder, frequently they found Jewish school teachers and principals on the rungs just above them, Jewish social workers and government bureaucrats, Jewish merchants and landlords, and Jewish civil rights officials, who whatever sympathy they had for black aspirations, now found that the positions they had gained, often through painful struggles with the "system," were threatened by the black surge forward. In spite of homage paid to the American creed, groups in our society, as often as not, are not let in automatically. Historically, they must use group power and disruption, forcing the "ins" to move over and make room.

For some blacks seeking to move up, the need to create a target secondary to the white oppressor now existed. The Jewish teacher and administrator are keeping black Johnny from learning how to read; it is the Jewish merchant selling Johnny's mother stale meat or gouging her in the purchase of a washing machine or television set. Ignored in this essentially ethnic collision is the fact of discrimination which had made small, and often marginal, businesses and positions in the lower bureaucracies of government the only means of livelihood open to Jews of an earlier generation, and postwar affluence and neighborhood change that had locked them into increasingly unprofitable and unsafe relationships in the slums.* The tragedy of the drama being played out by blacks and

* This essay is not the place to discuss in depth charges of exploitation by Jews of ghetto blacks. The issue is extremely complex. Whatever it may have been in the past, slum housing in recent years has often been unprofitable and a burden to many landlords who cannot break even. See "Many Landlords Abandon Solid Inner City Buildings," *Philadelphia Inquirer,* November 2, 1970. Doing business in the ghetto involves higher costs as a result of small-scale operations, pilferage, and the credit system often used in servicing the poor. Data have begun to accumulate also which suggests that inner city poor do not pay more for food. A study of pricing patterns in Philadelphia, undertaken in November 1967 by Temple University and the Academy of Food Marketing of St. Joseph's College, found that on the average the market-basket cost in the inner-city supermarkets was not higher than in the sample of higher-income supermarkets. Similarly, the market-basket cost for the small inner-city stores was not higher than that for the small stores in the higher income areas. The study showed that those who shop in small stores in the low-income area pay less than those who shop in small stores in the higher-income area. Donald F. Dixon and Daniel J. McLaughlin, Jr., "Do the Inner City Poor Pay More for Food?" *Economic and Business Bulletin* (Temple University) (Spring 1968), pp. 6–12. See also U.S. Department of Labor, Bureau of Labor Statistics, *A Study of*

Jews is that both groups have been placed in their roles by a hostile white society. Both are, in a sense, prisoners of history.

The Jewish community of the '60's had also been undergoing change. It, too, had grown increasingly group conscious as a result of black pressures and the psychological impact of the Six-Day War in 1967. The isolation of Israel as it faced the possibility of another holocaust, the failure of liberal and Christian friends to rally to her cause reopened many old wounds. The Six-Day War brought home to Jews the fact that, in the crunch, they could count only on themselves—and they must be ready to stand up and fight to protect their vital interests. The emergence of the Jewish Defense League and its motto, "Never Again," stems from these developments. By the late '60's, even many secularly oriented Jews began to feel the pull of their own racial identity.[8]

A second important development among Jews since World War II has been their extraordinary success and growing acceptance. Even less successful Jews have moved out of areas of immigrant settlement and into the lower rungs of civil service, modest businesses, and the professions. They have become in many important respects an establishment group and, as Richard Rubenstein has pointed out, this requires a new strategy.

> After at least a century of liberalism, there is a very strong likelihood that the Jewish community will turn somewhat conservative in the sense that its strategy for social change involves establishment politics rather than revolutionary violence. Jews have much to conserve in American life. It is no sin to conserve what one has worked with infinite difficulty to build.[9]

What has happened, therefore, is that the black movement of the '60's is colliding with a somewhat parallel movement among Jews. The black-Jewish confrontation today is an almost classic example of the tribal basis of American life.

The collision involves, also, differences in styles of life and values as well as conflicting interests. Jews have moved up in American

Prices Charged in Food Stores Located in Low and Higher Income Areas of Six Large Cities, February 1966, Washington, D.C., 28 pp. While there is exploitation by some Jewish merchants of black poor, the problem is less that of exploitation than the visibility of the Jewish merchant, like the Irish policeman, as close to hand symbols of an oppressive white society. In addition, the Jewish merchant in the black ghetto is a vulnerable target on which to vent "black rage."

life by utilizing middle-class skills—reason, orderliness, conservation of capital and a high valuation and use of education. In this respect, they were fortunate, as Nathan Glazer has pointed out, in entering a society that was itself becoming more middle class and celebrating the same virtues.[10] Finding that playing by the "rules of the game"—reward based on merit, training and seniority—has worked for them, many Jews wonder why Negroes do not utilize the same methods for getting ahead. In effect, they are asking why Negroes are not Jews.

But Negroes are not Jews. They come out of a different historical experience. Moreover, America in the 1960's and 1970's is sharply different from the society Jews entered in the first decades of this century. Since the "rules of the game" for the slum-shocked black and even his middle-class brother have not worked as well for him, he often asks that they be changed. He seeks to jump over the tedious in-between steps, demands compensation for past and present injustices, and insists that previous standards be relaxed or even abandoned. This has taken the form of demands for black quotas and group representation in admissions to colleges and graduate schools, in certain jobs and government service.

To the consternation of many Jews, they find the system bending under these pressures. Out of a mixture of guilt, and pressure from the Federal government, many colleges and universities have set aside a fixed percentage of admissions for disadvantaged, mostly black, students. The closing down of City College in the spring of 1969 following clashes between Jewish, Italian, and other lower middle-class white and black students stemmed from a plan to impose particularly generous black quotas. In 1971 and 1972, quotas and preferential treatment became a major issue in the Jewish community. *Commentary* devoted an unprecedented three articles to the subject.[11] Daniel Moynihan has spelled out his own and Jewish fears with regard to quotas:

> Once this process gets legitimated, there is no stopping it, and without intending anything of the sort, I fear it will be contributing significantly to the already well-developed tendency to politicize (and racialize) more and more aspects of modern life. . . . Let me be blunt. If ethnic quotas are to be imposed on American universities and similarly quasi public institutions, it is Jews who will be almost

driven out. They are not 3 percent of the population. This would be a misfortune to them, but a disaster to the nation. And I very much fear that there is a whiff of anti-Semitism in many of these demands.[12]

The increased use of anti-Semitic and anti-Zionist appeals by black extremists has been the most frightening aspect of the race revolution to most Jews. This surfaced most visibly in the Ocean Hill–Brownsville decentralization dispute and school strikes in New York City, the highly publicized and seemingly anti-Jewish Introduction in the Metropolitan Museum of Art show catalogue, *Harlem on My Mind,* and the statements of Black Panther leaders and publications. In a report released early in 1970, the American Jewish Committee charged that anti-Israel and anti-Zionist attacks by the Panthers were, in reality, a new shorthand for anti-Semitism.[13] Many Jews are convinced, also, that an ideology of anti-Semitism is being used by black extremists as a political tool to displace Jews in jobs and other positions in our society. In November 1970 a storm of protest arose from New York City Jews over announcement of replacement of a Jewish chief of pediatrics at the Lincoln Hospital in the Bronx serving Puerto Ricans and blacks.[14]

In turn, some Jewish leaders have not been above making use of Jewish fears to bolster their own establishment position. At the height of the Ocean Hill–Brownsville decentralization collision in New York, the predominantly Jewish teachers' union charged that Ocean Hill–Brownsville militants were "black Nazis" who printed and circulated anti-Semitic materials, which were allegedly being distributed in the area's schools.

Jewish community relations agencies have been caught between their roles as protective arms of the Jewish community and human relations groups working to extend minority rights for all. The Anti-Defamation League has commissioned studies dealing with anti-Semitism among Negroes and these report that in most important respects it is small and, in fact, less than among whites. The findings have been made available to Jews and to the community generally in an effort to cut down on the backlash. The evidence indicates, however, that young and better educated blacks score significantly higher on anti-Semitism than whites, a fact that does not augur well for the future of black-Jewish relations.[15]

Equally troubling to Jews, as it is for other Americans, is the growing violence and rhetoric of violence associated with efforts to bring about change in the status of Negroes, even though this has diminished in recent times. (Coming out of a "culture of inhibition"—to use Gertrude J. Selznick and Stephen Steinberg's phrase—they are reluctant themselves to act on passions and hatred and, have a special stake in orderly social change.) Violence has taken the form of assaults on Jewish teachers and students in schools in ghetto and racially changing neighborhoods, on elderly Jews who still worship in orthodox synagogues there, and harassment of merchants by Panther and other black extremists. The urban riots of 1964–68—perhaps the only way ghetto blacks could bring the tragedy of their situation to the attention of an indifferent and even hostile white community—found the chief victims, next to blacks, of course, to be Jews.

There has been little public discussion or knowledge about the victimization of Jewish merchants in the ghetto or racially changing neighborhoods. Their special problems have been swallowed up in the general violence and crime in which blacks and whites living and working there are victims alike. I began keeping a file on incidents in Philadelphia since September 1968 and found that in the following four years, 22 Jewish merchants had been killed in robberies and 27 shot or severely beaten. There are indications that a similar pattern has prevailed in Baltimore, New York, Chicago, and other major cities. By and large, assaults on Jewish merchants are a result of their presence in the ghetto rather than anti-Semitism. Nevertheless, these generally middle age and older men and women who for the most part earn modest and even marginal incomes live in great fear. Their precarious position has created much anxiety among their families and friends who press them to sell or abandon their property.[16]

Writers like Yves Simon, Bruno Bettelheim, and Milton Himmelfarb have noted parallels between ghetto violence and black uprisings of the '60's and pogroms against Jews by peasant and proletariat underclasses in Eastern Europe prior to 1939. ". . . current Jewish feelings and ways of thinking about Negroes," Himmelfarb writes, "will be affected by older feelings and ways of thinking about muzhiks."[17] In this respect, the willingness of police in some instances to look away as stores were being plundered during recent urban rioting—under orders to keep down casualties rather than sympathy for looters—has reinforced such feelings in the Jewish community. By the early 1970's, many Jews who had become comfortable as a result of post-World War II affluence and the decline of anti-Semitism were suddenly confronted by the recognition of their continued vulnerability.[18]

(In spite of this, the organized Jewish community has done relatively little to aid Jewish merchants in the ghetto. Many Jews have not experienced these problems directly and frequently accept as uncomfortably true the image of the ghetto merchant as an exploiter of helpless blacks. The Jewish community may reproach itself some day for its failure to aid and even rescue the Jewish merchants in the slums in the '60's in the same way it has agonized over its inability to act effectively during the Hitler holocaust.)

Fears of Jews of black violence and anti-Semitism have been heightened by "the Jewish nightmare": concern about a possible alliance between white upper classes and the black underclass at the expense of Jews. In recent months, Earl Rabb, Maurice Goldbloom, and Milton Himmelfarb have been sounding this alarm. As the Negro population becomes increasingly dominant in the major cities and black militants continue to use anti-Semitism as a political weapon, Rabb has written, the Establishment is likely to be forced to seek a political truce. "There is the possibility of a classic marriage, a manipulative symbiosis between the privileged class and the dis-privileged mass—in this case a WASP class and a black mass. . . . The anti-Semitic ideology developing in the black movement would be eminently suited to such purposes." [19]

This fear has been reinforced in the minds of many Jews living in modest economic circumstances by Mayor John Lindsay's support of the Ford Foundation plan for community control of the public schools in New York City. (Their more advantaged coreligionists further removed from urban problems were less concerned and often favored this.) Similarly, early in 1970, a WASP-led school administration in Philadelphia, also under black pressure, developed a widely publicized school administrators training plan—the wording was changed later following public protests—that seemed aimed at ridding the school system of Jews, Italians, and other "second and third generation" school officials.[20] In a number of cities, bank and other major corporate leaders have been funding various programs of black militants. This is no malevolent plot, as some have suggested. It represents a desire to alleviate the urban crisis and purchase community peace on the part of upper-class whites by helping blacks and insensitivity to the delicate ethnic balance of our cities. (At the height of the *Harlem On My Mind* controversy, in response to Jewish criticisms, Thomas Hoving, head of the Metropolitan Museum of Art, blurted out, "If the truth hurts, then so be it." Later he said he had been indiscreet.)[21] A desire to do good coupled with insufficient urban skills on the part of older stock and more affluent white leadership is exacerbating Jewish feelings toward blacks.

It is necessary at this point to define more clearly attitudes toward blacks of different groups of Jews. Prior to the racial explosions of the '60's, rich and poor Jews alike, by and large, identified with the black struggle for equal rights. In recent years, a sharp division has developed within the Jewish community largely along class lines. College-educated Jews employed in the arts, certain businesses, social service fields, and the professions who reside, for the most part, in the suburbs or more fashionable sections of the city tend to remain constant in their sympathy for and support of black causes including, in some instances, black extremist movements.

Their continued idealism or liberalism is a product of genuine empathy for the problems of the disadvantaged, memories of their own struggles with inequality, and, like upper-class WASPs, distance from many of the flashpoints of black-Jewish confrontation today. It is among elements of this group that we find what Tom Wolfe has labeled "radical chic"—a desire to be associated with the new, the fashionable, and daring in current, radical causes.[22] Upper-class Jews are more optimistic and tend to view blacks in terms of the older imagery that characterized the black-Jewish alliance of the '50's and early '60's.

Increased resistance on racial issues is chiefly found among lower middle-class Jews who send their children to city rather than suburban and private schools, to community or, in the case of New York City, municipal instead of élite colleges and universities, work at less glamorous jobs such as public-school teaching, operating a taxi, in small businesses and the lower or middle rungs of the civil service and live in deteriorating or racially changing neighborhoods where there is a rising crime rate and the schools are declining. A considerable number of older men and women are Orthodox.[23]

The tone of older and dissolving Jewish ghettos is demoralized, Samuel Z. Klausner and David P. Varady found in the study of one such area in Philadelphia, "It is not simply frustrated . . . There is a widespread conviction among residents . . . that the Jewish community there is declining, that the proportion of blacks is increasing . . . Everything seems harder and more difficult." [24] They are affected by the reality situation they face and are not necessarily racists. "They may have been less (or not at all) motivated by blind racial prejudice (Negroes are inferior, etc.)," a study of Brooklyn Jewish and Catholic attitudes on the civilian review board referendum in New York concluded, "than by fears of, and repugnance toward what they think Negroes typically represent: poverty, violence, crime, welfare, family disintegration, property deterioration, and low educational standards. To many middle class people, Negroes represent the very antithesis of their whole value structure and pose a threat to it." [25]

In the past, poor and lower-middle-class Jews were willing to be led by their upper-class coreligionists who had the time and the money to exercise these roles. The feeling has grown more recently, however, that those Jews who differ from them in style of life and affluence do not represent them and, frequently, work against their interests. It was liberal, upper-class Jews who supported desegregation in public schools and neighborhoods and, later, decentralization and who throw parties for Black Panthers. The clash is seen in the 1969 mayoralty elections in New York in 1969 and Philadelphia in 1971 where (according to CBS) most upper-middle to upper-class Jews voted for Lindsay and most lower-middle-class Jews for Procaccino and Rizzo. The growing split between blacks and Jews is mirrored in the widening chasm between Jews and Jews.

These substantial divisions are seen clearly in a poll of attitudes of Jews in New York City by Louis Harris and Associates, Inc., in July 1969. In response to the question, "Do Blacks want to tear down white society?" 54 per cent of the Orthodox Jews agreed, while 23 per cent disagreed. The percentage figures for those fifty and over were 49 per cent, "yes," and 26 per cent, "no," and for those with no more than an eighth-grade education, 58 per cent as against 14 per cent. Jews who did not agree were those earning over $15,000 (46 per cent to 38 per cent) and college graduates (45 per cent to 36 per cent). Twice as many Jews living in Manhattan (45 per cent) thought blacks in New York City justified in their demands than did those living in Brooklyn, the heartland of New York's lower-middle-class Jewry. On the question whether blacks tend to be anti-Semitic, the following table is revealing:

Blacks Tend To Be Anti-Semitic[26]

	Agree	*Disagree*	*Not Sure*
Total Jewish	*38*	*41*	*21*
Manhattan	23	61	16
Bronx	48	42	10
Queens	26	49	25
Brooklyn	49	23	28
Orthodox	50	26	24
Conservative	46	31	23
Reform	40	37	23
Non-Affiliated	*16*	*70*	*14*
21–34	27	48	25
35–49	34	48	18
50+	49	30	21
8th Grade	61	14	25
High School	45	34	21
College	24	54	22

The most vivid expression of the disaffection of lower-middle-class Jewry has been the emergence of the Jewish Defense League. Founded by Rabbi Meir Kahane, then Orthodox spiritual leader of a largely Jewish middle-income cooperative apartment community in Queens, following the 1968–69 New York City teacher strike—most of the 13 white teachers dismissed in Ocean Hill were Jewish—the JDL claimed at the end of 1971, 10,000 members in the New York metropolitan area, and 14,500 members nationally.[27] It has organized along military lines, teaches karate to its members, has stood uninvited outside Temple Emanu-El in Manhattan in a much celebrated incident with bats and chains at the ready to repel black reparationists, entered schools in New York City and Philadelphia to "protect" Jewish teachers and students, campaigned against John Lindsay, harassed Soviet and Arab officials in New York, and endorsed American involvement in Vietnam and Cambodia which, it notes, is opposed by the Black Panthers. Like the latter, their movement also represents a search for manhood.

JDL has been sharply and widely condemned as ineffective and a vigilante group by virtually all civic and religious groups in the Jewish community. The most slashing attack came from Rabbi Maurice N. Eisendrath, president of the Union of American Hebrew Congregations who charged that "Jews carrying baseball bats and chains, standing in phalanxes, like goon squads in front of synagogues, led by rabbis, are no less offensive and, in essence, no different from whites carrying robes and hoods, led by self-styled ministers of the gospel, standing in front of burning crosses."[28] Undaunted, JDL took a three-column advertisement in the *New York Times* following the Temple Emanu-El incident which argued that extremists have to be taught the Jew is not a patsy and Jewish organizations are too timid.

The emergence of JDL is more significant than its small numbers indicate. It has stimulated hope—false hope—among some poor and lower middle-class Jews that a show of force can solve the fundamental problems they face. Many post-Auschwitz Jews, especially a growing group of Jewishly oriented young people, vibrate to JDL's militant rhetoric and seemingly Israeli-like tactics. At the same time, most Jews are concerned about its use of violence. A Gallup poll commissioned by *Newsweek* reported on March 1, 1971, that 71 per cent of Jews in this country disapproved of JDL efforts to help Soviet Jewry by harassing Soviet diplomats.[29]

A number of voices have emerged recently that have moved

beyond denunciations of JDL to warn that established Jewish groups must begin to focus more effectively on the forces that have given rise to this militant group. "Somewhere along the way, Jewish agencies have lost touch with the rank and file of the Jewish community," Haskell L. Lazere, director of the New York City Chapter of the American Jewish Committee wrote recently, ". . . The Jewish Establishment has been dealing with the issues at top levels, not in the neighborhoods or the streets."[30] Another veteran community relations official, drawing upon the work of historians Daniel J. Boorstin and Richard Maxwell Brown, has argued that there is a case to be made for vigilantism—as on the American frontier—when legal processes are unable to function.[31]

The rise of JDL has stimulated the Jewish Establishment to take a closer look at the needs of Jewish underclasses. Recently, a number of Jewish community relations agencies have been exploring the use of neighborhood patrols, in cooperation with the police, to deal with crime and violence in "urban badlands," the Jewish Community Relations Council of Greater Philadelphia has been facilitating the sale of Jewish-owned businesses in the slums to black entrepreneurs, and the American Jewish Congress and the American Jewish Committee have been calling attention to the problems of the Jewish poor in conferences and publications.[32]

It is difficult to determine the number of poor and lower-middle-class Jews although there is reason to believe it is larger than generally believed.[33] The greater proportion of Jews are probably middle- and upper-middle-class in income and style and they tend to be moderately and often militantly pro black. It is largely from these sectors of the Jewish community that younger Jews continue to be drawn into various poverty and racial causes such as VISTA, Community Legal Services, and Left-leaning black militant movements. A high proportion of young Jewish teachers were hired in the experimental Ocean Hill–Brownsville school district during the confrontation there and a group of bright, radical Jewish interns and residents, sporting love beads and bell bottom trousers, sought to introduce a "pediatrics collective" and community control at Lincoln Hospital.

Perhaps the most difficult group of Jews to categorize simply are those younger people associated with extremist black and New Left movements that have adopted anti-Israel and anti-Jewish postures. Generally from upper-middle-class homes of pronounced liberal and left view, they are the celebrated "red diaper babies" in Kenneth Keniston's famous phrase. They are "turned off" from post-World War II Jewish affluence and materialism as well as from the Jewish "establishment" which they feel is incapable of challenging the property and other structural arrangements that keep blacks subordinated. However, they are not necessarily estranged from the prophetic traditions of the group they were born into. There is an attempt even by some radical Jews to utilize these traditions, as in Arthur Waskow's moving, "A Radical Haggadah for Passover," to bridge "the historic imperative of Jewish liberation and the urgency of today's black rebellion." [34]

At its most innocent, identification with black extremists is a matter of priorities. Commenting on the takeover of the 1967 New Politics Convention in Chicago by radical blacks and the demand for a resolution condemning "Israeli Imperialism," one Jewish delegate said, "I'm not going to quibble over words while Negroes are dying in the streets of Newark and Detroit." At its worst, Jewish acceptance of anti-Jewish postures by black extremists may be a form of self-hate, the familiar Jewish anti-Semitism. Nathan Glazer has speculated that Jews in the New Left may even ". . . take some actual pleasure in supporting positions that will hurt members of the Jewish group." [35]

I believe, however, that, in the main, this is too harsh. Jews in left-leaning movements tend to take the universalist side of the universalist vs. particularist battles that have raged in the Jewish community since the French Revolution. Having grown up without any direct exposure to the sufferings of Jews overseas and with no synagogue and Jewish organization identification, they believe that the interests of Jews, as a people, are best served by improving or even overturning the existing social and economic arrangements that oppress all men.[36] They are not so much "anti-Jewish" as "pro humanity," forgetting that one has to love a particular part of mankind before he is able to embrace all of it.

How can we sum up the attitude of Jews toward blacks and the prospects of restoring the deeply troubled black-Jewish alliance? It seems clear that in the short run there will be continued and even intensified resistance among many Jews to black pressures. Increased group identification and militancy of blacks and Jews, differences in values, styles of life, goals and strategies employed and, above all, efforts of blacks to displace Jews and other whites as they seek to move up in American life are bringing the two groups into collision.

It is pointless and even unfeeling to characterize Jewish resistance as racism, conservatism, or backlash, although obviously all these elements are present. The romanticism with which many Jews have viewed blacks traditionally was bound to give way under the impact of the forces that make for group confrontation in our society. ". . . When real Jews were forced to deal with real Negroes in the jungles of the cities," Berson writes,

> the language of artificial brotherhood failed completely. When they were forced to talk to each other about rents and credit, about school bussing and residential integration, they had no words. Negroes have not yet been able to convey to Jews the impact that the city confrontation has had on them. Nor are Jews willing to admit and understand their own reactions. A true dialogue has yet to begin . . .[37]

The conditions for such a dialogue, however, have begun to take shape as areas of collision between blacks and Jews narrow. The Jewish presence in black slums is declining. A study undertaken by the American Jewish Congress in 1968 reported that in two ten-block areas of Harlem, 58 per cent of the stores were owned by Negroes. Similarly, black businessmen comprised in 1970 almost one-third of the merchants in nine predominantly Negro sections of Philadelphia—in three areas, black businessmen outnumber Jewish merchants.[38]

As Jews move from "outs" to "ins" in the process of ethnic succession, lower-middle-class occupations such as public school teaching and the neighborhood small business no longer attract or are forced upon them. The son of the Jewish storekeeper in the ghetto is likely to be a college professor of history, a chemist at DuPont, or professional in some other higher status field of work. In short, Jews are becoming a middle- and upper-middle-class group similar in income and style of life to Episcopalians and

Presbyterians and, like them, able to focus more of their attention and energy on efforts to restore community peace and helping "outs" to get "in." The prospects, therefore, for an improvement of Jewish attitudes toward blacks is probably good in the long run.

It is important to note, also, that the black-Jewish alliance has *not* broken down in many parts of the country. The response of lower middle-class Jews in a Harris Poll in New York indicates that considerable numbers are still friendly or at least not opposed to what they consider legitimate Negro demands. Following the school strikes in New York, the United Federation of Teachers went on to organize the 14,000 paraprofessionals in the school system, most of whom are black and Puerto Rican, and won a contract virtually doubling their salaries. When the Board of Education balked at paying this the Union and the Philip Randolph Institute organized a city-wide coalition that included local decentralized school boards and forced the Board of Education to find the funds.[39]

Even though Mayor Sam Yorty played on Jewish fears of black militants, predominantly Jewish areas of Los Angeles voted for his Negro opponent, Thomas Bradley, by a margin of 5 to 4 in 1969.[40] (When Californians voted 2 to 1 several years earlier for Proposition 14 to repeal the state fair housing law, it is estimated Jews went 2 to 1 against.) Jews and blacks joined together in voting overwhelmingly against Conservative senatorial candidate James Buckley in New York in 1970 and Richard Nixon in 1972. In a political spectrum that has been marked in recent years by a shift to the right, Jews have backlashed, but considerably less than other groups.

In spite of extremist rhetoric, important black leaders like the late Martin Luther King and Whitney Young, Bayard Rustin, and Roy Wilkins, have responded to Jewish concerns with sensitivity and hard political support. It was Negro votes in Atlanta—the Jewish population there is small—that elected Atlanta's first Jewish mayor. On June 28, 1970, a full-page statement, AN APPEAL BY BLACK AMERICANS FOR UNITED STATES SUPPORT FOR ISRAEL, was published as an advertisement in the *New York Times, Washington Post,* and in many black newspapers around the country. The appeal signed by Mayors Richard Hatcher of Gary and Carl Stokes of Cleveland, Roy Wilkins, head of the nearly half-million member NAACP, and sixty-one other black leaders was described by the *Atlanta Constitution* as the largest display of solidarity by black leadership on any issue since the civil rights movement of the early '60's. Considerable attention has been given to the anti-Israel resolutions adopted by the National Black Political Convention in Gary, Indiana, in March 1972. The circumstances in which they were passed and the sharp attack on them subsequently by important black leaders, including the Congressional Black Caucus, suggests these views are not representative of the black community. As numerous surveys have shown, the vast majority of blacks and Jews support integration and are opposed to racial separation, anti-Semitism, and the use of violence to achieve racial and other needed changes.

In spite of recent tensions, therefore, a basis exists for renewed cooperation between the two groups. The relationship, however, will be a partnership of equals, less rooted in abstract notions of brotherhood and more in the realities of the way groups relate to one another in a pluralistic society.

The White Ethnics

PAUL WELKS

The signs were there, all right. The little photography studio on the corner of Harvey and 116th Street, where I had looked at the latest brides, their lips retouched deep red and eyebrows dark, was now a karate and judo school. A storefront church, Pilgrim Rest B. C., was on 93rd Street near Dickens. Protective grates guarded the front of Rosenbluth's, our local clothing store, whose recorded Santa Claus laugh had scared the patched corduroy pants right off me as a youngster. A public housing project rose from the mud. And in the streets there was a stillness.

As I drove back through my old neighborhood on the East Side of Cleveland last month, there was so little noise. No horns. At 8 o'clock in the evening, there were few cars on the street. There must have been more people walking around, but I remember only a handful at well-lit intersections.

There had been no dinner served on the flight to Cleveland, and as I turned onto Forest Avenue I thought it was just as well. There would be a pot of beef soup bubbling on the stove and huge lengths of garlic-spiced *kolbasz,* the soul food of my ethnic group, the Slovaks. Over such food a son could talk more easily with his father. Over such food it would be more comfortable to talk about the crime that appears to be sweeping this, the peaceful and benign neighborhood where I spent my first eighteen years. With hunks of rye bread in our hands and caraway seeds falling softly to the table, we could even talk about *them,* the new immigrants, the blacks who had broken the barrier and swept into this formerly homogeneous area of Cleveland. As the conversation began, though, it was embarrassing for me, always previously eager to shuck the ethnic business and a blue-collar background, to start asking questions about the family and the old neighborhood only because an idea had come to mind and an article had been assigned.

My father—his family name, Vilk, already Americanized to Wilkes—came to Cleveland with my mother and six brothers and sisters a year before I was born in 1938. They left an area that would soon stand for white poverty—Appalachia—and came to one where other Slovaks years before had found work in the factories that spread from the Cuyahoga River up the gentle slopes of streets like Kinsman, Union, Woodland, and Buckeye.

They soon bought a house that "wasn't much," my father explained through a wad of Havana Blossom chewing tobacco that remains virtually a part of his anatomy. "There wasn't any sheeting beneath the siding, the floors were wavy, but to your mother it was a mansion." The purchase price was $4000 and the monthly payments about $35, a third of my father's wages with the W.P.A.

Living on Forest Avenue after the war and through the first half of the 1950s surely fulfilled all the dreams of the Slovak and Hungarian immigrants and their offspring. There was regular work nearby, the brick streets were clean, lawns were mowed, and—except for some home-grown hooligans who might beat you up—it was safe. Blacks? Sure, we knew about blacks. They were a growing mass of look-alikes who flooded in after the war to produce fantastic basketball teams at East Tech. They lived on the crumbling rim of the downtown area seemingly content to wallow in their poverty. They were at once out of mind and a dull pain that would surely trouble us more in days to come.

For the Slovaks, the center of life was St. Benedict's Church, just four blocks from my house, the place where education, religion, and social life peacefully coexisted. When asked where I lived in Cleveland, the response was never the East Side, never the 29th Ward. I lived in St. Benedict's Parish.

In its neighborhood of modest older homes the new St. Benedict's Church, completed seventeen years ago, is something of a shock. It is a Byzantine mammoth, built at a cost of a million dollars by a blue-collar congregation that raised more than its share of children. As I rang the bell at the parish-house door, I could hear the chimes within, a long, majestic carillon whose frequent use would drive any but those with a Higher Calling right up the wall.

The pastor, Father Michael Jasko, hasn't changed much over the years. He is sixty-five now, his hair still regally silver, his voice nasal and high. As he began to talk about his parish, it was obviously painful. The glory that was St. Benedict's, the optimism that had built a church with a seating capacity of 1100 had faded.

"We had 2000 families and 8000 souls when you were here," he began. "Now it's 1000 families and 3000 souls, and most of them are pensioners. We stopped the Canteen [a weekly dance for teen-agers] ten years ago and hoped to reopen it, but never did. We made $45,000 in a big year at the bazaar; last year we got $24,000. Novenas and other night-time services have been stopped. The old ladies of the church were getting beaten and robbed on their way to early mass, so we stopped those. Now the first mass is at 7 o'clock, except in the summer when we have the 5:30. Early this year, we're starting a drive to pay off the $95,000 owing on the church. If we don't do it now, we'll never be able to.

"We had a lot of trouble with school children being beaten, in fact the entire baseball team and their coaches were overrun by a gang of thirty. I guess you heard about the eighth-grade girl who was raped by four boys from Audubon." I had, and Audubon, a public junior high school now almost entirely black though surrounded by a predominantly white neighborhood, was the reason given by many people for the old neighborhood's current state. "We stopped most of the problem by starting school a half hour before Audubon and letting out a half hour before them. The children can be safely home before they get out.

"The solution," the pastor said more than once, "is more police protection. My duty in these troubled times is to encourage the souls under my direction that we are in a changing world. I never mention 'black' from the pulpit, but I always talk about accepting *them.* No, we haven't visited the homes of these new people to ask them to join. They know about the church; they hear about it from their neighbors. We have a few blacks who attend." In a neighborhood that is 20 per cent black, with the percentage rising weekly, one Negro family is on the parish rolls.

A recent event had intensified the resentment in the neighborhood: the bludgeon slaying of Joe Toke, who was killed during a holdup at the service station he had run for more than forty years. Had his murder been mentioned from the pulpit? "No, my own judgment tells me it was best not to mention him," and Father Michael hesitated before saying, with no hint of expression on his face, "I wouldn't want to pinpoint the problem."

St. Benedict's School, which I had attended through the eighth grade, seemed to have changed little—the walls were still painted bland and restful beige and green, and the Blessed Virgin, who had looked out over us from her second-floor pedestal, was still standing firmly on the writhing serpent, though both he and she had been chipped and gouged over the years. But the appearance was deceptive.

While the 1100 of us in the student body had been stuffed 50 or 60 to a classroom, there were now only 350 students scattered loosely about the school, and precious space was allotted to an audio-visual room and a library. The student body now includes 25 or 30 non-Catholics—I can't remember a single one in my day—and four blacks.

A lunchroom has been built because even those parents who live only a few blocks away won't allow their children to come home at noon. It is considered too dangerous. A thousand lunches are served free each month, and 400 more go at half price. The full price for those who can pay is twenty cents.

Joe Toke's Sunoco station at Buckeye and E. 111th is one you could easily pass by: nothing fancy, no spinning aluminum or Dayglo disks, no posters proclaiming free glasses or soda pop. But for the neighborhood people there was always Joe, eternally growing bald, a taciturn man whose stern look was a veneer over a heart of gold. His hydraulic lift could be used without charge, credit was extended without a raised eyebrow, kids' bicycle tires were cheerfully filled with free air. Joe had been warned that the neighborhood was changing, that five merchants or property owners had been killed during holdups in the last few years. His response was, "Who would want to hurt me? Anyhow, they can take the money, I'll earn some more."

That night two weeks earlier, Marcella Toke had supper on the stove in the simple apartment, made uncomfortably warm by an oil burner in the middle of the living room floor. She saw the lights going out in the gas station next door, but began to wonder what had happened when Joe didn't appear. She found her husband in a pool of blood in the station. His eyes were open, and Marcella Toke thought at first that he was looking at her. His tire gauge had deflected a bullet, but his skull had been crushed in a remorseless beating.

"To people around here, Joe was a fixture, the honest businessman who had made it by hard work," his widow said. "We all knew the neighborhood was changing, but then this. . . . I think of leaving the neighborhood now, but where would I go? Everything I know is here. I just want those killers found, and I want them to get their due."

Each month the parishioners at St. Benedict's receive a copy of *The Post*, a paper put out by the church's Catholic War Veterans. Frank Stipkala, a 38-year-old bachelor, writes many of the stories and editorials, and he is proud to describe himself as a "superhawk and ultraconservative." Campus protest marches, such pop singers as Janis Joplin, new liturgy, and liberal Senators of the Kennedy and Church sort have all drawn his stern rebukes. Frank's rhetoric is still hard to take, but his concern for his nationality group and his love for the neighborhood were far more significant in our conversation.

Frank is an efficient man; he had outlined some things he wanted to tell me. A telephone booth on the corner of his street had been damaged so often that it was removed. A mail box had been burglarized on the day Social Security checks were to come. A doctor had installed a peep hole in his door and had gone to irregular office hours to thwart robbers. A mentally retarded boy whose joy was a paper route had to give it up after his collections were stolen and his papers thrown into the street. Somody's Delicatessen closed between 2:30 and 4 each afternoon to avoid harassment from the Audubon students.

"In everything I've told you," he said, "I've not once mentioned race. It isn't race; it's law and order. We Slovaks are too trusting, too honest, too open. There was never trouble here just because blacks moved in. In Murray Hill, the Italians told the blacks they would kill any who dared to move in. In Sowinski Park, the Polish pointed shotguns at them. That is not our way of life, but look what we are reaping now. Many people thought this neighborhood was a fortress, that we would never have trouble, but how we kidded ourselves. The streets are empty because people are afraid to go out and those that must go out are prey.

"We didn't even know the Hungarians in our neighborhood, and we certainly weren't prejudiced against them. Slovaks come from a country that was a collection of small villages; there was no such a thing as national spirit. Here in America, the center was the church, and our people did everything within that church. The Slovaks have been occupied before, by Russians and Germans, by the Hungarians, and now we are being occupied by the robber, the rapist, the murderer. But this is by far harder to live with, the unknowingness of it all. I see two solutions to help the neighborhood. One is very short-term, the other long: Post a policeman every 150 feet to start. Then go to work on the sociological problems like giving these people a better education."

Frank's sister Ethel stopped by, as she often does. She lived on Manor, several blocks away, and had just sold her house at a $4000 loss. She planned to move to the suburbs with her husband, a teacher, and their children. She flicked off her knitted cap, and—though she has a son ready to graduate from high school—looked like the lovely, shy, dark-haired girl she was twenty years ago. "One of the turning points for me was when I heard people were buying guns. I asked some of the women on the block and found three of them—just like that—who carry guns in their purses. Imagine, women who have never fired a gun in their lives carry one to go to the Pick 'n' Pay."

My next stop was at Bill's Grocery, the "corner store" for Forest Avenue and the most crowded store I have ever seen. Bill carries thread, dye, fruit, cough syrup, kites, canned goods, boiled ham, hand-dipped ice cream, socks, two brands of prophylactics (lubricated and plain—both good sellers, he admits), and now items required by his new clientele—canned okra and Jiffy corn-meal mix. He has had some call for chitterlings, but can't bring himself to stock them.

Bill Blissman never married, and it became obvious in our

conversation that if he had something, someone to go to, he would close up.

Bill smiles a lot these days. He has been fitted with a good set of uppers and it's a good smile, but beneath all that, he is afraid: "I used to stay open until 8 or so, now I close at 6. I keep the door locked most of the day and look through the window to see if I want to let the person in. Three of them drove up in a car the other day, and I was happy I had the door locked." Bill can see out reasonably well, but seeing in through his window and the labyrinth of key chains, suckers, Kits candy, Dark Shadows Bubble Gum, and novelties is impossible.

Bill's complaint was familiar. Things were bad before Mayor Stokes, a black, was elected, but since his election, the situation in the neighborhood had quickly become untenable. Stokes is responsible for encouraging blacks to come up from the South and get on Cleveland's welfare and crime rolls. Stokes has allowed a new permissiveness. The blacks are cocky because one of their own is downtown. It doesn't matter that crime has risen in cities with white mayors. In Cleveland, in the old neighborhood, it is largely Stokes's fault.

Bill and members of my own family had trouble remembering people my age who grew up in the neighborhood and were still there. Joe Kolenic, my buddy through St. Benedict's and Cathedral Latin School, had married and lived in the neighborhood until a few years ago, when, like all of our contemporaries who stayed in Cleveland, he joined the migration to the suburbs. Joe and his wife, Shirley, chose a tri-level tract house in Euclid.

We were sitting in their recreation room, where the Kolenics spend most of their time. Its floor is covered with indoor-outdoor carpeting, and there is a huge color television set and black imitation-leather furniture. Joe has gotten just a little pudgy over the years, but as we talked I saw him as a lean and physically mature eighth-grader on the St. Benedict's defensive line. He happily admits to being the stereotype young husband. He wants a safe home for his wife and children, one that he is buying, not renting; a steady job, a winning season for the Browns or Indians, and a good local golf course.

Joe, an accountant, was asked in 1967 to trade his white shirt for khaki and go down into the Hough area with his National Guard unit to quell the disturbance. "You remember our football games at Patrick Henry field; that was a nice neighborhood. And there we were with guns in our arms stepping over garbage in the streets, watching six- and seven-year-old kids running around in the middle of the night. It was a horror show. Our city. I wasn't a racist then and I'm not one now. But that time in Hough leaves its impression. To be honest, I didn't want to face that possibility every day in the neighborhood, so I left. But I'm not against the blacks. Hough taught me they need an education to help them help themselves. Back in the neighborhood we thought they'd never get across 93rd or in from Woodland Hills Park. The dam broke there; it can happen anyplace."

William Ternansky has taught at my high school, Cathedral Latin, for thirty-seven years. His remaining hair is now more gray than black, but otherwise he had changed little since I graduated from Latin in 1956. He still wore a nondescript suit, a V-neck sleeveless sweater beneath, and had a bunch of papers clutched to his chest. He smiled when I told him who I was and why I had come. He remembered me and he smiled—and for both I was immediately happy.

"The neighborhood lived by the Christian ethic of love thy neighbor," he began, "and that pales at the beginning of wrongdoing. The neighborhood is a new ghetto of fear. But for now it is a defensive fear, not an antagonistic fear that ethnic kids have, and that is what is so paralyzing. There is nothing to do but hide and shudder and withdraw with this kind of fear."

Rose Hrutkai is a strong-minded, strong-willed woman of Hungarian stock. She once discouraged a potential robber by going after him with a broom when he advanced toward her. When real estate agents call—they have been plaguing the neighborhood with panicky lines like "Sell while you can still get your money out"—Rose Hrutkai tells them off. Her house, down the street from mine, is in mint condition, a white double-decker with green trim that looks as though it goes through the weekly wash. Rose Hrutkai is boiling mad at what's happening, so angry she's going to stay in the neighborhood.

Rose sat in her living room in a shapeless cotton dress that didn't dare wrinkle. On her carpeted floor were a half dozen smaller rugs that protected her larger one.

"My husband is a maintenance man, and we've scrimped through all these years, raised two daughters, sent them to Catholic schools and paid off the $15,500 the house cost," she said. "That's about all we could get out of it if we sold it, because we would have to give points so the new people could get the down-payment money. I love this neighborhood, my garden; everything I have is here. My husband will be retiring soon, and we can't take on house payments. And what could we get for $15,500? A tarpaper shack, maybe. Every day you hear about a lady having her purse snatched, a house being broken into. It's that rough stuff coming up from the South. They drive up in a fancy car and even steal bags of groceries out of women's hands. It's sad when women have to pin their key inside their dress and put their grocery money in their shoes."

Her daughter, Mrs. Gloria Town, joined the conversation. Girls Gloria's age—middle twenties—were once commonplace on Forest Avenue, living upstairs in their parents' homes. Now they are a rarity. "We just couldn't face $250 a month in house payments," Gloria said. "I didn't want to live here, but listen, my husband isn't a $15,000-a-year man, not a $10,000-a-year man. I work, too. And we barely make the payments on our car and keep eating. We really wonder if we can ever afford kids. It's tough to just make ends meet, and then the neighborhood has to turn into a jungle. I hate to leave the house any more. But who wants to hear the complaints of the little American? The rich have power, the poor get attention. But we got nobody."

Her mother added: "I've got nothing against the colored that are moving in as long as they live the way we do. But so many of them are so lazy. The houses need paint, the lawns need cutting."

There had been peeling paint before and scrubby lawns. But in earlier years that was the extent of the neighborhood's blight—a few unkempt houses for a few years. Now the people of the neighborhood see it going downhill. These houses were built fifty to seventy-five years ago in the tradition of Middle Europe, with huge, sloping roofs for the mountain snowfalls that would never come to Cleveland. There were a few fine touches: Porch columns might have a scroll on top and bottom or a worked portion in the middle. Leaded glass graced living room windows. Not elegant homes, but big, substantial, ready to house families with many children. That was the appeal to people like my parents and those who had settled here directly from the "Old Country." What appeal do they have to the new immigrants, the people who were alternately received and cursed by the neighborhood?

"At our old place down on 81st and Kinsman, I'd get up in the morning and the smoke from the factories would just about make you sick; all I could see out my windows were chimneys and the filth in the air." Mrs. Mary Owing was talking in the simple gray house an aunt and uncle of mine had owned, diagonally across the street from my old home. "Here I walk out on the porch and the air is so fresh, the birds are chirping, and I feel like I'm in paradise. They tell me that tree on the front lawn will blossom so pretty in the spring. I can't wait for that. At the old place, all we had to look forward to was the next rotten building being torn down."

For eight years Mary lived with her husband, a mechanic and competition driver of dune buggies, and their four children in a $50-a-month apartment. Rats and roaches were unwelcome but regular visitors. A husky, good-looking woman with a smoky voice and a warm smile, even though two front teeth are missing, Mary went to school in the Kinsman area, dropped out in the 10th grade, and was married at sixteen. She is a neat housekeeper, but on Kinsman there was a constant battle with the black soot that invaded her house daily. On Forest Avenue she enjoys cleaning the house because the environment doesn't despoil her work.

Her husband replanted some burned-out patches of grass late in the summer and nursed them along so carefully that they look better than the rest of the lawn. He wants to replant the entire lawn this spring. Contrary to what the whites on Forest say, Mary Owing doesn't want the black influx and white outflow to continue indefinitely; she wants a racially mixed neighborhood, and she plans to keep her house up. No neighbors have stopped by to welcome the Owings, but some have said hello as they passed. Still others have stared icily at Mary, who enjoys sitting on a kitchen chair on the front porch. A woman a few doors away found her sidewalk cracked—the work of children with hammers—immediately called the police and told them it was the work of the Owing children. As it turned out, it was not, but the woman sold her house and moved in a few weeks. "I don't want them to move out," Mary says, "because most whites do keep up their houses better than blacks, but what can I do? Tell me and I'll do it."

Across the street from Mary Owing, two doors away from Rose Hrutkal, lives Mrs. Lorainne Gibson. She and her husband, a telephone-panel repairman, and their small daughter were the first blacks to move onto this part of Forest Avenue. They lived before on East 90th Street, off Euclid, where the neighborhood scenery included a house of prostitution across the street and flashily dressed pushers selling to shaky young addicts.

Lorainne was folding her baby's diapers in the living room, absent-mindedly watching an afternoon soap opera when I called. She opened the door readily after I introduced myself and told her what I was doing. (In white homes I was viewed with suspicion and forced to ask the first few questions through the pane of a storm door. When I was a boy, even the magazine salesmen were invited in to give their pitch before being turned down.) Lorainne was wearing a bright orange pants suit that seemed strange during the day in a Forest Avenue house; cotton dresses and aprons were the usual attire.

"If it does anything, renting down there makes you appreciate having your own home," she said. "I will never have roaches, I will never have rats here. I saw some roaches down at Bill's Grocery the other day, and I don't go there any more. I go up to Stevie's, a black-owned place; it's cleaner."

Her husband was able to secure a minimum-down-payment GI loan for their $18,000 two-family house, on which they pay $150 each month. The upstairs apartment brings $100 a month, and Lorainne supplements her husband's earnings by watching the two children of the woman upstairs, who works and receives child-care public assistance. "No two ways about it," Lorainne says, "we don't want this neighborhood all black; we have an investment to protect. But I'd like to see other young black couples, other white couples, move in because sometimes it gets a little boring around here for the housewife. The only thing wrong with the neighborhood is that there's a generation gap. Crime? The crime rate is going down. Mayor Stokes is doing a beautiful job."

Her attitude was typical. Most of the blacks in the neighborhood have come from high-crime areas, and they see their new homes as relatively safe. The older white residents, who remember when a mugging in the neighborhood was unheard of, feel that the area is crime-riddled and dangerous.

"Mostly," Mrs. Gibson said, "the white neighbors have been nice. One lady brought over a pitcher and glasses as a gift. Mrs. Martin showed me how to plant in the backyard. Then the lady next door buried a piece of rail—you know, like from the railroad—in her lawn, which is right by our driveway. Maybe somebody's car from our driveway ran over the grass a couple of times, but I never even saw a tire print. Now some of our friends have done hundreds of dollars of damage to their cars on the rail. That rail would have never happened if a white family had moved in. Listen, I'm more against all the lazy blacks on welfare than you are. I lived with all that down on East 90th."

I found Mrs. Ollie Slay, my father's next-door neighbor, at home on a Saturday morning. She works as a maid in a hotel during the week, and her husband is a carpenter and general handyman. In the Slays's backyard was a large German shepherd on a length of heavy chain. I can't forget his deep and menacing bark and the grating sound of the chain as it was pulled taut by his lunges.

"I didn't know much about this neighborhood, about all the ethnic business," Ollie said after she turned down the Wes Montgomery record on the stereo. "All I wanted was a place I could live and let live. Down at East 100th, where we lived, we were robbed three times. We bought the dog and started looking for a house. Originally I came from a farm in Louisiana; no electricity, no indoor plumbing. So this house, this neighborhood . . . well, I love it, I just love it.

"Everything we have, we worked for," she says. "Scraping together $1500 for a down-payment was the toughest thing we've ever done. So maybe blacks are the cause of crime in this area. But it isn't me out there bopping old ladies over the head. Talk about law and order—yes, sir, I'm for law and order. You can put me down as in love with the police."

In the City Council elections last year, the people in my old neighborhood did a strange thing. They elected a Republican—a Republican of Scottish ancestry, at that. Jayne Muir ordinarily could never have been elected, regardless of her intent and qualifications. But, by marrying a Ukranian named Zborowsky, she gained a name as politically potent as Kennedy, Roosevelt, or Taft. She is a former social worker whose constituency is distrustful of change and reform. Father Michael, for instance, says: "She's pushing the black movement too hard. She should listen more to the people."

In her storefront office on Buckeye Road, the usual complaints are handled by a group of New-Frontier-like college students. The water inspector will be sent out on Friday to see why Mrs. Kovach's bill was so high. Mrs. Sterpka's petition for a new streetlight where an elderly woman fell and broke her hip will be forwarded with a properly irate letter to the illuminating company. But Councilwoman Zborowsky wants to do more than party pols and hacks have done in the past. One morning while puffing her way through a half pack of Benson and Hedges and self-consciously trying to rearrange an uncooperative head of hair, she talked about her area.

"The 29th Ward is a ward in transition. That means whites move out, blacks move in, businesses close and everybody forgets about it until it's a slum, then Model Cities is supposed to rejuvenate it. We have 40 per cent black, a lot of ethnics and a few WASP types on the upper edges, where we touch on Shaker Heights. We have people who are used to taking care of things by themselves and of living within their own world. My job is to bring them together for cooperation and to let them know at the same time they don't have to go inviting each other over for supper. They can still be private people with their own traditions, but divided like this, they'll be eaten alive. Crime is up 25 or 30 per cent, and there's no reason why it won't go higher. Blacks are suffering, too, but they are used to it. The press on the ethnics is so strong, they want to kid themselves it's going to be O.K. tomorrow. So they wait and hope. Useless!"

Realizing that one of the irreparable casualties of "transitional neighborhoods" is often the shopping area, Mrs. Zborowsky—in an effort to head off the problem in her district—has organized the Buckeye Area (Cleveland) Development Corporation. "Through it we hope to get foundation money, local, state, federal money for development of the area that is beyond any businessman. There is no developer—as there would be for a suburban shopping center—ready to fly in here and be our angel." She found that of the 186 business locations in the Buckeye-E. 116th Street area, there were only eleven vacancies, and she wants to be sure that the number won't grow quickly.

The development corporation may or may not get off the ground, and Mrs. Zborowsky knows it, so she continues to work on smaller projects. She compiled a list of the more than thirty real-estate companies working in the area and hopes to coerce them into stopping their scare tactics. She has been instrumental in helping streets organize block organizations. Through her prodding, the abandoned house that was the scene of the gang rape has been torn down.

"I have to avoid the expedient, calling names, placing blame, merely getting more police in. That's what I'm pressured to do. Education is an overused word, but that's my job. The old residents of this ward have always relied on private institutions—their families, churches, clubs, lodges. Now they must be taught to report things to the police and not worry that they will in turn be prosecuted. This neighborhood has fantastic shops for ethnic baked goods, meats, renowned restaurants like Settlers Tavern and the Gypsy Cellar; there is something to be preserved. Right now I'm working to have an Outreach Station funded. It would be manned by an off-duty policeman and be a clearing house for complaints, a place where people could have problems taken care of. The reaction? Mixed. I get complaints like, 'You mean I get mugged down on East Boulevard and I have to run up to the station on 116th Street to report it?' It's hard to get a new idea across."

For every optimist like Jayne Muir Zborowsky in the neighborhood, there are ten nay-sayers. There were nay-sayers when I was a boy, but then the problems were cosmic and removed—like a pig-headed haberdasher named Truman or a war in a strange nation called Korea—or local but containable—like an increase in tax assessments or the placement of a stop sign. Then "bitching and moaning" was a part of ethnic life, our variation on "Nobody Knows the Trouble I've Seen."

On my visit I found people in the neighborhood, knowing that they are the forgotten Americans and no longer relishing the fact, doing two things. First, they leave. This is difficult to watch, but who can blame young families who want both good schools and safe streets for their children? The other reaction is frightening. These second- and third-generation Slovaks and Hungarians are digging in, hardening their attitudes because they are tired of being oppressed.

Take, for instance, one of the young policemen in the old neighborhood. He would talk only after I assured him I would not use his name. He admitted he was a typical Cleveland cop, ethnic, bitter, and not afraid to say he was afraid. He feels the old neighborhood is so unsafe that he has opted for the suburbs.

"I was off-duty the other day, and I walked into a bar on Buckeye and kiddingly—you know, like Dodge City or something —I said, "O.K., you guys, all the hardware on the bar." There were five guys in there. Four pulled out guns. I'm a bigot and I know it, but arming isn't the way. These people are going to get those guns rammed right up their own butts some day.

"Dope is the big problem beneath it all, and blacks who don't have or don't want work. In the old days, a black man couldn't even ride through the neighborhood without it being a big deal. Now they can move freely because blacks live here. The bad element has found a gold mine, and they're going to work it. The worst thing is that nobody's on the street any more. Those that have to go out are prey for the wolves. Half the crime would stop if more people would be out."

The anxiety and fear in the neighborhood have forged one significant group, the Buckeye Neighborhood Nationalities Civic Association. I attended a B.N.N.C.A. meeting one evening at the First Hungarian Lutheran Church. There were fifteen or twenty people there, but two of them dominated the proceedings. Ann Ganda, a woman with sharp features and a high, shrill voice talked about the proposed Outreach Center: "Those two colored kids have Legal Aid after they attacked us [there had been a street assault on an unnamed person], and what do we have? I'm in city housing. They demand tile in the kitchens and they get it. Sliding doors and they get it. We have to demand. We don't want an Outreach Center; we're too kind already. We want more police."

John Palasics, a scholarly-looking man with a graying tonsure, three-piece suit, and a low, calm voice, took me to the back of the room to display a street map another member had drawn. "This is our battle plan," he began slowly. "We want to have each house with a code number so that our police can get to any house in minutes. The city police won't cover us, so we are willing to give of ourselves. Special Police, Inc., has many people who have taken courses at their own expense to learn crime prevention and first aid, and if we can get the support, we'll have them on the street next year.

"I know people are calling us vigilantes," he said, and it was as if a switch was thrown someplace inside him. His eyes widened in their red rims, his voice became louder, and his right index finger jabbed at the air. "Anything the blacks say against us is out of ignorance. This neighborhood should be preserved as a national historic monument to mark the contribution of the nationalities. Monuments are WASP or black, nothing for us. We don't want our neighborhood liberated as a slum. And we don't want blacks in our group; we are for the preservation of the nationality way of life."

Words like "liberated" and "slum" came out of his mouth as if he had bitten down on some bitter fruit. "Listen, we know things the F.B.I. doesn't even know yet. When the blacks control this area," he said, sweeping his hand, now trembling, over the map, "they will put up roadblocks to keep the whites out of downtown. We know about all this. A black boy came up to me on the street the other day and said, 'We gonna keel you, whi' man, so get yo' —— out NOW.' Let the Anglo-Saxons turn their houses over to them. We demand the right of self-determination."

They are calling my neighborhood transitional, and it is not much fun to go home again. The old formula just doesn't seem to work anymore, and there are few people left who want to move along positive lines. So the ethnics continue to abandon the neighborhood, each saying he hates to go and he'll hate to come back in five or ten years when, as many of them say, it will be another Hough. Most major cities must have neighborhoods like it, neighborhoods that are being left to new immigrants who want to believe they have moved to Nirvana.

On a Monday morning I prepared for the trip back to New York, feeling confused and depressed at what I had found. As I walked my dog along Forest Avenue, he did his duty on the lawn of the new black family next door. I moved on, deep in contemplation. A few minutes later, John Slay walked up and, after saying good morning, hesitated. I expected a final plea, a demonstration that the black man wanted to do right by the neighborhood.

All that John Slay asked was, please, and don't take offense, clean off the lawn.

Politicians, Public Servants, and the People

Black Politicians

CHUCK STONE

On March 10, 1972, 7,000 Black people convened in Gary, Indiana for the historic National Black Political Convention. This effort marked the first time a national cross-section of Black elected officials and Black Nationalists joined together to work out a united Black strategy within the American electoral system; significantly this was in a Presidential election year.

The participation of the Black Nationalists was significant. Until their official participation in the Gary meeting, Black Nationalists had concentrated on developing a Black ethos, a Black value system whose emphasis was on education and thought rather than on political action. The Nationalists, led by such thinkers as Maulana Ron Karenga of Los Angeles, had previously been instrumental in the success of the three Black Power Conferences in Washington, D.C. (convened in 1966 by Rep. Adam Clayton Powell), Newark, N.J. (1967), and Philadelphia (1968). The purpose of these conferences had been to focus on the need to educate Black people, to unify under a banner of Blackness and move toward jurisdiction over their communities. "We must control the space we occupy," advised Karenga.

This Black territorial imperative was conceived largely in terms of spiritual, educational, and economic development. Political activity was eschewed essentially as the white oppressor's corrupt method of oppressing Black people. The Nationalists had considered politics "the white man's game."

In Gary, the involvement of all segments of the Black community represented the first coming together in modern times of a representative group of Blacks to make a public decision about the political and the national directions which Blacks should take.

In an address to the convention on Saturday, March 11th, the charismatic Rev. Jesse Jackson, a former close associate of the late Rev. Martin Luther King, Jr., and founder of a new Chicago-based organization called People United to Save Humanity (PUSH), outlined the thinking behind the convention:

> In this changing world that has changed so little that war, poverty, racism and economic oligarchies still devastate our lives, there is a permanent word which unifies and binds us as fiercely as the Zulu warriors who fought under Cetewayo. That word is Blackness.
>
> As Black people, declared Congressman William L. Clay last year, we must begin with the premise that we "have no permanent friends, no permanent enemies, just permanent interests." The permanence of these interests is what this Black political convention seeks to adjudicate. Politics is not merely the election of public officials or even a division of the spoils. Politics is the method by which the decision-making process of government is controlled. Politics is the determination of priorities—deciding whose neighborhood streets get paved first, what the tax base rate for new industry will be, where the next public housing project will be located, how many schools can be built in which communities, how many Federally funded economic development and manpower training programs can be used to lower unemployment rates and how the degrading increase of liquor stores in Black communities can be stopped and more stores and recreation centers built instead.

Rev. Jackson then placed the Black political process within the historical process of white ethnic political development. "While every other ethnic group in America has assiduously cultivated the art of politics and the skill of political manipulation, we have been busy buying more records than books and dancing away our lives."

The "every other ethnic group" which Rev. Jackson mentioned was a reference to the success of America's white ethnics who came to this country, plunged into the political process and achieved power, not only through a mastery of electoral politics, but a willingness to indulge in the savagery of organized crime, urban riots, labor union destruction, and any other violent act they believed necessary to achieve their ends. These ends varied from the empowerment of organizations to which they belonged to the empowerment of their ethnic communities.

No understanding of Black politicians is possible without a fuller appreciation of the historical role of white ethnics in American politics. This is particularly necessary since white ethnic groups emerged in 1972, after years of national quiescence, as the most potent force in a multi-ethnic electorate.

In the early years of their residence in the United States, various ethnic groups, particularly the Irish, the Italians, the Jews, and the Poles, experienced some form of political oppression in various regions of the country. As a result, they learned to practice an ethnic politics committed solely to the acquisition of power for their respective groups. Good government, better government, or reform politics was incorporated into each of these ethnic groups' political modus operandi only to the extent to which it reinforced group enhancement.

The politics of white ethnics was derived from geographical nationhood and was perpetuated through devotion to a transplanted nationalism. White ethnic politics also internalized the occasionally obligatory uses of violence as a response to a larger society attempting to limit their behavior. Whether this violence was masterminded by Irish mobs in New York City and Boston, Jewish gangsters in Chicago and New York City, the Italian Mafia or Polish thugs in Milwaukee and Chicago, white ethnics utilized disruptive tactics and organized violence as indispensable adjuncts to the political process in order to influence change and, frequently, control electoral decisions. In the labor revolution, the Irish-dominated Molly Maguires was but one of innumerable terroristic labor organizations which employed violence as a tool to promote the cause of collective bargaining.

But the white ethnics had at least one inherent advantage going for them: their white skin. If nothing else unified them in their disparate conditions of life, they were joined together by racist beliefs in white supremacy over all colored peoples, especially American "niggers."

In most of the big city political machines, the Irish were the first ethnic group to organize themselves for partial control of the political process. They were then challenged by the Jews who sought their proportionate share of ethnic political power. The Jews were subsequently challenged by the Italians who, in turn, had to make room for the Poles. Together, they all marched in cadence over the backs of the subjugated Blacks.

Newspaper editorials and magazine articles that today accuse Black advocates of Black political unity of being "separatists," "racists," or "practitioners of racial divisiveness" were notoriously absent when the white ethnic groups were "getting their thing together." Rather, these groups were applauded as members in good standing of the mythical "melting pot." A factor in the favorable early twentieth-century perception of white ethnic political unity was the editorial influence of representatives of these white ethnic groups as authors, reporters, editors, and publishers. Newspapers, magazines, and book publishing houses which still today practice the most unconscionable racism against Blacks in their employment policies, editorials, news reporting, and publication of books are, in many instances, controlled and dominated by the same white ethnic groups which were victims of WASP discrimination in the past.

As white ethnics established fiefs in large American cities, they were able to consolidate their power base and manipulate political machines to their groups' advantage. This concentration of white ethnic power flourished particularly in Baltimore, Boston, the Bronx, Chicago, Cleveland, Gary, Greenwich Village in New York City, Kansas City, Missouri, Milwaukee, Newark, and Philadelphia. There is a historical continuity to political machines. The corrupt spirit of New York City's W. M. (Boss) Tweed, one of the most larcenous politicians in history, has lived on in the conviction in 1970 of politicians such as Newark Mayor Hugh Addonizio for conspiracy and bribery.

From this historical perspective, it is important to emphasize the three basic features of the growth of white ethnic political power in America: its overriding commitment to ethnic nationhood; its utilization of violence whenever necessary (a kind of ethnic brinkmanship); and its savage corruption.

These historical facts have in the main been ignored by white political writers, for to admit to the pervasive influence of such a wholesale debasement of the political process is to indict an entire race of people, let alone a particular ethnic group. If there has been a central influence in American politics, it is the passionate agreement, implicit or explicit, among the white ethnics of this country—the Catholics, the French, the Greeks, the Germans, the Irish, the Italians, the Jews, the Poles, the Protestants, the Scandinavians, and the Scottish—that Blacks were at the bottom of the racial totem pole and should be contained in a "separate-but-equal" condition. Thus, did the American domestic policy of Black containment, officially sanctioned by the U.S. Supreme Court in the 1896 decision of Plessy *vs.* Ferguson, antedate the U.S. foreign policy of Russian containment. Plessy *vs.* Ferguson ruled that "separate-but-equal" facilities, or segregation, did not violate the U.S. Constitution. The historical racial segregation of Blacks was similar to the political quarantine of Russia. America could live in the same world with the Soviet Union as long as the Soviets were artfully "contained" within a prescribed geographic perimeter of activity while white Americans could "co-exist" with Black Americans so long as Blacks were contained as colonized racial inferiors from the days of slavery to their present subjugated condition.

Such is the historical basis for white racism and Black colonization in America. From the White House, the Congress of the United States, the Chicago Board of Trade, and the construction trades unions to the universities, the *New York Times*, the entire South, and General Motors, White Americans still believe in a preordained superiority over Black Americans as a moral justification for exploitation of the latter. Not necessarily violent or overtly crude, but always characterized by what a prominent Southern cracker writer, Henry Grady, labeled the "peaceful majesty of intelligence,"[1] the practicing ethic of white racism is as institutionalized in the United States as football, Sunday church services, corrupt public officials, and neon-lit hamburger stands. It is an ethic which white America has spent two hundred years denying as the major force responsible for the systematic destruction of Black Americans. But, finally, in 1968, in a quasi-official national document known as the Kerner Commission Report, the truth was blurted out in one breathless sentence: "White racism is essentially responsible for the explosive mixture which has been accumulating in our cities since the end of World War II."[2]

Most white Americans today who suffer from historical amnesia about the terrible lynchings of Blacks regard "white racism" as some kind of romanticized fiction that is tangential, if not totally unrelated, to their personal lives. But virtually all white Americans are racists. From the philosophical white racism of John Gardner and the academic white racism of Daniel Moynihan, author of *The Negro Family*,[3] to the political white racism of Richard Nixon whom Black voters continue to distrust[4] and the economic white racism of George Meany, whose labor unions continue to exclude Blacks, a racist colonial mentality influences all American politics. But most white political writers and white experts on the Black political experience find it convenient to obscure that state of affairs.

In the Black American's historical efforts to achieve so-called "racial equality," emphasis has been placed chiefly on both the tactics and the goal of racial integration. Black leaders were committed only to integration because they were all controlled by white money and ideas. They really had no choice. Periodically, however, Black voices have asked Black Americans to march to the beat of a different drummer—to seek repatriation back to Africa, to join the Communist Party, to become members of the Black Muslim sect, or to adopt any one of the Black Nationalist ideologies.

Until only a short time ago, these philosophical deviations from the mainstream doctrine of racial integration had been rejected by the Black masses. This is because Black Americans are, just as their white counterparts, political centrists. Furthermore, the white integrationist ethic has traditionally served as the basis for all Black community decisions. Black Americans have vigorously imitated the middle-class Calvinistic doctrine that hard work equals better homes and gardens and more fun in the sun. Even when radical Black political candidates have appealed to the Black instincts of the Black electorate by seeking support for Black nation-oriented politics, such candidates have been repudiated. Until the recent breakthroughs of Black mayors in Cleveland, Newark, Gary, Cincinnati, Washington, D.C. (a Presidential appointee and, by definition, a political "Uncle Tom"); Durham, North Carolina; and Fayette, Mississippi—all of whom heightened the national

Black consciousness of all Black Americans—widespread evidence could be found of Black Americans voting for a white candidate against a Black candidate, or of some white political machine-controlled Black mediocrity being supported in preference to a committed, adroit Black advocate of Black autonomy.

Despite the history of political white barbarism, educational white supremacy, and economic white élitism, Black Americans have inveterately remained committed to changing the system by working within it. They have submitted to a white legacy of hate, but have refused seriously to consider revolutionary solutions or truly radical action. This is not to suggest that Blacks have acted wisely or even in their best interests by completely eschewing violence. On the contrary, it is conceivable that, as America fails to ameliorate the legitimate grievances of its Black citizens, incidents of selected violence such as the Black rebellions of 1964, 1965, and 1966 that reached over 130 cities will occur again in the future. This is because an oppressed people can convince the oppressor of their manhood only by demonstrating their capacity to occasionally undermine his resources or selectively limit his options.

From the foregoing analysis, then, it is critical to the discussion of the American political process and its relationship to Black Americans that three major premises must first be affirmed: 1) White racism is the controlling ethic of American life; 2) Despite this ethic's dominance over their lives, Black Americans must paticipate fully in the political process, if only because their continued voluntary presence in this country demands that they either electorally confront their oppressor in his sanctuary of power or meekly suffer the certain probability of political genocide; and 3) As oppressed participants in the political process, Black Americans must manipulate the same wide diversity of political options which have been historically available to white American ethics—two-party politics, third-party politics, selective organized violence (urban guerrilla warfare, planned assassinations, blowing up of buildings), temporary political alliances (or what Samuel Gompers called the policy of "limited commitment"—reward your friends and punish your enemies), judicious electoral abstinence (stay home on election day), and ethnic nation-building—in order to gain political self-determination.

Until the last few years, the Black community was strait-jacketed by its usage of only one of these choices—two-party politics. And, even then, a politically dim-witted Black community prostituted itself within the province of this option by neurotically limiting its vote to one party.[5]

But the Black electorate has committed a far graver political sin than that of merely allowing itself to be imprisoned in the rumble seat of the Democratic party. Unlike succumbing, as has the white American electorate, to a chronic love affair with disruptive activities and carefully organized turmoil, the Black electorate has failed to condone any exhortation to organized violence as a powerful catalyst for change. Historically, the average white politician, especially in the South, has not publicly endorsed social violence, but he has rarely condemned its use by his own constituency or by any group sharing his own ideology when such groups sought to effect or prevent change. One hundred years of southern lynchings and northern race riots occurred because American leaders permitted them.

Thus, white politicians controlled by big labor bosses have introduced labor-written legislation to correct what labor conceived of as injustices only after labor unions went out on illegal, violence-riddled strikes. For example, the first sitdown strikes in the Michigan Chevrolet plants in 1937 were illegal. One unforgettable fact about the historical development of the labor movement must be continually emphasized: Without the tactic of organized terrorism, much of it inspired and orchestrated by union leaders, the causes of collective bargaining and recognition of labor unions would never have been successfully furthered. On the other hand, it is one of the supreme paradoxes of American history that the labor movement, which was itself suppressed by the same tyrannical ruling class which had founded and sustained racial apartheid, subsequently formed an immoral partnership with this very faction in order to expand the power of the white working class at the expense of Blacks. Once an oppressed class overthrows its shackles, it develops historical amnesia. When the semiliterate plumbers like George Meany came into power, they quickly chose to forget the horrors of the Haymarket massacre, the Homestead and Pullman strikes. It became labor's turn to act as oppressor and oppose Black equality, as it still does today, as rigorously as did its former enemies.

In the South, an entire culture was built on terrorism. White southern politicians were not only aggressively responsive to the prevailing Ku Klux Klan mentality, but have almost unanimously refused to censure any violence directed against the efforts of Blacks to attain political equality. There is some evidence of that in the 1970 Florida, Georgia, and South Carolina gubernatorial elections which elected liberal governors by Southern standards. The politics of niggerism is no longer as thoroughgoing as it was when lynchings and bombings flourished with official sanction. But the southern white capacity for murdering Blacks is as strong as ever. Black college students in Orangeburg, South Carolina, Jackson, Mississippi, and Baton Rouge, Louisiana, who lost their lives during various protests were as dead in 1970 and 1972 as their Black forebears who were lynched in 1870.

Even in the North, the tactic of preplanned disruption has been instrumental in reversing governmental decisions. For example, in Trenton, New Jersey, a group of Italian parents organized picket lines to prevent the busing of Black students into their Italian-populated schools at the beginning of the 1970 school year.

The parents did more than merely picket, however. They physically prevented the Black children from entering the schools. So successful was this venomously racist plan, which received the tacit cooperation of the Trenton police force, that the busing decision was reversed by the New Jersey Commissioner of Education. No state troops were called in to enforce the law, but organized violence, under the coloration of white law and white order won a significant political victory for white parents against Black children.

The Trenton incident is interesting because it occurred a full thirteen years after Little Rock, Arkansas, represented the same seething malicious hatred of Blacks by whites, and was just one more instance of the historical persistence of white racism. In Little Rock, the mobs were composed of white Anglo-Saxon Protestants. In Trenton, the mobs were predominantly Italian-American. But, as in the case of white hordes wearing white sheets or white hard hats or white collars to protest Black efforts to register to vote, obtain employment, or integrate a suburb, white-organized violence has been a spectacularly successful strategy for influencing the administrative decisions of politicians. While violence has not consistently been the final determinant in the political climate, it has been responsible for creating the climate itself.

In short, then, the two most important factors in the white ethnics' acquisition of political power on behalf of their respective ethnic groups have been their commitment to ethnic nationhood and their capacity for selective violence. White ethnics have never been restricted in the political process by a total reliance on the electoral process. Where expedient, they have been prepared to advance beyond the constitutional restraints of American society by obeying an immutable historical law: No subjugated group has ever achieved its freedom without using some form of violence at some time. One corollary of that historical law is: No ethnic group or people has ever achieved unity without external oppression. Israel and Pakistan owe their existence today to a history of oppression of their people.

What is astonishingly clear from a reading of American political history is that various communities of interest—all white—have been able to acquire and retain power by manipulating the political process for their own selfish ends without regard for the best interests of the country. This represents an attitude cogently expressed in 1954 by the Eisenhower-appointed Secretary of Defense, Charles Wilson, former president of General Motors: "What's good for General Motors is good for the country."

Black Americans are just beginning to arrive at this tactical philosophy in their political history. Through a demeaning reliance on the essentially white-determined strategy of integration, Black Americans had acted in just the opposite way of white groups by placing the welfare of America ahead of the welfare of the Black community. As a result, Black people have been politically retarded in their efforts to influence the electoral process.

But, in order to acquire and retain the same political power possessed at various times by white American ethnic groups such as the Irish, the Italians, the Jews, and the Poles, Black Americans have no alternative but to convert this electoral process to their own ends, exploiting all the same options—violence included.

Today in this era of computers and cybernetics, this strategy of options demands a mastery of all the oppressor's politico-scientific knowledge and paraphernalia (opinion polls, computer analyses, television spot announcements, and so forth), and turning them against white racism for the purposes of winning elections and eventually achieving Black autonomy.

This is known as Black multidimensional political activity.

Without it, the Black community can never function as a force to be reckoned with by all sectors of the white political process. The fact that Watts, Newark, and Detroit have become symbolic household words for more than 125 cities burned by Black rage in the summers of 1965–67 pointed to a new plateau of awareness in the struggle for power between Black Americans and white Americans. Black Americans were ready and willing to resort to communal violence against white racism for their struggle had attained a new level of sophistication. Like the white ethnics before them, Black Americans finally developed two requisites: a sense of nationhood and the determination to engage in selective violence. America reacted to Black guerrilla warfare just as it had reacted to labor guerrilla warfare: it expanded its military capability to contain any new violence and also embarked on a course of legislative repression.

At about the same time, a new Black group, casting its lot with a policy of self-defense which, to white Americans really meant open aggression "against whitey," had organized itself. The Black Panthers, apostles of revolutionary ferment, exploded on the scene with frightening unexpectedness. Small in number, dedicated, and disciplined, they were able to achieve a contemporary radicalization of the young Black mentality few would have believed possible twenty years ago. With their fearsome rhetoric and alliance with white revolutionary organizations, the Black Panthers became a political force demanding a response. At the ballot box, their impact was meaningless. But, as a convenient target for reactionary, white racist political aspirants, they were a made-to-order opposition factor. Unintentionally, the Black Panthers changed the political climate for the Black community. While the latter did not subscribe to the Panthers' doctrinaire coalition with the Communists or their imbalanced confrontations with the police, nonetheless the gruesome police assaults and genocidal tactics of the "authorities" in Chicago, Oakland, Los Angeles, and Philadelphia moved the Black community toward a new solidarity.

On the other hand, there is an obvious limit to the success the tactics of such a tiny minority within a minority can achieve. Excessive reliance by the Black community on any form of organized terrorism, including "vest pocket revolutions" in urban communities can unleash massive retaliation by the militarily superior and numerically preponderant white racist community, resulting in the possible institution of Hitlerian concentration camps for dissident Blacks.

To avoid this possibility, Blacks have wisely increased their involvement in electoral politics to achieve Black liberation. That is a slower process than launching a revolution, but as Mao Tse-tung pointed out in 1958: "A revolution does not march a straight line. It wanders where it can, retreats before superior forces, advances wherever it has room, attacks whenever the enemy retreats or bluffs, and, above all, is possessed of enormous patience." [6]

It does, indeed, take "enormous patience" for any oppressed people to participate in a political process designed to perpetuate their oppression, but upon which they are nonetheless dependent to liberate themselves.

Nonetheless, American Blacks must rely primarily on the more conventional mechanisms and traditional apparatus of the political process, political elections, if they are to survive as a people and achieve power.

One of the most telling definitions of the ultimate purpose of political elections for Black Americans has been provided by James Turner, director of Cornell University's African Studies Department, and a leading Black theoretician. In his article, "Blacks in the Cities: Land and Self-Determination," Turner states: "Political elections should be used to place Black nationalist-oriented party members in office who will claim the African areas as autonomous city states and develop and create planned economics based on African socialist models directed towards self-reliance." [7]

To attain the goals outlined by Turner would mean the loss to the white majority of vast land areas within the largest cities in America, which are rapidly assuming a Black personality because of the white flight to the suburbs. Despite the deteriorating quality of life in most major cities for all people, it is doubtful that white-controlled political machines will voluntarily relinquish power to Blacks. "Power concedes nothing without a demand," wrote Frederick Douglass. "It never has and it never will."[8] Consequently, governed by this immutable law of history, white Americans can be expected to resist any authentic exercise of power by Black Americans or any attempt by them to assume political power for ultimate self-reliance at the expense of the white power élite's prerogatives. To the extent that Black American politicians do succeed in moving toward the center of Blackness as a power, to the same extent will their viability as leaders be eviscerated by the white power structure. The political assassination of Adam Clayton Powell is an outstanding example.

The term, "white power structure," might be characterized as a very loosely connected, but nonetheless interlocking, confederation of powerful white businessmen, labor leaders, and politicians who run the country and determine how much freedom the Black community may have at any given time in history. A typical cross-section of the white power structure might include the president of the New York Stock Exchange, the chairman of the board of the Chase Manhattan Bank, the president of the AFL-CIO, the chairman of the Federal Reserve Board of Governors, the president of the Ford Foundation, the president of the Rockefeller Foundation, the Mayor of Chicago, the Capo of the Mafia, the director of the FBI, the publisher of the *New York Times*, the president of General Motors, the chairman of the U.S. House Appropriations Committee, the chairman of the House Ways and Means Committee, the chairman of the U.S. Senate Appropriations Committee, and, finally, the President of the United States. Those fifteen men are not dedicated to expanding Black autonomy.

Thus, white racism will never be eradicated in America until Black Americans are able, in some way, to limit the options of the white power structure to alone determine the course taken by the Black Community. Achieving Black political, economic, and educational autonomy is one way.

In 1972, Black political autonomy took a small step for the

American man and a giant leap for Black mankind with five significant breakthroughs for the Black electorate: 1.) the first Black person, Democratic Congresswoman Shirley Chisholm of Brooklyn, became a serious candidate for the Presidency by entering state primaries; 2.) the 13-member Congressional Black Caucus emerged as a united legislative voice; 3.) the National Black Political Convention was convened in Gary, Indiana on March 10–12; 4.) over 2,000 Black Republicans met in Washington, D.C., June 9–10 sponsored by the National Committee for the Re-election of the President; 5.) the first Black Congressman was elected from the Deep South since Robert H. White of North Carolina was defeated in 1901—Rev. Andrew Young of Atlanta, Georgia, a former aide to Rev. Martin Luther King, Jr.; 6.) two Black women were elected to Congress, State Assemblywoman Yvonne Braithwaite Burke of Los Angeles, California, and State Senator Barbara Jordan of Houston, Texas, the first Black woman to ever be elected to Congress from the South.

With the addition of three new Black Representatives in Congress, Black congressional strength achieved its highest total in history—16—yet still only 3.6 per cent of the 435 Congressmen, a far cry from the 52 Congressmen or 12 per cent Black people would need to elect to achieve full proportionate electoral representation.

Shirley Chisholm's abbreviated campaign for the Presidency was nonetheless unique because it was the first really serious Black candidacy and it was also the first one to be run by a Black Congresswoman.

It is one of the supreme paradoxes of American politics that the Democratic candidacy of this Northern Black woman committed to Women's Liberation for President received major recognition from a Republican President only when a southern white racist Democratic candidate was almost assassinated. The May 15 attempt on Alabama Gov. George Wallace's life at a Laurel, Maryland shopping center caused President Nixon to immediately assign Secret Service protection to Shirley Chisholm. Blacks had not legitimatized their candidate. The near assassination of a southern white racist had.

But the Black community had never taken Ms. Chisholm's candidacy too seriously. Most Blacks are nonsupporters of the white middle-class-oriented Women's Liberation movement. They were uncertain whether Ms. Chisholm was representing Blacks or Women's Liberation. Black voters are also political pragmatists to a fault. Most of them accurately concluded that she had no chance for the Presidency, so why waste votes and simultaneously hurt a white liberal candidate who might win. Another major factor inhibiting her candidacy's momentum was the manner in which she announced her decision. Not only did she boycott a Black politicians' strategy meeting at a Chicago O'Hare airport motel, but she never consulted with any of the Black politicians about her intentions. As far as they were then concerned, she was on her own.

Still, the changing face of America is reflected by her candidacy and its limited success can be compared to the crusade of another earlier American political reformer, Norman Thomas. The prominent advocate of socialism ran for the Presidency six times between 1928 and 1948, his highest total coming in 1932 with 884,649 votes or 2 per cent of the national vote. Those votes amounted to an average of 18,430 votes per state. In the first 6 primaries she entered, Rep. Chisholm's vote total was 189,969 votes or an average of 31,661 votes per state, nearly double that of Thomas's average per state.

The second major Black event in the 1972 Presidential race was the emergence of the Congressional Black Caucus as a united voice with a unifying strategy. As an outgrowth of the Black Power movement's nationalist consciousness, the Caucus's strategy represented that consciousness coming of age in 1972.

Its final hour came on June 1, 1972 when it announced that all 13 of them would lead a boycott of the Presidential election—"thus insuring the re-election of Richard Nixon"—unless the Democratic National Convention platform contained its "Black Bill of Rights."

This document, a more pragmatic distillation from the Gary convention contained 13 key provisions: busing to integrate public schools; Black control of schools with predominantly Black enrollments; full employment; a guaranteed annual income of $6,500 for a family of four; a new Homestead Act to utilize government lands for Black housing developments; rebuilding of inner city with large concentrations of Blacks; free medical care for all the poor and near poor; expansion of programs to aid minority enterprise; 15 per cent of all government contracts to Black-owned businesses; immediate withdrawal from Southeast Asia; heavily increased foreign aid for African nations; the severance of diplomatic relations with South Africa; and "Black Americans receiving a proportionate share of all appointed positions, up to and including the Cabinet."

The timing of the Caucus's statement was strategic. Sympathetic support for Wallace as a possible Vice Presidential candidate had begun to well up following his near assassination. The Caucus knew that its ultimatum to the Democratic party to accept their "bill of rights" or else would never be accepted by Wallace.

While many of the ideas in the Caucus's "Black Bill of Rights" can be traced directly to the Gary Convention's published "national Black Agenda," their document was their quietly diplomatic way of informing their constituencies and other Black communities that they still spoke for the national legislative mandates for Black people, not some of the more radical rhetoricians who fathered the document.

Moreover, more than one-third of the approximately 1600 elected Black officials come from the 11 Southern states. For the most part, southern Blacks tend to be more moderate and middle-class in their voting habits and legislative predilections than northern urban Blacks. A dashiki-clad candidate has virtually no appeal among Black voters who will, on the other hand, accept that symbol of African unity on its civil rights leaders such as the brilliant and eloquent Rev. Jesse Jackson.

Two issues on which the Gary convention nearly split asunder and which later caused the NAACP to withdraw from the convention's subsequently established National Black Assembly were opposition to busing and a resolution calling for the dismantling of "imperialist" Israel.

On the first issue, this historic convention of Black Americans had embarrassingly lined itself up squarely with the incorrigibly racist anti-busing positions of George Wallace and Richard Nixon. Whereas they were "coming from a Black thing" by demanding Black community control of schools and disavowing the white exracist educators' popularized notion that Black children can only achieve equal learning in integrated schools, the Convention's resolution on busing nonetheless caused many Northern suburban and Southern rural integration-oriented middle-class and middle-aged Blacks to reject the Convention's resolution.

The anti-Israel resolution was sheer political irresponsibility. That it was motivated by latent anti-Semitism cannot be denied. But, it forced unnecessary divisions between many Black legislators and their liberal and Jewish colleagues at a time when that alliance is already being eroded by an understandably disturbed Jewish community which feels threatened abroad and at home.

For a bloc vote that held the balance of power in the 1948 and 1960 Presidential elections, the Black vote fell on its hardest times in history in the 1972 Presidential election and raised some serious questions about the pivotal power of any bloc vote that defies a major trend among the majority of voters.

Of the 75,000,000 votes plus cast in the 1972 Presidential race, Richard M. Nixon won re-election with 61.3 per cent of that popular vote. Black voters, on the other hand, voted 85 per cent for Democratic challenger Sen. George McGovern. While the exact total of Black votes cast in the Presidential election is unknown, some projections are possible by assuming a 60 per cent registration of 14,000,000 Blacks of voting-age population, which is high, then a 54 per cent turn-out in the election (equal to the 54 per cent turn-out of white voters) and 85 per cent of those votes cast for McGovern. This would mean that Black voters accounted for only 13 per cent of the McGovern vote.

Blacks voted against Nixon with near unanimous disdain because of the openly racist strategies his campaign employed. In a nation whose political climate became dominated in 1972 by the politics of latent niggerism—busing and welfare—Black voters were literally caught in the crossfire of a disinterested Republican party, on the one hand anxious to woo both the traditionally Democratic blue-collar workers defecting to Nixon over the Vietnam War issue and bussing and the traditionally southern Democratic voter defecting for largely the same reasons, and on the other hand, a Democratic party anxious to not become too closely identified with Black voters lest that further alienate the racist electoral "hard hats."

Following the 1972 debacle for Black political strength at the national level, it has become clear to many Black political strategists that the emphasis must now shift away from the national to the local level where opportunities for Blacks to maximize their electoral strength in municipal and state elections are increasing.

For example, according to the U.S. Bureau of Census, 26 cities or 17 per cent of the 153 cities with populations of 100,000 or more have Black populations of at least 33 per cent.

Secondly, according to a report, "Black Politics '72," prepared by the Joint Center for Political Studies at Howard University, there are 59 congressional districts with 30 per cent or more Black populations.

Thus, in both major cities and congressional districts, Black voters can hope to reclaim some of the national luster that has been rubbed off their brilliant "balance of power" bloc vote by becoming the pivotal force in local and state elections.

Maximizing Black political power at the local level in an increasingly racist and repressive political climate will require a broad diversity of political skills among Black politicians. Like white politicians, Black politicians will be forced to adopt multiple strategies and styles.

Thus, Black Americans expect and want their leaders to have the political shrewdness of a Congressman, William L. Dawson, the charismatic flair of an Adam Clayton Powell, the good looks of a Julian Bond, the acceptable Uncle Tomism of a Senator Edward Brooke, the negotiating genius of a State Senator Leroy Johnson, the smoke-filled room organizational skills of a Congressman Ralph Metcalf, the radicalism of a Congressman Ronald Dellums, the administrative brilliance of a Mayor Carl Stokes, the skin-color blackness of a Mayor Richard Hatcher, and the incredible patience of a Mayor Charles Evers, who perhaps exemplifies the quintessence of today's Black politician by having got himself elected mayor in a city in the nation's most racist state, Mississippi, and managing to inspire Blacks to a bold unity without antagonizing whites to open political warfare.

Perhaps the contemporary Black politician, aware of the new dignity and power of Blackness, sensitive more than ever to the white racism dominating his community's lives, and yearning for the opportunity to help govern the body politic whose racism has almost destroyed his people, recognizes that he really has no choice but to become a successful schizophrenic in order to succeed.

A good example is Kenneth Gibson, who was authenticated as a serious candidate for Mayor of Newark only after a citywide convention of Blacks and Puerto Ricans organized by Imamu Amiri Baraka (also known as Leroi Jones) chose him as their nominee over several other candidates. Yet Gibson still had to negotiate with New Jersey Governor Cahill for state funds a year after his 1970 election to bring Newark out of a possible bankruptcy caused by a $60,000,000 deficit from the previous corrupt administration of Mayor Hugh Adonizio. It was a Black Nationalist, Baraka, who provided the organizing impetus for Gibson's victory, but it is only a white Republican governor who can guarantee the economic salvation of Newark. Baraka is totally unequipped to attract new industry or any significant white investment to Newark. If anything, he actively repels all such potential. Conversely, Governor Cahill as a nondescript white Republican to Newark's Black Democratic constituency would be of little assistance in insuring Gibson's re-election even if Gibson were to remind the Black electorate of Cahill's help.

The ability of a Mayor Kenneth Gibson to unite the Imamu Barakas and the Governor Cahills into some kind of functional political symbiosis is perhaps the real challenge of the Black politician for the 1970's. Charles Evers must function likewise in Mississippi, as must Leroy Johnson in Georgia and Ralph Metcalf (Dawson's successor) in Chicago. Ten years ago, a Black politician could mute his Blackness, if not ignore it altogether, and with the financial support of a white racist political oligarchy still win elections. Dawson proved it could be done by becoming the surrogate for Mayor Daley's plantation politics. But even in machine-controlled Chicago Blacks are defecting in large numbers from the Daley machine. In the 1971 mayoralty primary, Daley received approximately 30,000 fewer votes in eleven predominantly Black wards than he did in 1963. But it was in the 1972 Presidential election that Chicago Black Democrats worked one of those rare political miracles by splitting their tickets to vote for Democratic Presidential candidate McGovern and against Democratic candidate for State Attorney Edward Hanrahan. Blacks had never forgiven Hanrahan for ordering what they considered a phony raid on a Black Panther apartment in 1969 that resulted in the deaths of two prominent Panther leaders. The Black community held several large rallies to protest the killings as "murders."

Black Democratic leaders persuaded Daley to dump Hanrahan from the ticket, but Hanrahan ran in the Democratic primary and won the nomination. Angered by his continuing contemptuous treatment of the Black community, Black voters passed the word on election all over Chicago that "21-C is the survival key." (Hanrahan's opponent, Bernard Carey, was listed on line 21-C.) When the votes were counted, Hanrahan carried only four of the 14 Black wards that traditionally rack up whopping Black majorities for Democrats. (McGovern received, for example, 84 per cent of the Black vote, while Hanrahan only received 39 per cent.)

Black nationalism will surely grow and intensify in the 1970's in the Black community, as young Blacks, now motivated by the prospect of some form of Black political, economic, or educational autonomy, become the new voters and the new leaders. Integration as the only major philosophy in the Black community is dead. But as a political tactic, it is mandatory for Black survival.

The Black community has finally begun to "act like other folks," internalizing a capacity for organized violence and advocating a unity based on ethnic peoplehood. Though the Black political community is a hundred years late in acquiring these two dimensions of the political process, it will achieve greater power to the extent it is able to orchestrate them together in a symphony of brinkmanship with white American racism.

Just as America under the genius of John Foster Dulles practiced the art of brinkmanship in its coexistence with international communism, so must Black Americans in their drive toward the nationhood of Pan-Africanism adopt, where applicable, a similar strategy.

The Black community must exercise all its options, either at different times or simultaneously, weaving all of them into a tapestry of power politics. This means that at the same time we must have an Angela Davis; the Black Panthers; a Sen. Edward W. Brooke; Black Congressmen and women; Cincinnati Mayor Theodore Berry; a Mississippi Mayor Charles Evers; rebellion in Watts,

Newark, and Detroit; an Imamu Baraka; a Rev. Jesse Jackson; a Roy Innis of CORE; a Congresswoman Shirley Chisholm; and even unfortunately, a Presidential assistant like mediocre and meaningless Robert Brown in the White House.

The only political instrument lacking in the Black community's contemporary involvement with the electoral process is an ethnically controlled third party. And until Blacks can initiate a viable and visible third party, founded on a basic commitment to a Pan-African ideology (perhaps not so explicitly stated since most Black Americans are not yet emotionally prepared to accept the totality of Pan-Africanism as the spiritual yardstick for their political destiny), they cannot become a pivotal force in American politics.

The concept of a Black third party represents three political facts: a pragmatic option, an electoral necessity, and a balance of power. When both the Democratic and Republican parties, particularly at the local level, are closed to Black political advancement, then a third party becomes a pragmatic option. When both major parties refuse to accord Blacks their proportionate share of appointive offices, then the Black third party is an electoral necessity. When both parties ignore the legitimacy of Black demands and national candidates disregard the Black vote, as did Nixon and Humphrey in 1968 and Nixon again in 1972, then a Black third party must attempt to educate the Black electorate to its pivotal influence as an independent voting bloc. Only through the pressure of a contrapuntal political force, a Black third party, will the Democratic and Republican parties seriously consider the imperative to bring Blacks up to white economic and educational parity.

Third party movements must not be envisioned as sanctuaries of guaranteed political success. They rarely win major elections, but they occasionally decide Presidential elections, as did Theodore Roosevelt's Progressive party in 1912 when the split Republican vote between his party and the regular Republican party resulted in the election of Woodrow Wilson. Third parties have periodically forced the major parties to move closer to the third parties' perspective as did the Progressive party in 1948 when the Democratic party proposed one of its most aggressive civil rights platforms after the Progressive party advocated a strong civil rights program. The Democratic Convention's action set the stage for the Southern walkout and the formation of the Dixiecrat party.

In New York state, third party strength was reflected in the election of New York City Mayor Lindsay on the Liberal party ticket and the election of U.S. Senator James Buckley on the Conservative party ticket.

A Black political party remains the most urgent directive still neglected by the Black community. As have other third party movements, a Black political party would provide the philosophical option similar to that which existed for years when Americans voted for Norman Thomas's Socialist presidential candidacy as an alternative to the dreary me-tooism of both major parties. Norman Thomas never won office but he was respected as a recognized intellectual power in America.

In the 1970's, one of the heaviest burdens in Black history will fall on the Black politician who must negotiate from a Black situation of strength with a more powerful white configuration of dominant power.

As a successful schizophrenic, he must steer a course between what some might view as the Charybdis of Black Nationalism and the Scylla of white racism. When and under what circumstances the Black politician must elect to exploit which element of multi-dimensional political activity by boisterously encouraging the Black ethic, advocating a close alliance with white groups within the two-party system, maintaining a discreet silence on the imperatively disruptive and violent tactics of a few Black revolutionaries, or manipulating the prerogatives of office, are the crucial options confronting him or her today. The strengthening of Black nationhood until it becomes a reality in American society without dividing America is the Black politician's challenge.

The 1970's may well be the decade when America's two nations, one white and the other Black, decide whether they are going to co-exist as equals, wage war as unequals, or live grudgingly, but affectionately, as one in a land which has yet to deserve the political label democracy.

White Politicians

FRANK MUNGER

After we left the Mayor's office we went over to the printer's to see if the political name cards were ready. Sure enough, there they were, five thousand of them. "Just a starter," George had said. "Before the election's over we'll need fifty thousand of them."

They are really very good cards. In the left-hand corner there is a picture of me, and it is very flattering. At the top, across the card, is "Peter Martin" in big letters. Underneath that in italics is "Progressive and Militant"—which gives me a slogan with my own initials. At the bottom of the card it says "Democratic Representative" in big print. Next to my picture in smaller lettering is: "Lifelong Democrat, attended local schools and Chicago University. Capable, courageous, conscientious." George was great for having slogans that began with the same letter or with my initials. One of my opponents, Kelly, used to call me the CCC candidate and said I was still in the woods—but all that was much later in the campaign, of course. . . .

But as I was saying, George was very strong for cards and before the campaign was over I had cards printed in French, Polish, and Italian. There were sections of the city with big foreign votes and we wanted to get them. . . . The cards printed about me in the foreign languages were very good, I thought. The Italian cards had me as Pietro Martin, the French as Pierre Martin, and on the Polish it was Petrovich Martin. Joe thought "Petrovich" was Russian, but it was the closest we could come to a Polish name, so we used it. I began to wonder what my nationality really was supposed to be. . . .

We also had a card printed for the colored people. He mailed three thousand of them out two days before election—one to every voter in the colored section. It was George's idea. He had everything

> on it just like on my regular card except, instead of my picture, he had a picture of a colored fellow, and underneath the picture it said in very small letters, "Vote for Peter Martin, a friend of the colored." George said that *we* meant the colored man on the card to be saying that. "We don't mean you're the colored man," he told me, "and it's not our fault if the colored people think you're colored and vote for you because they think that. The colored fellow on the card is just a voter who's telling his friends to vote for you." Eddie and Joe finally agreed it was all right to send them out because nobody was going to get them but colored people anyway. "And," Joe pointed out, "before anybody finds out about it the election'll be over anyhow."
>
> "And anyhow," George pointed out, "we can say one of your opponents sent them out. Dirty politics against you. Something like that skunk Mason would pull." He was quiet for a long time after that and then he wanted to send postcards to the Irish and Italian section—postcards saying my opponent Murphy was a great guy and signed by the President of the Planned Parenthood League. "If the Irish think all the birth control people are for Murphy," George argued, "they'll be for anybody but Murphy."

This description of the use of the race issue by Peter Martin, a candidate, and George, his campaign manager, is in John Foster's fine novel of local politics in a northeastern state, *Let George Do It.*[1] And, with only slight reservations, it may be said to provide a fair description of the treatment given to race by most white politicians in American political campaigns for it includes all three of the most common elements of their approach: (1) personal detachment from the issue and from the consequences of its use; (2) an effort to manipulate the issue for maximum personal political advantage; and (3) a rather complete absence of scruple in such manipulation. The remainder of this essay will be devoted to elaborating upon these.

The White Politician as Covert Racist: Al Smith in 1928

The jump from Peter Martin to the presidency and from the 1970's to the 1920's may seem abrupt, but my illustration dates from 1928. In that year, Governor Alfred E. Smith of New York was the presidential candidate of the Democratic party. The central public issue of the campaign—despite Governor Smith's vain efforts to tie it to farm policy—was prohibition; the central private issue of the campaign was the fact that Al Smith was a Roman Catholic and his Republican opponent was not. And for those who assess Smith by the enemies he made—and read KKK as meaning "No Koons, No Kikes, No Katholics"—the widespread presumption has ordinarily been that he was a liberal on the issue of race. At the time many presumably knowledgeable observers made the assumption. Thus, one distinguished Southern publisher, George Fort Milton, conceived of Smith's campaign as an appeal "to every sort of group complex, inferiority attitude, and resentment to American standards and ideals which could be contrived. To the aliens, who feel that the elder America, the America of the Anglo-Saxon stock, is a hateful thing which must be overturned and humiliated; to the northern Negroes, who lust for social equality and racial dominance; to the Catholics who have been made to believe that they are entitled to the White House, and to the Jews who likewise are to be instilled with the feeling that this is the time for God's chosen people to chastise America yesteryear." [2]

There is actually little in the factual record, however, to justify such an interpretation of Smith's attitudes on the subject of race. During the 1920's, Tammany Hall, under the leadership of Charles F. Murphy, had in its pragmatic way begun to make overtures to the growing black population of Manhattan and in the South Smith was taxed with responsibility for the appointment of a Negro, Ferdinand Q. Morton, as a Civil Service Commissioner by New York City Mayor Michael Hylan in 1922. But as governor of the state, Smith had displayed no particular racial liberalism although, obviously, much of the social welfare legislation he sponsored benefited both the black and the white poor. During the 1928 campaign, W. E. B. DuBois wrote: "Smith is an excellent administrator and his attitude on liquor is at least honest, [but] he has consistently vetoed every bill and movement which Negroes advocated." [3] DuBois objected specifically to Smith's veto of a bill that would have authorized selection of a black magistrate in Harlem and to Smith's failure to appoint blacks to any major posts in state government. That his complaints had substance is perhaps sufficiently indicated by an official statement issued during the campaign rebutting charges made in the South that Smith had appointed numerous Negroes to office and had a black stenographer by noting that in fact only one Negro had received appointment from Governor Smith during four terms—as a messenger boy in the state capitol building.

Throughout his campaign for the presidency, apparently Smith made no reference of any kind to the questions of race relations; in the collection of twenty-one of his campaign speeches that he put together after his defeat, the closest to any allusion to race is the sentence, "Every race has made its contribution to the betterment of America," introduced as a preliminary to an appeal for the liberalization of immigration quotas.[4] (In his autobiographical writings and the adulatory biographical sketches written by his admirers and relatives, careful inspection of half a dozen sources discloses only one further mention of race: While sheriff of New York County, Smith went so far as to assure a newsboys' banquet that, "The flag of America stands for equal opportunity. It left open the gateway of opportunity irrespective of race, creed, or color so that the most humble in the land may rise to greater things; it made free institutions."[5])

That this silence on Smith's part was not accidental is clear enough. When Smith asked Walter White, national secretary of the NAACP, for his support, White replied that he would endorse Smith if the governor would issue an "unequivocal" statement "making it clear to the Negro and to the country" he would "not be ruled by the anti-Negro South." After consultation with his advisors and with his vice-presidential running mate, Senator Joseph T. Robinson of Arkansas, Smith decided "such a statement would too greatly antagonize the South" and declined.[6] And the tactical reason for Smith's silence is equally plain: On the ancient principle of fighting fire with fire, Smith's southern supporters were replying to criticism of their candidate's religion by mounting a virulently racist campaign. Loyal Democratic leaders, desperate to hold their states, played up the issue of white supremacy as it had not been necessary to do since the turn of the century when Reconstruction was in effect repealed and the "Redemption" of the South for its whites completed.

Alabama, where the Smith state campaign manager promised a campaign "on a high plane, disassociated from all prejudices, embittered personalities, or offensive recriminations," may be taken as typical of the loyal Democratic approach in the Deep South.[7] At the outset, the Democratic national committeewoman defined the "leading issue" of the campaign: "white rule." "The issue of this national campaign to the Democrats of the South is whether or not the civilization of the South shall be preserved." Smith's campaign manager assured Alabama voters that a vote for Smith was a vote for "white supremacy" and against "social equality." A Smith speaker in Montgomery reminded his listeners that the county was sixty percent black and in the surrounding counties blacks outnumbered whites three-to-one; this "black population" was not yet a "menace," but a Republican victory in Alabama could "light a spark" and "start a blaze more destructive than Sherman's barbaric and scourging march to the sea." Others warned that the "South is sleeping over a slumbering volcano"; a split in the white vote would be "very dangerous," since it might give the Negro the balance of power. Bolting Democrats were told they were joining the party that "brought the black heels of the ex-slaves down on the throats of Southern men and women." To assist the Smith campaign in Alabama a Women's League for White Supremacy was formed whose members pledged:

* I believe the white people of Alabama should make the laws for the citizens of Alabama.
* I am opposed to white children and negro children attending the same schools.
* I am opposed to whites and negroes being seated together on street cars.
* I am opposed to white girls and negroes working in the same offices as the order of Herbert Hoover has forced them to do.
* I am for the Democratic party and all its nominees for the reason that the principal laws have been made and upheld by the Democrats since the War Between the States.

As the pledge indicates, the speeches of Smith supporters also included personal attacks on Herbert Hoover, his opponent. As Secretary of Commerce, Hoover had ordered an end to the practice of segregating black and white employees in the Census Bureau; this was presented as proof he would "obey orders from the

Harlem black belt." Hoover had been nominated at the Republican convention with the help of 122 Negro delegates—one of whom had seconded his nomination—but "not a black face disgraced the Democratic convention." Or, couched in the more sensational rhetoric preferred by Senator Theodore G. Bilbo of Mississippi in stumping for Smith came the charge that Hoover had danced with a Negro while on a flood relief trip to Mound Bayou, Mississippi; that is, more bluntly, "Herbert Hoover dances with nigger women." Even Smith's seeming drawbacks were turned to his advantage. Hoover was prohibitionist—and so was Alabama—but Republican victory would bring as strict an enforcement of the 14th and 15th Amendments as of the 18th. Smith was a protégé of Tammany Hall, but before, during, and after the Civil War Tammany had been the South's "strongest and staunchest friend and supporter" and a Tammany leader had signed the bail bond for Jefferson Davis. Smith was a Catholic, but Hoover was a Quaker and, as the Alabama Attorney General assured his audiences: The Unknown Soldier buried at Arlington might have been white, yellow, red, or black, a Protestant, Jew, Catholic, or a non-believer, but he could not have been a Quaker because a Quaker would not "fight for his country in time of stress or peril."

Those Democrats who had deserted ranks reacted in kind with a reciprocal shower of abuse. Full-page advertisements were placed throughout the South, particularly in country newspapers, headed "Al Smith, the Negro Lover." The allegations included Morton's appointment as Civil Service Commissioner where he "had charge of hundreds of white girls"—in some versions he was slated for appointment to the Cabinet by Smith; that Smith had "refused to segregate white children from the negroes in the public schools" and permitted whites to dance with blacks in "Harlem cabarets"; that marriages between white women and black men had increased while Smith was governor of New York; and that New York [whether City or State was never made clear] employed more blacks than the entire national government. Bob Jones, Methodist minister and founder of Bob Jones University, guaranteed his audiences that Smith believed in racial intermarriage and was the "greatest nigger lover" and "nigger boot licker" of the country. Other speakers charged that prizefighter Jack Johnson—"the negro with the white wife"—was campaigning for Smith. One neat argument combined Smith's opposition to prohibition with his supposed support of "racial equality" to forecast a South overrun by "drunken Negroes" if Smith won. A statement from the Democratic National Committee alleged that Republican officials had hired Negroes to tour several southern states in automobiles carrying "Al Smith" streamers.

Hoover's own record on race was relatively clear. He had in fact ordered an end to segregation in the Census Bureau after receiving protests from Negro Republicans in the early stages of his pre-convention campaign for nomination. The Republican party platform had pledged support for a federal anti-lynching law—a promise often noted by Smith speakers in the South—and the candidate had himself declared in a campaign speech (albeit in Boston): "I think the place of the colored people is with the Republican party and I welcome you there and shall do all that is in my power to uphold the traditions of the party and the Constitution of the United States." The leading Negro spokesmen and editors in the South publicly endorsed him. The Republican National Campaign Committee established a colored voters division with Albon Holsey of the Tuskegee Institute as secretary. The one major party concession to the southern Democrats who had bolted to Hoover was the decision to nominate no Negro presidential electors anywhere in the South.

Al Smith does not stand alone, of course, as a candidate for office who engaged in no racist appeals but remained carefully silent while his supporters used them where they seemed likely to pay off; indeed, he is presented here as a type, summing up one kind of white political response to the race issue. What is perhaps unique to the Smith candidacy is the fact that a generation of biographers and historians in the years since have continued to severely criticize Hoover for his failure to speak out more strongly in rebuke of those of his supporters who made use of anti-Catholic entreaties but have remained as silent as Smith himself in reference to the "white supremacy" campaign waged against Hoover in the South.[8]

The White Politician as Uncommitted Liberal: John Kennedy in 1960

If many whites would—mistakenly—assume that Al Smith was a racial liberal, almost all will classify John Kennedy as one of the presidents most strongly committed to the cause of civil rights. For some, it is a matter for praise; for others, a matter for blame. Certainly his commitment to the cause of civil rights existed. In his campaign speeches of 1960 Kennedy spoke out strongly in favor of civil rights legislation. Black voters gave him heavy support (though his margin was probably not so high as that won by Adlai Stevenson in 1952, by Lyndon Johnson in 1964, or by Hubert Humphrey in 1968). Although few of the legislative civil rights proposals he presented to Congress were approved, some observers would regard the 1964 Civil Rights Act as a posthumous tribute to his life, and President Johnson urged its passage in just those terms. But a closer examination of John Kennedy's personal attitudes in racial questions would seem to suggest once again: (1) that he was emotionally uncommitted to the cause of civil rights; and (2) that the positions he adopted on the issue were essentially tactical.

These are painful evaluations to make and would be hard to defend if the evidence available from his close friends and associates were not so clearcut. Thus, Theodore Sorensen acknowledges: "As a Senator he simply did not give much thought to this subject. He had no background of association or activity in race relations. He was against discrimination as he was against colonialism or loyalty oaths—it was an academic judgment rather than a deep-rooted personal compulsion. He voted for every civil rights bill coming before him as Congressman and Senator more as a matter of course than of deep concern." [9]

So much for the matter of personal conviction. Sorensen then goes on to add: "In fact, when he talked privately about Negroes at all in those days, it was usually about winning Negro votes. He talked privately that way about every group—Poles, farmers, Jews, veterans, the aged, suburbanites, or any other. To him Negroes were no different from anyone else. He did not treat them differently, look at them differently, or speak of them differently. They were not set aside as a Special Problem or singled out as a special group—he simply sought their votes along with those of everyone else. Politics, in fact, helped to deepen his concern. He was a good politician—and in the 1960 convention and election Negroes more than most groups were his political friends and their enemies were often his enemies." [10]

Sorensen's assessments—based upon intimate personal acquaintance—can be corroborated easily enough from the record. At the 1960 Democratic convention, as Sorensen noted, Negroes were Kennedy's political friends, but four years earlier Kennedy had been a candidate before another Democratic national convention, seeking the nomination for vice-president as Stevenson's running-mate. Kennedy had sought unsuccessfully in 1956 to build a coalition into the right wing of the party; in 1960 he sought successfully to build a coalition toward the left wing of the party. It is hard to escape the conclusion that the change in strategy was tactical rather than the result of a sudden conversion to more liberal views, and was a frankly political response to the fact that his principal opponent was now Lyndon Johnson rather than Estes Kefauver.[11]

Nor is Kennedy unique among Democratic leaders in these ideological peregrinations.[12] Adlai Stevenson made a similar "tactical adjustment" in his racial stance between 1952 and 1956; but in a direction opposite to Kennedy's, as his later position was that of cultivating Southern support through "moderation." Lyndon Johnson seems to have been several different things at several different times. Franklin Roosevelt, though later identified with the cause of racial equality, won his first nomination in 1932 by building up support from an original base of strength in his own New York State and in the Deep South.[13] And Samuel Lubell, the political analyst, has contributed the anecdote that describes a Senator from Missouri, later to be President of the United States, telling his Southern senatorial colleagues when an antilynching bill was before the Congress in 1938: "All my sympathies are with you, but the Negro vote in Kansas City and St. Louis is too important." [14]

It seems a fair generalization to suggest that during the period from Al Smith's day to the present only two kinds of men have been nominated for President by the two major parties: men who have been prepared to profit from the use of racist anti-black arguments by some of their supporters but who have refrained from openly endorsing such a position themselves and men who have assumed positions as liberals in matters of race for essentially tactical reasons. During the same period there have been, of course, white politicians with strong convictions and commitments on the racial question, both pro and con, but some characteristic of the presidential nominating process has served to screen them out before they have emerged as serious contenders for the presidency.[15]

The White Politician as Overt Racist: The "New" Urban Politics

Also notable by its absence is another category of presidential candidate: the overt racist who—not by silent acquiescence but through active personal participation—seeks to secure white votes by direct anti-black appeals. If some quirk of the nominating process has functioned to screen out committed racial liberals, some rule of propriety in presidential campaigning has apparently restrained major party candidates active during the period in question from open personal involvement in a racist campaign. Even Barry Goldwater—whose pattern of electoral support in 1964 closely reflected a dividing line drawn by racism—refrained from any open bid for the racist votes he got. It has been left to third party candidates whose maximal hope has been the achievement of a position for bargained influence in the Electoral College to directly avow a racist position.

The same cannot be said for candidates for lesser office and one of the most widely discussed developments of the late 1960's in large-city politics in the United States was the emergence of a style of politics whereby candidates bid openly for the support of anti-black voters. By a kind of paradox—which is, of course, readily explicable—this political style is simultaneously in decline in southern state campaigns where it previously flourished and in the ascendant in political campaigns in the big cities of the North. It must be remembered, however, that for the latter it is not in fact a novelty but marks a return to the type of political practice that greeted Southern Negroes on their arrival in northern cities during and after the First World War.

Chicago may be taken as an example. The city's mayor throughout most of the 1920's was one of the nation's most colorful political personalities, William Hale Thompson, a Republican variously known as "Big Bill the Builder" and "Kaiser Bill." First winning national notoriety by his adamantly pro-German views during World War I, Thompson later became famous as the man who campaigned (successfully) for mayor in 1927 with the pledge to "make the King of England keep his snoot out of America." To tie the issue—expressed in national terms by opposition to American entry into the World Court—at least loosely to municipal politics he charged that the Chicago superintendent of schools was requiring the use of history textbooks filled with British propaganda and "all kinds of things belittling George Washington." Only somewhat less well-known were his close personal association with Al Capone and his fervent endorsement of the repeal of prohibition. (During his 1931 campaign Thompson paraded the streets with a camel bearing the sign, "I CAN GO EIGHT DAYS WITHOUT A DRINK BUT WHO THE HELL WANTS TO BE A CAMEL?")[16]

Little attention was paid outside Chicago, however, then or now, to Thompson's relationship with the black voters of the city. In his first mayoral campaign in 1915, Thompson actively sought the backing of the Negroes of the South Side, promising that jobs for Negroes would follow upon his election. An overwhelming 6,000 vote margin in the predominantly Negro Second Ward gave him his primary victory, counterbalancing a majority for his opponent in the rest of the city. In the general election, he wound up his campaign with a personal appearance in the Negro district. During his campaign for reelection in 1919, his manager deliberately and effectively concentrated on two groups, Negroes and Germans, as the core of his majority. Thompson carried the city by 21,000 votes and over half his margin was provided by a remarkable 11,000 vote plurality in the Second Ward.

Beset by personal and political scandals, Thompson did not seek reelection in 1923 and was succeeded by a Democrat, William E.

Dever. But in 1927 he decided to try again, this time with the campaign slogan of "America First, Last, and Always." Mayor Dever, running for reelection, offered the counter-slogan "Dever and Decency" and was endorsed by numerous reformers, including the University of Chicago Professor Charles E. Merriam, Harold L. Ickes (later to be Franklin Roosevelt's Secretary of the Interior), and Walter Dill Scott, president of Northwestern University. The racist character of the campaign was correctly forecast at the very beginning of Thompson's campaign. City police under Dever's direction invaded the Second and Third Wards (both now predominantly Negro), breaking into speakeasies, pool rooms, and private homes, and arrested more than a thousand men and women. All were released the following Monday without charges having been brought. Thompson's campaign manager accurately described the raids as "a plot . . . to terrorize and intimidate the colored voters so they will be deprived of their vote at the mayoralty election."

Thompson in turn opened his campaign in the Eighth Regiment Armory, drill hall for the city's Negro units of the state militia. He condemned his opponents as "traducers and liars and lily-white gentlemen." Toward the end of the meeting, he leaned over at one point to demonstratively hug a Negro child, the nephew of Oscar de Priest, one of his most faithful supporters and the first black to serve in Congress during the twentieth century. The Democratic managers thereupon had duplicated cartoons showing Thompson kissing Negro children and spread them throughout the city with the line: "Do You Want Negroes or White Men to Run Chicago? Bye, Bye, Blackbirds!" One Democratic speaker declared that during Thompson's first term as mayor he had invited Negro thugs and gamblers to Chicago. "He speaks 'America First' but he thinks 'Africa First.'" At Dever's meetings, bands played "Bye, Bye, Blackbird" and signs were posted: "Do You Want Negroes or White Men to Run Chicago? Ask Thompson!" The latter replied by claiming that "Dever and Brennan [Chicago's Democratic Party boss] are a disgrace to the Irish! They are trying to start a race riot to make white people hate Thompson and elect a crook mayor." (Despite the language it is beyond question that Al Capone lent Thompson strong support in this election; the Democratic campaign was, however, clearly inflammatory in a city that had been witness to a major race riot in 1919.) After Thompson's election, *The Emancipator*, a Negro journal, was one of the very few newspapers in the city to express approval of his victory; one editorial predicted that Thompson would be ranked some day with Washington and Lincoln in "the people's fight for democracy and human rights." (In the black Second Ward Thompson received 91 percent of the vote.)

The Thompson-Dever contest in 1927 was generally contemporaneous with the Al Smith campaign of 1928 described above and points to the degree of consistency between Democratic strategy at the national and at local levels. The style of politics it expressed, however, virtually disappeared in Chicago during the depression decade of the 1930's for what must appear from the local perspective to be essentially accidental reasons. Throughout the 1930's, black voters—for reasons associated with national presidential politics—were shifting from their traditional Republican affiliations to an identification with the Democratic party. Though the change came more slowly at the local level, most of the dominant Democratic party organizations in the big cities of the North found themselves blessed with an unearned increment of black support. (The process literally precluded two-party competition at the municipal level in cities such as Chicago where the Republican party had served as a viable alternative only through the votes of its black wing.) The minimum requirement demanded by the new black recruits was the silencing of overtly racist citywide campaigns, so the racist politics characteristic of many Northern cities in the 1920's gradually disappeared in the 1930's, the 1940's, and the 1950's. Only in the 1960's, with the extension of the civil rights movement into the North was this pattern challenged. The resulting "white backlash," first broached largely in terms of its possible effects on presidential politics, eventually proved to make its maximum impact on local politics.

The first important revival of the older style of politics based on open racism came in the least partisan of America's large cities, Los Angeles. Its foremost practitioner was the chameleon of big-city mayors, Samuel Yorty. Yorty had entered politics through election to the state legislature in 1938. Though a liberal on most social and economic issues, he early picked up on the political visibility of the communist issue and became the first chairman of the California Un-American Activities Committee. In 1954, he sought the Senate seat vacated by Richard Nixon and offered credentials good enough for endorsement by the highly liberal California Democratic Council, but broke with the CDC two years later when the group refused him further support. In 1960, he backed Nixon for president.

Yorty was first elected mayor of Los Angeles in 1961 and made no particular use of the race issue in his campaign.[17] It emerged as a major theme only during his third mayoral campaign in 1969, when he was opposed by a black candidate. More and more direct appeal to racism has characterized municipal elections then and since in Boston, New York, Newark, Philadelphia, Buffalo, Cleveland, Detroit, Minneapolis, and elsewhere. As in Yorty's case, the use of the issue has clearly been tactical; although some candidates have committed themselves to the racial issue totally more have played with it, picking it up or dropping it as calculations of political advantage have changed. It is for this reason that racist appeals have been almost unavoidable when black candidates have sought office as mayor. Only a strongly committed white would try vigorously to avoid picking up the anti-black votes that will come to him automatically and such men—it has been argued here—are few. In most such instances the choice made has lain between the two alternatives that have been described here as covert racism and overt racism.

The city conspicuous by its omission from the list in which the older style of politics still most conspicuously predominates is Chicago. Martin Meyerson and Edward C. Banfield have demonstrated that while the Democratic machine in Chicago is quite capable of quiet discrimination against blacks,[18] it has maintained intact the public style of black/blue-collar coalition, dating back to the 1930's and Mayor Richard Daley continues to win reelection with the same heavy black support that won him victory in the first place.[19] Thus one notable result of the 1970 off-year congressional elections was the first series of elections in which black candidates were elected to the House of Representatives in predominantly white districts. In two instances—Baltimore and Berkeley—the victories were won in atypical districts with unusual proportions of liberal Jewish and/or university voters. In only one instance—on Chicago's West Side—was the victory won in the classic machine pattern of the past with a minority candidate whose group has been accorded recognition ramrodded through a blue-collar district by precinct workers calling in their IOU's. Whether the Chicago Democratic organization can maintain such party unity through a mayoralty campaign in which it either offers or is challenged by a major black political figure only the future will tell.

The Consequences of Style: Electing Men to Office

To this point the discussion has been focused upon matters of campaign rhetoric: the kinds of campaign appeals employed, the symbols with which a candidate identifies himself, the image he seeks to present of himself and of his views on race. This rhetoric is important in itself, of course. But symbols and rhetoric are not the whole of politics; actions are important too, and perhaps are more important. Some white politicians rant like racists, others keep quiet, some talk like liberals. Does it make any difference in their performance in office? An attempt will be made to deal with that question in two parts: first, in terms of the selection of people for office; second, in respect to the making of public policy. Specifically, answers will be sought to two questions: Is there any evidence that opportunities for blacks to carve out political careers are affected by the attitudes of white politicians? Is there any evidence that legislation varies because white politicians regard race as they do?

Two alternative images of the nature of politics and the character of the politician are handy for analyzing these questions; unfortunately they point in opposite directions. One, the more traditional, emphasizes the role of the politician as a broker of interests. To get elected to office, particularly higher office, he must understand "human nature," he must realize that people will at times disagree with him, he must be prepared to compromise, he cannot always insist on having his own way. In a word, he must be tolerant. Applied to racial matters, this interpretation of the politician's role would imply that politicians, more than most whites, are sympathetic to black aspirations because they are accustomed to the sight of people pushing to get what they want; even when he considers it politically advantageous to assume an opposed position the actively pragmatic politician is not surprised at what he sees, is not outraged when he loses, does not really grow angry at his black opponents (even though he may pretend to do so for the benefit of other whites), and is always prepared to shift positions and "work something out" when circumstances change.

Comparatively recently, a different view of the politician has come into vogue, however, a view with differing emphasis and implications as to political behavior. It draws attention to the class background of the typical political activist, particularly in a big city or in its suburbs, and suggests that, disproportionately, politicians are drawn from the ranks of upwardly mobile white ethnics, especially such Catholic national stocks as Irish, Italians, and Poles. Having—as they see it—"made their own way" or "made it on their own," these men are most contemptuous of black demands for government assistance. Belonging to ethnic groups whose political culture prefers private goals to public needs,[20] they are prepared to yield no more than they have to. And as the individuals whose jobs, incomes, and status are most directly threatened by the demand for black political power, they are the most tenacious in organizing and leading a white resistance movement.

Each view is upheld in what purports to be descriptions of the realities of urban politics. On the one hand, William Osborne has argued that the Catholic Archdiocese of New York was racially liberalized by the pressure of white Catholic politicians whose "general rhetoric" of civic brotherhood and " 'feel' for popular opinion and group affiliations" attuned them to "the clashing loyalties and ambitions within the Negro population" and sensitized them to black demands.[21] On the other hand, James Q. Wilson, after a detailed study of Negro politics concluded: "In the case of the Negro, however, this resistance [to recognition of a new group in politics] is intensified by the frequent operation of personal prejudice and hostility. Negro entry into politics thus far has been less than proportional to their number. . . ."[22]

It is worth citing the fragment of empirical evidence that Wilson offers to support this proposition because it points the way to a resolution of the apparent contradiction. As an example backing his argument Wilson cites the fact that six St. Louis wards had elected Negro aldermen, but that only two had Negro ward leaders. Closely similar evidence could be culled, in fact, from other cities, including Chicago and New York. Thus, in Chicago, the first Negro was elected to the City Council in 1915, but the first ward committeeman, i.e., party leader, was not elected until 1920 and on into the 1920's the ward was actually in effect run by Mayor Thompson's white friend George Harding. Likewise, in New York City, the first Negro was elected to the New York State Assembly in 1917 and the following year a second assembly district fell to a black candidate, but it was not until 1935 that a black man was elected as Democratic leader in either one of the districts and not until 1941 that the second district was captured.

Obviously, white politicians have been more obstinate in fighting to hold on to party posts than in yielding up nominations for public office; the error is in the supposition that this pattern has applied only to exclude blacks. In the most elaborate study that has been made of ethnic succession in city politics, Marvin Weinbaum's study of the Republican party in Manhattan,[23] Weinbaum has identified a regular step-by-step procedure regarding the entrance of a new group into public office. First, candidates are nominated for lesser public office in elective posts; most often these nominations come earliest from the minority party in the district, which is employing a very obvious strategy to detach an element from the majority party coalition. Then candidates run for higher offices and, as the local district comes to be dominated by the new group, most or all of the nominations for public offices are awarded to it, but the party offices are retained to the last by those first in. Thus, at the turn of the century, though the Manhattan Republicans were nominating Irish, Jewish, and other ethnic candidates for many public offices, most party leadership remained in the hands of old-stock Americans. At the same time, at least 20 of the 29 Democratic district leaders were Irish. The Irish did not surrender leadership of Tammany Hall until 1949, many decades after the Manhattan Irish had learned to say to one another, "Well, there are a few of us left." [24]

The logic behind the distinction is easily apparent: Candidates come and go; party leaders go on for ever. Public offices—to a city politician—are just so many jobs; it is the party leader who distributes the jobs and it is his position, therefore, that is the more important. The history of the Harlem leaderships is instructive. By the best estimates, the 19th and 21st assembly districts in central Harlem would appear to have become predominantly black some time before 1930; by that year's census they both appear to be 70 percent Negro; by 1940 it was no more than 73 percent black. The adjacent 19th assembly district was 95 percent black by 1940, but nonetheless still had a white leader. (A bid for the leadership by J. Raymond Jones in 1939 was turned down when his nominating petitions were invalidated on minor technicalities.) Not until 1941 was a black district leader chosen. The difference between the two, as John Morsell notes,[25] was that the 19th was "job-rich" and loaded with patronage and the jobholders fought desperately to maintain their leadership. Similarly, because their job value was much less, the Republican leaderships were yielded up to blacks at much earlier stages.

Parallel patterns can be found in the appointment of blacks to city office. Theodore Lowi has argued, in fact, that it has been the regular function of the minority party to introduce new minority groups into the administrative life of the city. In New York City each of the three Republican-Fusion mayors (before Lindsay), Seth Low, John Purroy Mitchel, and Fiorello La Guardia, appointed substantially larger numbers of Jews, Italians, and Negroes to high political/administrative posts than did their Democratic predecessors. The numbers of such minority appointments then declined in subsequent Democratic city administrations, but never to their earlier levels. Each Republican-Fusion administration left behind, in other words, a legacy in the form of a new plateau defining the minimum acceptable minority representation.[26]

The pattern applies, if somewhat imperfectly, to Negroes in New York. The first Negro to serve in a major administrative post, Dr. Eugene P. Roberts, was appointed to the Board of Education by Mayor Mitchel in 1917. His position was soon thereafter eliminated when the Board of Education was reduced in size from 46 members to seven. The ethnic arrangements surrounding appointments to the seven-member Board thereafter prevented any Negro from serving and it was only by expanding the Board to nine members in 1948 that a vacancy for a black could be created. The appointment of Dr. Roberts was followed, however, by the appointment of Ferdinand Morton to the Civil Service Commission in 1922 (the Tammany-arranged appointment that was used against Smith in the South in 1928). The position was thereafter considered to be reserved for Negroes, and Robert's successors were all blacks. A Negro was appointed to the city Tax Commission in 1934 and another to the Board of Education after 1948. It is noteworthy, however, that all these appointments were made to boards or commissions where the black man was only one among others. This pattern likewise appears to have been widely followed in the introduction of other minority groups into city office. Not until 1954 was a Negro appointed to direct a department when Democratic Mayor Robert Wagner, Jr., appointed Arthur C. Ford as Commissioner of Water Supply, Gas, and Electricity.

The cycle through which blacks have moved in attaining city office, therefore, appears to be generally similar to that followed by other groups; the question remains, however, has their progress been slowed by the racial prejudices of white politicians or has it been eased by their tolerance? At the earliest stages—in New York City, at least—there is little evidence of unusual delays. By Morsell's calculations neither the 19th nor the 21st assembly district had black majorities by 1920 yet both had already elected Negro assemblymen. A more precise statement of relationship requires risky interpolations between census dates but at best guess the 19th can have been no more than a quarter black when it elected a Negro assemblyman and the 21st was perhaps a third black when it first elected a Negro to that office. If party leaderships came late, recognition in public office appears to have come early.[27]

A sharp line must be drawn, however, between recognition at such a level as this and acceptability at the most important levels of visibility in American politics. Certain offices—mayor of a city, governor of a state, President of the nation—appear to be regarded with special solicitude by the voters; an easy, but perhaps accurate interpretation would be that they are seen as paternal in character. Election of a member of a minority group to these posts—symbolically, to the position of head of the political family—is seen as the proof of arrival and acceptance for the entire group; by the same token these are the last posts to be yielded by the old to the new. Senator Edward Brooke has described this kind of reaction as the "captain of the ship" phenomenon, and used it at times to justify his own decision to run for the United States Senate rather than for governor of Massachusetts. He believed that white voters would be particularly hostile to the notion of a Negro in charge of things; in the Senate, however, he would have 99 colleagues to watch over him. (The parallel to administrative appointments on commissions and boards in the first instance, previously referred to, can be readily recognized.)[28]

Because these posts can be considered as rungs on a ladder of ascent to political recognition they take time to reach and one of the foremost difficulties in making too facile comparisons among ethnic groups in their political achievements is ignoring that fact. Politicians, especially organization politicians, recognize that many things have to be waited for. Before you can be a county leader, you must be a district leader. Before you can be a district leader, you must be a committeeman. Or: Before you can be Speaker of the House of Representatives, you must be Majority Leader. Before you can be Majority Leader—now, apparently—you must be Majority Whip. And so forth. Not all parts of the world of politics are run so neatly on the escalator principle, but the organization man who has learned to wait his turn is contemptuous of those who lack his patience and angry when those who will not wait are rewarded for their pushiness.

Some notion of waiting in line for ethnic recognition can be obtained by considering again the city of New York. To compare ethnic groups in this sense it is necessary to establish some kind of benchmark, identifying the point in time at which a group has arrived in sufficient numbers to justify the presumption it has placed a foot on the first rung of the ladder; though reliable data is mostly absent, an estimate that ten per cent of the city's population belonged to a given group may serve the purpose. By this criterion the Irish might be said to have arrived in the city by 1850 by which time New York was at least ten per cent Irish. The first Irish Catholic mayor was not elected until 1880, suggesting a wait of 30 years. The Jewish population of the city was probably—the census, which asks no questions about religion, does not tell us—about ten percent by 1890. Recognition of the Jews as a political group came—after a bitter struggle—in 1932 with the nomination and election of Herbert Lehman as governor. (The Irish Catholic state Democratic party leaders tried to shunt Lehman aside to run for the U.S. Senate.) This time the climb up the ladder appears to have taken about forty years. By 1910 the Italian population of New York City had exceeded ten per cent. If Fiorello La Guardia's election as mayor in 1933 is considered as a recognition of Italians, the process would appear to have speeded up; Nathan Glazer and Patrick Moynihan deny, however, that it can be so considered. They exclude the Episcopalian, half-Italian, half-Jewish La Guardia from their count and argue that the Italians really arrived in New York City politics only with the election of Vincent Impellitteri as mayor in 1950. If their evaluation is correct it would indicate that the Italians—like the Jews—had to wait forty years to reach the top of the city political ladder.[29]

On this basis, the white politician feels that blacks still have a time to wait and should recognize that fact. In 1940 blacks were six per cent of the population of the city; only by 1950 could they be properly said to have started to climb. Hulan Jack's election as Manhattan borough president in 1953 came at a time when blacks were only 21 per cent of the population of the island; this was in white eyes a generous and early recognition of the group. Since that time the post has been reserved for a black. According to our analysis, a black mayor may be due somewhere between 1980 and 1990 and a Puerto Rican between 2000 and 2010. And as for the presidency—it took the Irish 110 years to elect Kennedy; let others wait in line.[30] Rarely, of course, are the figures worked out so precisely, and the precise timing of the steps on the ladder would vary from one city to another, but the spirit they express is everywhere.

And in these feelings the white politician appears to echo the feelings of his constituents. Particularly because of the interest aroused by John Kennedy's candidacy for the presidency the American Institute of Public Opinion (the Gallup Poll) asked frequent questions about the acceptability of ethnic candidates in its national sample surveys in the late 1950's and early 1960's. The question was asked in the form: "If your party nominated a generally well-qualified man for President and he happened to be a (Catholic) (Jew) (Negro) would you vote for him?" Although it cannot be considered an accurate measure of the ticket-splitting such a candidacy actually would cause, precisely because of the "captain of the ship" phenomenon previously noted, it can be taken as a reasonable estimate of the levels of political prejudice. Since the emphasis here is upon the politics of ethnic recognition in urban areas the original sample has been reduced in secondary analysis to include only those interviews conducted in cities (with their suburbs) of 500,000 population or more. These large-city interviews have then been divided in turn into four categoric groups: white Protestants, white Catholics, Jews, and blacks.

In answering the question in respect to a Catholic the results show the following proportions of respondents in each category answering "yes," that is, that they would vote for a generally well-qualified man who happened to be a Catholic:

	White Protestants	*White Catholics*	*Jews*	*Blacks*
1959	80%	93%	85%	82%
1961	85	97	100	91
1963	87	99	100	93
1965	92	99	100	94

Even before the Kennedy nomination the results indicate that the idea of a Catholic "captain of the ship" was generally accepted in large cities. (Tabulations for smaller cities and rural areas would show very different percentages.) A few Catholics, thinking back presumably to the animosities aroused by the Smith campaign, were reluctant to see a Catholic candidate for President; as many as a fifth of the white Protestants were suspicious in 1959, but even these fragments of opposition were dissolved first with Kennedy's election (the change from 1959 to 1961), then by his record as President (from 1961 to 1963), and finally by his assassination (from 1963 to 1965).

The results are not notably different when the question is placed in terms of a Jewish candidate for the presidency. Once more confining the results to large-city populations only, the percentages answering that they would vote for a Jew are:

	White Protestants	*White Catholics*	*Jews*	*Blacks*
1959	84%	84%	98%	93%
1961	74	85	98	84
1963	88	92	96	77
1965	89	94	98	90

Although the differences are small it is perhaps worth noting that in 1959 when John Kennedy was being talked of as a presidential candidate but no Jew was under prominent discussion a Jewish president was actually considered more acceptable than a Catholic. Two other points can be singled out. While the general movement from 1959 to 1965 was a shift toward greater tolerance of a Jewish presidential candidate, blacks moved in the opposite direction from 1959 to 1963. Some might interpret this as evidence of the black anti-Semitism often affirmed and as often denied; such an interpretation might be correct but it is on the face of the data as plausible that the answers reflect the rise in prominence of Barry Goldwater as a presidential contender and then his disappearance from the scene after 1964. Secondly, the student of political behavior, particularly if suspicious of the validity of such small samples as here employed, may be interested to know that the minority of Jews opposed to a Jewish presidential candidate prove on further inspection to consist of women, all of whom report attending a religious service within the week. Presumably all Orthodox, they expressed willingness to vote either for a Catholic or a Negro.

The final tabulation concerns the big-city residents who say they would be willing to vote for a well-qualified Negro candidate for the Presidency (See next page). Again a small minority within the group itself opposed a potentially controversial presidential candidacy by a member, but the overwhelming majority of blacks—and of Jews—express willingness to vote for a Negro. Among Catholics and Protestants, however, skepticism is much greater. Though the movement of attitudes through time is clearly upward toward greater tolerance of a black candidate for President big-city white voters, like big-city white politicians, appear to believe the time is not yet right.

	White Protestants	*White Catholics*	*Jews*	*Blacks*
1959	47%	53%	80%	93%
1961	47	57	93	93
1963	45	51	96	92
1965	62	74	94	96

To summarize the argument to this point: the claim is made that there are elements of truth in both views of the intrinsic character of the white politician originally presented. He fights tenaciously to hold on to positions of party control and to preserve them from a black takeover just as in earlier times old-stock Americans fought to hold off the Irish, the Irish to hold off the Italians, the Italians to hold off the Jews, and so on and on and on. At the same time, however, he is sensitive to the claims of new groups for recognition and is prepared to distribute party nominations for public office—as well as a modicum of appointments—among all groups numerous enough in the electorate to warrant cultivation. In his willingness to balance party tickets ethnically the politician—because he is closer to political realities—is almost certainly more sensitive than the average voter, and can be said, therefore, to be more tolerant. The contrast is clear if the slates of candidates selected by party officials are compared with those nominated in open primaries. But the politician regards certain key posts as symbolic of paramountcy and believes that they should be awarded only after a period of time during which the group to be represented has proven itself. This view appears to be shared by both politicians and voters. Applied to black candidates for the highest offices it implies that they must not be too impatient because their turn has not yet come. Whether this constitutes a racial double standard depends upon the time scale adopted; to the white politician in a Northern city the black is newly arrived; from the viewpoint of the black he has been here for 350 years.

The Consequence of Style: Making Public Policy

At the beginning of the last section it was suggested that a new dimension of consideration had been entered: a concern for substance as opposed to rhetoric. In a way that promise was illusory. For most of the population the process of selection of individuals for election to office is as vague as the language they use in their campaigns. Even the terms of the discussion make that fact clear. "Recognition" through election or appointment to office is a way of saying "I'm as good as you are." The race, religion, and nationality of the slated candidates on a balanced ticket are just so many symbols of the kind of appeal the party wishes to make to the electorate. For aspirants to office "recognition" has substance; it's a job. For the rest of the group it has substance only if it affects the manner in which government is carried on, the kinds of policies adopted, and the way in which they are implemented. Does it have such meaning? This question is the more important but the more difficult to answer.

The more general form of the question might be stated as: in dealing with matters of race do the personal beliefs of the politician enter into his decisions and, if so, what is the direction of the influence they bring to bear? In the late 1950's, the Survey Research Center of the University of Michigan conducted an elaborate study of voting behavior in the U.S. House of Representatives. They conducted interviews within individual congressional constituencies and generated data on the public policy preferences of residents in 116 congressional districts. To supplement these data, interviews were conducted with the congressmen who represented these districts and information obtained both on the congressman's beliefs as to opinion within his constituency and his personal views on the sets of issues examined. From the records of congressional action the rollcall voting behavior of the congressman was noted and an attempt made to explain why the individual congressman had voted as he did.

Since one of the sets of issues studied concerned civil rights legislation the findings are clearly relevant to an understanding of the implications for public policy of the politician's personal views on the subject of race. In the model employed in analyzing the data it was assumed that either of two paths of influence might explain the vote of the congressman. The congressman might seek to "represent" his constituency's opinion, that is, to vote as the people in his district would vote if they were present in person. He might behave in this way either because he was afraid of the consequences of doing otherwise—potential defeat in an election focused upon his voting record on civil rights—or simply because that was his understanding of what a congressman was supposed to do. If he chose to vote this way his vote would be ultimately based upon opinion among his constituents, but the connection would not be direct for he could only vote as he thought his constituency wanted. If he was mistaken in his judgment of constituency opinion his very desire to reflect it might cause him to vote against it.

The second possibility was a path of influence running to the vote in which the congressman voted his own personal convictions. If this vote was his own choice the congressman would not need to consult the opinion of his constituency, and the rightness or wrongness of his evaluation of it would make no difference to his vote. Nevertheless his vote could not be said to be totally unrelated to the actual preferences of his constituency, for the possibility remained that his constituents had deliberately selected a congressman in whose views they had confidence, and his very presence in Congress holding the views that he held was a demonstration of constituency influence. Each of these possible associations was measured by the calculation of a coefficient of correlation showing the closeness of the relationship between the two variables (see Figure 1).

In attempting to answer the question at hand the most significant correlation would seem to be that between the attitude of the constituency and the rollcall record of the congressman; the correlation of .57 can be interpreted (by squaring) as meaning that about 32 per cent of the variation in voting among the congressmen can be attributed to differences in the views of their constituencies. Perhaps more to the point, however, is the correlation between what the representative thought opinion in his constituency supported and his vote; here the correlation of .82 suggests that about two-thirds of the variation in the vote (67%) can be associated with perceived differences in constituency opinion. The difference

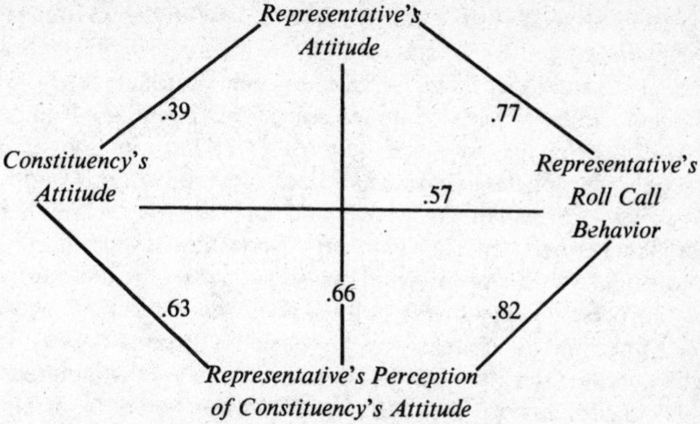

FIGURE I

between the two correlations lies in the relatively low correlation between constituency opinion as estimated by the congressman and as measured by the Survey Research Center. (Since the number of interviews taken in each congressional district was small it is quite possible that it is the congressman who was right and the poll that was wrong in judging opinion within any individual constituency.)

Since the personal preferences of the congressmen are correlated with their judgments as to what their constituencies want—partly because constituencies do have to a modest extent like-minded representatives, but partly also because a man sees what he wants to see and congressmen who wish to vote a given way imagine it also to be what their constituents want—it is impossible to separate the effects upon the rollcall votes of the two kinds of influence. It is possible, however, to add together the combined effects upon the vote of the representative's personal preferences and of his opinion of his constituency's opinion by calculating a multiple correlation. In this case it is reported as .9, that is, a little over 80 per cent of the variation in the vote on civil rights legislation can be explained by the combination of the two factors, leaving relatively little of the differences in rollcall voting unexplained.

These findings can be summarized: (1) Most of the difference in the voting behavior of the congressmen on civil rights matters can be explained by their judgments of constituency opinion without introducing any other factor; in this sense the personal views of the politician can be considered unnecessary for explaining adequately his voting behavior on racial questions; (2) introduction of the personal views of the congressman does serve, however, to add to the ability to explain his vote and may partly account for discrepancies between his judgment of constituency opinion and independent sources of information; stated generally, this suggests that the personal views of a politician on the subject of race do have some limited influence on his behavior, partly directly and partly by influencing the way in which he counts up the preferences of his constituents; (3) the data provide no lead to an understanding of the direction of the changes in voting behavior that may be attributed to personal views; they do not tell whether liberal-minded congressmen are voting in a fashion more liberal on civil rights than that supported in their districts, or whether, on the contrary, the personal racism of the representative causes him to distort the basic liberalism of his constituents.

Other data, however, strongly suggest that the former is the correct view: that the politicians are more liberal-minded than their constituents. Any quantity of data can be found to demonstrate, for example, that many, perhaps most southern congressmen have considered it politically necessary to take an intransigent stand on racial questions, but have not personally been so convinced of the folly of all civil rights measures as their speeches would suggest. And when the matter is considered in this light it must be recognized that there are many instances in which white politicians have been smacked down by their constituents for moving too far in a liberal direction—the cases might include John Lindsay's failure to secure a popular majority for his proposed Civilian Review Board for the New York police force, Governor Pat Brown's defeat over his open housing law in California, as well as the defeats and retirements of Southern congressmen who refused to sign the so-called Southern Manifesto regarding school segregation in the 1950's—but very few have been repudiated by white voters because they have moved too slowly.

Similar conclusions emerge from a consideration of city school decisions in respect to racial segregation. One breed of school board member has been excessively timid and hesitant to provide leadership of any kind in any direction. A second, much smaller group of leaders have been bold and liberal in orientation; some have been retired from office for their pains. In a few cases school board members who have fought integration have been defeated by black/white voting coalitions. It is hard to think of a case in a major city in which an elected school board member has been rejected by his white constituents because of his excessive conservatism on this matter.

One final piece of evidence can be offered. A study of 116 policy issues acted upon in the 50 states between 1954 and 1968 compared the actions of the state legislatures in enacting laws with the preferences of the adult populations of the states. On most issues there were wide discrepancies between public opinion and legislative action; in some cases, such as gun control legislation and the regulation of elections and political campaigns, the divergences were so great as to be grotesque. On a smaller set of issues a close fit was found between the preferences of the public and the decisions of the legislature. In most cases the similarity resulted from the existence of a broad consensus on the question: the appropriateness of laws permitting divorce after adultery, the inappropriateness of laws prohibiting the distribution of contraceptives, etc. In only one issue area was public opinion sharply divided yet the statutes, state by state, in almost perfect accord; that subject was race. If a state segregated the races in the schools it was because a majority of the eligible electorate favored the policy; if a majority in the electorate opposed segregation, the state did not have it. Later if a state adopted a public accommodations law, almost without exception it was because a majority of the electorate supported such a law; states without such laws were reflecting the opposition of majorities within their electorates. These findings reinforce and sharpen the conclusions of the congressional study first cited; both suggest that constituency pressures on matters related to race are so strong that politicians substitute their personal views for those of their constituents at great peril.

In a way, therefore, the final section of this essay denigrates the sections that have preceded it. That effect is chosen deliberately. The views of white politicians on the subject of race are intrinsically interesting; they are of sociological interest as illustrations of the crosspressures felt by professionals in an occupational role that forces compromise. They have political importance also in their effects upon the rhetoric of political campaigns, for campaign oratory in and of itself has an impact upon human lives. The attitudes of white politicians in respect to race help to define the political opportunities available to black careerists, making some jobs relatively easy to obtain, others difficult, and some well nigh impossible. The personal views of white politicians on racial matters may have some marginal effect upon the policy choices they make and the programs they implement; insofar as it is possible to discern the direction of that effect it would seem to encourage more liberal responses to racial issues. But such personal influences can be no more than marginal in importance when constituency pressures are so strong, and it would be folly to look to the practical politician for bold and creative leadership in matters such as these.

Welfare Workers

FRANKLIN ZWEIG

There can be little doubt that the racism so characteristic of all aspects of American life is confronted daily within the operational structures of the broad spectrum of organizations known as "welfare" agencies. That spectrum of organization cuts across such diverse fields as income maintenance, aging, primary and secondary education, health and mental health, manpower preparation in the human services, law enforcement and corrections, public housing, family planning, day care, drug treatment, and urban redevelopment. The organizations rendering services within these fields employ thousands of welfare workers who daily battle the consequences of racism in the course of delivering services to minority group members. In some organizations, welfare or social workers (the term is used interchangeably throughout this discussion) constitute the dominant professional group responsible for setting policy, administering and evaluating services. Social workers are the dominant professional groups in many public assistance, child adoption, and family counseling agencies, for example. In some organizations, social workers occupy a guest status; they are allocated circumscribed tasks by other dominant professional groups: by doctors in hospitals, for example; by public administrators in public housing; or by professional educators in public schools.

Whether dominant or subordinate in the range of services provided by welfare organizations, social workers face a host of dilemmas emanating from racist expressions within welfare agencies as well as from attempting to solve the personal and social issues which are triggered by racism in the larger society. It is ironic that such dilemmas place welfare workers and their organizations in a position to reduce racism and its injurious impacts on minority people, on the one hand, and assure that the oppressive consequences of racism are perpetuated, on the other.

The formal service mission of most agencies emphasizes the provision of opportunities by means of which disadvantaged members of minority groups can escape from the debilitating effects of racism. Yet, it is not uncommon to find that public assistance agencies enforce regulations more stringently with black than with white clients; that hospitals frequently continue to segregate minority patients under the guise of medical practices; that black prisoners are still regularly abused in county correctional institutions for real or suspected membership in militant organizations; that counseling agencies prefer to serve middle-class clientele, thereby de facto excluding much potential minority constituency; that minority representation in policy planning for the social services remains at a token level in many communities as well as at higher levels of government; that many professional schools in the human services fail to admit minority students in anywhere near the proportions that the volume of problems facing minority communities would require.

Balanced against such racist features of welfare agency practices is the long and deep tradition that the social services have voiced, represented, and embraced the nation's most fundamental set of ethical propositions designed to create equal opportunity for all to pursue life's benefits. Put another way, welfare agencies are the nation's conscience and are defined so in terms of policies, programs, and dollars. They are dedicated to furthering a better way of life, a mission embraced constantly even if frequently unattained. Their personnel are doubtless similar in temperamental make-up to professionals and managers in other fields of endeavor except for a vigorously stressed devotion to bettering the lot of people who are the underdogs in and of the society. Empirical observation and logical prediction indicate considerably less racial animosity and considerably more genuine racial openness among social workers as a group than may be found in industry, in the military, or in various other departments of government.

If, then, welfare agencies possess a unique sense of mission, and if the people staffing them are less prone to personal racism, what explains the fact that racism is nonetheless institutionalized among the social services? Why the existence of this paradox? Even more perplexing, why is it that welfare agencies are unable to exert significant influence on the rest of the nation such as to implement a more general reduction of prejudice souring our relationships? (After all, welfare organizations account for billions of dollars per year in expenditures. Surely such massive resources should be able to marshall incentives designed to reduce racism effectively, to lead to guided change in attitudes and actions based upon racial consideration.)

Some answers seem to lie in the basic dynamic of ambivalence which throws up a screen between perceptions and responses of welfare agencies and the actual significance that racism has for the problems facing Black Americans and other minorities. That ambivalence—experienced by welfare workers as wavering between advocacy of minorities and their situations, on the one hand, and maintenance of regulations which disadvantage minorities on the other—accounts for uncertainties of policy and practice within welfare agencies which permit institutionalized racism to be active continuously.

Before going on to explore the sources of ambivalence manifested in the operations of welfare organizations in greater detail, it is useful to point out in a general way that our society has been very hesitant to support the social services in much more than a very limited way; that the myth of rugged self-dependence and the stigma of seeking organized help still hold sway; that these fundamental values continue to call into question welfare policies and programs adopted largely out of the chaos of the great depression, and elaborated only with great reluctance and out of economic necessity since that time. The income maintenance system, and most related antipoverty, mental health, and family support efforts, have been caught continuously in a crossfire of controversy about their purposes, and about their consequences for those served, especially as regards minority people.

It is extremely difficult to develop stable, firm, and substantial allies for organizations required to respond to such constant criticism. With strong doubts on the part of powerful sponsors reflected in welfare operations, minority groups constituting the clientele also tend to regard welfare agencies as untrustworthy if not as outright enemies. A potential consumer constituency to fight on behalf of welfare organizations thus cannot become mobilized. And sympathetic observers in other segments of the society—the universities, the churches, in liberal political circles—observe the resultant interaction with criticism or despair.

It is extremely difficult to sustain and implement commitments to racial equality for organizations operating in a climate of such continuing suspiciousness. Welfare workers find that coping with the climate itself takes heavy tolls on energies otherwise directed to client service. In having to duck the brickbats thrown by friend and foe alike—as evidenced so clearly during recent, unresolved congressional debates about welfare reform—conditions become created wherein the basic ambivalence of the society about the social services seeps into welfare agencies, blurs their missions, and permits the emergence of racistlike responses.

Six more specific sources of ambivalence have been selected for attention in this essay. Some are directly derivative of the general lack of welfare agency support just described. Others are more directly related to the influence of professionalism sought by welfare organizations and workers. All exert important impacts upon welfare agency response to racial issues; all shape welfare worker performance in delivering services to minority people.

Source of Ambivalence I: Uncertain Political Priorities and Shifting Financial Fortunes

Welfare is a child of politics. The body politic has regarded welfare in cycles of favoritism and contempt since the milestone federal action of the early and mid-twentieth century translated social reform into public policy. Thus, the social services have experienced expansive eras and eras of severe restriction—with important consequences for the ways in which welfare agencies and welfare workers view their missions in terms of black clientele.

In those eras during which the social services have occupied a high place on the national political agenda, government has taken more responsibility for assisting the development of human resources and helping has been more respectable as a vocation. In more restrictive eras it has been common to find government moving away from supportive intervention in social problems, and the helping professions have lost their attractiveness along with some important sources of financial support. During expansive eras, the role of the private and church-supported social services has diminished as primary deliverers of welfare; they have tended to become specialists in expensive services not affordable under huge governmental programs. During restrictive eras, the welfare agencies and personnel of the private sector have curtailed their role in pioneering new forms of service and have become much more prominent as providers. Accordingly, emphasis on minority populations has been great during expansive periods, reduced greatly during restrictive periods; the bursts of social justice motivation fueling the expansive eras naturally have resulted in enhanced welfare services for Black Americans, while the same inspiration dims low when government moves away from responsibility for the human services.

The expansive periods of this century to the present time did not last long enough, however, to create permanent patterns for comprehensive social services. We have experienced developmental episodes full of hope and lofty objectives during the 1930's and 1960's which failed to achieve a sufficient level of financial support. They did not operate long enough to create the mechanisms to reach their objectives and they also failed to set dominant norms for helping which could protect them against the philosophical and financial encroachments of more restricted periods politically. And they created expectations for new opportunities on the parts of the minorities which became frustrated as the programs failed, perhaps with the result of enduring alienation of those minorities from the larger society.

During the last two decades we have witnessed extremes of favorable stimulation and rejection of welfare programs on the part of our climate-setting national administrations. Each extreme has had consequences for the minority-oriented missions of welfare agencies and welfare workers. The social improvement policies of the Kennedy-Johnson period, for example, ushered in a host of new and exciting innovations. Efforts intended to improve the quality of life were initiated across a broad spectrum of social problems. The antipoverty, community mental health, comprehensive health, and model cities efforts are the best known of such innovations. Emerging concurrently with sweeping efforts in the civil rights field, these bold efforts found their political springboard in the attempt of the federal administration to move the public purse away from foreign and military spending and more into domestic sectors in order to fortify political constituencies as well. Invariably the social services emerging from such efforts focused upon minority populations.

The new programs were established by Kennedy and Johnson people side by side with the large welfare bureaucracies created during the social service expansion of the Great Depression period. As they became operational realities, the new welfare organizations in many cases drew the best of the existing social service personnel away from the older bureaucracies. The new services promised fewer constraints to professional performance, offered more flexibility, and pledged to put their official missions ahead of organizational maintenance requirements. They helped create a following on college campuses which brought an unprecedented number of young people into the social sciences. They created an employment market among minority populations by means of "paraprofessional" and "new careers" efforts. By means of employment efforts, the new programs recruited, trained, and deployed thousands of new people, largely representing minorities, into new jobs.

The large federal, state, and local programs predating the new efforts of the Kennedy-Johnson era were weakened by the manpower drained from them to run the new organizations. Those who remained were often less than zealous in the pursuit of social justice for minorities than were their more adventurous colleagues. Yielding to comfort and tradition, the established welfare organizations seemed to possess reduced commitment to black and minority people; they were slow to move, bogged down in red tape, uninspired by the new climate of hope and bustle. It was common to find during the mid and late 1960's, moreover, that the new programs castigate the long-standing organizations publicly, highlighting their inadequacies and often alienating them. A civil war of sorts among the social services not only weakened attempts to create an enduring pattern of new opportunities for minorities, it blocked the motivation of the established housing, welfare, health, and education bureaucracies to adopt and incorporate pioneering efforts when continuous, independent funding of great society programs failed to materialize.

With the advent of the political era of President Richard Nixon, the pendulum began to swing away from the social services. The new welfare enterprises were first held at a steady state and later largely dismantled. Financial aid to long established state and local social service programs began to shrink. Assistance for the training of welfare workers and social service manpower in general was shut down. And a general withdrawal of social problems from the public agenda of the federal administration has taken place. As the responsibility of government for social development began to be downplayed, the privately supported and the church agencies re-emerged in greater importance as providers of services. And, consequently, the volume of attention directed toward minority populations became reduced.

The move toward withdrawal of involvement by the Nixon Administration has been accompanied by a political philosophy of marketing the social services. Those services which are popular, the philosophy would hold, will attract attention from revenue-sharing grants to the states, and people will pay for desired services otherwise. Supplementation for those below the poverty income level, according to the Nixon approaches, can be made by the private agencies. Considering the very limited financial and bureaucratic capacity of the voluntary agencies, however, and in light of their dependence upon the goodwill of the large corporations and the huge labor unions, minority people, never favored by voluntary social services largely oriented to more middle-class consumers, face wholesale reduction of services.

Shifts in political priorities and related sources of funding during the past few years, then, have created a psychology of impending famine among welfare agencies and welfare workers. Survival has become uppermost in the minds of agency administrators at all levels. "Don't rock the boat" has become a phrase which regulates the activities of welfare workers. In a climate of uncertainty and scarcity, the public and private agencies are reduced to conformity. In the attempt to remain viable, they adopt positions which mirror the general trend of political and social opinion; and actions are taken in the name of survival which come very close to carrying out the opposite of the intent for which the agencies were originally established.

In a recent meeting of the board of directors of a legal assistance organization, for example, the anticipated hostile reaction of the United Fund was introduced as a major element of a lengthy rebuke to a staff who had volunteered special assistance to the inmates of a well-known, nearby prison. The line of concern easily was traceable in the discussion: prison controversy, laced through with racial issues, was felt to be injurious to the collections potential of the United Fund; pressure to not initiate any departure from traditional service so as to threaten, even remotely, Fund collections, and thereby, the agency's budget—particularly felt to be important in light of the ending of the War on Poverty and its support for legal services. In the example, the situation was resolved when some progressive board members disguised the special service, but the conflict is illustrative of the sensitivity of service agencies, their felt financial vulnerability, and their tendency to accommodate their mission to racial minorities. In short, their ambivalence.

And this source of ambivalence, emanating from shifting political priorities and related threats to sources of funds, is a primary source of the ambivalence of welfare agencies and welfare workers toward minority peoples and problems.

Source of Ambivalence II: Help versus Riot Control

Motivations for establishing the social services on the part of the power structure have been diverse. They have ranged from altruism rooted in a conception of social justice to salvation rooted in a conception of religious mission to rehabilitation rooted in an economic conception of work to social control of large masses of people rooted in a conception of a constant potential for insurrection. Perhaps two general strains of motivation—one emphasizing help to the underdog to fulfill latent, blocked capacities for personal satisfaction and social responsibility, the other emphasizing the supply of needed resources and relationships in order to pacify people who need to be kept in check—can be viewed as dominant themes since American adoption of the English poor law provisions in colonial times. The first might be termed the "helping function," the second the "riot control function." The first is oriented to development of human potentials, the second to policing persons who for reason of age, or illness, or lack of education, or social discrimination do not fit into the economic production systems of the nation.

It is important to note that both motivational themes have required accommodation during expansive eras for the social services. Legislators and administrators have been persuaded to support welfare programs out of humanitarian principles and in order to keep potential offenders busy, channeled, moving toward the economic mainstream. The history of the social services has been permeated with these dual motivations, and their consequences have been handed down into the delivery of social services, resulting in regulations which are often in conflict, and which constrain welfare workers' actions on behalf of their clients. The public assistance agency and the caseworkers employed within it constitute a vivid example of the ambivalence-producing consequences of this motivational duality.

The job of the public assistance agency has been to supply economic resources to those in need for the purpose of providing a minimum level of living in the present and a potential for productive work in the future. The job of the public assistance agency has been to assure the society, however, that stringent regulations are followed by the recipients of such help. Thus, in the same day, a public assistance agency might authorize special medical help for a client and later barge into that client's home in order to check out a suspicion that an able-bodied man might be in secret residence there.

Since minority populations—particularly but not exclusively Black Americans—constitute a significant proportion of public assistance agency clientele, and since public pressures underpinned by racist features demand especially strong application of "police" regulations to minorities, the dual message of help and police control on client lives rings especially familiar in minority communities.

For the welfare worker attempting to serve both helping and police ends in carrying out his agency's mandate, an intolerable dilemma is imposed. Should the welfare worker emphasize the helping or police functions? The helping functions are likely to bring good responses from the client, but charges from the agency of being "soft" or "too identified with the client's interests" or "disloyal to the agency policy." The police functions are likely to bring agency approval, but charges from clients that the worker is "a stooge for the establishment" or a "cop in disguise." Obviously, the dilemma creates conditions of ambivalence for welfare workers, and especially salient in terms of minority communities which most welfare workers know to be alienated, disenfranchised, and in need of special opportunity.

Ambivalence on a grand scale is impossible to avoid for welfare agency administrators. When he enforces "police" regulations expected of him by those in power, the public assistance administrator creates conditions perfect for establishing the agency as an enemy of the poor and oppressed. The consequences of following the "helping" emphasis may be loss of job; the consequences of following the "police" emphasis may be ostracism from clientele. Juggling both functions constitutes an energy- and time-consuming task for all who can master it and remain true to themselves. If enforcement of regulations is less than satisfactory from the point of view of policy makers, threats to legal and financial supports for the agency are engendered. Both agency and administrator become whipping boys for claims from all sides, because neither helping nor enforcement can be perfect. Nothing is more painful than watching a well-motivated agency official defend his agency's riot control mission to consumers and his helping mission to hostile policy makers. Nothing is more detestable than watching a poorly motivated agency official denigrate his consumer constituency to policy makers and other critics and thereby add to the sum total of manifest racism in his community. So the agency and its employees are always treading a narrow line. In not wanting to alienate either its consumer constituency or its policy constituency, many welfare agencies will simply equivocate, stall for time, and in the process lose credibility from both constituencies. And the efficiency and morale costs created by the pervasive ambivalence escalate within the agency and among welfare workers.

Source of Ambivalence III: Responses to Client Militancy

Out of the various civil rights movements of the 1960's a demand arose for consumer participation in the decision-making mechanisms of the social services. Initially expressed in civil disobedience directed against service agencies, the trend has been for militant client groups to become bureaucratized pressure organizations, negotiating for goods and services and pushing toward more complete political consciousness on the part of their membership. The mass media have familiarized much of America with dramatic rent strikes, waiting-room sit-ins and other confrontation tactics used by consumers as they initially became caught up with the activism of the civil rights movement. Organizational reactions of the social services to incorporation of consumers on boards of directors, participation in fair hearing procedures and operation of various collective bargaining schemes have received less widespread attention. And the employment of the poor in social work jobs has received little publicity outside of professional circles. But the activist, bureaucratized, and employment-arrested factions of militant client groups have made important impacts upon social service agencies and personnel. Among those reactions has been ambivalence toward minority consumers generated by fear of attack and fear of replacement.

Client militancy is geared to the achievement of power. And in order to solidify a constituency behind a militant group, the leadership of that group must target an enemy who can be attacked with confidence that a return attack will not be costly. If a series of such tactics can result in visible results, constituencies can be attracted. If such tactics can yield tangible benefits to members, constituencies can be solidified. And the attraction and solidification of members of client organizations, such as Welfare Rights Organization, for example, is necessary in order to attain increments of power across any bargaining table.

Thus it has been common to find that social agencies have been targeted as villains—for power gain as well as for substantive reasons relating to shortcomings of service. And welfare agency administrators and personnel have found themselves rallying to their agency's defense oftentimes because they found themselves under mutual attack. When meetings are disrupted in welfare agencies, for example, the client critics make no differentiation between friendly and antagonistic welfare workers. Lumped together as the "enemy," social service personnel have found themselves united in spite of fundamental differences previously in their attitudes toward minority clientele. Basic moral and professional commitments have been undermined by attacks from client groups, sometimes resulting in double feelings toward minority clientele.

Philosophically, welfare workers tend to regard the rights of client self-determination and participation as desirable. When that philosophy becomes operationalized against them, however, the abstract goodness of principles tends to fade in favor of reflexive self-defense. And welfare workers who at an earlier time were overheard at lunch to say that client conditions will not change until client groups learn to help themselves currently may be overheard to say that organization of client interests is fine but oftentimes "they go too far."

Fear of being replaced is somewhat new to social service personnel. In earlier times, however, it was common to encounter the sentiment that the job of social workers was to work themselves out of their jobs—in short to end the social conditions requiring their presence. Today, client militancy expressed in political terms tends to press for the hiring of persons representing the client groups served. Not the end of conditions; rather, a new type of personnel.

Thus, we find with increasing frequency that negotiations between client organizations and welfare bureaucracies include provisions for hiring blacks and other minority people with low levels of education to deliver services formerly staffed by middle-class people of college and higher educational attainment. The negotiations have been made possible by the enhanced power position of client groups, their increased political savvy, and the training programs which have invented the techniques for career development on the part of the poor—people whose only former career was dependency on the social services.

Fear of replacement on the part of welfare workers has been exacerbated by reduced funding of the social services characteristic of President Nixon's posture toward those services. If jobs are mandated to be reduced, who will remain and who will be released? And if the political skill of client groups exceeds that of the professional social work association, is it not possible that scarce jobs will go to minority Americans as a further inducement to keep things quiet among the poor? Regardless of the realities, such as the psychology of the climate in which welfare workers currently operate. And that psychology serves to induce ambivalence toward the client groups that welfare agencies and workers are pledged to assist.

Source of Ambivalence IV: Individual Adjustment versus Social Change

Most professions produce people who are primarily concerned either with the private interests of individuals or the public interests of groups. Very few doctors, for example, practice cardiology and public health at the same time. Very few social workers practice counseling and community organization as part of one job. A few might be skilled in both, but rarely can both be practiced together.

In point of fact, most professions produce practitioners who focus on the individual. Only in the more expansive eras of the social services has a sizeable group concerned with the public interest in that field been recruited, trained, and deployed in any number. The social services are currently encountering a large surplus of young professionals who were trained in War on Poverty programs—community organizers and social planners. And individual welfare organizations have sent a large number of "untrained" people to professional school on the crest of benefits from the War on Poverty period and have found that their returnees are full of new ideas, are troublemakers, are inciting the clientele. In short, a corps of professionals in a number of welfare agencies is upsetting the apple cart by maximizing public interest issues, lending support to client groups, and otherwise promoting system change rather than sticking to the traditional casework more desirable in agency administration eyes. The conflict between stress on social change, on the one hand, and stress on casework on the other, grew so bitter in New York State that the State Welfare Association, composed of county directors of public welfare, instituted a boycott against New York schools of social work because the schools were, from the agency point of view, seducing and subverting social service manpower.

Continuing controversy and bitter battles have been experienced by schools of social welfare over favored methods of intervention—casework or community organization. Casework emphasizes individual adjustment; community organization emphasizes social change by harnessing unrealized power of the disadvantaged. Since the connections between professional schools and welfare agencies are strong and enduring it is not surprising to find reverberations over individual adjustment and social change postures similarly confronted in both arenas. Sharp lines have been drawn to achieve the supremacy of each position. The fact that minority populations largely have rejected adjustment to intolerable conditions and favor social reform adds fuel to the conflict. In-fighting among professionals is exacerbated by the tendency of black leadership to side with the community organizers. Caseworkers tend to be denigrated for being irrelevant. Community organizers tend to be cited by caseworkers as aiding troublemakers or fostering reverse racism. And so colleagues are torn apart in wasteful internecine warfare which drains the energy of all away from substantive help to black people.

Obviously connected with ambivalences relating to client militancy, the schism between emphases on individual adjustment and social change constitute a fundamental philosophical and operating dilemma.

Source of Ambivalence V: The Failure Taboo

The internal morale of and the public confidence in welfare agencies have been severely restricted by the agencies' inability to point to evidence of real, long-range success in their work. That inability has been reinforced by the fact that less than one per cent of all social service expenditures has been allocated to evaluative research. Yet, for the professional to talk of failure is to commit the worst sin of all. In the absence of data, faith has been relied upon to guide the welfare worker and to raise the issue of failure is seriously to encroach upon that faith. Thus, a circularity has evolved wherein failure in extending the social services is a forbidden topic but the continuing absence of evaluative research seems only to support fundamental doubts about their effectiveness.

Indeed, the literature of the social services includes virtually no reporting of failures; yet the few studies of significance which have attempted to systematically gauge the impact of the social services have come to the conclusion that welfare agencies do little more than does the passage of time to alleviate social suffering. Both casework and community organizing bear the burden of that indictment, although the latter has been subject to even less research than the former.

The value of casework services nevertheless has been severely questioned. This is true to such an extent that at least one major social service agency, New York City's prestigious Community Service Society, has finally abandoned services to individuals and families and has embarked upon a community organizing enterprise as a primary means to help the most disadvantaged. Such a wholesale shift in faith, however, is not characteristic of the welfare field in general, and casework services continue largely unmodified and without benefit of evaluative research in spite of deep suspicions as to their effectiveness.

One obvious reason for the failure to evaluate casework programs adequately obviously lies in the long chainlike supervisory hierarchy so endemic to welfare agencies. This hierarchy consistently refuses to evaluate the success or failure of case work. The issue, indeed, is almost unmentionable, and statistics as to the number of persons serviced are substituted for studies of the qualitative impact of case work on the life of the client. One suspects that many welfare bureaucrats fear that investigations of this type would open a Pandora's box and seriously threaten the tenuous support they have received from over the years from clients and policy makers alike.

Client groups are also fearful of research, of course. Having been exploited by social researchers in the past, access by welfare agencies for measuring the impact of welfare services cannot be assured.

The suspicion of failure, then, and the remoteness of useful evaluation, constitutes a forceful feature of ambivalence resonating between social services and minority communities.

Source of Ambivalence VI: Second-Class Professionalism

The ambivalences discussed earlier add up to a terrific toll upon the performances and the self-images of career social workers. Without a clear literature to bank upon, without an arsenal of surefire tools to be used to help, with the constant crossfire of public and official opinion descending upon the social workers, a climate of despair seeps into and spreads through the operating agencies of the welfare field. When that climate extends to the educational apparatus of the social services as well, all conditions are present for the creation of a pervasive feeling of second-class professionalism.

The mainstay of that apparatus are the eighty-plus graduate schools of social work in the United States and Canada. And the ambivalence of the agencies in approaching issues of race are mirrored, indeed concentrated, in those schools.

One would expect that social work schools would have given clear priority to the problems of minorities, but not until the late 1960's did official accreditation standards incorporate such sentiment effectively. Except for the schools of the large cities of the east and west coast, action to recruit, train, and deploy blacks and others at the graduate level has been far less than the need could be measured in terms of the proportion of black people crowded into public housing, shunted onto welfare, lined up at the unemployment offices, and packed into the clinic areas of large hospitals.

Those schools of social work which have attempted to develop affirmative action programs with respect to black graduate students and other minorities have inevitably faced conflict, sometimes of a crippling nature, from within their own walls. The conflict has sometimes been limited to faculty concern about establishing precedents of a "reverse racism" by setting affirmative objectives for minority recruitment. At other times, strikes have closed schools grappling with charges by enrolled minority students and white allies that the educational content and faculty have revealed significant racist features.

It should be pointed out that social work schools have demonstrated more willingness to recruit blacks and other minority students than have schools linked to many other professions. And the track record of social work schools in enrolling minority students when 1960 and 1970 admission figures are compared is very favorable. But the record still falls short of the need of minority communities for social service personnel. And many welfare school faculty seem less than enthusiastic about heavy investments in minority education for another reason: that road does not appear to lead to first-class professionalism.

Professionalism in the educational field, as it is within the social agencies, is linked to the issue of whether to emphasize individual adjustment or social change. In the schools, the former seems to lead to status among the other professions, and a tradition of association with psychiatry dating from the First World War has drawn much of the profession toward counseling and psychotherapy. While the success rates of therapy are indeterminable, the prestige and respect accorded to psychiatrists and psychologists are shared by social workers and generate the *feeling* of professionalism. Community organizing, on the other hand, and to some extent the political activities associated with social planning, have fewer associations with established prestige groups; this service emphasis is often considered more akin with labor organizing than with professional practice. And there is far less *feeling* of professionalism.

Yet, it is clear that blacks and other minorities want power, want a place in the society, want a competitive position within the economic market and within the body politic. Middle-class therapists are rejected as irrelevant. An important message of the '60's was clearly that the black community will conduct its own welfare functions, will generate its own unique therapies if it can organize to get the power to conduct its own affairs.

Thus, the polarities creating the conditions for painful ambivalence are present. On the one hand, the desires of the minorities are to organize, to gain power, to run their own service; on the other hand, agencies. Organizing is not viewed as fully "professional" by the graduate schools which move toward the agencies associated with medicine and public administration in order to become more professional. This policy is reinforced within social work schools by continuing conflict over how many minority people will be favored with professional education as well as the fear that social service techniques are inadequate.

Professional schools and their constituent social service agencies thereby are torn and crippled by the dilemmas of professionalism coupled with the realities of race. To many, emphasis of minority problems leads to second-class professionalism.

Finding Friends

Just as our nation's future will be heavily influenced by the successful incorporation of black and other minorities into the mainstream of the society, the future of the social services will continue to be largely enmeshed with issues of race. The survival of welfare organizations, of professional social services, seems to depend in large measure upon the ability of the agencies to find friends in the minority communities, that is, among their consumers. Perseverance, commitment, and the ability to plan effectively for the location of such allies somehow must come to the fore in light of the restrictive climate facing the social services.

It is neither clear that the forces impinging upon the welfare agencies can be remedied, nor that it will be possible in the foreseeable future for the social services to overcome basic ambivalences toward black and minority people. One cannot be sanguine that welfare agencies will be able to express the solidarity with disadvantaged peoples that will cause alliances to form, which will cause a constituency to solidify on behalf of those agencies.

Reason for doubt goes beyond the depth of ambivalence experienced by the social services. The sheer number of agencies, and their varied sources of support, scopes, jurisdictions, mandates, and competitive needs mitigate against the kind of collaborative planning which must be undertaken. Without collaborative planning among service agencies, it will be impossible to bring coherence out of the confusion and cross-fires so characteristic of welfare agencies' relationship to racial issues. Literally thousands of organizations tend to the business of health, welfare, education, corrections, and the like. Literally billions of dollars and hundreds of thousands of people play caretaker to the underdog minorities. Our understanding of the nature of organizations leads to the conclusion that only the most modest gains can be expected to emerge from the agency morass. There currently exist few mechanisms which can effectively lead to rational planning.

Beyond the tangled net of organizations lie other fundamental problems. The nation's priorities must favor the human services in a way not currently in evidence. A determined shift of the basic economy must move the nation from military spending to peace and development spending. Some threat of agency starvation must be lightened thereby. And new social services delivery mechanisms, emphasizing adjustment services and organizing services in equal quantity and quality, must be forthcoming.

Moreover, the future of the social services depends upon a greater sense of client confidence in the ability of welfare agencies to make a difference. The large social service bureaucracies must be supplemented with organizations able to bring wanted and acceptable forms of service to minority people.

If there is hope for imparting a coherence to the current scene, for developing an effective planning thrust during this era of retrenchment in human services, it seems to lie with the schools of social work. In spite of the issues which confront them internally, the schools possess the most creative, flexible, plentiful, and concertible resources to be found in the nation for planning the future of the social services. Over a thousand full-time faculty constitute the instructional staffs of the schools. If the equivalent of ten per cent of that faculty resource were available per year to staff interschool commissions to develop policy proposals and mechanisms, to consult with the best motivated of the welfare agencies and their managements and clients, a significant contribution to creating coherence might be forthcoming. Using graduate students as the staff contingent of such a planning effort, a manpower device for social services planning second to none is potentially available.

And by taking a few of the best motivated faculty and students from the many schools and combining them into a planning body concerned with racial and minority issues and the underlying schisms and dilemmas which attend them, it is possible that the ambivalences confronting the schools themselves might be effectively dealt with. Such a planning enterprise would be very negligent if it did not attend to the issue of the failure of the social services. Working with the schools and the agencies, it might be possible to classify the conditions of useful practice in such a way that the examination of failure could lead to guidelines for successful work.

How such a planning enterprise could be organized remains an open question, one which is answerable, but which requires a basic commitment and resolution to attend to the issues of the day before any technical designs will have meaning. It is clear, however, that planning of this scale is necessary to find friends for support of the social services; a first step in overcoming several fundamental sources of ambivalence which block welfare agencies and welfare workers in their service missions with minority communities.

Policemen

LAWRENCE ROSEN

The tensions and conflicts between police and blacks have been very near the center (if not at the very center) of the civil rights turmoil of the 1960's. Unfortunately, objective and dispassionate investigations and analyses of the issue, especially from the perspective of the police, have been far too few. Instead the major attempt at understanding has simply been to label the police as "racists." Although some natural desires to castigate and accuse may be satisfied by continuing to engage in the ideological exercise of offering "racism" as an explanation of police conduct and attitudes, it seems fairly clear that very little will be added to an understanding of the problem.

The task or problem of this paper is to construct an empirical picture from whatever *systematic* evidence exists, not only of how police[1] view blacks, but also how they treat them.

The "conventional wisdom" of the social scientists has argued that the police hold "prejudicial" attitudes toward blacks and, as a direct consequence of that prejudice, engage in discriminatory treatment of blacks in the form of harassment, brutality, differential arrest, and so forth. As I will argue in some detail, this is a grossly oversimplified view of the problem. Although there is little doubt that white policemen are anything but sympathetic toward blacks, there is also no simple one-to-one correspondence between the way police feel about and the way in which they behave toward blacks. In order to argue this position effectively it is important to keep attitudes and behavior analytically distinct.

Before beginning, it should be made clear that this discussion is concerned with police in large northern urban areas (population greater than 100,000) during the 1960's. Perhaps the most notorious character in the black-white drama, the small-town Southern sheriff, is excluded from any of the generalizations and conclusions. The principal reason for the limitations is that almost all of the systematic research of police is confined within these boundaries of space and time. In addition, the focus is almost exclusively on the day-to-day work routines and experiences of the patrolman, rather than on riots and mass civil disorders.

Rather than discuss the more general aspects (sampling, methodology, limitations, and so forth) of each of the studies in the body of the paper, I have described these in an appendix. The five studies included in the appendix represent the basic source material for this paper and are referred to by geographic labels (e.g. Philadelphia Study, Denver Study, etc.).

Generalized Sentiment Toward Blacks

The consensus among many observers of police is that a significant proportion of policemen can be classified as being antiblack in their generalized beliefs and feelings. However, the exact proportion is difficult to determine because the evidence is contradictory or difficult to interpret. For example, Black and Reiss (1957, p. 135) report that approximately 72 per cent of the white patrolmen had informally expressed at one time or another, "prejudiced" or "highly prejudiced" [2] views in front of neutral observers. In sharp contrast to this finding is the 5 per cent of the Denver police (Bayley and Mendelsohn, 1969, p. 145) who said they, "on the whole disliked Negroes." (An identical proportion of a sample of non-Spanish white citizens expressed the same sentiment.) Although some difference must be expected between cities, it is unlikely that it would account for the very large difference between the two studies. A more likely reason can be attributed to differences in methodology. In the "three-city" study (Black and Reiss, 1967), the policemen were classified on the basis of verbal statements uttered in front of observers, rather than on how they might respond to formalized questions in an interview or questionnaire. The Denver study utilized a formal question ("On the whole do you like or dislike Negroes") in an interview situation. Without additional evidence it is difficult to evaluate the relative merits of each technique. It might appear that utterances in an informal setting are more indicative of "true" sentiments than formal responses to an interviewer. However, the validity of this conclusion is far from self-evident. The major difficulty with the informal observational approach is that the nature of the stimulus is uncontrolled. We do not know, for example, if the prejudiced statements were made in the presence of other policemen, or just observers; or whether the references were to all blacks, or only those with whom the policemen have had some negative confrontation (e.g. offender, complainant). Were they stress situations or relaxed informal settings? How are statements that reflect a basic and sincere dislike of blacks separated from conventional statements of a lower-middle or lower-class male subculture? The more conventional approach in this Denver study does at least represent responses to a fairly homogeneous stimulus presented to all the policemen interviewed. Of course, this does not say anything about the adequacy of the technique for measuring antiblack feelings. The fact that 42 per cent of the policemen responded with "don't care," "neither," or "doesn't apply," would indicate that it was a poor question.

Somewhat less direct evidence of generalized sentiment can be found in the fifteen-city study (Ross et al., 1968). Although no direct question about "liking" blacks was asked, questions concerning reactions to "Negroes taking over political power," "moving into white areas," and "socializing with whites" were included. Undoubtedly, responses to these questions are in part a function of the respondents' general attitude toward blacks; but they are probably better interpreted as indicators of the fears and anxieties of increased progress of blacks. The data on these questions are presented in Table 1 for police and five other occupational groups that have daily contact with ghetto residents. For all three areas of concern the police are more likely, with the major exception of merchants, to express extreme concern over increased competition and interaction with blacks. (Note that 25 per cent of the police were black, so that in all likelihood the percentages for white policemen would be slightly larger. It is significant to note that the largest portion of policemen did not express *strong* misgivings in these areas. Even if it is assumed that all black policemen did not respond in a negative way, no more than 25 per cent of the white policemen would have been "very disturbed" by at least one of these issues.)

Table 1

Percentage of Six Occupational Groups Servicing the Ghetto Who Expressed Themselves as Being "Very Disturbed" About Blacks Making Inroads in Selected Areas

			Areas of Concern about Blacks		
Occupational Group	*N*	*% Black*	*Taking over Political Power*	*Moving into White Areas*	*Socializing with Whites*
Police	437	25	9	18	16
Educators	273	50	7	8	1
Social Workers	264	50	4	4	2
Political Workers	103	100	14	7	4
Merchants	442	26	14	17	15
Employers	434	0	5	6	7

SOURCE: Rossi et al. (1968), Table 3.9 (adapted), p. 90.

One of the more classic and traditional issues in the study of "prejudice" and "racism" is the extent to which sentiments toward blacks are based on (or rationalized by) beliefs of innate biological inferiority of blacks. Although this dimension has been researched quite sparingly for police, there are two questions, among the various studies, that address themselves to some extent to this issue.

In the Philadelphia study (Savitz, 1971) patrolmen who were on the force for three years were asked if they thought "hereditary factors" could account for the "Negro crime rate." About 10 per cent of the white policemen (N = 118) and 19 per cent of the black patrolmen (N = 36) agreed that "hereditary factors" were responsible. However, it is not clear if the respondents interpreted "hereditary factors" as genetic factors. Furthermore, since there was no corresponding question about a "white crime rate" it is impossible to determine if the policemen believed in a specific racial characteristic, or simply that biology would explain crime in general.

Perhaps a more direct measure of belief in biological inferiority are the responses in the Western Michigan study (Bouma, 1969, p. 104) to: "Even if Negroes had the same living conditions as white people most Negroes would have lower morals than whites." Approximately 52 per cent of the police questioned (N = 310) agreed with the statement. Because of the reference to "white people," it is plausible that the idea being offered for acceptance or rejection was racial in character. Even though there is no direct reference to biologic or genetic factors, it is also plausible that the subjects interpreted the phrase "same living conditions" as making the entire statement an idea about biology. But, of course, with no additional evidence, it is difficult to be certain about this conclusion.

On the basis of the limited evidence on generalized sentiment toward blacks, the most reasonable conclusion that can be offered is that no reliable estimate about the amount or intensity of antiblack feelings among police can be made.

Admittedly, attempts at measuring generalized attitudes are not easy. However, of more importance and immediate interest, and somewhat more amenable to research, are the views on more specific issues. For example: How sympathetic are police toward the goals of the civil rights movement? Do they believe the blacks to be treated unfairly? Are they willing to attribute any legitimacy to the blacks' demands for better treatment from police? Fortunately there is substantially more evidence on specific attitudes than on generalized attitudes.

Specific Attitude I: Societal Treatment of Blacks

What are the policemen's views on how blacks are treated in our society? The findings from the fifteen-city study (Table 2) indicate quite clearly that there is almost complete unanimity (88 per cent) among white policemen that blacks are treated "no worse" than others. This finding is especially dramatic when compared with the more pessimistic views of black policemen and other occupational groups (with the exception of merchants and employers) in the ghetto.

Table 2

Per Cent Distribution of the Responses of Various Occupational Groups Servicing the Black Ghetto to the Question: "In Your Opinion, How Well Are Negroes Treated in (City) ?"

		Responses			
Occupational Group	*N*	*Same or Better*[a]	*Worse*[b]	*Don't Know*	*Total*
White Police	335	88	10	2	100
Black Police	101	32	64	5	101
Educators	273	26	71	3	100
Social Workers	264	28	70	2	100
Political Workers	103	24	71	5	100
Merchants	442	74	25	1	100
Employers	434	63	35	2	100

a Included the following response categories: "Treated better than any other part of the population," "treated equally," and "treated as other people of the same income."

b Includes the following response categories: "Treated worse than other police of the same income" and "treated worse than any other part of the population."

SOURCE: Rossi et al. (1968), Tables 3.2 (p. 288) and 6.12 (p. 109).

When queried about their treatment in specific social or institutional areas they tend, however, to exhibit some variability (Table 3). For example, the police are more likely to accept the notion of unfair treatment in housing and employment, but far less likely to see matters this way in education, law enforcement, health, and so forth. The Detroit study indicates that large differentials exist for white and black policemen for all areas. Also of interest in the Detroit study is that inspectors and lieutenants differed appreciably in their opinions from white patrolmen. In some instances the higher ranking officers came very close to the views of the black patrolmen (Mendelsohn, 1970, p. 750).

In the light of this evidence it comes as no surprise that between 50 and 60 per cent of the police (Rossi et al., 1968, p. 89; Bayley and Mendelsohn, 1969, p. 150) feel that blacks are "moving too fast" in attempting to gain equality with whites.

Specific Attitudes II: Police Treatment of Blacks

On the issue of police treatment of blacks, it again is not unexpected that white policemen are very unlikely to give much credence to the view that police mistreat blacks (Bayley and Mendelsohn, 1969, p. 148; Rossi et al., 1968, p. 108). For example, Savitz (1971) found that white policemen on the force for three years were far more likely to see police treating blacks "fairly" (84 per cent) than they believed magistrates (56 per cent), trial judges (40 per cent), and juries (58 per cent) to do. It is not that they viewed these other law enforcement agencies as treating blacks more "severely"; on the contrary, they believed them to treat blacks "too leniently." (The percentage of white policemen responding "too leniently" were: police, 11 per cent, magistrates, 44 per cent, trial judges, 60 per cent, and juries, 41 per cent). In short, a significant portion of white policemen saw the judicial system as leaning over "blackwards," and only the police were seen as fair and impartial. The black policemen had a somewhat different view. They believed that blacks were getting more equitable (not lenient or severe) treatment from the judicial system than from the police. Rossi (1968, p. 108) has also found that the black policeman is far more likely to believe that the police mistreat blacks.

Specific Attitudes III: Blacks and Social Disorder

Popular explanation of the riots and civil disorders in the black ghettos during the 1960's tend to fall into two major areas. One interpretation, usually labeled as liberal, sees the disorders as emanating from the frustrations and grievances of ghetto life (that is, poverty, poor housing, police mistreatment, and so forth).

Table 3

Percentage of Policemen in Two Studies that Believe Blacks to be Treated Favorably or the Same as Others by Various Institutional Areas

	15-Cities Study[a]	*Detroit Study*[b]	
Institution	*Police (Both Races) (N = 437)*	*White Patrolmen (N = 86)*	*Black Police, All Ranks (N = 36)*
Schools or Education	72	99	17
Housing	42	56	6
Jobs or Employment	51	74	8
Welfare Agencies	—[c]	96	67
Stores	—[c]	83	39
Medical Care	72	—[c]	—[c]
Recreation	83	—[c]	—[c]
Public Officials	81	—[c]	—[c]
Police	82	—[c]	—[c]
Law Enforcement	—[c]	91	9

a. Includes the percent who answered "as well off" or "better off" to the question: "Compared to other groups in the city of the same income and education, do you think Negroes are about as well off, less well off, or better off with respect to. . . ."

b. Includes the percent who answered "the same as whites" or "things are in their favor" to the question: "Here is a list of areas in which some people say Negroes are not treated fairly. Do you think they are treated very unfairly, slightly unfairly, the same as whites, or that things are in their favor?"

c. Not included in study.

SOURCE: Rossi et al. (1968), Table 3.4, p. 89; Mendelsohn (1970), Table 3, p. 750.

The second set of explanations centers on factors that are intrinsic to blacks or black culture—outside agitators, immorality, disrespect for authority and law, and the like. This latter view is often defined as a conservative view, and in some instances as a "racist" explanation. It is easily seen that the first approach is often interpreted as being sympathetic toward blacks, whereas the latter view is unwilling to give much legitimacy to the assertions that the blacks have "real" grievances. Therefore, which position policemen subscribe to is, in all likelihood, some indication of the degree of sympathy with blacks.

The evidence indicates that the white policeman is more likely to agree with the conservative explanation of ghetto disorders, whereas the black policeman had to agree with the liberal positions (Rossi et al., 1968, p. 111; Mendelsohn, 1970, p. 749). In addition, Mendelsohn (1970, p. 752) found that not a single Detroit inspector (most of whom were white) was willing to attribute the disorders to the "antisocial" nature of blacks.

White policemen also tend to believe that blacks are disproportionately involved in crime (see Table 4).[3] Although this estimation is objectively correct they tend to overestimate the degree of involvement (again this is seen in Table 4; the actual percentage of crime in Philadelphia committed by blacks is substantially less than 90 per cent).[4]

Fairly large numbers of police feel that blacks are more difficult to arrest and in general place them in relatively greater danger. In Philadelphia (Savitz, 1971), for example, 48 per cent of the white policemen and 39 per cent of the black policemen agree that it required more force in arresting blacks than whites. Likewise in Denver (Bayley and Mendelsohn, 1969, pp. 90–91) police tended to indicate that resistance to arrest was more likely to occur in "minority group areas." These areas were also seen as places where crimes of violence (assault, homicide, and so forth) were more common. The expectation would be then, that assignments in ghettos would be seen by the patrolmen as more hazardous and undesirable. To some extent the evidence indicates this to be true. Sixty per cent of the police in the fifteen-city study (Rossi et al., 1968, p. 104) found their assignment in the black ghetto to be "harder" and "more dangerous" than elsewhere. However, a smaller portion (26 per cent) found it sufficiently intolerable to prefer a different assignment.

Specific Attitude IV: The Perception of Black Hostility

The evidence is quite clear that the police perceive the black public in general to be nonsupportive or even overtly hostile toward them (Bayley and Mendelsohn, 1969; Bouma, 1969; Mendelsohn, 1970; Rossi et al., 1968; Savitz, 1971). However, there is important variation, in terms of which group of blacks is being considered. Rossi (1968, p. 106), for example, found that over 90 per cent of the police believed that "most old persons" in the ghetto were "on their side"; whereas only 16 per cent evaluated most young adults and adolescents in this way. There was a fair amount of agreement between white (52 per cent) and black (46 per cent) policemen that adolescents viewed police as their "enemies." Findings from surveys of ghetto residents indicate that the policemen's perception of the attitudes of young and old blacks is basically an accurate one.

Table 4

Percentage Distribution of Responses to the Statement: "Ninety Per Cent of Crime in Philadelphia Is Committed by Negroes" (Philadelphia Police Who Have Been on the Force for Three Years)

	White (*N* = *118*)	*Black* (*N* = *36*)
Agree	42%	14%
Disagree	53	83
Unknown	4	3
Total	99	100

SOURCE: Savitz (1971).

Groves and Rossi (1970), after a fairly sophisticated analysis of the fifteen-city study data, conclude that much of the perceived hostility is due more to the projected fears and "prejudices" of white policemen than objective experiences with blacks. However, their conclusions must be viewed with some reservation. For one, as the authors themselves admit, they had no direct measure of objective or actual black hostility and were, therefore, unable to assess adequately the effect of this factor. Secondly, the conclusion is inconsistent with the very strong evidence (from surveys of blacks) that blacks are quite willing to express open dislike or hostility toward police.

Some interesting and relevant data on this issue are provided by the Philadelphia study. A sample of recruits was questioned at three different time periods about their beliefs on how the black public viewed police: (1) just prior to their training, (2) at the end of their eleven-week training period, and (3) after three years on the force. As can be seen from Table 5 the major shift in beliefs, for both white and black policemen, occurred during the eleven-week training period. Whereas 16 per cent of the recruits saw the black public as holding unfavorable or very unfavorable views of the police, over 50 per cent of the same groups made this assessment immediately after their training was completed. Much smaller shifts in thinking were noted three years later.[5] To some extent these findings contradict the Groves and Rossi conclusion. If prejudices and fear of blacks were primarily responsible for the perception of black hostility, we would expect a much larger difference in the responses of black and white recruits (T 1) before they have had any significant exposure to police culture. One possible interpretation of these findings is that policemen are taught by their police academy instructors that blacks are more hostile to police (in all likelihood citing the available social science evidence to this effect), and that subsequent experiences do little to change their view. The thesis that direct experience with black citizens or socialization by veteran police results in perception of black hostility is also not supported because the recruit is almost never involved in either police assignments or has direct interaction with veteran officers during his training period.

Specific Attitude V: Civil Rights Organizations

Considering the evidence presented to this point, we would expect that the police would have little sympathy with organizations or individuals that argue for or promote the cause of the blacks. The research findings support this expectation. For example, 75 per cent of the white policemen in the fifteen-city study (Rossi et al., 1968, p. 112) indicated that groups like SNCC, CORE, NAACP, etc., "hinder or make more difficult the work of the police." This percentage is substantially higher than the 39 per cent of the black policemen who express the same view. Similar sentiments were found in the Denver study (Bayley and Mendelsohn, 1969, pp. 151–52) and the Philadelphia study (Savitz, 1971).

Table 5

Beliefs About How Negroes View Police at Three Different Periods of Time for a Cohort of Philadelphia Police

	T_1 (1)		T_2 (2)		T_3 (3)	
Blacks View of Police	*Whites (N = 176)*	*Blacks (N = 57)*	*Whites (N = 175)*	*Blacks (N = 57)*	*Whites (N = 126)*	*Blacks (N = 36)*
Very favorable or favorable	41%	46%	19%	28%	18%	19%
Neutral	43	39	27	21	14	22
Very unfavorable or unfavorable	16	16	54	52	64	53
Unknown	0	0	0	0	3	5
Total	100	101	100	101	99	99

1. Immediately at start of training.
2. After eleven weeks of training.
3. After three years on the police force.

SOURCE: Savitz (1971).

Although there is no question that attitudes toward blacks play an important part in the formation of attitudes toward civil rights organizations, these attitudes are also somewhat confounded with highly specific ideological issues.[6] Since most of the spokesmen of civil rights organizations often voice criticism of the police, the police tend to see these organizations and individuals as antipolice. Considering the extreme sensitivity and in-group loyalty of police organizations, it is highly likely that the police will express dislike of any organization or individual that they define as antipolice (which might explain the sizable percentage of black policemen that are critical of these organizations).

To some extent these forces seem to be operating in the recent Black Panther party-police conflicts. Although there is no evidence, it would be somewhat naïve to attribute the strong actions and public expressions on the part of the police toward the Black Panther party entirely to whatever antiblack sentiment exists among police. In all likelihood the police would behave in similar fashion if a white group of low power and status equivalent to that of the Black Panther party were as overtly strident in their actions and public statements in regard to the police as the Black Panther party.

Summary and Conclusions on Attitudes

On the basis of the available evidence the following general points can be made about the attitudes of police:

1. There are no reliable and consistent findings that would enable one to make a reasonable estimate about the amount or intensity of general antiblack sentiment.
2. White policemen are fairly unanimous in expressing strong beliefs that, for the most part, blacks are not treated any worse than other groups in society.
3. A sizable portion (20 to 50 per cent) of white policemen feel that the black demands for equality or better treatment are at best ill advised, if not illegitimate.
4. More than half of the white policemen believe that blacks are being treated quite fairly by police; even more so than by judges and juries (who are seen as being too lenient).
5. They tend to view the black community as somewhat antisocial, and as reluctant to accept the "liberal" explanations for riots

and crime rates. However, they are more likely to reserve this view for young blacks.

6. Both white and black policemen tend to see the black public (especially young blacks) as being hostile toward police.
7. Their assignments in the ghetto are seen as being more difficult and hazardous, although they do not tend to express any strong dissatisfaction about actually working such assignments.
8. There is strong antipathy (especially among white policemen) toward civil rights organizations and spokesmen.

Thus the evidence in general is fairly clear-cut: Policemen—whites more than blacks, and patrolmen more than officers—are not very sympathetic toward blacks, at least relative to several other occupational groups. However, at the same time, one should not overlook the fact that a significant proportion of white policemen cannot be classified in this way. Depending upon the issue or question being asked, 10 to 70 per cent of police have been unwilling to express strong views against blacks.

Attempts to explain the attitudes of police in this area have tended to fall into two general categories: (1) the antecedent characteristic that a policeman brings with him to the job; and (2) the daily work experiences of policing the ghetto.

One popular argument is that police work attracts or selects individuals with strong elements of "prejudice" and "racism" or personality types (that is, authoritarianism) that are supportive of strong hostility toward ethnic groups. A somewhat different argument, but still in the same category of antecedent characteristics, is that policemen exhibit the same attitudinal tendencies as the stratum of society from which they are recruited. In most instances they come from the lower-middle or lower class (as measured by father's occupation) and have completed high school. Thus, if people with these characteristics are somewhat antiblack in their views, then policemen will also be antiblack. Despite a fair amount of speculation there is virtually no systematic empirical evidence to assess the relative worth of these positions. There is some scattered evidence, however, to indicate that certain personality or character predispositions often associated with "prejudice" (that is, authoritarianism, anomie) are no more likely to be exhibited by police than by persons of similar social background (Nierderhoffer, 1967, p. 150; McNamara, 1967, p. 194; Smith, et al., 1968; Bayley and Mendelsohn, 1969, pp. 16–18). This evidence, of course, tends to support the argument that policemen exhibit the same attitudes as members of their social class.

The second major set of explanations, expressed in their simplest and most basic terms, states that policemen are more likely to express antiblack attitudes because they are more often (relative to other occupational groups) placed in negative situations with blacks. Thus it is argued the experiences in the black ghetto, with its relatively high levels of conflict, violence, law-violating behavior, and hostility toward police would either produce antiblack feelings or as a minimum enhance and support whatever negative sentiments exist. This position is articulated very well by a police officer:

> [The police have to] associate with lower-class people, slobs, drunks, criminals, riff-raff of the worst sort. Most of those . . . now in [this city] are Negroes. The police officer sees these people through middle-class or lower-middle-class eyeballs. But even if he saw them through highly sophisticated eyeballs, he can't go on the street . . . and take this night after night. When some Negro criminal says to you a few times, "you white motherfucker, take that badge off and I'll shove it up your ass," well, it's bound to affect you after a while. Pretty soon you decide they're all just niggers and they'll never be anything else but niggers. It would take not just an average man to resist this feeling, it would take an extraordinary man to resist it, and there are very few ways by which the police department can attract extraordinary men to join it.
>
> (CITED IN J. Q. WILSON, 1968b, P. 43.)

Again, as with the previous arguments, there is little evidence to support this explanation. Mendelsohn (1970, p. 758), for example, finds very little difference in attitudes toward blacks between white officers whose major experience is patrolling white areas from those who work the black areas. Likewise, the three-city study (Black and Reiss, 1967, p. 135) found very minor differences in verbalized "prejudice" between patrolmen in black ghettos from those working in other neighborhoods. In opposition to this view is the report of an ongoing study in Miami that "bigotry" is "inculcated" partly because of direct contact with blacks (reported in the *New York Times*, November 29, 1970, p. 32).

Quite obviously the problem of what explains policemen's attitudes is a difficult one to study. However, it is also fairly obvious that we are unable to provide an adequate explanation of these attitudes without undertaking research.

Attitudes and Behavior—General Comments

In a certain sense the attempts to document and explain attitudes are of little practical consequence (although intellectually it is quite a legitimate practice). For many the more critical issue centers on the behavior of police, and the attitudes are only of interest insofar as they can be used to explain or understand that behavior.

Perhaps the simplest thesis connecting attitudes and behavior is the one that states there is a one-to-one correspondence between the two. In other words, an individual will behave toward a certain object in a manner predicted by his attitudes toward that object. For example, if a person likes ice cream, it can be predicted that the person will eat ice cream. Similarly, if police dislike blacks, then they will behave negatively toward blacks in the exercise of their duties. It is a simple and straightforward proposition, and one which many people regard as a self-evident truth requiring only the evidence of antiblack sentiment on the part of police to verify. However, the proposition is *not* self-evident. For one, there is some question about its theoretical adequacy, and secondly systematic evidence of racial discrimination on the part of the police has been somewhat sparse.

Within the last decade the hypothesis of a one-to-one correspondence between attitudes and behavior has been questioned on both empirical and theoretical grounds. However, rather than review this debate, a theoretical position that seems to be a reasonable compromise will be offered. To some extent, the notion that attitudes cause behavior is probably a fairly valid one, but the causal connection is far more complex than suggested by the "one-to-one" hypothesis. The major difficulty with the "one-to-one" thesis is that it erroneously assumes that we encounter single objects in isolation. It is fairly obvious that this is not the case; we react to complex social situations and our behavior is an outcome of a calculus (of which we have little knowledge) of attitudes toward all the objects and issues that are involved in the particular social situation. Thus, in reference to the example of ice cream, it would be necessary to know if the individual was hungry, on a diet, his view about the "healthfulness" of ice cream, the situation he is part of (it might be a funeral), and the like, before predicting whether or not he will eat the ice cream. Considering a more germane illustration, the decision to arrest a black—what are some of the possible factors that will be weighed in that decision on the part of an officer:

> What ever he may say . . . his actual decision whether and how to intervene involves such questions as these: Has anyone been hurt or deprived? Will anyone be hurt or deprived if I do nothing? Will an arrest improve the situation or only make matters worse? Is a complaint more likely if there is no arrest, or if there is an arrest? What does the sergeant expect of me? Am I getting near the end of my tour of duty? Will I have to go to court on my day off? If I do appear in court, will the charge stand up or will it be withdrawn or dismissed by the prosecutor? Will my partner think that an arrest shows I can handle things or that I can't handle things? What will the guy do if I let him go?
>
> (WILSON, 1968b, P. 84.)

All of these concerns might be weighed (some with great care and time, others on a more implicit level) along with such other concerns as the age, sex, race, demeanor, style of dress, personal appearance, and so forth, of the suspect; not to mention the policeman's feelings about professionalism (which directs him to disregard status attributes of the suspect) and his assessment of the degree of control or supervision of him by the department. In order for the policemen to make an arrest *solely* on the basis of the suspect's race, his feelings about blacks would have to be so strong that they would override all other considerations. This would seem highly unlikely to happen in a *large* number of situations in large urban areas.

Therefore, even if the position that attitudes completely determine behavior is taken, it is far from simple to account for the relationship between the two. What this all means, for the purpose of the present discussion, is that because police may be antiblack (or "prejudiced") in their attitudes does not necessarily mean that they will discriminate against blacks (or vice versa).

However, no matter what theoretical argument is being pursued, it is still important to determine empirically the extent of discriminatory treatment by police. The three major issues to be explored in this paper will be arrest practices, harassment, and brutality. Unfortunately, there is an even greater scarcity of data on these issues than was the case for policemen's attitudes. In fact, with the exception of the arrest decision, the only study available is the "three-city" observation study (Black and Reiss, 1967). Consequently, almost all conclusions and generalizations are based on this one investigation. (See the appendix for a brief description of the study.)

Police Behavior I: Arrest

From a legal standpoint police are required "to arrest everyone whom they see committing an offense or, with regard to the more serious offenses (felonies), everyone who they have reasonable cause to believe has committed an offense" (Wilson, 1968, p. 7). In actual practice, however, they fail to follow this legal mandate. This is due in part in some situations to the fact that the policeman finds it problematic that a crime has occurred. But in many situations there is little question about the crime or the suspect, and the policeman decides that for one reason or another an arrest is inappropriate. Although there is debate among legal scholars about the correctness of police discretion, it is somewhat difficult to see how "discretion" could be eliminated from the arrest procedure.

Given the fact that police do exercise some discretion, it is plausible that the race of the offender or suspect becomes a factor in the arrest decision. However, there is debate over exactly what effect it might have. On the one hand it has been argued that blacks are more likely to be arrested than whites given the same amount of evidence that the suspect committed the offense. Partly in opposition to this argument is the belief that in instances where the victim is black the police will tend *not* to arrest the black offender. Given both of these arguments, any difference in arrest rates between whites and blacks can be taken as evidence of discrimination.

James Q. Wilson (1968) has argued that tendency for "under-arrest" of blacks is related to the basic policies of a police department. Wilson distinguishes between two major types of departments: "watchman" and "legalistic." "Watchman" style departments are primarily concerned with "order maintenance" which consists of minimizing community conflict and maintaining a level of public behavior that is consistent with the normative guidelines of the community (even though some of these may be in violation of criminal statutes). "Legalistic" departments stress "law enforcement" in the sense that they attempt to enforce all criminal laws, even if they are in opposition to some sentiment in the community that the behavior should be tolerated. "Order maintenance" tends to be associated with more traditional police procedures, whereas universalistic law enforcement is often seen as indicative of the modern professional police department.

According to Wilson, "watchman" style departments, as a direct consequence of the "order maintenance" philosophy are more likely to see blacks as wanting and deserving:

> . . . less law enforcement because to the police their conduct suggests a low level of public and private morality, or unwillingness to cooperate with the police or offer information, and wide-spread criminality. Serious crimes, of course, should be dealt with seriously; further when Negroes offend whites, who in the eyes of the police, have a different standard of public order then an arrest must be made.
>
> (WILSON, 1968b, P. 141.)

Thus, in such departments private disputes that involve assaultive behavior are often handled informally or ignored (hence the lower arrest rates for blacks for this specific offense) because they are seen as not being potentially disruptive of "public order." As one detective cogently expressed it:

> When one of them [a Negro] gets cut, they don't come in here and tell us. He handles it on his own. He or his brother will cut the guy back. If we do get to question the victim . . . he'll suddenly be unable to remember who did it. And if we can file a complaint, often

> he'll shake down the guy who cut him for fifty bucks, and withdraw the complaint.
>
> (CITED IN WILSON, 1968b, P. 163.)

This does not mean that there will be no arrest for all offenses involving a black offender and black victim, but only for those that are not seen as very serious (that is, excluding homicide), or potentially disruptive (e.g., petty theft, assault). In sharp contrast, "legalistic" departments, with their primary emphasis on law enforcement will be less likely to underarrest blacks. Although substantially more research is needed, the idea of the general policy of local police departments infiuencing arrest practices of black offenders is worthwhile considering in evaluating this issue.

Almost all of the systematic evidence related to discriminatory arrest practices describes the apprehension of juvenile suspects (usually defined as below the age of eighteen). However, before reviewing this evidence it is important to indicate what is meant by an arrest in most of these studies. In the case of juveniles, most large urban jurisdictions have special divisions of the police department charged with the responsibility of formally handling juvenile suspects. It is usually these divisions that make the formal decision to arrest, even though an ordinary patrolman may have been the one to take the youth in custody and transport him to the "station." It is important to keep this distinction in mind, because, with the exception of the "three-city study" it is the decision of this special division and not the uniformed patrolman that is being researched. There is only one study (Black and Reiss, 1967) that deals with the uniformed patrolmen's decision to take into custody and transport to the station (for both adults and juveniles).[7] For juveniles the decision to arrest is taken to mean that the youth was being referred to juvenile court to receive a hearing.

The findings from seven different geographical locations are summarized in Table 6. The table includes, in addition to the percent of suspects arrested for both races, a measure (Goodman and Kruskal Tau b) of strength of association between the variables of race and the decision to arrest. This measure enables us to provide a more adequate way of comparing the various studies. Although we will not elaborate on the statistical technicalities of the measure, suffice it to say that its value varies between zero and one, with a very weak association being less than 0.10.

The findings with respect to the arrest rates indicate that in almost every instance blacks were more likely to be arrested than whites. However, in every one of the studies not a single Tau b exceeded 0.07, which means that the relationship between arrest and race is an extremely weak one. In other words, knowing the race of the suspect would not be very helpful in predicting whether or not the suspect will be arrested. It is interesting to note that the city demonstrating the largest difference ("Eastern City") was policed by a "traditional" police department, which seems to contradict Wilson's notion that such departments will underarrest blacks.[8]

The existence of differences in arrest rates, even if relatively small, does not necessarily mean the presence of racial discrimination. Other factors like social class of the offender, seriousness of the offense, attitude of the suspect and victim, and so forth, must be ruled out as accounting for the differences if the hypothesis of racial discrimination is to be accepted. Although controlling for age, sex, socioeconomic class of the suspect, seriousness of the offense, does reduce the racial differences to some extent, they fail to eliminate it entirely (Black and Reiss, 1966; Black and Reiss, 1970; Ferdinand and Luchterhand, 1970; Hohenstein, 1969).

One factor which has received a fair amount of attention in recent years, and seems to be strongly implicated in the arrest decision, is the attitude of the victim or complainant toward the police disposition of the suspect.[9] The evidence has shown that the police tend to arrest, especially in the case of misdemeanors, when the victim either prefers that an arrest be made or at least makes no statement against an arrest (Hohenstein, 1969). Given the importance of the citizen complainant in this process, is it possible that the reason blacks tend to have slightly higher arrest rates is that the black complainant (a large majority of offenses are intraracial) is more likely to favor the arrest than the white complainant. Black and Reiss (1970) have in fact strongly suggested that this might be the case, at least for juvenile suspects. However, because of the small number of cases, their analysis fails to demonstrate this effectively. In order to provide a more adequate empirical basis to

Table 6

Relationship Between Arrest and Race of Offender for Seven Different Geographic Areas

Place	*Year*	*N*	*Arrest Rates* *Black*	*White*	*Tau b*
Washington, Boston, Chicago[1]	1966	1423	25%	12%	.026
"Large N.E. City" (pop. 225,000)[2]	1957–60	1811	58	44	.016
"Easton" (fictitious) (pop. 150,000)[3]	1964	288	76	63	.020
Los Angeles County and Santa Monica[4]	1940–60	951	28	26	.000
"Midwest industrialized city" (pop. 100,000)[5]	1958–62	7919	8	8	.000
"Western City" (pop. 300,000)[6]	1962	5223	51	46	.000
"Eastern City" (pop. 300,000)[7]	1959–61	350	43	16	.067

1. Black and Reiss (1967, p. 76). Includes all suspects, both adult and juvenile, for all types of offenses. A suspect was defined as anyone the police treated as such, or against whom a citizen alleged to that effect. An arrest was defined as any transportation to the police station (not a technical arrest).
2. Bodine (1964, Table 1a). Includes all male suspects, ages 7–15, included in the "central registry of juvenile offenders" (police record). An arrest was defined as being sent to juvenile court.
3. Ferdinand and Luchterhand (1970, p. 512). A sample of inner-city youths (7–17), male and female, who had a police record for a first offense only. Arrest means being referred to juvenile court (excludes traffic offenses).
4. McEachern and Bauzer (1967, p. 155). A sample of records from Los Angeles County Sheriff's Department and all records from Santa Monica (1940–60), including both male and female juveniles. Arrest is referral to juvenile court (excludes traffic offenses).
5. Terry (1967, p. 224). Includes all offenses committed by a juvenile (excluding traffic offenses) from 1958 to 1962 recorded in the files of the "Juvenile Bureau." The basic unit is offenses and not offenders. Arrest is a referral to "probation department."
6. Wilson (1968a, p. 13). "Western City" is viewed by the author as having a "highly professionalized" police department. The analysis is for all juvenile offenses (not offenders) processed by the police in 1962.
7. Wilson (1968a, p. 14). "Eastern City" is viewed by the author as having a "non-professional" police department. The analysis is for a 1 in 25 sample of a juvenile processed by the police between 1959 and 1961.

explore this issue the data for juveniles (Black and Reiss, 1970) have been combined with the data for adults (Black, 1968). The results of this analysis are tabulated in Table 7 and do indicate that racial differences in arrest rates still remain when controlled for the complainant's preference. However, once again the Tau b's demonstrate that in each instance the race of the suspect is weakly related to the arrest decision. Thus, Black and Reiss's contention does not seem to be supported by their own data. In addition, the same differentials are generally true for those situations in which the police confront a suspect with no complainant present (Black, 1968, pp. 226 and 250).

Table 7

Percentage of White and Black Suspects Arrested in Police-Citizen Encounters Involving a Suspect and a Complainant, Controlled for Preference of Complainant*

	Complainant's Preference											
	Prefers Arrest				*Prefers No Arrest*				*Unclear*			
	White		*Black*		*White*		*Black*		*White*		*Black*	
	N	%	*N*	%	*N*	%	*N*	%	*N*	%	*N*	%
Arrest	14	58.3	31	72.1	1	4.3	4	16.0	5	27.8	24	41.4
Release	10	41.7	12	27.9	22	95.7	21	84.0	13	72.2	34	58.6
Total	24	100.0	43	100.0	23	100.0	25	100.0	18	100.0	58	100.0
Tau *b*	.020				.036				.014			

* All traffic offenses are excluded. For juvenile suspects includes only those involving a misdemeanor; and for adult suspects, felonies and misdemeanors for encounters that were initiated by a citizen.

SOURCE: Black and Reiss (1970, Table 4, p. 71), and Black (1968, Tables 39–41, pp. 218–20).

To conclude, very small differences in arrest rates tend to remain after controlling for several other factors. Therefore, it is possible (unless a factor or factors yet to be tested eliminates the differences) to interpret these findings as indicating a small amount of racial discrimination, at least in the case of juveniles on the arrest decision. However, it should also be stressed that other factors have proved to be far more important than race in explaining the arrest decision, especially the attitude of the victim and the demeanor of the suspect (Hohenstein, 1960; Pilivan and Briar, 1964).

Police Behavior II: Brutality

Police brutality is perhaps the one issue in police-black relationships that generates the most emotion. However, before looking at the evidence in this area it is important that the term "brutality" be defined with some precision.

The police have a *legal* right to employ physical force, but only in sufficient degree necessary to make an arrest, keep "public order," or protect themselves (in which case an arrest should follow, since the citizen has committed the offense of assaulting an officer). Anything in excess of that necessary legal force constitutes "brutality." Of course, the limits of "necessary force" are difficult to articulate and to reach some agreement on. However, there is probably little question that to date both the judiciary and the community (with the exception of blacks and other minorities) have given the benefit of the doubt to the policemen. The term "brutality" has also often been used to refer to such nonphysical acts as name-calling, disrespect, condescending demeanor, sneers, and so forth. Admittedly, these acts can be as damaging to police community relations as illegal violence, but they clearly represent phenomena quite different from illegal violence, and therefore should be kept analytically distinct.

In order to document brutality in the sense in which we are using it, it is necessary to indicate that (1) physical force was used and (2) it failed to satisfy the conditions of legality. In about the only systematic study (three-city study) of the issue Reiss (1968) spelled out the operational conditions that had to be present for the observers to classify a police action as brutality (a physical assault had to be present in all):

1. If a policeman physically assaulted a citizen and then failed to make an arrest; or
2. if the citizen being arrested did not by word or deed resist the policeman; or

3. if the policeman, even though there was resistance to the arrest, could easily have restrained the citizen in other ways; or
4. if a large number of policemen were present and could have assisted in subduing the citizen in the station, in lockup, and in the interrogation rooms; or
5. if an offender was handcuffed and made no attempt to flee or offer violent resistance; or
6. if the citizen resisted arrest, but the use of force continued even after the citizen was subdued.

(REISS, 1968, P. 12.)

Within a period of about fifty days the trained observers witnessed "improper" force being used against 44 citizens. (A total of over 10,000 citizens were observed as having contact with police during that period of time.) Of these 44 citizens, 17 were black and 27 white, representing a rate of about 4.2 white victims of illegal police violence per 100 white suspects and 2.3 black victims per 100 black suspects. These findings fail to support the contention that blacks are the principal victims of police brutality. In addition, Reiss argues that black policemen are as likely (when controlled for the number of white and black policemen patrolling blacks) as the white policeman to victimize black suspects.

To conclude, racial discrimination or "prejudice" seems to be a poor explanation of who is likely to be a victim of police brutality. (Reiss argues that social class is far more significant.)

Police Behavior III: Harassment

There are many police practices that fall short of illegal violence, but at the same time prove to be troublesome and annoying to these citizens who are the object of such treatment. These include such practices as verbal ridicule or abuse, stopping citizens for what seems to them unwarranted reasons, unnecessary questioning and searching, and so forth. In some instances it is fairly clear that a policeman oversteps reasonable limits in his treatment of citizens. In other instances, however, it is somewhat difficult to say what is reasonable (that is, stopping citizens for questioning). For most of these practices the police are operating within legal limits (as contrasted with brutality), but in spite of this such practices are often viewed as harassment (or the deliberate attempt to annoy citizens). And a widely held belief is that blacks are more likely to be objects of these practices.

Although it is difficult to characterize "harassment" the Black and Reiss study (1967) does provide some data on procedures that could be viewed as harassment. The extent to which police are likely to abuse citizens verbally, or treat them in an overtly hostile manner, depends in part on how the citizens behave toward the policeman. Citizens who evidence antagonism, represent, at least in the eyes of the police, a potential threat to authority. Given the fact that maintaining authority is quite critical to a policeman (Reiss and Bordua, 1967, pp. 47–48), he is very likely to take steps to restore or protect his control over the situation and in doing so he often reacts in an authoritarian and brusque manner. Observers in the Black and Reiss study classified each transaction with a citizen according to both the behavior of the citizen and the conduct of the policemen. Unfortunately, no data were presented on which party (citizen or policeman) initiated hostile action. Therefore, no assessments can be made on causal priority, but only about the characteristics of the interaction. The data are presented in Table 8. First of all, it is quite evident that as the citizen becomes less cooperative the more likely it is that the policeman will be classified as hostile or authoritarian. Secondly, the findings indicate that blacks are *not* more likely to be objects of harsh treatment by police, in fact, the opposite is true. (However, the differences are small.)

In addition, Black and Reiss found no evidence of a greater likelihood for blacks to be threatened by an arrest or detention (p. 115), not to be informed of their legal rights (p. 115), to be transported to the station without booking (p. 107), to be interrogated (p. 70), or to have an officer be "brusque or nasty" in his questioning of suspects (p. 98). About the only instances of greater involvement of blacks in a potential harassment practice is the likelihood of personal searches and the "constraining" of a suspect. For personal searches there was a slightly greater chance that blacks would be the objects of such procedures. However, they

Table 8

Behavior of Police Toward White and Black Citizens Controlled for Behavior of Citizen Toward Policeman

	Black		White	
	N	%	*N*	%
Police Behavior				
	Very Deferential Citizens			
Good-humored or jovial	220	21.6	207	33.0
Businesslike or routinized	710	69.7	348	55.4
Ridiculed, brusque, provocative, authoritarian, or hostile	89	8.7	73	11.6
Total	1019	100.0	628	100.0
	Civil Citizens			
Good-humored or jovial	723	10.8	911	20.5
Businesslike or routinized	544	81.1	3000	67.7
Ridiculed, brusque, provocative, authoritarian, or hostile	546	8.1	522	11.7
Total	6710	100.0	4433	99.9
	Antagonistic Citizens			
Good-humored or jovial	45	6.3	27	6.3
Businesslike or routinized	418	58.1	175	40.7
Ridiculed, brusque, provocative, authoritarian, or hostile	256	35.6	228	53.0
Total	719	100.0	430	100.0
	Demeanor of Citizen Not Ascertained			
Good-humored or jovial	31	6.6	21	9.1
Businesslike or routinized	414	87.9	179	77.8
Ridiculed, brusque, provocative, authoritarian, or hostile	26	5.5	30	13.0
Total	471	100.0	230	99.9

SOURCE: Black and Reiss (1966, Table 5, p. 34).

were also more likely to have concealed weapons found on them thus, in part at least, justifying the increased likelihood of searching blacks (p. 87). Finally, there was a small difference between blacks and whites (Tau b = .026) in placing constraints on a suspect (transport to a station, made to sit in a police car, physical and verbal constraints, and so forth) (p. 103).

The one practice that has seemed to generate the most conflict between the police and the black community is the "aggressive patrol" (that is, the stopping of "suspicious" persons for purposes of gathering information about recent offenses in the area and/or searching for weapons and illegal goods). The police feel that this tactic is an important one for purposes of investigating and solving crime, and not a discriminatory practice designed to harass blacks. The black community, however, tends to see it purely as a harassment device. Unfortunately, there is no relevant data to determine if in fact blacks, relative to population numbers, are more likely to be stopped by such patrols. Considering the circumstances and rationale for its use, however, it is highly likely that blacks, especially young black males, are stopped more often.

No matter what the objective evidence may indicate about the probability of blacks being stopped by aggressive patrols, there seems to be little question that the practice is a major source of conflict between blacks and police (in those cities in which it is employed with some frequency). When police departments are urged or pressured to "do something" about crime they are more likely to react by placing more policemen on the streets at the same time and increase the aggressiveness of the patrols which

> . . . increases the likelihood of the patrolman coming into an adversary relationship with citizens—innocent people, to say nothing of guilty ones, usually do not like being stopped, questioned, or frisked. Furthermore, the patrolman cannot stop everyone, and in deciding who "ought" to be stopped he will rely on whatever clues he can. Persons who appear to be lower class are more likely than others to commit crimes; Negroes are more likely than whites to commit the crimes of violence about which the public is most concerned; young men are more likely than older ones to steal automobiles. Intensifying surveillance will be experienced by people in these categories as "harassment"; failure to intensify surveillance

will be regarded by people not in these categories as being "soft" on crime.

(WILSON, 1968b, PP. 63–64.)

In all likelihood the police are fairly sincere in their contention that "aggressive patrols" are necessary in the "war against crime," and are not using this idea as a rationalization or cover for discrimination. (When they are accused of such intentions they often become annoyed and angered about being "misunderstood.") But the policeman's sincerity in no way lessens what the blacks subjectively experience as a result of such practices, and it seems that the police are insensitive to this fact. They have been reluctant to change these tactics, even when it is not clear that such tactics achieve their intended goal, for the sake of improving community relations.

To sum up the evidence on police behavior:

1. Arrest rates for blacks tend to be slightly higher than the rates for whites, and the differences are not completely eliminated when controlled for such factors as age, seriousness of offense, attitudes of victim, etc. Until a set of variables can be found to eliminate the differences, the hypothesis of small amounts of racial discrimination in the arrest procedure remains a plausible one. However, other variables (e.g. attitude of victim, demeanor of citizen) prove to be far more important than race in predicting the arrest decision.
2. The hypothesis of "underarresting blacks" as a form of discrimination has yet to be tested in any adequate fashion. J. Q. Wilson has argued, with some evidence, that the practice is more likely to occur in "traditional" police departments.
3. The only systematic empirical study of police brutality has failed to demonstrate that blacks are more likely than whites to be victims of illegal police violence.
4. The same holds true for possible harassment techniques as for the issue of brutality.

Conclusions

Even though we would like to see more research in order to be more confident about our assessment, we must conclude that the best available evidence on police behavior fails to support any assertion of widespread and blatant racial discrimination on the part of contemporary urban police. This does not mean that there have not been individual acts of police discrimination; quite clearly, such acts have undoubtedly occurred. But in the aggregate, and as a characteristic of the police system, major patterns of discrimination have yet to be documented.

In addition, the findings in this area again remind us that the attitudes on a specific issue must be treated separately from the corresponding behavior. Because in some instances we were able to conclude that policemen are somewhat negative in their views and feelings about blacks, it was far from certain that they would behave as policemen in negative ways toward blacks.

Finally, there is no denying that policemen are somewhat insensitive to the desires and needs of blacks, but it also seems likely that the black community has also tended to be insensitive to the problems of police. And this seems to be the real tragedy: Police and blacks caught in an escalation of conflict, distrust, and hatred. In this vicious circle it is extremely difficult to determine who is the hero and who is the villain.

APPENDIX

Description of Major Police Studies Surveyed: Fifteen-City Study (Rossi et al., 1968; Groves and Rossi, 1970)

As part of the investigations of the National Advisory Commission on Civil Disorders (Kerner Commission), the authors of this study were commissioned to investigate the attitudes toward blacks and related issues of various occupational groups (among them, police) serving the ghetto. Samples from fifteen cities were selected, representing a wide range of riot experience in 1967. The fifteen cities were Newark, Detroit, Milwaukee, Cincinnati, Boston, Brooklyn, Cleveland, Chicago, San Francisco, Philadelphia, Washington, D.C., Baltimore, Gary, Pittsburgh, and St. Louis. The police departments of Milwaukee and Boston refused to cooperate, and thus the policemen from these two cities were not included in the study. In addition, the published findings in the major report (1968) did not include data on the police from Detroit and Chicago. These two cities were included, however, in a later paper (1970). Finally, data were also unavailable for Detroit social workers.

The police were selected after first eliciting cooperation from the individual police departments involved, which were asked to supply a list of patrolmen in designated precincts (those serving the ghetto areas) who would be interviewed. Thus, the sample was not a probability one, since police officials were left free to choose, for whatever reasons, those patrolmen who would be included in the sample. What biases were introduced by this procedure is difficult to say, but the authors feel that the distortion was a conservative one. In other words, it was felt that the degree of antiblack feeling was underestimated because the likelihood was that the police department tended to choose those with the least amount of antipathy toward blacks. Whether this is true is of course impossible to tell without further evidence. It would seem that the officials might exclude the blatant and vocal policemen on this issue; however, it is rather difficult for them to know their policemen sufficiently well to predicate how they might answer a set of standardized questions. In other words it is not necessarily clear that a strong distortion in the conservative direction was introduced.

The aim was to include about forty policemen from each sample. (Since the sample of police is not proportional to the population of police in each city one cannot use the findings to estimate any population parameters.) About 435 police were included in the major report (1968) and 515 in the later paper (1970).

Three-City Study (*Black, 1968; Black and Reiss, 1966, 1970; Reiss, 1968*)

The study was commissioned by the now defunct President's Commission on Law Enforcement and the Administration of Justice and is perhaps the most comprehensive and systematic study of police utilizing observational techniques in a natural setting.

The principal goal was to investigate police-citizen interaction in high-crime areas of large cities. The cities included in the study were Boston, Chicago, and Washington, D.C. A total of eight police precincts, all high in crime, low socioeconomic, and racially homogeneous areas. The observations were conducted during a six-week period in the summer of 1966.

Principal investigators were thirty-six trained observers who rode with patrolmen (and somewhat less often walked the beat) during all shifts on all days of the week. They recorded certain selected characteristics of police encounters with citizens, with most of the information being recorded after the event had occurred. A total of 5,360 such events were observed involving more than 11,000 citizens and 700 police officers (92 were black).

Some possible limitations of the study are:

1. The events recorded were not a probability sample of all police-citizen interactions, but were restricted to only those events that:
   —occurred in a high crime, low socioeconomic, racially homogeneous areas,
   —involved patrolmen and not detectives or special investigation officers,
   —were initiated by a citizen complaint over the phone or in the field to a police officer, or by a patrolman on the street.

Thus, any attempts to generalize the findings must be done with these limits in mind.

2. In almost all of the analyses of the data there was no information given about about the race of the patrolmen. This is unfortunate for the purposes of this paper because our primary interest centers on the behavior of white policemen. However, there is some information given which allows one to bracket certain findings: For one, almost all the white citizens were policed by white patrolmen, thus the behavior of white police toward white citizens is easily determined. Secondly, about one-half of the black citizens encountered white policemen, which means there is a possibility that the treatment of blacks (as measured by rates and percentages) by white policemen would be different from what the published findings indicate. However, it is not clear how they would be different or in what direction. On the one issue, where data by race of policemen are given, Reiss (1968) reports about an equal tendency on the part of white and black policemen to use illegal force against citizens. If the argument of police work experiences and the police subculture as being of more influence in the behavior of patrolmen is accepted, then there would be some expectation that the treatment of black citizens would be very similar for white and black policemen.

3. The most obvious criticism concerns the effect of neutral observers on the behavior of policemen. In other words did the policemen alter their behavior for the observers in order to protect themselves against criticism and possible punitive action? Or would their behavior have been the same if no observer had been present? Although it is impossible to assess this effect directly without having evidence of behavior without the presence of an observer, the authors argue that distortions are small because:
   a. the policemen were informed that the observers were there to study citizen behavior and not the police;
   b. the observers were trained to "fit into a role of trust" with the officer;
   c. in many instances the policeman must react quickly, giving him little time or forethought to choose the behavior he thinks might impress the observer favorably;

> " . . . people cannot change their behavior in the presence of others as easily as many think. This is particularly true when people become deeply involved in certain situations. The policeman not only comes to 'trust' the observer in the law enforcement situation, regarding him as a source of additional help if necessary, but, when he becomes involved in a dispute with a citizen, he easily forgets that an observer is present. Partly because he does not know what else to do, in such situations, the policeman behaves 'normally.' " (Reiss, 1968, p. 15.)

Since no substantial evidence is given on the lack of distortion, the defense presented by Black and Reiss can either be rejected or accepted. Either way, the assessment remains a matter of faith. The reasonable position seems to be that until strong evidence is presented to the contrary, the thesis that the study represents "artificial" behavior on the part of the police remains plausible, and any conclusions on the basis of the evidence should be evaluated accordingly.

Denver Study (Bayley and Mendelsohn, 1969)

The study is based upon interviews of Denver policemen conducted in 1966. The total number of patrolmen, randomly selected, was 100 (less than 5 per cent were black). In addition to the policemen, samples of the general public (N = 806), blacks (N = 100), Spanish-named persons (N = 100), and community leaders were surveyed.

Western Michigan Study (Bouma, 1969)

The study basically is a collection of smaller studies of about 10,000 public school students and 310 police officers in western Michigan. The three cities from which the sample of police was drawn were: Grand Rapids, population of 200,000 (N=150); Kalamazoo, population of 100,000 (N=120); and Muskegon Heights, population of 20,000 (N=40). No breakdown by race was given for the sample of policemen. If the other cities are any guide, the percentage of blacks on the total force should be no greater than 10 per cent.

The interviews were carried out after the riots of the summer of 1967.

Detroit Study (Mendelsohn, 1970)

The sample of policemen was random, stratified by rank and race. Of the white officers interviewed, 57 were inspectors, 33 lieutenants, 36 sergeants, 36 detectives, and 86 patrolmen. Included in the sample of 36 black policemen were all levels of rank.

The data were collected by interviews conducted shortly after the Detroit riot of 1967, from about November 1967 to March 1968.

Philadelphia Study (Savitz, 1971)

The project was primarily concerned with the socialization of new police recruits and followed a cohort of policemen for a period of three years.

The sample (N=245) consisted of all members of two nonconsecutive training classes in 1967, of which 25 per cent were black. The recruits were first interviewed (T1) during their first week of training at the Police Academy. The second wave of interviews (T2) was completed immediately after the completion of the formal training period (eleven weeks). The third (T3) and fourth (T4) sets of interviews were carried out after six months and three years, respectively.

As one would expect there was some loss in the cohort during the three-year period. By the end of the study 7 per cent of the original group had been forced or dismissed from the force, and 10 per cent resigned. The problems in interpreting the findings because of this attrition are discussed in note 5.

I am extremely thankful to Professor Savitz for the use of his data.

Teachers

LAWRENCE A. FINK

Throughout the last decade, educational institutions, both public and private, have found themselves embroiled in the massive national struggle against racial discrimination. The Supreme Court decisions against school segregation and imbalance, directed ultimately to all sections of the country, were implemented by slow and laborious steps that left much to be done and more to be hoped for. It is not surprising that the public would focus its moral indignation and action on the educational field, since one aspect in the circular reasoning that has been used for so long to explain the social inequality of American black people is that they are academically ill-prepared to compete for the better-paying jobs.

Of course, the public school system is huge and affects the lives of so many children that, undeniably, much more than racial imbalance needs correcting. Increasingly, leaders of black communities have accused public schools of failing in their appointed tasks. The mis-education of today's black children who, in substantial numbers, are reacting to their learning experience with apathetic or disruptive behavior, has led some of these leaders to charge educators with inefficiency if not conspiracy. The neighborhood school system, the apparent quota of black teachers, the presentation of classroom material, especially in the field of history, and the emphasis of the curriculum as a whole are condemned as inadequate or wrong for the encouragement of confidence and the development of "success patterns" among the black people.

Some educators have responded to this criticism by maintaining that the fault lies less with the school than with the larger society, and that a heritage of discrimination, poverty, and family dissolution is the key element preventing black youth from taking full advantage of the educational opportunities that exist. Such assumptions underlie many programs which have been initiated to reach black children even before they begin conventional schooling and to add compensatory programs to the standard curriculum once they have.

Other, more radical, educators have argued that the "negativism" of black students is merely part of a more widespread dissatisfaction with the general quality and direction of public education. Such authors as John Holt, George Leonard, Neil Postman, and Jonathan Kozol, among others, feel that the basic character and purposes of education are ill-suited to encouraging either intellectual or emotional growth, and that a total overhaul of the educational system is required. Thus far, at least, most teachers remain somewhat skeptical of the reorientation schemes which these authors regard as necessary, and, indeed, find their blueprints somewhat less than realistic.

Traditionally, college teachers have expressed small satisfaction with the results of their public school colleagues in preparing students for higher learning. Noting that college freshmen seem ill-prepared in writing and verbal skills, professors attribute this to unimaginative and poor teaching throughout the lower grades. The public school teacher's commitment-to-nonacademic and extracurricular activities is considered a significant detriment to the advancement of his teaching abilities. And, indeed, this may be. Yet, recent experiences of conflict on the university level indicate that not all learning and communication between faculty and students is confined to the classroom.

For the first time in their lives, today's professors have had angry hands laid on them. They were ignored, they were heckled and attacked, their offices were ransacked, and, most devastating, their very integrity was put in question. One might suspect that this kind of encounter is their initiation into the daily life of an urban teacher in a comprehensive public school. Perhaps the endless hours spent in setting up and attending committees, in meeting with student groups and organizing rebuttals and proposals, and in checking out the validity of allegations and counterclaims will engender greater sympathy for the dedicated public school teacher involved with the extra-classroom commitments common to troubled urban areas.

While these criticisms have some merit, many of them are mutually contradictory. However, before they can be evaluated, a somewhat broader perspective must be provided to place the problems of contemporary urban education within the framework of the educational system as it has evolved during the past fifty years.

As of September 1971, more than three million full-time teachers were employed in U.S. public and private institutions: 1,232,000 in elementary schools, teaching 36,600,000 children; 1,013,000 at the secondary level, instructing 15,000,000 students; and 833,000 at institutions of higher education with an enrollment of 7,377,000. Under the best of circumstances, a human enterprise of such immensity would be continually evolving and producing change and reform. Given the disparity of political and economic conditions and social and academic aspirations marking the different regions and localities of our country, conflicts in educational philosophy and practice are inevitable. This applies equally to attitudes and approaches demonstrated by teachers toward race problems in the schools. The dimensions of the educational enterprise and the variability and complexity of its relationship to the issues of racial discord limit any essay on this subject to a few cautious observations and generalizations.

At an ever-quickening pace, the expansion of the concept of public school education and the proliferation of in-school services have brought into focus the redefinition of the terms "education" and "teaching." Until the last decade or so, the public school teacher was regarded somewhat romantically as a Don Quixote, unconcerned about personal economic advancement and preoccupied along with his students, in searching out and comprehending man's highest ideals of truth and beauty. While teachers traditionally have been the confidants of their students, they were respected primarily for their role as educators. Accordingly, the schools in which they taught were considered solely as academic institutions whose function was to provide students with the intellectual tools necessary for an understanding of the social, economic, and political processes of our society. It was assumed that this basic knowledge would lead to a widened opportunity in the selection of one's vocation and in the promotion of one's welfare.

Over the past several decades, however, the concept of the public school has changed in fundamental ways, as has the image of the teacher. Perhaps the most important change has been a redefinition of the term "education." In today's comprehensive school, the curriculum includes a far greater variety of activities. In addition to the classical studies and their modern derivatives, students may now select from an astonishingly long list of vocational courses. Auto mechanics, woodworking, pottery-making, cooking, sewing, hair-styling and grooming, typing, photography, film-making, and horticulture do not exhaust the offerings available to a secondary school student. In fact, a vast apprenticeship system has been incorporated into the school program. Meanwhile, counseling programs have proliferated in schools throughout the country. Students receive academic and career guidance counseling, instruction in mental and physical hygiene, referrals to psychiatric and family aid services for emotional problems, and medical attention. But it is, above all, concern and careful observation on the part of classroom teachers that leads to administrative awareness of individual students whose education is hampered by poor eyesight, hearing deficiency, malnutrition, drug addiction, and other physical problems. The new, expanded self-image of today's school is reflected by some of the specific goals of a recent teacher strike in a predominantly black school area in the Northeast: obtaining more reading specialists, establishing day-care centers, and introducing medical tests for lead poisoning and sickle cell anemia.

Ironically, the all-embracing commitment of our present educational system to the general welfare of its students has made it increasingly vulnerable to criticism and attack. Assuming responsibilities in so many sectors only multiplies the number of ways in which the school can fail. It might almost seem that what is *not* accomplished by the school constitutes a deliberate evasion of educational effort. Disagreement about the extent to which the school should become the instrument for further amelioration of social ills presents a serious conflict in the minds of concerned parents, reformers, and educators. While the truest definition of education admits to no boundaries, any institutional framework must of necessity operate within a limited field. More than nostalgia induces people to recall when schools were essentially academic in nature. There is a prevailing sense of desperation over the number and kind of battles being fought through the schools since their crucial effects are to weaken the educational process and afflict our children prematurely with the burdens of strife that should and must be shouldered by adults.

The redefinition of the scope of education has, quite naturally, added considerably to the work of the teacher. He (or she) has continued to teach five academic classes per day (college professors are well-known to complain if their "teaching load" amounts to more than six contact hours per week). His daily preparation usually covers more than one subject and must be presented in each class at a different level according to student competence. In addition to meeting 150 or so students every day, he is expected to supervise a homeroom in which he collects money for a variety of school reasons and maintains attendance reports: to oversee a study-hall probably held in a basement cafeteria with large posts and occupied by thirty to five hundred students, to run a club, and to take on some other nonteaching duty such as cafeteria clean-up, hall guard, or washroom patrol. Correcting of papers and examinations continues unabated during his "off" time, when he is also attempting to study for a course he is taking at the local university.

As the national economy expanded and as labor unions realized higher wages and better working conditions, teacher frustration and anger over the inability to earn a salary at all commensurate with the growing nonteaching and classroom work load led many professionals to turn to the American Federation of Teachers for help. The traditionally conservative National Education Association was forced to adopt a more militant posture in order to have a chance in a new teacher participant activity—the collective bargaining election. Contracts were negotiated for higher salaries which permitted many teachers to give up second jobs formerly needed to maintain their families at even a subsistence level. Also included were provisions for extra pay for club sponsorship and athletic coaching, ground rules for leaves, absences, vacations and lunch hours, and, in some cases, stipulations for police protection when needed. In the effort to ameliorate their economic disadvantage and to gain a reasonable position of influence in the educational policies of school systems, teachers assumed trade union attitudes and employed trade union practices such as strikes which temporarily hurt the educational process. The dislike of teachers for any self-serving technique which disrupts learning has led most to feel a reluctant allegiance to teacher unions. Half-hearted though it may be, this new allegiance, however, makes teachers more vulnerable to accusations that they are thinking more of themselves and of their personal gain and security than of the students who are their professional responsibility.

I

Most teachers accept with humility the contention of blacks that no one outside the pale of the black experience can fully comprehend the psychic dislocation they have endured because of their history of slavery and racial discrimination. Many significant reforms in the school come as the result of teacher pressure to comply with the needs and sentiments of the black community in which they teach. However, as with all American communities, members of black communities are not always in accord among themselves as to the best methods of effecting their ultimate betterment. Middle-class black parents seem to support a rigorous academic school system heavy on discipline and do not condone the use of schools as a laboratory for social experiments. They see their own future in the context of American society and the advancement of their children as dependent upon a solid intellectual foundation. At the same time, they generally are in favor of demands for black teachers and principals, and for curricular revision designed to include and emphasize black contributions to American society throughout American history.

In any black community, however, one cannot help but focus on the small but extreme militant groups whose aims are essentially political and who embrace the concept of black nationalism. A more "moderate" wing of these groups proposes a "renegotiation of the social contract" with the white power structure, while a more extreme element contends with profoundly cynical conviction that black equality can never become a reality until all the power structures, including schools, that maintain "this white racist society" are destroyed. Some militants go so far as to propose the creation of a black nation in a number of states, equal but "separate" from white America politically, economically, socially, and even militarily. Another group is interested only in the institution of a separate black school system. This faction argues that integrated schools are exploitative and reactionary and that black children will thrive in institutions with exclusively black teachers and principals.

Among those militants involved primarily with curricular "reform," the more radical demand that all courses deal with "black truth" as opposed to "white truth." Educators are responsive to the call for reorganizing the humanities and social sciences to more fully illuminate the contributions and experiences of black people, but they are baffled by any similar demands to apply these efforts to the objective field of science. Are the methods or the conclusions of scientific inquiry offensive to the black reformers? Scholarship and the investigative method are theoretically characterized by an intrinsic discipline and intellectual honesty that reject tampering with conclusions that would stand the scrutiny of time. However, it is more than likely that the militants are fully aware of this and ultimately are in accord with accepted logical ground rules. Perhaps their need for evidence corroborative of their position on black problems is short range and tactical in nature. An exchange between a black student and a white author who had cast doubt in his book on the heroic nature of a famous black man may illustrate this point. The author said: "All the evidence led me to the truth of my conclusions." The student replied, "But 'the truth' is that we black people today 'need' our hero."

Many teachers attempt to present "two truths" in the course of their classroom teaching, but many others are disturbed by the element of condescension they feel is implicit in this approach. False heroes, even for a good cause, are nonetheless false. Teacher ambivalence in regard to the needs of black people and the methods black leaders often employ can be seen in their attitude toward acts of disruption by black students in public schools, many of which are organized and instigated by militant parents and leaders to dramatize their demands for educational reform. The teachers understand the purposes of disruption and, in fact, are quite familiar with boycotts, sit-ins, and picketings. What they find fruitless and self-destructive, however, is the victimization of children for what they feel should be accomplished by adults.

The resulting lack of respect for the school and for schoolroom discipline has already provoked disastrous repercussions both in and out of the school building. In many urban schools, black youngsters returning to the classroom after taking part in mass demonstrations aimed at inciting anger against local school officials feel they no longer need to obey the regular school rules. Essentially, the public school teacher's allegiance lies with the continuation of the learning process, however shaped or modified or arranged. But both teaching and learning function only when discipline is maintained. Militant black leaders have at times failed to recognize that their efforts to achieve reforms in the schools might better be accomplished without the exploitation of their youngsters.

The consequences of such irresponsibility can be disastrous for American education and society. It is not a far cry from participation in a school boycott and breaches in classroom discipline to the rock-throwing and looting which have marked riots in the recent past in predominantly black neighborhoods.

Indeed, the effects of such practices could lead to increased racism rather than deepened understanding, greater hatred rather than broader love, and more rioting rather than reform. In the end such developments, while they may provide a temporary lip service to the narcissism of the reckless educational militant, are hardly likely to contribute to the long-range welfare of the black masses. Responsible leadership such as that of A. Philip Randolph, Roy Wilkins, Floyd McKissick, Roy Innes, the late Martin Luther King, Jr., and Whitney Young provides a real alternative which can encourage black people away from apartheid, away from permanent poverty, and away from violent actions that bring suffering to all.

II

It is mainly toward the black separatist philosophy that teachers and their unions have expressed their greatest antagonism and over which bitter dispute has polarized whole urban communities. There is no doubt that matters of principle are of the essence to both teachers and black radicals in this struggle, but it would be naïve to ignore the fact that power is at stake here, too. Referring movingly to the perpetual economic defeat of too many Black Americans, black nationalists and other more moderate groups alike are calling for community control of schools that, as distinguished from decentralization, would place them beyond educational regulatory agencies at least on the city and perhaps even on the state level. With community parents and leaders hiring teachers and administrators and establishing the curriculum, thereby localizing the educational format and criteria, the reason for the existence of any central school board or teacher unions would end. With their possible demise in view, teachers take a strong position against community-run schools, basing their arguments on the pernicious effects of community control in southern states and on the efforts of southern black people to break the provincial strangleholds on their schools. Teachers also express grave concern about the long-range success of students, after graduating from community-run schools, in competing for jobs or college placement. Why not work for decentralization, they suggest, which combines the advantages of greater community influence with the preservation of regional or national academic accreditation?

Teachers have expressed a profound sympathy for the pain and problems inflicted upon black children by racial discrimination in America. A large number of the teachers in urban schools, where racial strife is most severe, have entered their profession in part because they were anxious to reach and help these very children. But the ability of teachers to function efficiently and happily with their students is directly related to such factors as the magnitude and intensity of school building disruption. One can cite instances in which militant school reformers aroused such bitterness between the school and the community that education all but ended. However, in the midst of a situation in which very little successful teaching is being accomplished, one may still find a teaching zealot whose professionalism, energy, and dedication to his "kids" and their future raise him above the fracas. Indeed, in many cases, he might have chosen a particularly difficult school as a matter of altruistic preference. At the other end of the spectrum exist many schools within whose walls good students are allowed to be trapped in classes presided over by zombie teachers.

Most instructors fall somewhere in between these extremes. A good many who are quite competent in their fields and who can teach effectively under orderly conditions lack the ability to cope with the kind of disorder and chaos which have increasingly come to characterize the schools of the inner city. They may feel personally attacked and will be overwhelmed by the frustration inherent in trying to interest apathetic students in their subject areas. Their best intentions for becoming teachers seem thwarted by a school environment which counters their teaching strengths and magnifies their weaknesses. A large number of these teachers originally had requested placement in college-oriented schools, but were assigned or transferred by the school system to more heterogeneous schools which were understaffed. Similarly, many teachers who began their careers in predominantly college-preparatory schools, where their role was indisputably academic, find that a shift in neighborhood population has changed the orientation of the student body and the emphasis of the school. These teachers in middle age suffer from a form of professional dislocation that adversely affects their classroom relationships and jeopardizes their success as educators. Either of these types could conceivably evolve into the stereotyped ghetto teacher depicted in exposé articles as a dehumanized policeman, making little or no effort to teach or communicate on any effective level.

The personal predispositions of teachers, however, should not bear the entire blame for the low standards of education prevalent in the economically poorer sections of our nation. The deleterious effects on the entire school system of a minimal budgetary expenditure are also of decisive importance. An inadequate number of teachers and a deficiency of facilities to handle an increasing number of students present a situation conducive to failure. Overloaded classes and inadequate teaching materials unquestionably undermine students' ability to learn at an optimum level of accomplishment. One of the premises of the concept of equality of opportunity is equitable availability of quality education. The quality of education offered to Black Americans in the South can be measured in many ways, not the least pertinent of which is the amount of money spent. The United States Department of the Interior, through its Office of Education, in 1934 sponsored a National Conference on Fundamental Problems in the Education of Negroes. The findings of the Committee on Finance of that Conference provide some interesting facts. The average expenditure for every public school pupil throughout the United States in 1930 was $99.00; the expenditure for white children in the South was $44.31 (less than half the national average), while the expenditure for Negro children in the same states was $12.57, slightly more than one-fourth that for southern white children and about one-eighth the national average. In certain southern states with a huge Negro population, the fiscal discrimination was even greater: Georgia spent $35.42 for each white pupil and $6.38 for each Negro; the comparison in Mississippi was $45.34 against $5.45. The children of the million Negroes of the deep South had less than one-fifteenth the opportunity for education of the average American child. To paraphrase Booker T. Washington: It is too great a compliment to the Negro to suppose he can learn fifteen times more easily than his white neighbor. Those who complain that the Negro cannot gain complete equality overnight must also admit that the Negro cannot always prepare himself overnight to take advantage of new opportunities offered to him.

The seventies are ushering in a new breed of public school teacher—a man of today who grew up with civil rights marches, encounter sessions, and political activism committees. He has touched upon at least the fringes of the youth culture and shares many of the sentiments of the present alienated generation. He not only sympathizes with the black militants but is comfortable with them, their aims and their methods. Monolithic centralism, bureaucracy, school boards, and Regents requirements seem to him archaic, dehumanizing, and far-removed from the practical needs of diverse communities.

He continues along a path of reform that can be traced through the late nineteenth and twentieth centuries. Since the first charges of inadequacy were hurled at the public school establishment during the 1880's and 1890's, reformers have offered solutions that were hoped would finally end many of the problems that have seemed insoluble. Progressive education was simply the educational phase of the progressive movement of the late nineteenth and early twentieth centuries. It was an effort to adapt school reform to the new industrial, urban civilization. It was a period of protest against formalism. The schools and their curricula, it was said, were divorced from real life—were irrelevant. The Progressives wanted to bring the schools into touch with the life of the majority of Americans and use them as the means for far-reaching social reform. They envisoned the schools as the most important lever for improvement in a democratic society. Change your school, invest it with concern for social issues and causes, and the school becomes the instrument by which society can change itself.

When one reads certain contemporary critics and self-styled reformers, one gets the impression of having seen it all somewhere before. John Dewey's definition of education as being "life itself"; Thorstein Veblen's idea that culture and education had been devices by which the leisure class could assert its superiority as an élite; John Ruskin and others' statements of a sense of alienation attributable to the new industrialism and appeals to intellectuals to commit themselves to the re-establishment of the human community; Jane Addams and others' advocacy of the establishment of a new Christianity, leading to the foundation of the social settlement movement in this country; G. Stanley Hall and the child-study movement; Dewey and William James and the child-centered curriculum. All these and more are being reaffirmed by today's contemporary writers without the benefit of footnote.

The various attempts at reform by the Progressives led to the development of the core-curriculum in the 1930's, followed, among other things, by increasing emphasis on science in the 1950's and team-teaching, modular scheduling, and nongraded schools in the 1960's. Two major reform efforts have been made in the early 1970's and their success or failure could very well determine whether or not any schools at all will survive into the 1980's. The first, underway as the decade began, is the concept of the open school or open campus which is based on the belief that the traditional classroom as a unique setting for learning is in many ways too constrictive. The application of this concept can lead to corridor classrooms or to entire schools "without walls," a term referring to many learning areas scattered about a huge open building. Some systems are extending learning centers around the community, expanding the "walls" of the school to encompass the entire community or more.

The second imminent reform has to do with teacher accountability. As the decade progresses, teachers and their unions are joining with school boards and community dissidents to establish objective criteria of professional responsibility. Strangely enough, all these factions seem to support this approach and to regard it, for their own different reasons, as a solid answer to much of the criticism leveled at teachers and the results or lack of results they obtain. The dissidents see a system of teacher accountability as a way of proving their charges of poor and indifferent teaching and a way of improving what goes on in the schools by cleaning the rascals out if they don't measure up. The new teacher of the '70's is responsive to the concept of accountability because of his desire to better education and his feeling that he is and will continue to be quite effective in the role of teacher. School boards go along because this is the first possible crack to show itself in the armor of permanent tenure. Any system of accountability will, by definition, incorporate a basic revision of the tenure system. Older teachers and the unions see accountability as a means of vindication. Honestly constructed, it will put the quietus on much of what they consider irresponsible and baseless criticism of what they have done and are doing. Many of them see accountability as the greatest protection that could be devised for their professionalism.

Without question, the open classroom and teacher accountability will have a great deal of influence on teachers and the education of all students—black and white—in the decade ahead.

Prison Personnel

WINSTON E. MOORE

The recent prison riots and killings at Attica, N.Y., and San Quentin, Calif., and similar eruptions in other jails and prisons throughout the United States have come as no surprise to me. In fact, I am expecting more explosions of this type if drastic changes in the U.S. penal system are not undertaken at once.

I maintain that Attica and all the other outbreaks could have been avoided without any bloodshed. I further maintain that an Attica-type riot will never occur in the Cook County Jail and the Chicago House of Correction, the two institutions under my care, as long as I am in charge. This is not meant to be a boast, but a statement based on insights I have gained during many years of working with juveniles and adults in correctional institutions.

The key to the effective operation of correctional institutions, I am convinced, is communication. There must be at all times communication and meaningful interaction between inmates and prison staff.

In Attica, such communication was virtually nonexistent because the guards were *incapable* of communicating with the inmates. Not only were all the guards white, but they were mostly residents of a small, ultra-conservative community (pop. 2,800) that was totally alienated from the urban blacks and Puerto Ricans who make up 85 percent of Attica Prison's inmates. Even the remaining white inmates were mostly from the New York City area and had little in common with the rural-oriented guards. I am not saying that black prison guards are better guards than white ones. But I am saying that in an institution in which the majority of inmates are urban blacks, you are inviting trouble when you have them guarded by rural redneck types.

Proof that there was no communication at Attica is the fact that the inmates were able to instigate such a confrontation without any of the prison officials hearing as much as a rumor of the plan. The prisoners had to carefully map their strategy regarding what they intended to do, whom to seize as hostages, how to cut off communications, how to block entrance, how to set up a line of defense. All this required elaborate organization. I insist that if there had been dialogue between the inmates and guards, such as exists in my institutions, it would have been impossible for the inmates to handle all the necessary logistics without some knowledge of their plan leaking to the guards.

Attica was not a spontaneous outbreak but the climax of an intolerable situation that had been permitted to arise over a period of at least a year. During that time, the inmates had submitted a number of just demands such as better food, improved recreational facilities, and an end to administrative mistreatment and physical brutality. Most of these grievances could have been easily handled by the authorities without any fanfare or approval from the legislature or governor. Although he was hailed as a great reform penologist, Russell Oswald, New York State Commissioner of Corrections, procrastinated in dealing with the prisoners' entreaties. At the same time, the NAACP Legal Defense Fund had a class action pending in behalf of the inmates, charging cruel and unusual punishment. The courts, like the Attica Prison administrators, procrastinated with their decision until the inmates felt that the only way to get relief was to dramatize their plight to the whole nation. And that is exactly what they did when they seized the hostages. I don't think that they ever intended to kill their hostages, if indeed they killed any of them.

If we stop to analyze Attica and all the other prison eruptions, we find that the underlying cause in each case was racism—plain and simple white racism aimed at blacks. Racism is more intense, more vicious, and thus more inhuman in correctional institutions than anywhere else. What is happening in these prisons is essentially what is happening throughout the country outside prison walls: Black people and other minorities are becoming ever more vocal and militant in demanding basic rights that still are being denied them. But whereas on the outside the system has given in to the pressure and made some changes, such as the dropping of certain racial barriers in the South, practically nothing has changed inside correctional institutions. The attitude of most wardens and other correctional officers is still that of "lock 'em up and throw away the key." This is, of course, not surprising, since the American Correctional Association (ACA), penology's counterpart of the American Medical Association, is, itself, an ultra-conservative, racist organization and, consequently, has not been vocal in pressing for change. U.S. correctional institutions are still run according to the archaic and outdated mandates set forth by the ACA more than a hundred years ago in 1870. The effect of this has been that these have become citadels of dictatorship and right-wing thinking. It is only within the last eighteen months, as the result of prisoners' refusal to put up with this dictatorship, that penological administrators, wardens and superintendents in particular, have been held accountable for their incompetency and indifference by the public and the press. The killings in Attica and other prisons have served notice that racist practices will no longer be tolerated by inmates.

I think what the inmates are saying with their rebellions is simply this: "Treat us like human beings." I wholeheartedly support that demand. Some people are hung-up on the term "penal institution" and feel that jails and prisons must be punitive. They oppose any attempt at reform with the contention that correctional institutions must not become places where inmates are being "coddled" or allowed to have "a good time." Such sentiment, I believe, is shortsighted and counterproductive. I happen to be of the opinion that locking a person up is plenty punishment. Depriving a man of the freedom to come and go as he pleases, the right to make certain basic decisions, the right to be with his family and friends, the ability to advance himself in society—all this I think is punishment. I don't think prison officials should arbitrarily allot more punishment to an inmate simply because they don't like him or the crime he committed. The only justification for additional punishment beyond that ordered in sentencing by the courts would be found if the prisoner continues to violate rules governing behavior in the way in which he used to break the law outside the prison walls.

One way of assuring humane and fair treatment for inmates, as I said earlier, is to eliminate the hostility based on racism which too many guards feel toward the inmates. This cannot be done without altering the lopsided racial ratio between guards and inmates. At present, more than 60 per cent of the nation's jail and prison population is urban black and Spanish-speaking (Puerto Rican, Chicano, etc.), but not even two per cent of that majority is employed in corrections as guards and other personnel, not to mention wardens or superintendents. Consequently, the prison communication gap exists not only at Attica but throughout the U.S. correctional system. At the two institutions under my supervision, we have a balanced racial ratio between inmates and guards—approximately 85 per cent black inmates and 15 per cent white inmates to 85 per cent black guards and 15 per cent white guards.

Another important aspect of guaranteeing fair treatment to inmates is the protection of inmates. All inmates must be protected at all times from fellow inmates as well as from prison personnel. In my institutions, we do not tolerate the abuse of inmates by anyone and no inmate is obliged to make himself a knife or other weapon with which to defend himself. We keep our institutions clean of weapons. And the only way to do that is by regular shakedowns.

I think it is about time, too, that someone discusses what happened at Attica not only in terms of racism, brutality, needless bloodletting and murder, but in terms of the impact of the decision of Governor Nelson Rockefeller and Director Oswald to storm the prison on the correctional system. Heretofore, the idea of taking prison personnel as hostages seemed to most inmates an almost foolproof method of gaining extended negotiations with institution officials, and in cases where the correctional officials felt that the hostages had to be saved at any cost, taking hostages might even have proved the most expedient method of escape. The actions taken at Attica have erased that theory. The deaths of more than forty persons deemed expendable by Rockefeller and Oswald have categorically proved that taking hostages is a dead-end street. Now rebellious inmates will have to—and I am sure are going to—find other means of defiance, which could come in the form of property damage or staff beatings and murder.

Outsiders, especially white and black radical groups, will increasingly try to influence the more impressionable inmates to disrupt and destroy penal institutions, in some cases even at the risk of suicide to the inmates, certainly never at any risk to themselves. Some outsiders who have been promoting this radical conduct have already labeled all black inmates as "political prisoners," charging that black criminals are "victims of the system." While being strongly in favor of treating inmates as human beings and respecting their dignity at all times, I am just as strongly opposed to this notion. It is my contention that persons who support that ideal are sabotaging any possibility of rehabilitating black felons. It is a well-established psychological fact that all criminals, black or white, have a deep-rooted need to justify their criminal act to themselves. Thus, a holdup man who shot and killed an unarmed storekeeper invariably convinces himself that, somehow, he acted in self-defense. In rehabilitating such a criminal, the first and most important job facing correctional personnel is to break down the criminal's self-denial of his offense and to make him realize and admit to himself that he did wrong. If, however, the criminal is told that not he, but society is to blame for his crime, that he is a victim and political prisoner of "the system," the process of rehabilitation is short-circuited and the criminal feels justified in continuing his life of crime. Strangely enough, the majority of crimes committed by black criminals are being committed against other black people. I fail to see how "the system" makes blacks kill black people, rob black people, rape black people, and run black people out of business.

Some proponents of the "political prisoner" notion point to the ghetto background of the criminals. But, I ask, how many black people come from the same dismal ghettos without turning to crime? The answer is, more than 98 per cent of all Black Americans are law-abiding citizens despite racism, ghetto background, and other handicaps resulting from being black in a white racist-dominated country. Then there is the argument that many of these criminals turned to crime because of high unemployment. But some six or seven years back, when jobs were plentiful, these same people who are committing robberies today were committing robberies then, instead of holding jobs.

This brings me to an area that should go hand in hand with prison reform—the re-establishment of law and order in the black community. Some people wonder why there is such a disproportionately large number of black prisoners in US penal institutions. Apart from the fact of glaring injustices in the judicial process, one incontrovertible point is that black people are committing more than their share of violent crimes, particularly violent crimes against black people; it's as simple as that. If one considers for a moment that last year 749 blacks, as compared with 99 whites, charged with murder passed through my department, one can begin to understand how dangerous the ghettos are—not only for white people passing through but especially for the vast majority of law-abiding black residents.

Unfortunately, what has happened in the black community is that whites have taught us to hate authority, to regard police and the courts as our enemies, and to hate or be frightened of the words "law and order" because, for the most part, they have meant the oppression of black people by white cops.

Today there are those—so-called militants and radicals—who exploit blacks' apprehension toward law and order for their own ends. In addition, blacks who live outside the law find the anti-law and order sentiment of their black brothers and sisters very convenient for committing crimes since it enables them to victimize the black community with impunity.

Robbing, raping, and murdering black people has nothing to do with the black liberation struggle. The sooner decent black people realize this, the sooner will they be liberated from these "soul brothers" and "soul sisters" who make their neighborhoods unsafe. Decent black people have to become aware that crime is bad wherever it takes place—be it in a white neighborhood or in a black one—and that law and order are desirable and needed by both blacks and whites. Decent black people must demand the same thing white people are demanding in their communities: first-class police protection and fair and impartial treatment in the courts.

I believe that black leaders have shortchanged the black

communities by giving the impression that black people are against law and order. So far, only one black organization, the Harlem branch of the NAACP, has had the guts to openly condemn black crime in the black community and to support stronger sentences for blacks convicted of violent crimes.

I don't think that law and order are the same as ultra-conservatism and police brutality. I feel that the black community wants law and order because it needs law and order for its own survival.

I mainly blame the white press for its having failed to communicate that need. The white press, which is basically a racist press, has created monsters in the form of street gangs and other criminal types by giving credence and publicity to these undesirable elements in the black community while remaining silent whenever responsible black people have been speaking out. Remember, the white press never paid much attention to the black community until Watts erupted. Only when a riot erupted was the white press out there in any numbers. As far as the daily struggle of decent blacks against black gangs and other criminal types was concerned, the white press could not have cared less. This attitude of indifference goes straight across the board from the police to the courts who have encouraged crime in the ghetto by the leniency of sentences whenever the victim is black. Whites simply don't care when both victims and offenders are black. It appears that justice prevails only when both the defendant and the victim are white.

But I hope I will see the day when black citizens will insist on law enforcement that will drive home the message to criminals that crime—whether committed against a white person or a black person—does not pay. When that happens, I predict, we blacks will stop making up 85 per cent of our prison and jail inmate population if we represent only 15 per cent of the general population of a given city. At this point, we are a long way from that and we don't get there by saying that jailed criminals are "political prisoners."

Meanwhile, the threat of further jail and prison explosions is imminent. Throughout the nation, correctional administrators are now flooding their budgets with superficial and worthless "instant appeasement" programs as a quick and easy alternative to genuine rehabilitative efforts. Somehow, they seem to think that throwing up a library overnight and stocking it full of black literature and records, along with slating furloughs to the more militant inmates whose antisocial behavior still prevails inside the institution, will "soothe the savage beast" and rid their jails and prisons of incorrigibles. They are grasping at straws. There are no alternatives in corrections to sincere concern for the welfare of the inmates. Money cannot buy the most basic and important commodities in dealing with adult behavior modification: human understanding and respect in the form of fair and impartial treatment of all inmates by everyone involved in penology.

Wardens must get off their behinds, away from their desks, and into their institutions. They must make it their business to get to know personally as many inmates as possible. They must make themselves accessible to their inmates and become responsive to the prisoners' grievances. They must understand that running a prison is not a nine-to-five job and that it cannot be done from one end of a three-foot riot baton.

What American correctional officers must do is offer their inmates consistent educational, vocational, recreational, and spiritual programs that provide constructive and realistic alternatives to crime inside and outside of prisons. Any failure to do so is bound to have catastrophic consequences that might dwarf the tragedy of Attica.

Those correctional administrators who have been sweeping their problems under the proverbial ol' rug for many years are now going to have to establish themselves as correctionists or else reap the whirlwind.

On the Campus

White Professors

ROBERT BLAUNER

In the late 1960s the hallowed university, long seen as the institution with the most enlightened race relations, became the focus of intense racial conflict. In the year and a half following the assassination of Martin Luther King, the thrust of militant black protest shifted from the streets of the ghetto to the administration building and the tree-lined malls of the college campus. Predominately liberal in politics, professors experienced their own version of the crisis of racial attitude that white liberals as a group underwent during the decade. Liberals had long been committed to the goals of the civil rights movement: ending discrimination and achieving social and economic equality through the strategy of integration. As long as the battlefield was in the South or in the "inner city" comfortably distant from his suburban residence,the liberal's commitment was free of inner conflict, though perhaps somewhat abstract. But when racial protest moved northward, when a new philosophy of black power came into ascendancy, and when the militants began to adopt more aggressive, even violent, methods, the issues were no longer abstract and distant.[1] As in the case of the Harlem and Bedford-Stuyvesant teachers, the white liberal's material and professional interests were threatened. Individually, and as a group, he was subject to intense attack. He was termed as much the racist as the worst Southern bigot, indeed at times even the more so, since a liberal "facade" in the face of racial privilege added up to personal hypocrisy.

Were race relations on the campus during the premilitant period really so enlightened? * If they were relatively liberal and low key, the fundamental reason is that there were so little of them. Though precise figures are not available, a number of studies indicate that between 3 and 5 percent of all undergraduates in the early 1960s were black. Since 50 to 60 percent of Afro-American students were then in Negro colleges, the proportion in predominantly white schools must have been 2 to 3 percent.[3] With these "integrated" students concentrated in state and city colleges, probably no more than 1 to 2 percent of the enrollments at the better universities and élite colleges were Negro. And as late as 1969 when the Carnegie Foundation surveyed a random sample of faculty, black professors made up less than one-half of one percent of the sample at the universities the study classed as "high and medium quality," and less than one percent at the "high and medium quality" four-year colleges.** Thus the exclusion of third world students, faculty, and administrators from the major universities was virtually total, with the exception of Asian-Americans who were fairly well represented as students and professors. But when black students (and to a lesser degree Chicanos and Puerto Ricans) entered the campuses in somewhat more than token numbers during the late 1960s, "race relations" came to the university with a vengeance, bringing the racial crisis of the larger society home to roost for the white professor.

In this essay I shall examine the situation and the outlook of the white professor, particularly how he responded in action and in shift of perspective to the new immediacy of racial issues. Assuming that the dominant philosophy of the professoriat has been liberalism, and that liberal values are institutionalized within the structure of the university, I shall argue that the liberal framework of most faculty members was severely tried by the changing conditions, notably new university commitments to roll back racial exclusion and the educational and political challenges

* It may be impossible to generalize about the thousand or more institutions of higher learning, but minority students who have written about this period are more likely to stress the pervasiveness of racism, sometimes petty and overt, more often subtle and subconscious, even on the most cosmopolitan campuses.[2]

** Among the "low quality" universities, blacks were 1.8 percent of the faculty sample. They made up 10.4 percent at the "low quality" four-year colleges, yet only 0.3 percent at the junior colleges.[4]

of third world students. Over a period of time that has now extended about five years, a dialogue from conflicting perspectives between white faculty and students of color over the nature of the university and the role and relevance of race and racism in the society at large has been taking place. This dialogue has been expressed in specific confrontations, both in the classroom and in the arenas of campus decision making. The concrete issues that have divided the contestants have been many, varying with the unique situations on particular campuses. The two most pressing and frequent ones have been admissions policy and black or ethnic studies departments. These controversies have exposed underlying conflicts of interests and values between the two main protagonists. On one side we find the faculty defending its privileged position in the university, its distinctive academic values, and its general liberal social philosophy. On the other side stand previously excluded student groups with an interest in establishing a base in higher educational institutions, and newly equipped with perspectives on race and society (black, Chicano and third world consciousness) that in no small degree have grown out of the failure of civil rights liberalism to achieve its ends. Although this conflict has a material basis in the struggle for educational resources and is played out in concrete terms, on the level of ideas it is succinctly crystallized in different "definitions of the situation," particularly with respect to the characterization of "the race problem" and explanations of racial inequality. The liberal faculty began with (and to a degree clings to) the notions of the 1950s, that prejudice and discrimination lie at the heart of racial injustice, whereas third world students conceive of *racism* as an overriding reality, a systematic process structuring the entire society and its institutions. As of 1971 the students appear to have had more educational impact on faculty conceptions of race relations than vice versa. For the general dialogue and specific crises have resulted in an erosion of the liberal position, which previously had appeared to be based on a consistent philosophy that made sense of social issues and indicated policies for their amelioration. The racial perspectives of most white professors are now in a state of flux.

Despite their liberalism and commitment to reform through

democratic political participation, white professors were largely passive on racial matters during the past decade or two. Of course, some individuals were activists during the civil rights period, many advised federal and local governments or wrote about urban problems, and there were others who worked quietly behind the scenes to integrate their professions and campuses. But by and large the faculty was content with the university as an institution and its position within it;* it did not act until jolted from this complacency by movements that effectively disrupted the tranquility of teaching, research, and the leisurely walks from classroom to faculty club to library. Thus faculties as collective bodies were not the primary forces that initiated challenges to the institutional racism of their universities. Professors responded to other initiators, usually students, at times the administration; and with few exceptions they took action only when their own college, their department, or their professional association was threatened.**

One could account for the white faculty's role or lack of role on the grounds of its essential and ingrained racism, and let it go at that. But such a dismissal would be an oversimplification, as well as unjust. This is not to deny that professors, like all white Americans, share many of the racist assumptions of our culture, and partake of certain privilege and advantage because of their color and European background. But if racism is to be a useful concept for understanding oppression and social change in America, it cannot be used as a magical catchphrase to be applied mechanically to every situation without analyzing its specifics. Crucial for an adequate understanding is the context in which university and professorial racism is embedded. The struggle against racism is not primarily a matter of the clash of individual attitudes and

* This has been most true at the major universities. At less prestigious universities and colleges the faculty is relatively less privileged, and often considerably dissatisfied about salary, teaching load, and lack of autonomy. Studies at Columbia and San Francisco State suggest that the less privileged faculty is more likely to support student protest on the campus.

** It is important to stress that the faculties of some universities responded much more rapidly to third world movements and student aspirations than at others. Certain private universities, such as Harvard, Yale, Northwestern, and Stanford, moved rather quickly to initiate black studies curricula. These institutions tend to be better protected from political pressures than public ones. On the other hand, some of the first Afro-American studies departments were established in junior or community colleges such as Merritt College in Oakland, California.

preferences, but instead a clash of group values and interests, which vary in different classes, occupations, and institutional settings. Thus, in order to understand the white professor in the face of the recent racial challenge, we must look at his political outlook, the structure of the university and its academic culture, and, in particular, the dominant philosophy of liberalism—as these factors relate to present-day racial controversies.

There are many reasons why the analysis I put forward must be tentative. My ideas are based primarily on my participation and involvement in campus race relations at one university, and not on systematic research within the thousand or more institutions of higher learning, which differ in regional climate, proportion of minority students, academic level, and private versus public status. No studies yet exist on the subject of the racial attitudes of the faculty, though the Carnegie-sponsored investigation of higher education will contain important material. The many books on major crises that I have drawn upon reveal very little about faculty thinking, and the same is true of detailed journalistic accounts, such as the *New York Times* coverage. To some degree this is an indication of the weak political role of faculty, to which I have alluded; it also reflects the general reluctance of professors to speak out on public issues, especially such sensitive matters as race. Those who have spoken out undoubtedly represent the attitudes of others than themselves, and I have incorporated their perspectives in this paper. But to a considerable degree I generalize on the basis of my experiences at the University of California in Berkeley.

Limited as these are, I think it likely that students and professors on other campuses will recognize themselves in the discussion that follows. For the central issues of controversy have been the same at all major Northern universities; on most campuses students of color, though diverse in many ways, are characteristic of a "new breed," and the faculty is composed of roughly similar distributions of political and social positions. Thus radical professors are a minority at Berkeley just as elsewhere, the dominant consensus is liberal, not conservative, and I therefore assume that the values and conflicts of the liberal colleagues with whom I have worked and argued at the University of California are shared by their counterparts at other institutions. As a fellow professor, I have tried to examine the outlook of this liberal majority in a spirit of appreciation and fairness, but, as a radical often operating with different assumptions and priorities, I have most likely not always succeeded.*

Some Observations on Faculty Politics

Many commentators have noted an apparent paradox in faculty politics. On matters affecting their work, profession, and home institution, professors are remarkably conservative. On issues of national and international scope, college teachers tend to be one of the most liberal, even left-wing, occupational groups in our society. University and college professors are probably the most consistent supporters of civil liberties;[5] they are more concerned than the average citizen with issues of social justice; they tend to favor liberal economic reforms; and of course they have been especially active in opposition to the Vietnam War.[6]

The conservatism of the professor on his own turf is in part a matter of the bureaucratic sclerosis that affects every organization and institution. The scientific and professional fields within the academic world are much like traditional guilds. The faculty is jealous of its craft autonomy, its authority over the standards of entrance into its discipline—hence the notion that only graduate training in the major universities provides apprenticeship and socialization into its specialized field of learning and, therefore, the union card for membership in the academic community. The professor is oriented toward molding the student in his own image, and he is likely to feel that the only satisfactory training is the kind of education he himself received in graduate school.

* My essay is an attempt to characterize the faculty as a whole and important tendencies within it. Therefore I do not deal with those individual professors who have been heavily involved in race relations through controversial public action or publication. Here I refer to such people as Arthur Jensen, Professor of Education at Berkeley, who has raised the issue of genetic differences in "intelligence" by race; Harvard's D. P. Moynihan, famous for his report *The Negro Family* and advocacy of "benign neglect"; Edward Banfield, author of *The Unheavenly City* and others.

Some critics of this essay have questioned the prominence given to the liberal professor. For example, one reviewer of this book in manuscript suggests that faculties have experienced a significant infusion of younger and more radically oriented professors, and that these new elements have been actively challenging academic racism. I have not observed this at Berkeley, where the lack of expansion has kept new blood at a minimum; if this has been an important trend at other institutions it points up the problems of generalizing from a case study.

The professor tends to be conservative in his method of work also. The scholar and teacher respect the authority of past knowledge; the research worker is governed by scientific norms that he rarely questions. The methodology of men of learning is based on the painstaking accretion of new findings that result in the gradual improvement of previous formulations rather than the dramatic and "revolutionary" breakthroughs sought by artists, for example.*

The departmental organization of the university is another factor. The professor is primarily a member of a department, a segment of the university, that represents his special discipline. His primary loyalty to his own field prevents him from developing a vision of the University as a whole, particularly of the need for institutional change and responsiveness to new publics. Here administrators have an advantage. We tend to think of college presidents and deans as men of more conservative mettle than their faculties. And yet, with some exceptions, administrators have generally been more innovative than professors on racial issues in the recent period. At the University of California, the significant opposition to the kind of Black Studies Department the students advocated came from influential faculty and not the administration. Many college presidents—Berkeley's Roger Heyns, Cornell's James Perkins, John Summerskill of San Francisco State—were ahead of their faculties on such issues as admissions policy and the hiring of minority faculty.

It is true that university personnel in general, professors as well as administrators, operate within a social context that limits their political options. The control over budget exercised by state

* I am indebted to Jessie Reichek for this point.

Probably the most well publicized exception to this rule was Columbia where President Grayson Kirk appeared less sensitive than many professors to the concern of black students, with the building of the gymnasium in Harlem. There were also important universities, such as Harvard and Yale, where the faculty appears to have supported and participated in racial reform. Still, one might speculate as to why administrators often have been more change oriented than their faculties, particularly with respect to the interests of third world communities. One hypothesis is that college presidents are in contact with a wider range of publics and advisors than is the typical faculty member. In urban centers they meet with representatives of ethnic communities. And whereas the typical professor in an all-white department rarely or never talks with third world colleagues, some of these few minority professors on the campus will have the ear of the President, and thus his perspective on racial matters is likely to be broader.[7]

officials and trustees, the priorities that have been put forward long in advance by various educational master plans, make up the larger picture in which the faculty response to the demands of new constituencies unfolds. Thus, professors frequently do not have the freedom and power to put their views into practice.

Yet when forced to choose, the faculty has tended to defend its own interests and values. Here I refer to its privileged position in society: a virtual monopoly on intellectual work; tenured employment and freedom from accountability for the consequences of its ideas; relatively high social status and income; the free time, vacations, opportunity to travel, and leisurely routine absent from most work-a-day jobs.[8] The liberal professor is also defending certain values that have been institutionalized in the university and have generally been nonexistent or precarious elsewhere. These make up the "academic freedom" complex: freedom of inquiry; the pursuit of universal questions about the nature of life, art, and society; the commitment to dialogue; the clash of ideas; and the intellectual life. That universities do not always live up to these ideals is beside the point. They are part of the liberal culture of the academy, and the professor will resist change to defend them.[9]

Paradoxically, the strength of this commitment to liberalism may explain, in part, faculty conservatism. Institutionalized within the university format, liberal values tend to take on the rigidity associated with organized structures and procedures. The inflexibility that results threatens to make these same values conservative ones, for liberal principles must adapt to new conditions in order to retain their essence.

With respect to racial matters in the recent period, the predominant liberalism of the faculty has been a mixed blessing. Initially professors were predisposed positively toward minority students, to equal access to higher education, and to integration of the university through reform. But at the same time, and unbeknownst to most faculty, the liberal outlook also contained a number of tenets that were to become obstacles to fundamental change in race relations in the 1960's. These assumptions and values came into serious conflict with the values and assumptions of the new ethnic consciousness that college students from third world backgrounds were developing. We can see this process at work if we examine a number of new issues and situations that posed dilemmas for the faculty: changes in admissions policies, the increasing third world presence in the classroom and in campus politics, and the demand for ethnic studies departments.

Admissions Policy and Liberal Universalism

Professors played, at most, a minor role in the special admissions programs that set the stage for later events in the campus racial drama. Until the 1960s only a handful of Northern colleges, such as Oberlin, had taken any special interest in recruiting Negro students. The programs that existed were small; they concentrated on promising youth with middle-class backgrounds and aspirations, and were often criticized for paternalism. Awakened by the civil rights movement and its growing militancy, a number of universities and colleges began, in the mid-1960s, to set up "educational opportunity programs," particularly at the undergraduate level.*

Traditional entrance criteria were expanded to emphasize such qualities as potential and motivation; the rigidity of grade point and test requirements were correspondingly relaxed. These "special students" were typically afforded financial assistance to cover tuition, books, and sometimes other costs, and tutoring programs were introduced to make up academic deficiencies. The result on many campuses was a rapid increase in the visibility of black students, though their numbers remained relatively small, especially in proportion to the student body as a whole. Thus, at the University of California in Berkeley the black student enrollment at the end of the 1960s stood at about 1000 (4 percent), compared with about 100 (0.4 percent) at the beginning of the decade. The freshman class of Dartmouth in 1969 included 90 blacks (10 percent), compared with 30 in 1968, and 8 to 10 during previous years. Similar increases took place at Harvard, Brown, Yale, Northwestern, and many other campuses.[12] Government figures

* One of the first, at Hofstra University, began in 1964 and was called NOAH (Negro Opportunity at Hofstra).[10] Other early programs were the E.O.P.'s (Educational Opportunity Programs) at Berkeley and San Francisco State College. Northwestern University began an aggressive effort to recruit black freshmen in the summer of 1965.[11]

suggest that the most dramatic gains came between 1968 and 1970. In this brief period the proportion of black students virtually doubled at many of the best institutions, and among freshmen the percentage rose from 5.8 to 9.1.[13] Characteristically, the increase in enrollment of other third world groups, Chicanos, Puerto Ricans, and Native Americans, has not kept up with that of the blacks.

At the outset, those faculty who were aware of the new programs probably approved them, though with a certain ambivalence. The university was doing something about racial exclusion; it was assumed that with adequate tutoring and compensatory study black students would eventually relate to the university much as white students did. Many professors were troubled to see these new students clustering together at defined campus hangouts; this was not the way integration was supposed to look.*

These early programs were usually under the aegis of the president, administered by a special office. Few faculty participated in their operation, nor were they or their departments much affected by the new campus presence. The departments, which typically control the admission of graduate students, were much slower to take notice of and act upon the exclusion of minorities from their programs and their professions. However, stimulated by the undergraduate example, administrative prodding, or the special initiative of a chairman or faculty member, some began to move to change the situation. As of 1969 a survey of graduate department minority programs revealed that special admission or recruitment efforts were in operation in at least 96 specific graduate departments and 111 professional schools in addition to university-wide policies at 42 graduate institutions. Law, medicine, business administration, social work, and theology among the professional schools, and sociology, history, and English among academic fields, were the most frequently represented.[16] By 1971 the proportion of black graduate students was about 5 percent at many of the most prestigious universities. Institutions lesser in repute were, in

* Friedland and Edwards report from Cornell, "Blacks moved around the campus in groups and were never found fraternizing with whites. This was upsetting to most faculty and students." [14] And at the University of Connecticut, the editor of the student paper noted that "The Blacks are suddenly visible around the campus. They walk around in groups of fives and sixes to classes, and the whites eye them nervously." [15]

general, still predominantly segregated at the graduate level.[17] The one event that spurred many universities and departments into action was the assassination of Martin Luther King.*

As the number of minority students began to increase, many professors became uneasy about admissions developments. The idea of a special recruiting effort could be tolerated, especially since each applicant was to be treated individually and no determinate number was promised. But third world students on many campuses "upped the ante" and demanded that a certain number, or a certain proportion, of each class must be black, Chicano, Puerto Rican, or of other ethnic background. Many professors attacked such formulas as equivalent to the kinds of restrictive quotas the Jews at one time had suffered under. Administrators who accepted or negotiated compromises with the demands were seen as submitting to student pressure or the threat of disruption. On urban campuses, like City College of New York and San Francisco State, students demanded open enrollment for all peoples of color. In general the faculty has felt that such a policy would be undesirable (if not disastrous) as well as unrealistic; the fear most commonly expressed has been of the probable undermining of academic standards, intellectual eminence, and cultural style of the university.**

* The failure of departments to act sooner (and many still have not acted) can be attributed as much to faculty inertia and the traditionalism of admissions procedures, as to principled objections. When I proposed a plan for vigorous third world student recruiting to the Berkeley Graduate Department of Sociology in 1967, I received the strong support of the chairman, whose political orientation was made up of conservative as well as liberal elements, and a unanimous mandate to proceed from the faculty as a whole, representing a wide range of political persuasions. Some fears of the institutionalization of quotas were expressed, the advisability and ambiguity of special "remedial" seminars was debated, but the general reaction was enthusiastic. In my own department, and on university campuses in general, problems developed later—when third world students came on the scene in large enough numbers to make a difference.

** In an influential paper delivered to a state-wide University of California meeting on urban issues, the Berkeley sociologist Martin Trow attributed the increasing racial conflict at Berkeley to an admissions policy that emphasized recruitment from ghetto high schools and overselection of politicized youth, whose militancy was viewed as evidence of academic potential. Trow suggested that minority admissions be focused on middle-class blacks and that emphasis be shifted from undergraduate to graduate and professional training.[18] At the same time, black student organizations were often demanding that the University reverse policies that had been favoring the "assimilated" Negroes; at Northwestern, for example, in April 1968 they demanded "that at least half of each year's incoming black students be from the inner city school systems." [19]

Special admissions policies favoring students of color came into conflict with the central value of the liberal philosophy, universalism. The universalistic ethic insists that everyone be viewed and treated in terms of the same criteria. The sociologist Talcott Parsons considers universalism one of the dominant value orientations of modern industrial societies, and he contrasts it with particularism, the orientation to men and action on the basis of group affiliations, such as family, clan, race, religion, sex, or place of origin. Liberal universalism has been one of the great progressive ideas, affirming the essential humanity of all people; it has also been a wedge against graft and favoritism in public life. For my purposes in this essay, the importance of universalism is its implication that race and ethnicity should not be taken into account in judgments about people and in the arrangement of institutions.

The liberal wants to judge a man in terms of his individual uniqueness and his universal humanity, not in terms of "accidental" features like skin color. Universalism thus goes hand in hand with individualism, and in the area of race the two join in the ideal of "color blindness." Unlike the conservatives, who make up only a minority of college faculty, the liberal is uncomfortable with the consciousness of color. Again, unlike the conservative, particularly the Southern breed, the liberal does not like to think of himself as *white*—why, therefore, should minority people make so much of their blackness or brownness?[20] People are human beings first. Then they are unique individuals. The group identities appropriate to the modern world are the more universalistic ones, like occupation and associational membership. For the professorial generation of the 1950s and 1960s, the period of the Second World War was the crucial political experience; color consciousness brings unpleasant memories of Nazism—and the fact that a considerable proportion of professors at prestige universities are Jewish has been significant in reinforcing such an association.

Related to universalism is the faculty's general commitment to assimilation as the solution for racial and ethnic inequalities. Most liberals accept, at least in theory, the idea that no important differences exist between whites and blacks in America—either biologically or culturally. When distinctive attitudes, values, and life styles are recognized, they are usually explained in terms of social class rather than ethnicity or culture. Assimilation is seen as part of the ineluctable logic of the large-scale social trends that characterize modern, urban, industrial societies.

The Carnegie survey of university and college faculty documents the prevailing universalistic perspective, indicates a considerable split among the faculty, and suggests that there may be significant internal conflict within individual minds on this matter. Fifty-nine percent of the sample disagreed with the statement that "more minority group undergraduates should be admitted even if it means relaxing normal academic standards of admission." However, the higher the quality of the university or college, the more likely faculty were to favor special admissions. At the high prestige universities, professors were evenly split between those who agreed with the statement and those who disagreed, though most of those who agreed did so with reservations, and the proportion who strongly disagreed was markedly higher than the proportion who strongly agreed. The faculty confirmed its color-blind perspective even more convincingly on the question whether "any special academic program for Black students should be administered and controlled by Black people." Here only 4 percent agreed strongly and 21 percent with reservations; there was no real variation by type of institution.

The color-blind ethos of the liberal ideology has been shaken by the increasing prominence of race in the social upheavals of the past years. Whereas a significant minority of professors have presumably given up this belief as an anachronism, the majority have not. Commitment to the color-blind ideal lies behind the faculty's distress at the general thrust of third world student politics. But many professors must also sense the truth of an NYU Law Dean's dictum that "the fact of the matter is that if you're color-blind you don't admit minority groups,"[21] and they have therefore reluctantly supported some particularistic programs. As Lawrence Fein points out, this is not really a break with present actualities, for "the structure of the system, which is to say, of our institutions, and the rules according to which they are managed, preserve, in many ways, a reality of particularism and of ascription, elaborately disguised by a mythology of universalism and achievement orientation." [22]*

Racial Conflict in Campus Politics and the Classroom

It is obvious that black students—and, on some campuses, Chicanos, Puerto Ricans, and other third world groups—have become a significant force within the political life of American colleges and universities, though their activity and militancy has varied from one place to another. Because the patterns of racial exclusion have been virtually identical throughout higher education, third world students, once their numbers are sufficient for a political base, have a built-in agenda for action against the all-white character of their institutions. This explains why the demands of black students, for example, have been remarkably similar at campuses across the nation.**

At various times and places, some faculty have supported these demands, others have opposed them, and a large number, sometimes the majority, have been indifferent or neutral. The alienation that has developed between many white professors and the black movement on campus is not only a matter of different views of the content or legitimacy of proposals for change. The faculty has a

* In response to these dilemmas, new positions are emerging. One advocates ethnic consciousness for a number of years in the immediate future in order to bring about the conditions in academic and professional life that will make color blindedness possible eventually. Whether realistic or not, such a formula seems to be in the spirit of liberalism, which historically in the United States has based its strength on a flexible social doctrine and pragmatic adaptation to new realities rather than on a set of dogmatic principles.

** The number of demands varies with the specific campus crisis, but in almost every case three have been included: first, a rapid increase in the admission of black and other third world students through changing traditional entrance criteria and providing financial aid; second, the hiring of black and third world professors and administrators; and, third, the establishment of a relatively autonomous department or school of Afro-American or ethnic studies. Other frequent demands have been for the disciplining or dismissal of a particular professor or administrative aide charged with racism or insensitivity (Cornell and San Francisco State are examples) and the provision of separate facilities, residence halls, or cultural centers for black students (Northwestern and Cornell). A type of concern that is becoming more central is the university's relation to, or exploitation of, nearby ethnic communities (for example, the case of the Columbia gym) and its financial involvement with corporations doing business in South Africa (Princeton, Cornell, Stanford, among others).

different set of priorities from that of the students, and the liberal professor in particular maintains a belief in the sacredness of procedures—a conception of the "means-ends" problem in political action that diverges from the assumptions of contemporary student movements, both white and third world.

Thus professors may agree that racism should be eliminated from the university, but they see this goal as only one of many reforms that are needed to improve the viability of the institution and its educational mission. The faculty is a heterogeneous body, ranging widely in interests and values. If a hierarchy of its priorities could be drawn up, racial justice would not lead the list. Professional, academic, and intellectual values are much more important, for the majority. The radical faculty has not seen university racism and third world issues as its main concern, either. In recent years its politics has been directed toward antiwar protest and restructuring the university in response to white student interests.*

Third world students have a different set of priorities. Whereas they are not necessarily opposed to traditional academic values—although many professors think they are—the struggle against the racism of the university appears to them to be absolutely essential to their presence and survival in the academic environment. The single-mindedness of minority students on this issue, and the organizational unity that has emerged in certain crisis situations, strikes many professors as narrowminded, anti-intellectual, and totalitarian—not to mention, uncouth. From the student standpoint, the faculty's defense of other values appears to be a self-serving clinging to class and racial privileges, a copping out of the central struggle against racial injustice, and, therefore, a confirmation of deep-seated racism. Such a student perception, when articulated, seems like "arrogant nonsense" to many professors.

When priorities are clear-cut and unequivocal, the means of

* The low priority of racism on the faculty's political agenda is one of the reasons for the passivity and indifference I have alluded to. During the Harvard strike of April, 1969, the faculty discussion on the black students' proposal for a black studies program revealed that few professors had even read the Rosovsky Report (The Report of the Faculty Committee on African and Afro-American Studies), though they swore by this document, which was the focus for their deliberations.[23]

reaching one's goals may become secondary. It is the wholehearted dedication of the black movement to ending racism that makes "by any means necessary" something more than a rhetorical slogan. When priorities are diffuse, diverse, or conflicting, the means or procedures by which decisions are made often become as important as, or even more important than, the content of the political issues. Further, liberal philosophers like John Dewey have argued that, in the chain of public action, every means to an end is also an end or goal itself at some point in the cycle. From such a framework, liberals have come to view the procedures or rules of the "political game" as the essence of the democratic system.[24]

Malcolm X's expression "by any means necessary" was therefore a calculated attack on this liberal position and its implicit sanction of the racial *status quo.* Third world people have pointed out that an explicit policy of racial discrimination has not been the primary means by which they have been excluded from various institutions or denied power and autonomy therein. Today, the mechanisms and procedures of admission, hiring, promotion, and decision making, the distribution of income, and the allocation of other resources are much more effective in this regard. On campus, racial confrontations have often erupted because the procedural mechanisms of faculty decision making (secrecy, the slow movement through a series of bureaucratic channels) created a climate of suspicion and a pace of response that could not satisfy the zeal and seriousness of ethnic students. Strikes and confrontational forms of protest attempt to change the means of decision making to the advantage of excluded and relatively powerless groups, and these pressures have usually speeded up the resolution of concrete issues. The faculty, on the other hand, tends to resist negotiation in a situation seen as threatening or involving undue pressure. The widely publicized events at Cornell illustrate these attitudes. There black students seized Straight Hall, and administrators negotiated a settlement of their grievances in exchange for their exodus from the building. In its first meeting the faculty refused to recognize this agreement, many feeling that they were being blackmailed by threats of violence.*

* The event was overdramatized by the media's emphasis on the blacks' possession of guns; the photo of armed students was flashed around the world. Two days later,

The presence of more than token numbers of third world students has had special effects on the climate of the classroom as well as on the larger politics of the university.* Minority students, especially blacks, have proved to be extremely vocal in classroom discussions. Among the various student groups at Berkeley they are probably the most likely to challenge a professor's lecture, breaking away from the prevailing patterns of passive absorption and indifference to the form and content of the classroom monologue. Third world people are particularly alert to any implications of racism in a professor's interpretation and presentation of social issues. By now there is probably not a sociology department on a major campus in the country whose chairman has not faced a caucus of very upset black students protesting the overt or covert racism of a particular course or professor.[26] Not only professors, but white students also are regularly challenged for their approach to the issues under discussion and for their racial attitudes. In the past five years at Berkeley I have noted a tendency for whites to refrain from a frank and vigorous presentation of their views, generally out of deference to the superior credentials in life experience of third world students; but in some cases they are intimidated by the possibility of being attacked as racists.

The third world presence has catalyzed many lethargic lecture halls. Though the negative implications for free discussion should not be overlooked, the reactions of the faculty are my central interest. I would guess that only a minority have had the security of personality and flexibility of style to respond well to these classroom confrontations. As professors, we tend to be defensive in the face of challenges to our authority, particularly when students question our competence to expound upon a topic within the purview of our presumed expertise. White students, especially the political radicals, also question faculty interpretations of social science problems, but third world students—and particularly the

after a long student convocation, the faculty agreed to uphold the *entente* with the blacks. Some professors, however, continued to feel that the week of disruption to the orderly procedures of campus life had dealt a death blow to academic freedom and the university itself; several eminent professors resigned.[25]

* These effects are probably most felt in the social sciences and the humanities, and it is sometimes difficult to separate the impact of third world students from effects of other shifts in student behavior and attitude during the past few years.

blacks—do so with an aggressive manner and an ethnic flavor which is more abrasive to the professorial mentality.

The most intense expression of this conflict involves those white professors who teach black history, race relations, social problems, poverty, and a host of other courses where racial issues are central. The influx of third world students has radically changed the teaching atmosphere in these fields. When there were few or no third world students, it was possible for the professor to do his academic thing, analyzing racial problems in the abstract, dissecting ethnic groups, their histories, communities, culture, and social movements, as if under a microscope. On the Berkeley campus a number of developments converged in the spring of 1968 to change this situation: the murders of Martin Luther King and Bobby Hutton, the local Panther leader, the rise in black enrollment, and increased acceptance of black power and third world perspectives. The white professor's prevailing monopoly of the analysis of racial conflict and third world experience was seen (and correctly, in my view) as a reflection of academic colonialism.*

The presence of students of color in the classroom and as political actors threatening the disruption of business-as-usual on campus, has had a disquieting effect on many professors. In the late 1960s liberals began to realize that these students were different

* In the spring of 1968 I was teaching an experimental course in race and culture with two other white professors. Though that was the last quarter in which there was still little direct challenge to our authority, the restlessness and tension in the classroom communicated to us the inauthenticity of a race relations course without instructors from racially oppressed groups. The students, black and white—there were still few Chicanos at Berkeley and Asian-American identity remained relatively undeveloped—wanted to hear about the big issues: the black and Mexican communities; the black family, which Moynihan's report had converted into a loaded subject; black culture; and trends within the third world movements. As white instructors we could only "know" about these crucial matters from books, newspapers, and second-hand accounts. The areas in which our expertise seemed legitimate, expostulating theories of race relations, the dynamics of prejudice and racism, were the more abstract and academic issues, which did not grab the students' attention. Pragmatically oriented young people today are also more interested in discussing solutions than intellectual analyses, and our training and situation made us as incompetent to focus on strategies of change as to inject passion and moral indignation into the classroom situation. My own adaptation to this situation has been to use books by third world writers, to deemphasize the lecture format, to encourage students to organize project groups, often ethnically based, and to invite people of color to lecture. But these adjustments have been only partly successful, which underscores the need for both the rapid integration of the teaching faculty and the establishment of ethnic studies departments.

from whites in some important respects despite their own universalistic theories. For the most part, the white professor has not appreciated or respected these differences. But confronted by outspoken third world students, he began to recognize in himself attitudes that were very similar to the "prejudices" he had always associated with less educated, less sophisticated people. In short (though there are important exceptions) many if not most faculty found that they didn't like third world students and were not particularly interested in teaching them. In the abstract, and from a distance, the liberal professor had "identified" with blacks and their causes, but in the flesh he was often offended by their style, their demands, and a conception of education that differed from his own. It appears that this sympathy and identification had often stemmed from paternalistic motives, the perhaps natural desire of an educator to "help" people progress along his own path, to mold the minority student in his image. Those who had participated in programs to bring in third world students expected that they would respond with gratitude and appreciation. But paternalism was no longer accepted nor gratitude dispensed; the racist games of an earlier period were finished.

In many graduate departments that had "brought in" third world students, liberal professors (and even some radicals) were disturbed by their hostility or apparent indifference to them and their courses. They assumed they were being avoided because they were white, and they searched for techniques to bring about better communication. In fact, the tensions were often due to conflicts in style, personality, politics, and professional methodology rather than to skin color per se. Many third world students found it difficult and unrewarding to relate to professors who were "uptight," overintellectual, and excessively professional in their concerns and mannerisms. And, indeed, this type of professor, perhaps the modal one in today's academy, often appeared to me to be extremely uncomfortable in interaction with students of color.

A typical response to this situation was to view the students as less able and less well prepared than whites, rather than different in their interests and reasons for attending the university. The third world student was seen as anti-intellectual, rather than as being concerned with the fusion of reason and emotion, ideas and social relevance.[27] The great fear of the faculty was that large numbers of minority students would result in the lowering of standards. Obviously, mistakes in admission decisions were made, and there were and are some students who lack either the aptitude or the interest to succeed in a particular field. But this reality inevitably became contaminated through interaction with the classic dynamics of racism. Thus a third world student who was dumb or hopelessly conflicted raised questions about the ability of nonwhites in general and the success of the "special program," while white students who were dumb and messed up were just dumb and messed up, their race or ethnicity never the issue. The professor also faced dilemmas of a "double standard" concerning classroom response, grading, and criticism of papers. Instead of offering a frank evaluation and grading the minority student down when he felt it was deserved, too often he eased up. This tendency was quickly perceived by the students, who resented the patronization involved. Of course racial games were not played by one side only. Many third world students became adept at hustling for grades, working on the professor's guilt, confusion, and general ignorance of the cultural patterns and survival techniques of the racially oppressed.*

Conflicting Conceptions of Racism

The conflict in perspective between white faculty and third world students is related to contrasting conceptions of racial oppression. Though both groups talk about racism, they talk past each other. Contending interests typically define crucial terms in ways that reflect their group position and further its collective needs. Since the Kerner report introduced the idea to white liberals, racism has become perhaps the most loaded and overloaded word in public discourse. Militants expand its meaning in an attempt to force

* It must be pointed out that race and racism are not the only matters involved in these conflicts: many minority professors also have been critical of the third world students and their politics. At Cornell a black economist resigned because he felt that university judiciary procedures had been too lenient in the case of a black student. And some of the strongest attacks on Afro-American studies programs, particularly in their "separatist" tendencies, have come from such liberal blacks as Bayard Rustin, Kenneth Clark, and Roy Wilkins.[28]

far-reaching changes upon institutions reluctant to share power with the oppressed. Those who want to contain the pace and style of racial revolution evoke its stigma to attack radical reforms that appear to deviate from accepted procedures. Thus on the campus, proposals for special consideration of racial minorities are often viewed as racism-in-reverse by traditional faculty, just as many liberals experience the most militant trends in the black power and nationalist movements as black racism. The Kerner report may have contributed to this state of affairs by failing to define and analyze racism seriously. But the realities of American racism are full of complexity and ambiguity, and in situations of group and value conflict, words will become political weapons.

I am placing considerable stress on what might appear to be simply a semantic problem. This is because I think the racist label, aimed at individual professors and the university as a whole, has contributed significantly to the faculty's disaffection with the student movement. Of course, if the shoe fits, wear it. Much of the hurt must have come because the validity of the charge was understood or intuited at some level of consciousness; the sensitivity would be the greater because the professor prided himself on his equalitarianism and his sympathy with the underdog. But many professors could make no sense of these allegations because they were working with a totally different idea. Particularly galling to the liberal was the militant's tendency to castigate all whites as prima facie racist (rationalized by the idea that embattled people cannot afford the luxury of making distinctions).* An eminent professor of left-liberal persuasion at Cornell compared this phenomenon to the indiscriminate branding of people as Communists during the McCarthy era.[30]

The liberal professor tends to define racism in a much more restricted sense than do people of color and white radicals today. For him, racism connotes conscious acts, where there is an intent to

* I personally have found that third world militants who use this rhetoric do make distinctions among various whites in their day-to-day relations and political work. One of the problems of the white response to blacks is that we take their rhetoric too seriously, but we do not take them seriously enough as individuals and groups with specific needs and interests. Thus Friedland and Edwards note that Cornell professors were hung-up behind the black student assertion that their demands were nonnegotiable, at the same time that negotiations were taking place.[29]

hurt or degrade or disadvantage others because of their color or ethnicity. It implies bigotry and prejudice, hatred and hostility, concrete individual acts, and clear-cut organizational policies of exclusion or segregation on the basis of race. He does not consider the all-white or predominantly white character of an occupation or an institution in itself to be racism.* He does not understand the notion of covert racism, that white people maintain a system of racial oppression by acts of omission, indifference, and failure to challenge the *status quo.* The fact that he leads his daily life in the ambience of an all-white department and neighborhood does not seem racist to him, because he did not choose his colleagues or neighbors for their color. For many liberals the notion of institutional racism is obscurantist propaganda; in another parallel to the McCarthy era they resent its implications of "guilt by association." **

The third world definition of racism tends to be broader and

* Only 38 percent of the professors in the Carnegie sample agreed that "most American colleges and universities are racist whether they mean to be or not." Sixty percent disagreed. More surprising to me was the finding that a majority (52 percent) disagreed with the conclusion of the Kerner report, that "the main cause of Negro riots in the cities is white racism." Only at the highest prestige universities did a slight majority (52 percent) accept the Kerner findings.

These attitudes underscore the significance of an official position paper of Northwestern University, in which a group of administrators, professors, and students boldly noted that campus's institutional racism. Evidently the students in pushing for the following statement were testing Sartre's dictum, applied by Stokely Carmichael to white America, that "man cannot condemn himself":

> Northwestern University recognizes that throughout its history it has been an institution of the white establishment. This is not to gainsay that many members of its administration, its faculty, and its student body have engaged themselves in activities directed to the righting of racial wrongs. It is also true that for many years a few Blacks have been members of its administration, faculty, and student body. But the fact remains that the University in its overwhelming character has been a white institution. This it has had in common with virtually all institutions of higher learning in the United States. Its members have also had in common with the white community in America, in greater or lesser degree, the racist attitudes that have prevailed historically in the society and which continue to constitute the most important social problem of our times. This University with other institutions must share responsibility for the continuance over many past years of these racist attitudes.[31]

** At certain universities many professors bristle at this term because they see their campuses, Cornell, Berkeley, Stanford, San Francisco State, for example, as well ahead of others in programs relevant to minority students. With the administration already fighting racism, the charge of institutional racism appears as irresponsible rhetorical distortion. From the student standpoint the beginnings of change do not affect the larger picture; the fact that we're more liberal than Columbia or UCLA is irrelevant.

more sociological. It focuses on the society as a whole and on structured relations between people rather than on individual personalities and actions. From this standpoint, the university is racist because people of color are and have been so systematically excluded from full and equal participation and power—as students, professors, administrators, and, particularly, in the historical definition of the character of the institution and its curriculum. Third world students experience racism in the subtle vibrations that emanate from the climate of the classroom and the quadrangle, in the university's dispassionate, intellectual interest in poor people and their problems, and in a myriad of other specifics—that the custodians and dormitory maids are usually black, for example. The students start from the premise that the society and its basic institutions are all based on the dominant position of whites and the subjugation of people of color; in an essentially racist culture all people share racist assumptions and beliefs in varying degrees of intensity and sophistication. Although for many professors third world protest has been an educational challenge, which has deepened their understanding of racism, the majority have probably been antagonized by the blanket condemnation of themselves and their institutions that is implied in the students' usage. Perhaps the faculty feels even more affronted because, as a group of scholars and educators, it believes that it possesses the legitimate monopoly on the correct interpretation of words and ideas, including changes in such interpretations!

Probably the central demand of black students has been the establishment of an Afro-American Studies Department. Since this falls within the faculty's jurisdiction over curriculum, the setting up of black studies has probably aroused more campus controversy than any other racial issue. The debate over black studies illustrated the great disparity between faculty and student definitions of racism and how it should be eliminated. The two sides in the struggle were coming from totally different places as they invoked divergent conceptions of racism to buttress their arguments. For the liberal professor, the strategic idea has been that of *reverse racism.*

The charge of reverse racism is often used to discredit various projects for preferential treatment. In the university context this means special admissions programs for minority students and deliberate efforts to hire third world faculty and other employees. The classical liberal position holds that color and ethnicity should be irrelevant to all such decisions and that the elimination of overt discrimination is as far as any institution should move toward the goal of racial equality. The error in this view is the assumption that patterns of racial subjugation, the exclusion of people of color from an equitable share of social opportunity, can be eliminated by simply ending discrimination. Since much of racial exclusion is the present-day reflection or residue of past racial discrimination and the disadvantages suffered by peoples of color earlier in their lives, special energies must be expended in an active effort to reverse inequality.[32] Preferential treatment is not racism in reverse because its purpose and goal is not to turn our racial order on its head so that nonwhites will be in the position of dominance. Why administrators have often been able to see this point more readily than professors is again puzzling. The cry of reverse racism is raised not only by white liberals who have been personally dedicated to civil rights and integration; it is more and more raised by conservatives, including professors, who have never raised a finger in the past about white racism. This would seem to confirm the observation made earlier that, in a context of social change, principles originally associated with liberalism become conservative in character, just as many ideas that were once radical are now widely accepted by liberals.

Racism in reverse is a central argument also against black studies programs and other efforts of third world groups to celebrate and develop their culture, their ethnic institutions, and their racial pride and identity. Because a concern with color is in itself supposed to be racist, according to the universalistic *weltanschauung* of the liberal, black consciousness, especially in its militant and more abrasive expressions, is perceived as "black racism." Here, I think, white liberals in general, and many professors in particular, are guilty of a number of sociological misconceptions. The fundamental point is a confusion of racism with *ethnocentrism.* As William Graham Sumner pointed out in his classic *Folkways*, every tribe, ethnic group, and nation tends to feel that its own values, customs, and ways of life are the most natural ones, superior to those of its neighbors. Whereas ethnocentrism can be a component of and a contributor to the systematic racism that would aggressively deny the value and humanity of "lesser peoples," it is not the main cause of racism. The ethnocentric impulse remains strong among other ethnic groups in America. Liberals do not deny Jews, Italians, or even Chinese the right to such attitudes, but when developed by Afro-Americans it is offensive, another example of the truly racist double standard. The experience of slavery and the system of racial subordination that followed Emancipation weakened or virtually eliminated the healthy ethnocentrism of Africans and Afro-Americans. Thus from the past to the present the most significant racism that exists among black people in America is not the antiwhite racism that liberals react to, but an antiblack racism derived from the larger society and culture, that is, assumptions and beliefs about their own incapacities. From this perspective, black studies, black cultural movements, and black institution building are antiracist and not racist, for they are efforts to recoup the losses in group integrity and ethnocentric pride that white racist America has historically undermined.

I am not suggesting that there is no racism at all in the third world movements, or among students in particular. The example that has most bothered me is a tendency on the part of some black students to refuse to read books by whites. The interest in black writers and the insight that many students learn best from professors with a similar cultural experience have led in some cases to the feeling that the goal of learning from any source of knowledge that might prove useful is not applicable to black people.* This strikes me as not only racist, but foolish and anti-intellectual. Harold Cruse has put it well: "All race hate is self-defeating in the long run because it distorts the critical faculties."[33] But my example illustrates another fallacy of the liberal's alarmist equation of white and black racism. Because black people are for the most part without effective power, black

* It is also a reaction to the exclusion of the black perspective from the university curriculum, a historic pattern that still remains in some institutions and departments. An informant in Berkeley's School of Education tells me that no white professor has included a book by a black or Chicano author on a required or suggested reading list in the past few years, despite the department's emphasis on urban and minority problems.

racism only hurts blacks themselves, though in the short run it can yield psychic comfort. White racism, on the other hand, obviously harms people of color and not primarily whites.

Liberals often fail to recognize this difference because their perspective emphasizes attitudes and intentions, underplaying issues of group power. Attitudes may be similar, but since people of color lack power they cannot impose their will on whites in the same way that white power has been imposed on them for centuries. If we recognize that racism is a system of domination as well as a complex of beliefs and attitudes, and that this objective dimension of racial oppression is the more determining one, the separatist impulse in third world movements cannot be seen as analogous to white racism.

Though most professors have reacted negatively and with defensiveness to such ideas and to the new claims addressed to "their" jurisdiction and authority, the faculty of many major universities has not stood pat in its views on race and the role of higher education in the process of social change. Everywhere there are college teachers who have become educated about racial oppression in America, understanding and, to a degree, accepting the perspectives of third world students.[34] Others, and this includes a number of older civil rights era liberals, have been antagonized by the action, style, rhetoric, and goals of black student movements; they have reacted with disgust and hostility much as have the "backlashers"of Middle America. But the most common response may be another. The modal professor, liberal in his attitudes, finds himself accepting principles and solutions that are not mutually consistent. The liberal consensus of the 1950s is shattered, not only as a coherent social philosophy, but also in terms of the corporate group that shared the outlook, the liberal center having moved toward the left or toward the right.

Conclusion

Just as the civil rights movement of an earlier period exposed basic problems of American life that transcended race (poverty, the quality of education and of the larger culture), the recent student movement has had an impact on campus life broader than its own goals and the racial relations on which I have focused my analysis. In emphasizing the systematic exclusion of people of color, the third world movement set the stage for the growing reaction against the university's class elitism and male domination. Though women have been fairly well represented as college undergraduates, their participation in most graduate programs and professional schools has been systematically discouraged. On many campuses today, however, women's liberation groups are challenging this historical pattern; in some situations third world and women's movements find themselves in competition for a limited number of graduate school openings and faculty positions. The white working class also continues to be systematically disadvantaged in higher education, and it is possible, though by no means certain, that significant movements will arise to defend its still unrepresented interests.

The ethnic presence has given new immediacy also to the relation between university education and contemporary life and society outside its walls. On this issue, often trivialized as the "search for relevance," third world groups were preceded by the general student movement, which was predominantly white. But racial minorities have provided a distinctive approach to the problem in their concern with linking both the educational process and their future careers to those ethnic communities that most colleges and universities had either ignored or exploited.

Furthermore, the racial crisis on campus contributed to the overall weakening of the old liberal consensus and to the rearrangement of political perspectives, which is still going on. As I have stressed in this essay, the liberal philosophy on race failed to provide either the general orientation or the specific guidelines to deal with the changing situations of the 1960s. This has been true in the nation as a whole, and on the campus. The racial crisis was only one among many that rendered obsolete old political labels. It is now more and more difficult to characterize specific people as liberal, conservative, radical, or what-have-you. An innovative approach to racial issues may sometimes appear in combination with a hard-line position on traditional academic questions; a professor may be radical on the university's connection with the military and conservative with respect to standards of admission, curriculum, and classroom ceremony.

Finally, a brief consideration of the long-term implications of the changing racial situation within higher education is in order. If current trends continue for the next few years, the proportion of black students on the major campuses will approach the proportion in the general population. Although other third world groups (with the exception of Asian-Americans) are entering at a slower rate, their numbers also will increase. What impact will such a significant presence of people of color have on the university as a whole, on the future course of campus conflict, and on the direction of third world student movements?

Only a fool would try to answer these questions. However alternative outcomes can be examined. At one extreme, it is possible that there will be no significant transformation in the university's organization and charter of purpose and that third world students will be "co-opted" or absorbed into the present system, which will undergo only minor adaptations. If this turns out to be the case, then future sociologists will interpret the racial conflicts of the late 1960s as a transitional phenomenon, which opened up wedges in the educational monolith through which new groups were able to enter. But an opposite outcome also is possible. Students of color, with a growing number of white allies, may continue to hammer at the racist assumptions buttressing the organization, curriculum, and politics inside the university monolith, to the point that serious cracks appear in its structure. The pieces could then be put together in such a way that cultural pluralism, decentralization, and significant space for group self-determination inform a new concept of higher education.

If neither co-optation nor the institutionalization of a genuine pluralism is likely to occur in the period immediately ahead, how will racial protest develop in a situation offering some possibility of compromise between the two poles? The first wave of racial conflict at the major universities has produced victories for third world students, specifically, black or ethnic studies departments and more favorable admission policies. Slower, more incremental gains in the composition of the faculty are next in the offing, as many professors have come to accept the fact that their institutions and they themselves bear the major responsibility for its all-white character, and as the number of ethnic graduate students grows—

for whom, at least at present, the job market has never been more favorable. The question that arises is whether student groups will be relatively satisfied with such reforms and will slow down their political activism, or whether these gains, along with emerging issues, will raise racial conflict to new and more intensified levels.

Thus far the trickling-in of minority (mostly black) faculty seems to have contained militancy. The third world professor or administrator plays a go-between role. To the whites he interprets the students' views and problems; for the students of color he mediates grievances and whenever possible wins concessions from a department or a particular professor. And his availability as a teacher has taken some of the heat off the white faculty. But such middle-man roles are compromising; how long third world faculty will continue to play them is in doubt.[35]

If on some campuses there appears to be a standoff between white faculty and third world students, this is probably only a temporary *modus vivendi.* Also apparent is a retrenchment in the form of an alliance between conservative and liberal professors based on a mutual determination to restore standards and to end past tendencies to make concessions to the demands of students—white as well as colored. But the future of campus race relations probably depends on other uncertainties beyond the political competence of the professoriat. One factor is the larger political context, both national and statewide, and its meaning for higher education. Matters of resources and budget will be important here; a militant student response is to be expected whenever funds are cut back, as Reagan almost carried out with respect to the California State Colleges' Educational Opportunity Program in 1971. At the same time, a repressive national atmosphere tends to take some of the steam out of student activism, as the first three years of Nixon's administration indicates. But events on campus will be most affected by race relations in the nation as a whole and the choices that third world students make about their own social and political direction. On both these counts, the situation is extremely dynamic at present.

*Radical Students**

JAN E. DIZARD

The current generation of American student radicalism had its genesis in the late 1950's and early 1960's, in some measure coincidental with and in much larger measure as a direct consequence of the assault southern blacks were launching on the legal edifice of racism. Contemporary student radicalism is, thus, very much a product of the crisis in race relations. As might be expected, considerations of race and racism are central to current radical thought, in terms of both the radicals' diagnosis of the ills of society and their active attempts to improve society. At the same time, however, relations between white student radicals and blacks have been anything but harmonious. The difficulties, too, are a product of race relations in America—the gulf of suspicion and hostility created by centuries of oppression (and manifest in both the oppressed and the oppressor) is not easily bridged, even for those who are committed to change. In this sense, white student radicals have had thrust upon them a complex and frustrating role in the racial conflict that has marked our recent history—they are offspring of that conflict; they are actors in the conflict; and they are also articulate commentators on the conflict and its likely resolution.

The task of analyzing white student radicals and their relations with black people is not made any easier by the diversity of the student radicals themselves. The term "student radical" covers an enormous range of individuals—from teenagers in high school to graduate students in their early to middle thirties. Moreover, many properly seen as "student radicals" are technically not students at all, though their identifications are largely with those in university or college communities and they typically live in or around the student "ghettos" of Berkeley, Ann Arbor, Cambridge, and the host of other similar enclaves. And, needless to say, although race is a central preoccupation for most radicals, considerable differences obtain as to what the ideologies of various radicals say about race. What links together such an array of individuals and conflicting ideologies, making it feasible to speak of radical students as a group, is a fundamental set of attitudes toward American society. These attitudes, held more or less in common within the group, are reinforced by a network of crosscutting associations, similarities in major aspects of life experience (e.g. college),[1] and the network of radical and underground presses that keep people aware of "what's happening."

Since radical students, unlike most other groups within the white community, are both analysts of, as well as participants in, contemporary racial conflicts, we must take care to examine each role carefully. The two are, of course, intimately connected. The experiences of whites in the Civil Rights Movement demanded a continual series of modifications in the interpretations which the student radicals made of American society; and these modifications in turn called for shifts in the nature of the relationships radical students maintained with black people. Although we cannot here go into the historical detail necessary to fully unravel the complexities of this interaction between analysis and action, the major lines of development can be set forth briefly.[2]

The initial impulses that prompted white youths in the South to join the civil rights movement in the early 1960's were less ideological than they were moral. Among the few who actively proselytized for radical political theory and analysis, the absence of ideology was a matter of principle—advancing an ideology was regarded as the surest way to relive the sectarian squabbles that had sapped the vigor of earlier generations of American radicals. This disdain for ideology was ultimately codified in what remains one of the most inspired documents of the student left—The Port Huron Statement of SDS. For the vast majority of the young radicals, however, the lack of ideology was a fact of life, not a principle. Evils were abundantly present and one needed, it seemed, no theories or theoretically derived programs of action to see that poverty, racism, and war needed to be opposed. Moreover, even for many of the most radical students, there existed in the early days of the Kennedy administration the conviction that the coalition of liberals, labor, youth, and blacks could unite, and within the system solve through reform the great problems confronting the country then—and confronting the country still.[3]

Thus it was that the early protests of the New Left were largely *ad hoc.* The student radicals confronted what they believed was evil where it was most obvious and they expected a national movement to grow out of these confrontations. This movement, would, in turn, strengthen the hand of the liberals in the White House and Congress who would then implement the necessary reforms. This was the primary strategy of emergent student radicalism. Events were allowed to provide their own linkages and so the issues dramatized were never terribly abstract. In a technical sense, these early activists were not "radicals," if by that term we take radicals to be those who see specific problems as manifestations of a larger systemic crisis, the resolution of which requires the thorough transformation of the social order. The activists were self-consciously reformers (although for many of the new activists this was a pragmatic adaptation to the fact that no radical movement was then in existence); they had not yet become radicals.

Activism, however, soon began to turn into radicalism. In the late 1950's only a small group of young radicals existed but they nonetheless managed to keep alive the central theme of radicalism—anticapitalism and pro-socialism—primarily through the now defunct journal *Studies on the Left.* But, as it developed, it was the logic of events, the lessons learned from demonstrations, more than abstract socialist analysis that propelled the activists leftward. In counseling a "go slow" and "be realistic" approach, even the most liberal politicians appeared to student radicals to undermine the movement for equality. It soon became clear, to both black and white student activists, that desegregation of public facilities represented only the tip of the iceberg. They also realized that the hoped-for coalition of liberal and labor groups within the Democratic Party was not adequate to the tasks facing it and that a long-term struggle, not *ad hoc* demonstrations, was going to be necessary.

The practical experiences of the northern white students in the South had other, complementary effects on the process of radicalization. Foremost was the realization that racism was not a disease confined to southern whites. Participation of white students in the southern struggles was most often a summer vacation project: They returned to their homes and schools in the North transformed people. Part of the transformation was, by all accounts, a heightened sense of the hypocrisy that Northerners indulged in as they condemned the South while they ignored the systematic brutalization practiced on blacks in the North. Close and intimate contact with black activists destroyed the convenient liberal rationales of "qualifications" and "motivations" and the like that had long been used to explain why blacks fared so poorly even in the enlightened North. What started out as a "Southern Problem" was now seen as a truly national failure.

Returning to school also presented rude shocks for many. Long accustomed to excelling without much questioning of the criteria of excellence or the reasons for aspiring to excellence in terms of those criteria, activists suddenly had questions about how society works (or doesn't work) that were in no way dealt with in any of their coursework. By now, ambivalent over traditional career goals, they began to seek a new "relevancy" in their educations that would help them make sense of the world in which they found themselves while at the same time providing for the exploration of new ways, apart from traditional careers, of relating to and changing that society. Needless to say, the Academy did not exactly welcome this disconcerting thirst for new knowledge. Disenchantment simply deepened, culminating in the Free Speech Movement at Berkeley in the fall of 1964 and the countless subsequent student demonstrations whose goals have been a New Academy.

Participation in the civil rights movement thus deepened commitment to change and, perhaps more important, created intellectual needs that could be met only by breaking away from conventional analysis and cultivating a radical critique of American society. Students had begun to move from reform to radical politics. As we have said, this shift did not result from abstract analysis but, rather, it grew directly out of experiences of trying to change aspects of the society. Opposition, especially the opposition from national political leaders whose rhetoric had done much to legitimate the early protests, demanded reappraisal of the political possibilities facing the student radicals. This reappraisal quickly became a sweeping indictment of the economy, the political order, and the entire social order of American society.[4]

By August 1963, all these trends were in full force and the Movement was on the verge of going its own way, separate from the liberal coalition that had served, up until then, as the dominant public voice of dissent. The historic 1963 March on Washington was the last event of this era—black and white radicals had begun to turn away from erstwhile liberal allies who had urged patience and cooperation with the Kennedy administration. By the summer of 1963 many in SNCC and SDS had started the long process of searching for and developing constituencies independent of the "liberal-labor" coalition that had backed Kennedy's election in 1960.[5] Voter registration drives were accelerated in the South; in the North, SDS launched organizing drives in twelve cities where large concentrations of poor blacks and whites were present. The vision of a "new politics" was dawning, based on widely dispersed groups of the disinherited and disenfranchised which the New Left's analysis at that point suggested were the prime sources for a mass base supportive of radical transformation.[6]

This associated shift in tactics and analysis placed white radicals in more direct contact with black people than had been usual during the early period of mobilizing for demonstrations. Up to this point, whites had more or less been sheltered from much of the ever present hostility toward whites that black communities have sustained as a condition of their own survival. This hostility—and passivity and superficial compliance are characteristic of it—has typically been expressed in roundabout ways that, themselves, acted to obscure real feelings of suspicion and mistrust. But however disguised the hostility, whites were having difficulties getting along with blacks, especially non-Movement black people. At the same time, the young black students in SNCC were discovering the potential strengths of black people, and many were rediscovering traditions that they themselves had largely rejected for the middle-class world black college students usually entered. The combination proved fateful for the coalition between white radicals and blacks. By 1965, it became apparent to both blacks and whites that racism, past and present, had created two separate communities and that it was the task of blacks themselves to consolidate and mobilize their own. With considerable reluctance and anguish, the movement split again, this time more on racial than on ideological grounds.[7]

By the time of this split and the emergence of black power as the dominant rallying cry of the Movement's black wing, student radicalism had increased its influence on the youth of the nation. Its radicalism had become much more than *ad hoc* responses to injustice, and with the escalation of the Vietnam War in 1965, student radicals were making a bid to become a serious political force in America. While the evolution of the New Left was by no means complete at that point, still, the major foundations for subsequent developments had been well founded by this time.

Thus, we can turn now to a closer look at the specific views of the black liberation struggle that have informed the student Left. There are essentially two connected issues with which student radicals had to come to terms and with which we shall deal in the remainder of this paper. The first was to articulate an analysis of American society that would solve the constituency problem faced by the student radicals, and the second was to overcome, if possible, the barriers to effective cooperation between blacks and the student radicals.

From the very earliest eruption of the current radical stirrings among white college youth, student radicals confronted an essentially passive white community. The classical radical constituency, the industrial working class, appeared complacent and self-seeking, certainly anything but the militant and selfless proletarians that earlier generations of American radicals thought they had found in the labor organizing struggles of the '20's and '30's. The educated middle class, the origin of the student radicals, was also quiescent, concerned more with consumption than with peace or social justice. The civil rights movement seemed, for a while, to have changed all this, as the dormant liberal forces began to mobilize behind black demands for an end to segregation. As we have seen, the cooperation between liberals and the student radicals did not work for long. The collapse of the coalition once again made it mandatory for the student radicals to seek out a new constituency.

The need to relate to and incorporate social strata in the larger society who are, ideally at least, more numerous and thus more capable of exerting decisive influence on the shape of politics than are students themselves has given rise to some of the most cogent analysis that has emanated from the student radicals.[8] Here, of course, our focus is specifically on the relationships of radical students to black people and, therefore, we will not discuss this analysis in its general form. The radical students now saw quite clearly that their power to shape politics in the larger society was extremely limited. Though their Movement had grown rapidly, by 1965 they still comprised only a small proportion of college-aged youth. Moreover, any leverage they could exert was limited, at least at that time, to their capacity to dramatize issues through demonstrations, media publicity, and local organizing projects whose objective was mobilization of specific populations around specific grievances. In the case of all these actions, the hope was to stir larger numbers to action around the critiques and the essentially reformist programs that their plans projected.[9] What was requisite, clearly, were groups in the population who could demand more than momentary attention by virtue of their capacity to seriously affect the interests of those who held power in the society—corporate leaders and members of the executive branch of the federal government.

For obvious reasons, black people constituted such a group. Not only was their condition in America wretched—and that alone was enough for the radical students—but also, the experiences of the preceding ten years of civil rights activity had proven that even reforms which might appear superficial required massive mobilization to dislodge the powerful interests that, if left undisturbed, would simply perpetuate the gross inequity that has characterized America's treatment of her black citizens. It is not just that individuals held racist attitudes; more important was the fact that major institutions were committed, directly and indirectly, in whole or in part, to racism.

The analysis made by the radical students suggested, then, that the very stability of the political economy of the US rested, albeit in sometimes complex and indirect ways, on keeping black people in a position subordinate to that of whites. The lessons of the Mississippi Freedom Democratic Party's attempt to gain recognition from the Democratic Party convention in 1964 indicated that the major parties in America maintain seemingly irreversible commitments to constituencies which will not tolerate substantive moves toward racial equality. Thus, little more than token gains could be expected from the political process as it is. Organized labor and the large corporations dominating the economic landscape of American society came to be seen in terms of an unwritten gentleman's agreement which rests, at least in part, on the willingness of both to exclude blacks from important sectors of the industrial labor force. As a result, minority employment schemes were constantly frustrated. The myriad of small businessmen and merchants, shut out from the major arenas of profit-making by the huge corporations, were kept within the fold of consensus politics by having available to them the opportunity to reap exorbitant rents, high prices for inferior products, and usurious interest rates from the captive market of the black community. In short, to the student radicals, there appeared no substantial segment of the white population, save poor whites, who did not see their own interests challenged by even the most modest of black demands for equality. The conclusion was obvious—black people could not achieve equality in a society such as ours, dominated by a corporate capitalism dependent at all levels on a stability based on keeping blacks "in their place."

The black uprisings during the summers of 1964, '65, '66, and '67 seemed to confirm this analysis. Instead of meeting legitimate demands for justice with even minor reforms, the powerful responded with either symbolic and ultimately ineffectual gestures or with straightforwardly repressive measures. The result was to widen the contradictions and to harden lines. In short, attempts at amelioration generally failed to stem the assertiveness of blacks held down for so long.

But, even for all this, blacks remained a difficult constituency for the white student radicals. On the one hand, the latter were up against a growing sense of nationalism that rather explicitly ruled out collaboration with whites; on the other, the white radicals felt increasingly estranged from those black groups whose goals remained integration. It was not that the student radicals were not committed to integration; they were—and I daresay they remain so—and this was the basis for much of the ambivalence they felt toward the moves within SNCC and CORE toward nationalism and the exclusion of whites.[10] Divergence from the integrationist thesis came not over the goal of integration *per se* but, rather, over the question "Integration into what?" The white students saw the old-line civil rights groups, such as the NAACP and the Urban League, as naïvely uncritical of the dominant society, at best, or, at worst (and this was the most popular position), as cooperating with established corporate and political élites in an effort to defuse the potential radicalism of black demands.

Of special importance in the critique of black groups that remained oriented to integration was the notion that these groups went out of their way to avoid contact with ongoing grass-roots organizations of black and white people and avoided involving rank-and-file blacks in the struggles for equality. Somehow, the New Left argued, the masses of blacks and whites had to be reached directly if more than superficial changes in society were to be made. At every turn, it seemed to the student radicals, the integrationists discouraged such involvement, preferring to work through the courts (NAACP) or behind the scenes in private negotiations (Urban League) or through occasional mass demonstrations that left no self-sustaining structures or goals around which large numbers of people could sustain the struggle (SCLC).[11]

It was felt that the victories thus won seemed regularly to prove pyrrhic. In the first place, consolidation of gains or concessions won on paper required mobilized masses of people who could continue to press for implementation. As a result of the discouragement of such mobilization, the most that was achieved were token gains—a few blacks hired here and there in previously all-white companies, a few conspicuous black students enrolled at once all-white schools, and so on. Moreover, to proceed in such a fashion ran the twin dangers of perpetuating apathy ("Let someone else do it") and/or lulling people into the illusion that genuine progress was being made, thereby reducing militancy and the likelihood that even the moderate gains made would be consolidated, much less advanced.[12]

Beyond this important disagreement over tactics between the student radicals and the integrationists, there was in evidence a deep disappointment with the fact that the integrationists—SCLC being the lone, though hesitating exception—were reluctant to entertain any critique of the dominant society that went beyond the issues of discrimination and racism. (Even with SCLC, it took two years of agonizing before Martin Luther King was willing to publicly declare his opposition to the Vietnam War and to spell out the relationship between that war and the subjugation of blacks in the United States.) As a result of the narrowness of program as well as the élitist organizational principles of the integrationist groups, the student radicals' relations with them steadily grew worse and private misgivings soon became public criticism.

At the same time, however, relations with the more militant black groups had also grown difficult, if not impossible, on all but an individual basis. SNCC and CORE had come to see that only a well-organized and militant black *community* could possibly stand up to the challenges facing blacks—and, they argued, whites, whether radical or not, simply had no positive contribution to make to this effort. Blacks had to act themselves and by themselves in order to create an independent black force for political change. The student radicals could follow the logic here and their initial responses were favorable and supportive. There were, to be sure, misgivings, not so much about the need for blacks to organize themselves as about their own abilities to relate effectively to the new agenda. After all, experiences in the South had made obvious the difficulties that many whites had in relating successfully to non-Movement blacks. Within the newly emerging frame of reference, blacks were to organize blacks and white radicals were to organize in white communities around the demands of black people as well as the needs that the white communities themselves had. But it was precisely the lack of a clearcut white constituency for the white student radical that created dependence upon the black community in the first place.

Initially seen as a tactical division of labor, black nationalism soon increased to account for further splits within both the black and white sections of the Movement. Some blacks held to the logistical interpretation of nationalism and were thus willing to entertain joint programs with white radicals (SNCC for a time; more recently the Black Panther Party has expressed this position). For others (most notably, CORE from among the "old civil rights groups" as well as a host of more localized groups such as the Los Angeles-based US led by Ron Karenga), nationalism came to mean a very different thing, most easily summarized as the development of institutions within the black community that parallelled those of the white community—including calls for black capitalism. Needless to say, white student radicals greeted this latter development with anything but enthusiasm—not just because their help was shunned, but because they could not support what they saw as bourgeois nationalist goals.[13]

This lack of "enthusiasm" for the growing nationalism among black activists was rarely aired publicly.[14] The demise, to all purposes, of SNCC had left the radical students temporarily without a viable counterpart within the black community. The theoretical basis for a critique of this nascent nationalism was available—black nationalism simply had no program capable of wresting power, economic or political, from dominant whites and, as such, could at best carve out only minor niches in the administrative labyrinth which the dominant society sets up to supervise and control blacks. But the critique was not forthcoming. The failure of the white student radicals to articulate a program independent of the black nationalists was, I think, a direct result of the fact that the nationalists were then the most vociferous representatives of black discontent. White radicals knew they had to relate to this discontent and were thus unwilling to attack the nationalist position for fear of losing all contact with blacks.

The student radicals in general abdicated their leadership role with respect to white students and, in the years 1966 to 1968, were essentially led on issues of race by an increasingly reformist nationalism.[15] Cynicism and despair too often resulted as white students supported black demands about which they often had deep but unexpressed reservations. The radical students should have been the agents for the publicizing of these uncertainties, if only to deepen understanding of and sympathy for the issues being raised. The Movement had reached the point where fundamental honesty between blacks and whites was virtually nonexistent. Judgment was suspended and distrust and mutual recrimination grew apace.

Concerned with a resolution of their predicament, radical whites discovered Malcolm X—*after* his assassination. Here was someone who combined, after his split with the Nation of Islam, a deep sense of nationalism with an expansive vision of a new order in which blacks and whites could create a more humane community. With this discovery, the considerable critical powers of the student radicals began to manifest themselves in public. This dovetailed with the rise of the Black Panther party. The Panthers, as we suggested above, represented the re-emergence of a "tactical nationalism" and thus opened the door to cooperation with white student radicals. The now greatly enlarged ranks of student radicals began immediately to respond—a clear indication of their earlier ambivalence over and dissatisfaction with the antiwhite nationalism that had prevailed for some time.[16]

If a rapprochement had begun, it still remains far from complete. The Black Panthers themselves have tolerated little criticism and the student radicals, still plagued by the problem of constituency, were largely unwilling to assert themselves on racial issues in their own terms. The divisions within the black community—the old-line integrationists, the black nationalists, and the much more universalistic revolutionary nationalists like the Black Panthers—have allowed for much more open discussion within the New Left, but an independent position has yet to be clearly stated. The result has been, as Julius Lester suggested recently, that both radical whites and blacks have been trapped in some extremely compromised positions.[17] Even if one assumes, as many on the student Left do today, that the uniqueness of contemporary America has created circumstances in which blacks will lead the struggle for a revolutionary new society, the question remains, "Which blacks should one follow and on what terms?" In short, there is no escaping the need for the student Left to handle the issue of black liberation much more concretely than it has yet done.

As I have suggested at several points in this discussion, the student Left has not evolved an independent position on black liberation—except, obviously, to conclude that it is compulsory and that it cannot be achieved without eliminating inequality in general and, specifically, without drastic changes in the American economy and polity—because they depend upon blacks for a constituency. Up to now we have given, I think, only a partial explanation as to why a constituency beyond students and young people themselves is a necessity. Only part of the answer lies in the objective political requisites mentioned earlier. The other part rests in the nature of the student radicals themselves. I do not propose here to discuss the student Left's psychology, since this has been done elsewhere by others;[18] rather, I am interested in looking a bit more closely at the process of radicalization undergone by many of the new radicals, and, from this, I will go on to explore how the student radicals have come to perceive the world as they have.

The student radicals originally were mobilized essentially around other peoples' oppression—most notably, of course, black peoples' continuing poverty and subjugation. To be sure, more personal concerns were also a factor—they always are—but the general character of early involvement has been based on a deep sense of moral outrage at what was being done to others. It was not long, however, before perspectives began to change. Part of the effect of the experiences we have outlined above was to create, piece by piece, a sense of one's own oppression and need for liberation. This development—from a commitment to relieving others' to a commitment to freeing oneself—has been a continuing feature of the New Left throughout the last half of the 1960's and the early '70's. It found its earliest expression in the discovery of the "Student as Nigger"[19] and the correlative demand, paralleling the cry for black power, for "student power." The more recent development of a movement around women's liberation is equally an outgrowth of the process whereby an ever broader critique of the institutions and culture of American society has come to be felt in specific ways by the student radicals themselves.

In a very real sense, this process represents a turning inward and, thus, at least a partial solution to the constituency impasse that we have been discussing. That is, as the student radicals began to discover the ways in which the society has stifled their own aspirations and attempted to repress their own ideas and experiments with alternative life styles, modes of education, and modes of political expression, they began to see young people in general as their primary constituency. The process has continued beyond this point, to produce more delimited constituencies, some of which are indeed potentially large—e.g., women—and others that are quite narrowly defined—e.g., specific occupational groups as well as groups which are deviant from the cultural norms of the larger society, as the Gay Liberation Front. In other words, as the radicals' analysis of the social ills of contemporary society expanded, the list of "victims" was also expanded and the radicals came to see themselves as "victims"—all with the result that heretofore unimagined constituencies were exposed.

As the analysis made by the new student radicals came to include a conception of their own oppressions, their relation with black militants began to change. Part of this change took the form of a growing willingness to criticize certain expressions of militancy; and that was also facilitated, as we have seen, by the political splits within the ranks of blacks themselves. In effect, as the radicals came to see themselves as oppressed, they began to seek out and demand a more open political exchange with blacks in what was now seen more profoundly as a joint struggle—not simply a black struggle to which whites should give support. As a result, the taint of paternalism which had haunted much of the early civil rights involvement of white radicals was vanishing. Of course, all of this could be regarded simply as convenient self-deception on the part of the white radicals—but a complementary process was also, it seems to me, at work among a sector of the black movement such that a mutual reinforcement has begun to assert itself.

If white radicals began with a deep awareness only of others' oppression, the opposite can be said of blacks. Their mobilization flowed directly out of a desperate sense of their own immediate suffering at the hands of whites and the legal and institutional structures developed by whites. Black nationalism, then, is the extreme manifestation of this consciousness—the oppression of blacks has been so extreme and unique as to rule out any relationships with nonblacks. At the expense of simplifying a complex issue, it is sufficient for our purpose to note that some within the black community became aware, in the process of their own struggle, that their oppression was in fact linked with a whole range of cultural, political, and economic forces that had created oppressive conditions for large numbers beyond the confines of the black community. In *Soul on Ice*, Eldridge Cleaver expressed this realization trenchantly:[20]

> There is in America today a generation of white youth that is truly worthy of a black man's respect, and this is a rare event in the foul annals of American history. From the beginning of the contact between blacks and whites, there has been very little reason for a black man to respect a white, with such exceptions as John Brown and others lesser known. But respect commands itself and it can neither be given nor withheld when it is due. If a man like Malcolm X could change and repudiate racism, if I myself and other former Muslims can change, if young whites can change, then there is hope for America.

This development set a new tone in the relationships between black and white radicals. The resultant new cooperation has been recently manifested in the "Constitutional Convention" called by the Black Panthers to which all movements of the "new" and "old" oppressed were invited—with delegations attending from the Women's Liberation Movement, from a host of white radical student groups, from the Gay Liberation Front, and from the Chicano, Asian, and American Indian communities—united by their respective senses of alienation from and oppression by the larger society.

While it is too early to suggest that these developments mark the end of the contradictions and difficulties that beset the relations between the student radicals and blacks, it does seem safe to conclude that such relations are entering a new phase in which a stable rapprochement is possible. The growing sense of a generalized cultural, economic, and political oppression, tangibly augmented by the increasingly repressive atmosphere in which both whites and blacks are harassed and jailed has laid a foundation upon which many of the issues that have separated white radicals and blacks can conceivably be resolved.

Whatever the actual eventual outcome, it is now clear that substantial numbers of young whites share an increasing alienation from the larger society, an alienation that now goes considerably beyond dissatisfaction with the way black people have been treated and beyond anger with the Vietnam War. The issue now is whether these young people can help create a vision of how our society ought to be structured that goes beyond expressions of rage and alienation and which is capable of strengthening the as yet tentative and precarious links between blacks and whites.

Black Professors

SETHARD FISHER

One of the most significant accomplishments of the black liberation movement in the United States to date has been its impact on institutions of higher learning. Black students and black professors are currently in great demand throughout the country. Employment of black professors is a top-priority item at many formerly all-white colleges and universities, even though employment opportunity at these institutions for whites is scant. This is a reversal of the employment picture in the country as a whole, in which blacks are customarily unemployed and underemployed. Too little time has passed to know whether this situation is a temporary aberration or whether it will be an enduring trend reflecting real flexibility and capability within the American institutional system to meet black demands for proportional representation in the class structure of the society.

This new burgeoning prosperity for Black Americans has brought profound change to many college and university campuses. The American experience from a black viewpoint is now being widely aired and new visions are emerging among black people and white people alike that are grievously at variance with traditional images of American society. For white America to know the reality of the black experience, and to take seriously its implications and imperatives for liberation, is to undergo deeply unsettling questioning, and to newly discover an oppressive and shameful reality. It is of utmost importance that this new concern and awareness within the university setting grow and progressively generate the idealism, skill, and strategy necessary to eradicate the scourge of racism in both this country and the rest of the world. Whether or not this degree of prosperity is achieved depends in part, though by no means exclusively, on what happens within the ranks of those blacks who have chosen the academic profession. It is, then, timely to consider the subject of black professors, for what they make or fail to make of the black experience on campus can be a crucial factor of the broader movement on which their new prosperity rests.

It has been my experience that there are at least three distinctly different orientations among black professors. In describing these, I use the issues of racial militancy and radical change as axial criteria, in the manner that Samuel Strong some years ago used the concept of axes of life in his study of an ethnic group. Strong saw the preoccupation among minorities with the race issue in its various manifestations and subtleties as a demanding central issue claiming their attention in some way most of the time. Varying postures within the group, based on adaptation and adjustment to this central preoccupation, provided the basis for Strong's delineation of a social typology.

Some black professors take a militant and aggressive problack attitude about racial inequality, its causes and consequences, and the means leading to its demise, and consider their involvement in the university community as an integral part of this concern. This group of professors is absorbed in the search for ways by which they can more effectively use themselves and the resources at their disposal to further the cause of racial equality. Very often, such persons adopt strong concomitant antiwhite sentiment. I hasten to add, however, that this latter trait is not generic to the militant orientation but, rather, is only one of its possible variations. Enthusiasm for it generally waxes or wanes according to the extent to which separatist or integrationist motives predominate in the black equality movement as a whole.

It is among these professors that one finds the closest ties with students. Frequently, the former interact with selected elements of the student population—namely, the black students, mainly the black student leadership—as peers, sometimes approaching near-total defection from the rank-related collegial relationship traditionally characteristic of university life. Bonds of friendship, loyalty, and respect, that is, primary relations, often develop between this group and students which may be so enduring as to render other more conventional relationships secondary. Sometimes even formal, or official, obligations such as departmental staff meetings, committee activities, publications, and so forth, are neglected in deference to these associations.

University administrative practices and officials usually find their most vociferous, articulate, and legitimate critics among black faculty who share the militant outlook. The very real grievances confronting black students in adapting to campus life are well-known by these instructors, who vigorously protest administrative insensitivity and indifference (a frequent reality), and who sometimes join student protests and demonstrations aimed at achieving grievance correction through administrative channels. Often this leads to temporary breakdown of part of the administrative apparatus, either because university officials are unsympathetic to black student complaints, or because "satisfaction" cannot be offered within the conventional structure of university policy.

One more characteristic of the militant orientation is its view of the need for immediate social change as an urgent imperative. It derives from black professors' keen sensitivity to the racist oppression of black people, their lively intelligence and idealism, and their emancipation from traditional interpretations of the plight of blacks.

Within this group there has evolved what I shall call a system interpretation of black oppression, a thesis that contrasts markedly with the commonly held individualist interpretation. The ration of liberal individualism and self-reliance which has been the primary ideological source of social and personal orientation among Americans is seriously questioned, challenged, and, for the most part, rejected by this group. Its weaknesses are too blatantly obvious. The Darwinian myth through which this ideology has been passed on suggests that social life is essentially a struggle for survival and that those who are better suited to survive do indeed survive. Thus, members of the various disadvantaged groups could explain their unfortunate condition only in terms of imperfections within themselves as individuals.

In opposition to this attitude, militant black professors have inclined toward a view that stresses the importance of social opportunity rather than the idiosyncratic qualities of individuals. They find it impossible to comprehend the oppression of black people in the United States in terms of a lack of certain essential innate qualities on the part of blacks. They find a more accurate interpretation in the historical actuality of chronic exploitative manipulation of the social condition of black people by whites who hold blacks in perpetual low regard. They see segregated and inferior schools, job and housing discrimination, egregious bias in administration of criminal justice, and so forth, as circumstances actively created by white racists. In addition, many among this group see such conditions not as random evils arising from the insanity of a few, but as evils inherent to the basic institutions of American life. For some, racism is so integrally a part of our ongoing social system that only as the entire system itself is changed can one reasonably expect significant improvement among its member institutions.

The number of militant black professors is small. Yet, their influence is considerable, owing both to their expressive pinpointing of realities to which many are oblivious and to their vociferous idealistic appeal.

A second orientation among black professors is more traditional. It places primary emphasis on professional commitment and achievement but admits to an abiding uneasiness and inner turmoil about black oppression. The issue of black inequality is put in abeyance, though sometimes only superficially, by identification with and dedication to one's profession and one's professional obligations. This is not to say that this group is exactly inert or neutral concerning matters of racial inequality, but only that this is a secondary preoccupation as regards their participation in university life. Frequently, the private lives and informal affiliations of this group are more or less wholly given over to active struggle against racial inequality. But these faculty members generally endorse traditional patterns of association and codes of conduct on campus.

The relation of this group to students does not lead to the intensity or kind of involvement described above as affecting faculty of the militant persuasion. Rather, they assign first priority to the use of the university by students for the development of professional expertise and acquisition of a liberal education, and while they may be exposed to extensive contact with black students, the student-professor characterization of the relationship is seldom repudiated. They see virtue in helping black students master the ongoing conditions of campus life, not in attempting to convert that way of life to large-scale change. This does not mean that this group is necessarily insensitive to the need for change, either within the university or within the broader community. It does mean that they feel the best way to effect improvement is by building up the educational and professional skills of the black community itself. Thus, successful student mastery of academic difficulties has a special meaning for this group. Their counsel to students is usually that of hard work and discipline.

This second group of black faculty are by no means entirely satisfied or completely happy with administrative machinations. Yet, they experience an ambivalence about the matter. On the one hand, the memory of the nearly total inaccessibility of Academe to blacks is still vivid, and thus their very presence in the sacred grove is seen as a substantial accomplishment. On the other hand, they suffer apprehension over the precariousness and insecurity of their position, as most black family members occupy the lower ranks and untenured. Their efforts to achieve some degree of autonomy and independence—from both black students and administration—are severely handicapped by this. They are continually reminded by the more militant and coercive students that their membership on the faculty is a direct result of agitation by black students, and that thus some reciprocal favor is expected. Failure to show such favor may generate the kind of embroilment that would lead to official dismissal, whereby they would lose forever their already tenuous position in the academic world. Considerable psychological and moral discomfort devolves from this situation, as acquiescence to militant demands and/or administrative pressures, for it implies serious compromise of their fundamental beliefs concerning the proper role of a professor. And, usually, members of this group are sooner or later forced into some form of compromise. That may mean a degree of concession to certain unpalatable student demands for "involvement" and selective treatment or, contrastingly, it may mean a closer than ideally desirable alliance with authorities on particular issues. The guiding criteria are determined by whatever line of conduct appears safest in the interest of keeping their jobs, with least possible affront to their essentially traditional view of the university.

The orientation described here is, in a sense, pragmatic, but not completely so, in view of the deep underlying sympathy for and concern about the well-being of the new black presence on college campuses. It is, however, a very typically American view in that, while increasingly exposed to alternative theories, members of this group are largely content to settle for the liberal American reformist view as a means to black equality.

However, this group has undeniably suffered profound disillusionment as to the practical efficacy of the liberal individualistic ethic. Thus, while initiative, hard work, and individual excellence are foremost among its directives to students—black and white—yet, private despair and doubt persist that breed cynicism. The white American middle-class world is taken extremely seriously by this group. Its accomplishments and aspirations are also seen as theirs, but with an important difference namely, the ordeal of racism is an ever vivid, disquieting, and painful reality to them. The slow pace of social reform, occasioned by adamant white resistance to racial equality, cause disturbing questions about its commitment to American society. It is, indeed, as Frazier has derisively claimed, a black bourgeoisie, but it is a group more easily susceptible to disaffection than its white counterpart on account of the persisting vitality of white racism.

The third orientation among black professors, subscribed to by far fewer persons than either of those described above, is one that totally ignores the race issue and the activist or militant posture both on campus and in private life. For this group, it is as if the problem of racial oppression did not exist, at least for them. Highly self-reliant, individualistic, and private in outlook, such persons generally do not extensively socialize with either black students or professors. They do not maintain an extensive network of informal contacts among their white colleagues either, for that matter. They appear to be highly motivated towards academic accomplishment, indeed excellence, in their fields and generally are considered among their black and white associates to be highly competent.

These black teachers do not recognize, or accept, race-based demands from students and none wish to be classed as "the Negro professor." They are disinterested in black student demands for concessions, as well as demands from any other student source. They assiduously avoid entanglements with black students that would enmesh them in anything other than their relentless striving for professional superiority. They are severely affronted by and resist efforts at intimidation by militant black students and steadfastly refuse to be coerced. Black students often take the attitude that these men are ashamed of their race or that "they think they're better than anybody else." And, very often, they are considerably better professionals than equally placed colleagues, black or white.

This group seldom comes to the attention of administrators within the university, except when there arises unwarranted interference with the conduct of their professional life. In such instances as this, they can be implacable and ruthless critics of administrative blundering or injudiciousness. About one such black professor, a university dean once commented to me: "He thinks he's too good for this place." This was said in the course of a general private critique of the black professor for his recent contentiousness with the dean over computer installations.

The black professors of this group apparently have resolved their preoccupation with race and racial oppression by relying on individual professional prestige. Very often being in fact highly gifted, or at least highly motivated to excellence, they have persuaded themselves that this is the means for overcoming the problem. They are often disdainful of those with lesser motivation and professional stamina than they themselves possess. They appear to believe without equivocation in the liberal individualist ethic that personal qualities of character, will, and ability can subdue such forms of social pathology as racial inequality, poverty, and so forth. The militance and commitment to the black movement by other black professors and students is frequently viewed with some repugnance by these scholars. Such related activities are seen as entirely inappropriate within the context of

Academe, and even their meaningfulness in the broader community is seen as dubious.

I should emphasize the point that the above three characterizations of orientation among black professors represent perspectives. That is, they are general viewpoints that should be seen as positions into which individual professors may move and from which they emerge, depending on decisions made at given points in their own experience. This means that, over time, a given faculty member may be classified in one of these categories as he responds to the everyday events of his life and career situations. On the other hand, the categories themselves I consider to be generic, or basic, to the condition of black professors in the context of white universities in a racist society. The usefulness of this kind of categorization is that, in terms of its differential attractiveness to proportions of the black academic community, crucial questions are raised. Such questions involve events in the larger academic community as well as those in the social community as a whole that may have a causal bearing on these proportions. For example, it could reasonably be assumed that the conditions of both campus and social life associated with high proportions of black professors gravitating to the first—or last—described category are basically different from conditions associated with large numbers in the second category.

The majority of black faculty appear to be most accurately classified in the second group described. As will be recalled, this group was basically traditional in orientation. But, a suffusive ambivalence was said to mark the group that weakened its identification with a white middle-class American outlook. It was found to be amenable to alternative orientations owing to its basic uncertainty about the future indefinite resolution of American racism. It may be well to consider some of the campus and more general social conditions that may sway the direction of their university orientation.

On many campuses, black faculty are almost without exception among the lowest-ranked, and by far the majority are on one-year, or limited, contracts. This leaves them vulnerable to a range of pressures against which they would otherwise have some protection. The basic problem here is that the traditional racist bar against black people in academic life has not allowed the build-up of any black tradition on most college campuses. Were such a tradition in evidence, a less insecure and anxiety-filled introduction of new black professors to academic life would be possible. The traditional collegial orientation is likewise not available to many because they are largely hired to run recently created black studies programs, or departments, in which the availability of colleagues is limited. On one large western university campus known to me as of September 1969, there were approximately fifteen black faculty, twelve of whom were at that time beginning their teaching experience at this university. Only three of the twelve were "ladder" faculty members and only one had tenure. The vast majority were one-year or one-quarter appointments with some possibility of renewal of their contracts. Four were Ph.D.s.

A second issue of concern to black professors of the middle group is use of them by university administrators, and by some white colleagues, as buffers to deal with issues touching black students. It is à propos, of course, that those black professors who wish to assume responsibility of this kind should do so. The problem is, however, that there is a rather subtle assumption that a black instructor's mere presence in a university setting presupposes his usefulness in this regard. Such instructors, as mentioned earlier, are caught in a double bind. Usually not having tenure, they can be readily dismissed. Should they arouse the ire of black students, they may be subjected to student abrasiveness and ridicule. Yet, should they allow themselves to be used too extensively on behalf of the various causes and conflicts initiated by black students, the sincerity of their professional commitment is sometimes questioned and their jobs may be jeopardized. This is not a context for professional development and growth enjoyed by most white professors who come fresh to college faculty life.

A third matter of grave concern to these scholars is the vague status of black studies departments and programs and their limited capacity to take on tenured faculty. Being new, many of the course offerings are funded on an *ad hoc* basis and are seriously short of slots for tenured personnel. Effort to increase the number often involves the arbitrary removal of unfilled openings from other departments which can create interdepartmental jealousy and ill-will.

Given conditions such as these, it is amazing that alienation among black professors is not deeper than it is. The absence of a deeper cynicism is in part accounted for by the largely pragmatic attitude of this group and by their typically American hope for, and expectation of, significant improvement soon.

Another important matter for those instructors sharing the second perspective sketched above has to do with prescriptions for black-white relations. The pattern of these, both on campus and off, has increasingly become that urged by the militant-activist group. This warrants consideration, as it involves the active practice of separatism and segregation, practices drastically at variance with their traditional integrationist aims of Black Americans. However, before continuing this discussion, note must be taken of a new secular awareness and its growing influence among black people.

Commenting on the importance of man's knowledge of his society, Kenneth Boulding has written the following:

> It is only within the last two hundred years, and in a sense almost within this generation, that man has become widely conscious of his own societies and of the larger socio-sphere of which they are a part. This movement of the social system into self-consciousness is perhaps one of the most significant phenomena of our time, and it represents a very fundamental break with the past, as did the development of personal self-consciousness many millennia ago.
>
> (*The Impact of the Social Sciences*, p. 4)

What, then, are the consequences of acceptance of this new secular knowledge among blacks? What is its relationship to the perceptives found among black professors described earlier?

Knowledge of social systems is gradually being infused into the black community. Its impact, especially on youth, is energizing and liberating, for it removes the racist-imposed burden of personal inadequacy as an explanation for the black man's social condition. It is a healthy counter to the Darwinist stereotypes which have persisted unrivaled as the ideological underpinnings of a virulent racism. Further, this knowledge counteracts the other-worldly emphasis which has long dominated the outlook of Black Americans. Precisely the secular emphasis, new to the American black, community on a broad scale, informs the orientation of the activist-militant black professors and increases the likelihood of a wide appeal for their outlook. The long hidden realization that black poverty, disease, and general social degradation are not caused by failings of blacks themselves is a revealing insight. And, moreover, the fact that racial oppression can be seen as a product, indeed a necessity, of certain kinds of social arrangements clearly invites alteration of these arrangements. The new secular knowledge may be taken as an important impetus to mobilization for social change.

The militant-activist perspective interprets the need for fundamental modification in America's social order as an imperative, and it employs certain tactics among blacks and among whites to achieve this change. From this derives their prescription, increasingly popular among blacks, for black-white relations.

The militant-activist group is basically oriented to the "black masses," combined with a disdainful view of the black bourgeosie. The needs, wishes, desires, condition, and views of dispossessed black people are a central concern of their rhetoric and their raison d'être. The hypothesis that only militance leads to radical system change will freedom and equality be achieved for blacks is combined with a reversal of the white Protestant disdain for blackness. This assumption exerts a powerful influence in the entire black community. It is an influence whose strength among blacks rests on its reversal of value priorities traditional to the white racist community. "Black is beautiful" epitomizes and symbolizes this reversal. The appeal of this, and other such slogans that cast black people in a sympathetic, positive, and prideful light, is profound among black people, most especially black youth. Its liberating influence is seen daily in the many attempts by blacks to make public their identity with the Third World, particularly with blacks of the African continent. The dashiki and the "Afro" hair style are perhaps the most common symbolic manifestations of this new identity.

It must be remembered that the militant-activist professors' rejection of white American culture is not essentially selective. That is, it is not a simple matter of disclaiming racism, but of rejecting the entire culture of capitalist "Amerika." This total repudiation usually accompanies the appeal of black pride, power, and dignity. In many instances, particularly where black youth are affected, black pride basically means a blanket dismissal of white people and "white culture" and the necessity of confining one's contact and associations to black people exclusively. College communities have felt the impact of this disposition among black youth as they demand separate living quarters, separate dining accommodations, and separate places of informal contact such as black centers on campus. In many instances, black students, in cooperation with the militant-activist black faculty, have even demanded separate classes, claiming their learning experience to be seriously compromised by the presence of white students. The rationale given for such separatist actions by this group is that "black people have to get their thing together" before they can interact meaningfully with whites. The effect of this on black students is often profound, involving as it does considerable coercive insistence that a refusal to participate in segregationist activities is to be "a traitor to your race." To the charge of this being racism in reverse, separatists argue that it is but a phase in a process of redefinition of self and world. The emphasis on black pride, once a matter of black solidarity, may also lead to black separatism. This is currently a forceful imperative governing black-white relations at all levels on university campuses.

Separatism must not be understood as an inevitable outcome of the stress on black pride and black solidarity. Both pride and solidarity can exist without it. It is, rather, an outcome actively promoted as political strategy by that segment of the radical and revolutionary Left that views the black movement as a "vanguard" movement, of which Richard John Neuhaus, in his exciting essay, "The Thorough Revolutionary," has written as follows:

> The vanguard mission of blacks in the Movement is based in part on blacks being the group of the most evidently exploited. In addition to this basis, which is related to conventional notions of class warfare, the blacks have the assets of demonstrated moral virility, a capacity for social fury, and no alternative to radical action in order to gain wider recognition of their asserted identity.
>
> (*Movement and Revolution*, p. 108.)

The formula for black-white relations traditional to the middle group of black professors is also based on a sense of black pride, as well as on a somewhat more diffuse sense of black solidarity. Being less idealistic and less committed to the black masses (though by no means indifferent), and being basically unconvinced of the prognostic accuracy of the revolutionary vision, this group emphasizes a more selective attitude toward white people. A distinction is made between white racists and whites who are problack and nonracist. As the overall society is not condemned *in toto,* emphasis is given to reducing its racist features and progressively creating a condition of racial equality within existing institutional areas—with the aid of whites and other nonblacks so disposed.

In the context of current university life, this nonseparatist viewpoint is in serious decline. This is partially due to the extensive vulnerability of black faculty to black militant-activist pressure, both physical and symbolic, which seems far out of proportion to its possible benefit to any movement toward black equality. It is largely explained by the ascendancy to black student leadership of militant-activist students who, along with the militant-activist professors, share a basically revolutionary view of the achievement of black equality. Their control over black students derives in part from the idealism of their appeal, and sometimes from the use of strong-arm methods to stifle dissent. Those students who would share in campus community life on a nonseparatist basis are sometimes subjected to considerable harassment. Being "together" is taken as a mandatory condition according to the militant-activist viewpoint, and important evidence of this attitude is seen in a pattern of limited-to-nonexistent association with whites.

Because of the creation of black militant-activist dynasties on college campuses throughout the country many academically qualified, creative black professors are loathe to become engaged in black studies programs and departments. This is a serious setback because the value of this new academic and intellectual emphasis on black people is yet only potential in terms of its contribution to the struggle for black equality. Only as competent, committed scholars lend their energies in reconceptualizing and redefining black people and their proper relationship to their society and world will it be possible to reorient Americans (black and white) to the new and prideful interpretations of blackness.

The demand for more blacks, both students and faculty, within the major university systems throughout the country is likely to continue. The black community feels strong motivation in this direction. Education has long been thought of by many blacks as *the* way out of racism. Thus, the liklihood of a deceleration of this trend is not very great. As the years advance, increasingly large numbers of highly competent black scholars can be expected to emerge, a group that will eventually form an influential intellectual class among blacks. Their emergence, the outlines of which are clearly visible now, will mark an important shift in the nature of leadership among Black Americans—a shift from a traditionally religious outlook to a more secular point of view. Black professors will be an integral and perhaps predominant part of this new intelligentsia, though by no stretch of the imagination will it be made up only of academic types. This means, however, that their dispositions regarding American society will become more and more important as tactical and strategic thought and planning for equality move from a sacred to a secular approach.

To this point three different orientations among black professors have been briefly described, and several different responses to academia related to them. The three groups analyzed were seen to differ in their relations with students, colleagues, and administration, as well as in their ideas about the particular way academic life can best serve black people. But before ending this essay, a few words may serve as a reminder that black professors, and the academy in general, do not function in isolation. Their deliberations and prevailing strategic options are very much dependent on certain factors.

Black deprivation in the United States, and the growth today of a mobilized militant-activist outlook, must be seen as due to the class position of black people. It has been estimated that 25 per cent of the lower class in America is black. This encompasses an overwhelming majority of the Black American population, referred to in radical jargon as the "black masses." As long as this class arrangement persists, intensifying radicalization of black people can be expected. This generalization applies equally to black professors. Such disproportionate class stratification, combined with a general affluence and ideology of equality, will not permit continued black passivity and quiescence. This means that only accelerated gains by Black Americans in income, employment, and education sufficient to more equitable distribution of blacks throughout the class spectrum will change the radicalization process.

Perhaps the most important, influential, and ominous reality external to campus life that bears directly on black leadership orientations is rising unemployment throughout the United States. Only under conditions of economic prosperity can substantial upward mobility by Black Americans be achieved. Economic scarcity will result in a general halt of this process, at a time prior to the build-up of lasting and significant gain. Broom and Glen have reminded us that the recent rate of progress by blacks in white-collar, crafts, and foreman occupational groups is not enough to lead to occupational equality in the near future. They contend that, even at the 1940–1960 rate, it would take black males another 530 years after 1960—until the year 2490—to gain proportional representation as professional, technical, and kindred workers. By similar calculation, proportional representation of Negro males as managers, officials, and proprietors would take 415 years from 1960.

Clearly, recent rates of improvement are insufficient to assuage the ever-rising legitimate demands and expectations of Black Americans. The precarious employment situation of black professors is consistent with the nature of black gains throughout the country: as yet they are not stable and continuous. A period of successful and successive black incumbency across the economic, political, and social spectrum must precede the achievement of any stable black prosperity. While there is no absolute certainty that general economic prosperity will be accompanied by black equality, there is certainty that without economic prosperity black equality will not be effected. The point is that with economic prosperity and an organized, strategically oriented black community, accelerated gains are possible. This is because the range of antiracist sentiment in the country is much broader than within the black community alone. Thus, barring circumstances such as economic stagnation and/or depression, a formidable segment of the American population will enlist itself in necessary black-led efforts to achieve proportional representation. Under conditions of economic scarcity, however, support for black interest will narrow to a level of near insignificance. Economic prosperity means an expansion of the influence of moderate black professors. Economic stagnation or depression means more rapid radicalization.

A second equally important general social condition vitally related to orientations among black professors is continued adherence to the democratic principle. The fact must not be overlooked that this principle has never been fully operative, particularly with reference to black people, within American society. Yet, only as faith in it is sustained and it is progressively expanded in reality are interest-group operation and achievement possible. The point at which this tenet is abandoned marks the juncture at which the principle of blacks as countervailing power is abandoned. This means abrogation by government of its role of balancing power and building needed countervailing forces. The vitality of this essential process requires the exercise of those civil liberties and freedoms that are the basic constituents of democratic government. Freedom of assembly, and of speech, for example, are absolutely necessary to the development of black solidarity. And only through the build-up of black solidarity can the sufficient pressure be amassed to force recognition by government, and other recalcitrant sectors of the society, of the black community as a significant power.

The decline of the democratic principle in American society would mean elevation of special interests to pinnacles of power and depression or paralysis of others. The demise of racism in the United States, I submit, cannot be effectively achieved in this way, even in the unlikely event that black interests are among those specially elevated. This is because such elevation would lack the element of legitimacy required to make of the equality so obtained an enduring feature of the society. In other words, the extirpation of racism as a social institution, necessarily involves the kind of learning within a society that interest-group mobilization, strategy, and struggle make necessary. It is only out of this struggle that new visions appropriate to black equality will emerge. This I take to be a central meaning of the statement by Stokely Carmichael that freedom cannot be given; it must be taken.

Black expectations of equality in America are growing apace, and should the opportunity structure of the society not be flexible enough to fulfill these expectations in reasonable measure, intense radicalization of the entire black community, not just of black professors, seems likely. Such a shift by black professors would, under that circumstance, be in the interest of both the black community and the wider society as a whole, the reason being that the unrelenting black thrust for equality is one among several such efforts to achieve equality as women, young people, old people, and others, forge out more satisfactory ways to live in a world that now recognizes happier alternatives. As Ernest Becker has reminded us, it is precisely this creative process that must go on if man's rational and humane dispositions are ever to determine, rather than be determined by, his way of life. The black struggle for equality must be seen as a vital component of this original Enlightenment vision.

Black Students

CLEVELAND DONALD, JR.

I

One way to analyze the behavior, assumptions, and strategies of militant black activists on white campuses during the 1960's is through an application of Karl Mannheim's notion that the ideology of a group grows from the social situation of the group. The tensions within the group and within individual members derive from conflicting or opposing ideologies and generally occur among groups or individuals who are socially mobile—those confronted with conflicting life styles. On the predominantly white campus, the frustrations of black students during the 1960's came from the independent action and interaction of two sets of antagonisms. The first set occurred between the white institutions and the black community, that is, between a white life style and a black life style. The second set occurred within the group and within individual members of the group. The first set of conflicts necessitated black student activism; the second set defined the process by which most black students became engaged in reformist or activist activity.

It is difficult to observe a common denominator for the variety of blacks who attended the predominantly white college during the 1960's. Most of the black college students resided in the ghetto; a few of them did not. Some came from families that earned comfortable incomes, while others came from families that struggled to survive. Some had received their secondary school education in ghetto schools, and others had been educated at prep schools. But without exception and regardless of geographical or economic situation, most black students entered the white university because of the greater mobility they might have within the predominantly white society.

The major motive for the black student's desire for greater mobility was escape from the black community. Because of the racist nature of his earlier education, the black student generally held a negative image of his community. By the time the black student had entered college the process of alienation had already begun. Thus escape from the ghetto became a rejection of tenement flats with eight children and no father. However, because he had not yet lost the deeper sense of love of family and community, often there existed a duality in the black student's attitude toward the black community. This attitude was exemplified by those few students who had nothing whatsoever to do with most of the other blacks on campus. For the vast majority of black students, the escape was perceived as a positive contribution to the improvement of the black community and was shrouded in the complex but sincere rationalization that the general uplift and improvement of the black community could best occur through the individual efforts of those members whose lives became a tribute to the race. In the latter instance, the black community, that is, the part with which the student was familiar, such as family and friends, encouraged the student to escape, assuming that it was indeed the only alternative, given the limitations placed on black self-expression, for the uplifting of black people.

Indirectly, the liberal paternalism of the predominantly white university inadvertently retarded the process of escape and forced a common identity upon black students. Figuratively, every black university student, whether he lived there or not, lived within the shadow of the ghetto. In one sense, the ghetto was analogous to the plantation, and as the concept slave defined the status of blacks on the plantation, so the special programs for bringing black students to white campuses defined their status. Whenever a white student encountered a black student, and indeed whenever one black met another, it was assumed a priori that he participated in the "special" program and that he came from the ghetto.

Unlike the status slave on the plantation, the special status accorded black students at white schools offered more benefits. For one thing, there was more money. For another, the black student was encouraged to conform to the stereotype of the ghetto life. This allowed the student to add new dimensions to the narrow role he had played as high school intellectual. Ultimately the performing of other roles that were identified as characteristic of the ghetto made the black student receptive to a more profound understanding of his community and its problems.

II

Yet neither the enthusiastic endorsement of whites nor the latent altruistic motivation of the black students themselves would have been sufficient to bring about the black-led confrontations of the late 1960's. In fact, a delicate balance existed on most integrated campuses in such a way as to allow the optimum co-optation of the black student. Sanctioned by whites, the black could finish four years of college with only the trappings of ideology that would be beneficial to the black struggle. At graduation and upon re-entering a black world, if indeed he felt motivated to do so, he would have discovered a void in the development of his blackness that actually would have made him irrelevant to the black people. The point should be emphasized: the university is a laboratory where an experiment in black-white relations is being performed to bring about greater social control of the black community, or at least a particular segment of that community. Given ideal conditions, and if it were possible to isolate the university as some academics claim, the experiment would have been carried out with predictability and according to plan. But, like the impact of the African Independence Movement on the Afro-American experience, the rise of black nationalism within the black community intruded into the Cornell laboratory. In 1966, Stokely Carmichael marched through Mississippi and the echo of black power and its demands for immediacy terminated another period of peaceful co-existence in black-white relations.

The reverberations of black nationalism came to most predominantly white colleges in this way. Before the Meredith march, at least one generation of black students had spent one or more years on the predominantly white campus; a second group or generation was to enter in the fall. In the fall, following the march through Mississippi, white students called upon the first generation, whom all along they had considered experts on the black community, to explain the new phenomenon. In explaining the new cry from the black community, this generation had to deal once more with the true effect of the white university upon their lives. When they had returned home during the summer, they had already had to deal with the changed mood of their community. Most importantly, they had to reassess their roles given the new demands of the black community. These demands raised the old contradictions in the apparent inconsistency between their aspiration and the needs of the community. The second generation, which came in the fall, had not been a party to the social contract that existed between whites and the black first generation. Having less of a need to justify the modus vivendi, since they had not constructed it, and arriving newly from a black community fired up by black power, this generation stridently attacked the whites and the black first generation for the racial situation on the campus. In the process they legitimated themselves as the oracles of black power on the predominantly white college campus. Whites turned to them, and this challenged the pre-eminent influence of the first generation.

The challenge to the first or older generation's authority as experts on the black community in white eyes was minor compared with the challenge to their influence among other blacks on campus. At most white colleges, the black student's background of segregated living and his relations with white students had resulted in the germination of informal and unstructured black associations convened in corners of cafeterias and student unions. The older generation ruled these groups which exerted powerful informal control over the behavior of black collegiates. Ideologically, the new generation had to face the fact that their ability to enter into dialogue with whites ran counter to the Black Power position that blacks had nothing to say to whites and ought to withdraw unto themselves. To avoid being called counterrevolutionary, the new generation gradually abandoned their position vis-à-vis whites and sought ways of increasing their influence within informal black campus groups. The older generation regarded with horror the possibility that their influence might be diluted by the younger pretenders. The older generation resisted, battle lines were drawn, and all that remained was an issue that could be used by either generation to discredit the other.

The latent issue on most coeducational campuses involved the question of who might be the champion of the black woman. In the original social contract between whites and the black first generation, the black woman had occupied a nebulous, undefined position. The typical black woman arriving at a white college was innocent sexually. But since college has a liberating influence on sex attitude, she should have made certain changes in her sexual behavior. However, several factors prevented the black woman from dealing creatively with the question of sex. Because of social myths associated with her color, she was considered loose and immoral. Particularly, the black sister suffered from the stereotype, with its stigma in white eyes, that every black woman will be an unwed mother. Her suffering came not from the fact that she considered an unwed mother morally reprehensible, but that it meant the end of her upward mobility, her major reason for being at college. Usually her own family was upwardly mobile or was concerned about her mobility. With Victorian rhetoric her parents had already warned her that to get a good man she must get a good education, that black men were no good, that above all she had to be independent and able to fend for herself. In one sense, such an attitude contributed to the alienation of black women from black men.

If she had been the only female available, the black woman could have controlled the black man by holding over him the promise but not the actuality of sex. But at the white college white women offered black men an alternative to black women. The black man said that he was attracted to the white woman partly because a relationship with her appeared to be less complicated than one with a black woman, since neither party initially contemplated that their relationship might lead to marriage. In reality, by not allowing him to develop a relationship with a black woman, however complicated that relationship might have been, interracial dating restricted the maturation of the black man's personality and limited his ability to understand himself.

Often the black man-white woman relationship forced the black woman to make premature decisions concerning her relationship with black men. Frequently it relieved the black woman from having to deal with black men by providing her with the convenient rationalization that her predicament was primarily the fault of black men or white women. This attitude appeared in the justification put forward by some black women on coed campuses that most of the marriages between black women and white men, which occur as often as those between black men and white women, if not more often, were due to the shortcomings of black men. They argued that every sister who married a white man had had a miserable experience with a black man. In all instances, whatever the rationale, the tensions between black men and women increased, inevitably affecting their perception of themselves and the black community.

Before the advent of black power, the black woman's life on campus was degrading and frustrating. In her own mind, the only possible justification for dating white men had to be marriage—not sex. In addition, it had to be directly related to some real and unpleasant affair with a black man. Whenever she did date interracially, the black coed had to endure the vigorous condemnation of the black male, who did not hesitate to apply the double standard. On the other hand, her childhood education, provided by the racists' society and reinforced by her perceived experience with black men, argued for the essentially negative concept of the black male.

The black woman developed two solutions to her problems. She dated only light-complexioned black males. As one dark-complexioned male reported, before black power, a dark-complexioned brother could not get a date or a dance with a black woman. Or the black woman was attracted to the black men whom white women found attractive. Both approaches to the dilemma reflected the inner tensions of an upwardly mobile individual who felt that she had to reject her own culture and accept the dominant values of society in order to succeed. Such a rejection was suicidal, for it generated self-degradation and self-hatred.

Black power, or more precisely black nationalism, sought to redefine and expand the traditional concept of manhood in such a manner that it took into account the realistic condition of a black community. In the process it reaffirmed the old idea that the black man could be understood best by contrasting him physically and emotionally with black women. Furthermore, the new ideology incorporated the former understanding that authentication of one's manhood depended not only on a personal recognition of its validity but on its acceptance by other men and especially women.

Manhood as expressed in the black nationalism that came to the integrated campus said, "We must protect our women; we must love women." Love and protection of women became synonymous with the acceptance of oneself and of the black community. Other men, specifically white male students on the campus, had to show their acceptance of the new definition of the new black manhood by respecting the black women. The black man had to reject white women. Although inclined to be independent, even distrustful, black women accepted the ideology and the self-subordination it required because it brought them to center stage, focusing attention on them. The black woman rewarded the philosophy's exponents by showering them with attention. The first generation of black collegians, that is, those whose members professed a genuine concern for the black community, had to consider this new outlook because it came from the black community and because the new generation of blacks was using it to challenge the influence of the first within the college community.

Black nationalism also drew black men and women together by removing much of the stigma attached to premarital sex. Prior to black power, a black woman who engaged in premarital sex was thought to have relinquished her principal weapon for attracting black men. Moreover, the rejection of sex before marriage provided another opportunity to escape from the black community, for ghettoites were reputed to be sexually loose. Black Power said that sex was important as a cultural function rather than as a biological one, and it maintained that blacks were better at it than whites. The romanticizing of the ghetto, inherent in Black Power, brought respect to some of its activities—in this case, its reputed sexual habits. At the theoretical level, meaningful premarital sexual intercourse became a legitimate expression of one's humanity and one's blackness. Practically, it made women more open to sex, particularly since Black Power also assured them of the love and protection of black men. It also destroyed the basic rationale that black men had presented for dating white women.

Ultimately the significance of a major issue agreed upon by both generations lay in its irresolvability or lack of clear-cut resolution. The continuing existence of an issue like the role of black women on the white campus served as the central thread that united disparate incidents affecting black students into a logical pattern. Every event, particularly every act emanating from those labeled as the enemy, was made to appear as an act of hostility or a challenge which when confronted proved that one was a defender of the crucial issue and consequently relevant to the black experience. To the extent that black leaders or their opponents led black students to see the relations between any incident and an underlying issue or issues, to that degree they were able to seize control and move blacks to engage in activism.

III

The advent of Black Power coincided with and grew out of the failure of this country to fulfill Martin Luther King's dream. Before Black Power idealistic reformers had been critical of the society, but implicit in their actions was the belief that the society would correct its own inequities. The failure of integration, which was supposed to be society's way of self-preservation, spawned black power. Black Power grew because, despite civil rights laws, the condition of the average black man worsened. It tried to give the black man a modicum of control over his own fate and attempted to prevent the total psychological emasculation of the black race. While the new ideology continued to blame society for the condition of black people, it maintained that black people themselves, not society, would be their own salvation. Under the new order, the black man retained his pride since he had ultimate control over his fate.

Attributing to an individual ultimate, but not immediate, control over his fate encourages introspection and self-criticism since the inevitable question, "Why wait?" raises itself. With proper supervision, this introspection was absolutely necessary to understanding the black community and self-actualization. But black students on white campuses found it difficult to develop a critical self-analysis because, observed by whites, they felt the need to manifest a continuous display of unity. Nevertheless, when a group has separated itself from the dominant society, factions do develop which affect its ability to function. After black collegians had developed a separate identity, the old and simple division between first and second generation gave way to three extremely complex factions which exhibited more intricate variations of the tendencies developed in the simpler division. The success of the college Afro-American societies in dealing with the problems posed by factionalization did not come without struggle and conflict. Since black student activism occurred after a long period of developing internal consensus and unity, the process itself must be examined to understand the implication of the strategies and assumptions of black students.

Among most black student groups on predominantly white campuses there existed at least three major factions: the Yippies, the Converts, the Radicals. The Yippies, as the Radicals labeled them, were artistic and "super cool." In their practice and philosophy one found the notion of black people as a loving people given its most extreme expression. They resisted the constant preoccupation of the other factions with the white devils by asking black students to forget the honkey and to concentrate on love and respect within the black community. The implication of their philosophy meant withdrawal from the politics of dealing with white society and the development of strong interpersonal relationships among black students. The group's members, most of whom came from first-generation students, were known to date white women, although they managed to evade detection. They enjoyed the notorious reputation of being both heartbreakers and able to date any black woman they desired. The Yippies lived their philosophy and rarely involved themselves as a group or as individuals in the contest for power.

The Yippie leader had great difficulty in accepting the practical implications of militant black power. Usually one of the original founders of the college's Afro-American society, he had become disenchanted with the political development of black students and frustrated with his incapacity to understand his own political role. A promising young writer, he generally served as editor of the black literary magazine. But his frustrations affected his ability to write or to function well. His dilemma was probably compounded by the thought that black people were as angry with him as he was with himself.

The typical Convert was also from the first generation. The failure of the fraternity system to accept him pushed him initially toward more radical expressions of concern for the black community and black separatism. After conversion to black separatism, Converts stopped interracial dating and through their political activism gained the allegiance of many of the black women. The Converts had close ties with the Yippies and a few of them, except for their political involvement, were actually a part of that group.

Any attempt to describe the Converts poses certain difficulties. One should not refer to them as moderates, for that would make the Yippies appear more conservative and the Radicals more radical. In fact, the Converts exhibited a political naïveté far more rudimentary than the complex Yippie philosophy. On occasions they would vehemently give the university fifteen minutes to live. At other times they would observe that whites could be trusted, a reactionary notion within the organization, and looked disappointed and angry when white liberals did not do what they had expected of them. I have called them Converts, but they were charter members of most Afro-American societies. Yet, they had infrequently attended meetings. The Converts tried harder, but their earnest political concern often far outdistanced their political grasp of the cause. One could interpret the Yippies' emphasis on love rather than politics as "unpolitical" and consequently either conservative or radical because it went beyond politics. But the Yippies at least had a program distinctively different from that of the Radicals. The Converts and Radicals sometimes said the same things but with competing and conflicting meanings. Because they had chosen the political avenue to relevancy, the Converts rather than the Yippies offered the real challenge to the Radicals.

In the beginning there was blackness; blackness was Radical leadership and Radical leaders were radical. Brilliant students, the

Radical leaders' minds plowed through fertile fields of unconventional thought. Nearly every militant or revolutionary concept known to black college students had issued first from their mouths. To black students, Radical leaders were not super cool, or so super black as to be uncool, rather they were so super cool and super black as to be super serious. The Yippies often said that if radical leaders slept with a white woman they would change their ideological perspective. To which the Radicals replied, probably so, but if Radical leaders ever slept with a white woman, they would not be radical. In a group of black students where the disease known as blacker-than-thou had not been eradicated completely, the radical leader was truly black.

The contrasts between the Radicals and other groups were remarkably subtle and often confusing. Blacks were concerned about relevant education. In the integrationist period, blacks on a white campus constituted the highest act of commitment to the black community. Those integrationists became the vanguard, whether at the University of Alabama or at the Woolworth lunch counter, of the black struggle for survival and uplift. The black community bestowed upon these students the badge of courage because they bore the scars of police clubs and the stench of rotten eggs on their bodies. On the Northern white campus these integrationists, the "firsters" as the barrier-breakers were labeled, engaged themselves in the battle to destroy the stereotypes that whites used to justify oppression of the black community. Following the development of black separatism, this old vanguard was declared irrelevant, and in one brief moment the revolutionaries of the old era became the counterrevolutionaries of the new.

Given the existence of the new order, black students on white campuses sought ways to make themselves relevant to their community. The Radicals argued that they ought to leave the university as the SNCC members had left the Negro institutions in the days of integration. If they remained, they should constantly *heighten the contradictions,* that is, they ought to raise and prove, through word and deed, that integration had not worked for the black community and could only result in the alienation of a Negro elite from their black brothers. To avoid this, blacks had constantly to make the integrationists' life unpleasant for themselves and the white community. Tactically this could be done through the process known as *confrontation.*

Implicit in the way they used the technique was the assumption that an individual, particularly one who is not highly politicized, rarely consciously acted contrary to his own self-interest. Consequently, the radicals desired to *raise the level of awareness* by heightening the contradiction through the process of confrontation. That is, they wanted blacks to redefine self-interest so that it would become indistinguishable from identification with the black community, and so that it would lead blacks to reject the white college. Simultaneously, Radical ideology combined the objective of raising the level of awareness among blacks with another objective, the destruction of the university—if not its complete destruction, at least its disruption. Once a black student had become aware of the contradictions inherent in his presence on the white campus, reflected on the contradictions inherent in the presence of black people within the racist American society, he was expected to continue participating in the process of confrontation in order to raise the level of awareness of his less politicized brother, and to disrupt and destroy the society. It could even be said that Radical ideology made the process of disruption and destruction indistinguishable from the process of raising the level of awareness.

The Radicals believed that the heightening of the contradiction through the process of confrontation would result in the ejection of blacks from the white campus. Unconsciously, they created situations in which their predictions seemed to come true. That is, most black students reacted in this manner to everything they did. On the other hand, although the Converts used the same rhetoric as the Radicals, they did not mean the same thing. They advocated heightening the contradiction, the process of confrontation, raising the level of awareness, and disrupting and destroying the university; but they could not bring themselves to accept the consequence of the argument that all these would ultimately result in their expulsion from the campus. The Converts were careful never to state the probability of expulsion in their action. Because the larger society outside the university was just as oppressive as the university environment, they saw no point in leaving the latter for the former. Where, they asked, was the revolutionary structure that would receive them? Everywhere one lived, they argued, one had to attempt to work for the survival and uplifting of blacks. Conceding that they lacked the skill that was needed in the black community, the Converts asked how they could be relevant by returning to the black community in the same condition as when they left. Furthermore, students who left would only be replaced by others—less politicized or uncommitted blacks. Within the racist establishment they could serve as conduits through which knowledge and information about the enemy could be channeled to the black community. They could send money and material to less advantaged blacks elsewhere.

IV

Our society possesses almost unlimited capacity to absorb the rhetoric of new ideas. At one level this involves commercializing the rhetoric and co-opting the rhetoricians; at another it requires declaring the rhetoric off limits and eliminating or destroying the exponents of the new ideologies. As in the larger society, white students and liberal faculty moved at first to co-opt the militants and their cause. That is, they decided to allow them the forms but not the substance of their militancy. The university community rapidly learned the militant new vocabulary and eagerly sought the expertise of the militant on all matters relevant to the black community.

No doubt the act of haranguing whites, which characterized such consultations, had the initial effect of creating a vehicle for the release of the frustrations blacks experienced while living in a university environment that was hostile to their cultural needs. The implicit "children will be children" notion involved in the tolerance of the black students' verbal attack on the system was accepted by all but the most conservative members of the university. They either took blacks more seriously or held onto the old child-rearing idea that children must be disciplined. In fact, the rising level of verbal militancy within black campus groups coincided with the intensification of black frustration. This frustration grew because blacks knew that whites enjoyed the punishment, indeed, they enjoyed it to the point of not actually taking blacks seriously. Blacks began to feel that they were entertaining rather than educating the university community. Black frustration increased because whites, by enjoying the punishment, deprived blacks of the therapeutic value inherent in the act of punishing.

If the higher level of frustration were given political rather than emotional expression, black students would have been extremely dangerous. Otherwise, unguided and undirected, the increased frustration increased the likelihood that blacks would be co-opted, since the simple absorption of the new militancy by the whites seemed to instruct blacks in the futility of attempting to change or destroy the system.

The desire to direct the frustrations of black students into political and reformist activities functioned as the major ideological explanation for the actions of black activist leaders and for their struggle for control of black groups. The pattern of struggle itself was simple: initially a moderate leader of a group found his power wrested from him by a more militant group. During the course of the struggle, a dictatorial maverick would emerge to temporarily repress internal dissension. Gradually, a conservative or moderate reaction would be built among black students that would culminate in the ouster of the maverick and his replacement by a moderate apolitical individual. If the new leader did not become radicalized on the road to power or by the assumption of power, he would be removed by radical leadership. At this point, radical leadership, sincerely committed to activism, would attempt to involve black students in political activity that would intensify after each successful attainment of a specific goal. When a stated goal was not reached, and no explanation given, a period of severe internal criticism—often expressions of self-hatred—would set in, only to be terminated with radical leadership intensifying its demands on an increasingly hostile group of followers. Ultimately, radical leadership would be replaced by moderate leadership which, enjoying the support of a coalition of the majority of black students, might successfully implement aspects of the radical program. Success and the leadership position would in turn radicalize the new leadership, and consequently contribute to its downfall. When there no longer existed any opposition or potential opposition leadership, a lull would envelop the black student organization. Throughout this process, a great deal of attention would have been paid to the observance of established rules and precedents, which often would never have been set down on paper. No contestant would have reached a position of power by other than established practices; roles and precedents could be bent and distorted, but they could not be broken.

An example of the process of leadership alienation exists in changing attitudes toward the black woman. According to Radical thought, political black women should date only political black men to avoid being corrupted by unpolitical men. Or they should politicize those unpolitical men whom they dated. Unpolitical women should always relate to political men if they wanted to be political. From the Radical viewpoint the other two factions, especially the Yippies, were unpolitical. The Radicals had a small cadre of women, but the other two factions, particularly the Yippies, had the largest number of women. The Radicals believed that the political black woman not only was unable to politicize her lesser political brother, but actually was being corrupted by him. Consequently, while they understood why an unpolitical woman might be attracted to an unpolitical man, they never saw how a political woman could be. When the black coed did not conform to the ideal model of the black woman, the Radicals concluded that she was unpolitical. When the black female made no effort to change, the Radicals grew more disappointed and angry with her. Upon sensing the attitude of the Radicals, the black woman found it even more difficult to communicate with them and turned more and more to the men in the other two factions. To complicate matters further, the Radicals blamed the Yippies and the Converts for exploiting black women sexually and for not trying to politicize them.

As Radicals' estrangement grew, their dislike for Yippie and Convert men also increased. The Radicals had an impenetrable case against the Yippies, the Converts, and most of the black women. So non-Radical black men and women comforted each other by drawing closer together. From this experience, the Radicals decided that all blacks in the organization were not worth fighting for. Thus Radicals exonerated radical leaders by saying it was useless for them to waste their time in a futile effort to change a lot of worthless blacks. Ultimately, such an attitude tended to give radical leadership's assessment of blacks an unrealistic distortion, and contribute to their downfall.

v

The rapid alienation of extremely militant black students from their less radical brothers provides the clue to the character of militant activism during the 1960's and to its future in the 1970's. Caught up in the vibrations of revolutionary confrontation rhetoric, militant leaders really thought a cataclysm, spearheaded primarily by black college students, was imminent. They felt that black collegians, especially those at white universities, were at or near the stage where they would rebel and join the crucial vanguard of the black revolution; they believed this despite their cries of their own irrelevancy—cries which consequently were uttered more to mobilize black students than to judge and condemn them. While the wider Afro-American community found its role determined by its location in the eye of a racist and imperialistic octopus, black students discovered theirs determined by their position in the octopus's brain and nerve center. However, militant black student leaders could not see that the white university was not the center of Armageddon; more importantly, most black students were not revolutionary but conservative and establishmentarian. This has been proven by the fact that after they had created institutions like Black Studies Programs, they tried to use them to get an easy grade, not to make the university education relevant to their experience. Militant black student activists of the 1970's must deal with the problems left by the recent failure of militant activism, with a growing body of black teachers in white universities often displaying bourgeois tendencies, with blacks who will have been immunized against the emotionalism of black power before they enter college, and with Black Studies Programs that are little more than Negro colleges in miniature. Yet, their task will be no greater than that of their predecessors of the 1960's. They too must translate the black frustration caused by a racist system into a constructive force that can be used to uplift and improve the black community.

Epilogue

The Significance of Social and Racial Prisms

WILLIAM J. WILSON

The essays in this book demonstrate that perceptions of race relations are determined not only by skin color but also by socioeconomic position. Blacks and whites of the general public tend to view American race relations "through different eyes," but it is likewise true that within each racial group perceptions vary according to income, occupation, education, and place of residence. However, there is no simple one-to-one relationship between individuals' views on racial matters and their respective positions in the social structure because racial attitudes are in major measure shaped by an important intervening variable—feelings of apprehension that outgroup racial members plan to undermine, encroach on, or challenge in-group claims to certain rights and privileges. People of high social status, for example, tend to be less virulent in their racial attitudes because their position in society is more secure and they have fewer fears that their interests or prerogatives will be jeopardized by outgroup racial members.

Thus, for whites the most intense forms of racial animosity emerge when blacks compete directly with them for scarce goods or when blacks challenge the very prerogatives (that is, exclusive or prior rights in housing, occupation, education) that have historically set the races apart. And, as I shall endeavor to show, fear of black encroachment varies among the white population depending on their geographical location and social position in society. For blacks, on the other hand, the most bitter forms of racial hostility emerge when their social position vis-à-vis whites is marginal, ambiguous, or insecure; when they feel that whites have prevented them from gaining high status and respect; when they are apprehensive that whites will take away hard won positions of status; or when their accomplishments are belittled, undermined, and denied the privileges that automatically flow to whites who have experienced similar achievements.

In short, the less threatened individual whites are by black advancement or encroachment, the less hostile their attitudes toward blacks and the lower their degree of racial tension; likewise the more secure individual blacks are in their socioeconomic positions, the less belligerent their attitudes toward whites and the lower their level of racial tension. The crucial underlying assumption of these propositions is that racial groups, like other social groups, engage in a constant competitive struggle for control of scarce resources.[1]

In the United States whites have been successful in this struggle by either eliminating or neutralizing blacks as competitors or by exploiting black labor in order to maximize scarce resources. White gains from black subordination is the historic pattern of American race relations. However, the recent surge of black protest has presented a serious challenge to white prerogatives. Blacks have not only revolted against labor exploitation, but also have confronted whites in areas where the latter had almost exclusive control (e.g., places of residence, upper status jobs, higher education, and politics). Racial tension and hostility has spread, therefore, into institutions occupied by whites who, in the past, could smugly sit back and blame racial problems on lower-class ignorance or on Southern racism. Disillusionment and hostility have, in turn, increased among blacks as they attempt to overcome new obstacles to racial equality erected by the very groups once defining themselves as either liberal or tolerant toward racial differences.

The shifting of racial tensions from the South to the North in the middle twentieth century provides the clearest examples of the foregoing generalizations. Lewis Killian's essay stresses the fact that until recent decades, Northerners, unlike Southerners, could virtually ignore blacks. Only a small percentage of the total population above the Mason-Dixon line was black. They were invisible—"hidden in small islands within large cities"—and, unlike European immigrants, they occupied peripheral positions in the region's economy. In short, they hardly presented a threat to the northern white's sense of superior position. In the South, on the other hand, just the reverse situation prevailed: blacks made up nearly 40 per cent of the population in the years following the Civil War; they were central to the economy as cheap laborers; and they were visible in virtually every region of the South. As Killian notes, the combination of black emancipation and citizenship, and white illiteracy and poverty threatened to "destroy the sort of white supremacy which made the poorest white superior to any black" and the activities of northern Republicans during Reconstruction "seem to endanger the color line itself."

It is little wonder then that the most threatened of white Southerners set about to re-establish white supremacy after the collapse of Reconstruction. And they did it well. The Jim Crow system of segregation was virtually unchallenged until the early 1950's. As long as blacks kept "their place," white Southerners exhibited little outward racial hostility; but the 1954 Supreme Court Decision, Brown vs Board of Education and the nonviolent demonstrations in the South threatened the southern way of life, and the most violent resistance to racial change came from marginal status whites who felt they had the most to lose by black advancement. As white resistance to civil rights protests increased in the South, black bitterness, disgust, and disappointment over the pace of social change also increased.

However, the fear of black advancement or encroachment in areas where whites "have prior claim" is no longer a preoccupation of only white Southerners. It is now a major concern of whites across the nation. Killian observes that the southern white is pleased to see increasing numbers of his race in other parts of the country developing perspectives on American race relations quite similar to his own.

Just how northern whites are changing their views is seen in Friedman's essay on American Jews. Friedman points out that whereas both upper- and lower-status Jews identified with the black man's struggle for racial equality prior to the 1960's, sharp division along class lines now characterizes Jewish reactions to blacks. Hostile feelings have emerged among lower middle-class Jews who are most "threatened by the black surge forward." Their children attend municipal rather than private suburban schools, and community or city colleges rather than élite private institutions of higher learning; they live in racially changing neighborhoods, work in marginal status jobs, and are the most visible and vulnerable targets upon which blacks in the ghettoes can vent their rage. Upper-status Jews can keep the liberal tradition alive because they do not face the day-to-day challenge from blacks for scarce resources within the inner city whereas lower status Jews are in the immediate path of black efforts to improve their status. The black threat comes from many directions—in the policy of open enrollment which could reduce their competitive advantage in entering municipal colleges; in the increasing number of blacks residing in their neighborhoods which in turn is accelerating the white (Jewish) exodus; in the emerging black capitalism which is challenging Jewish-owned stores in the ghetto; in the quest for black control of community schools which could make their positions as teachers less secure; and in the anti-Semitic rhetoric of black militancy which increases their insecurity in central cities where they are highly visible.

But the lower-middle class Jew's reaction to black encroachment is not unique. In Welks's essay on white ethnics it is clear that very intense and hostile feelings toward blacks are expressed by other ethnic groups such as the Slovaks (the group most discussed in Welks's article), the Italians, and the Poles—whose communities border black ghettoes and who are gripped by the fear that blacks threaten to invade their communities, terrorize their people, lower the status of their property, and ultimately force whites to leave. The specific issue is whether neighborhood ethnic churches, private ethnic schools, and ethnic social clubs can survive if whites leave their communities in great numbers and move to other parts of the city or to the suburbs. The growing specter of black political power in urban areas, where blacks are now heavily concentrated, exacerbates racial tensions and animosity in ethnic neighborhoods. For example, in Welks's former neighborhood in Cleveland, whites were concerned that Carl Stokes, the then black mayor, would encourage blacks to move to the city, invade white neighborhoods, and get on the crime and welfare rolls.

Norbert Wiley's essay, however, presents a much more fundamental explanation for lower-status white hostility toward blacks. He argues that the white working class exhibits the highest degree of racism in the United States because of its precarious economic position. The general view among the "silent majority," according to Wiley, is that "if Negroes can be kept from better paid jobs, better quality housing, and more comfortable schools, there is all the more for whites to enjoy." The competition between low-status whites and blacks is basically economic. Wiley contends that, in the final analysis, these two groups are merely fighting "over crumbs," that the dividends low-status whites receive from black subordination are meager when compared with the gains enjoyed by the rich and the powerful.

However, whether poor whites defend their opposition to blacks in solely economic terms or in the use of widely held racial stereotypes (e.g., "Negroes run down their property"), their rationalizations frequently represent a concern that blacks plan to undermine, encroach on, or challenge their claims to certain rights and privileges. That this feeling is not restricted to lower-class whites is seen in the reaction of intellectuals to black protest on college campuses.

Robert Blauner states that as long as the "racial crisis" was concentrated in the South or in the central cities, white professionals could maintain an abstract liberal philosophy toward race that was free of inner conflict. Prior to the middle 1960's black and other Third World students on white campuses were virtually invisible comprising no more than one or two per cent of the total student population in the better universities and élite colleges. "But when black students (and to a lesser degree Chicanos and Puerto Ricans) entered campuses in somewhat more than token numbers during the late 1960's, 'race relations' came to the university with a vengeance, bringing the racial crisis of the larger society home to roost for the white professor." Whereas white ethnics develop hostile racial feelings when blacks threaten their proprietary claims to certain neighborhoods, jobs, and schools, white professors, according to Blauner, develop inimical reactions when the increasing number of minority students on campuses begin to press for programs such as open enrollments and ethnic studies, and denounce the traditional way professors teach their classes. The concern of white professors is what they perceive to be "an undermining of academic standards, intellectual eminence, and cultural style of the university" and their liberal views on race relations were "severely tried" by minority students challenging the traditional rights and privileges of scholars and teachers.

If racial animosity among whites is related to fears that their rights and privileges will be undermined by black encroachment, racial hostility among blacks stems from beliefs that they have been forced into marginal, ambiguous, or insecure positions. It really doesn't matter that the degree of bitterness does not always correspond with the extent of racial suppression. What is important, in the final analysis, is the way blacks perceive both their inferior status and the efforts of whites to keep them in subordinate positions. So, despite the fact that racial subjugation in the last several decades is no greater, and in many cases is less, than the oppression of previous decades, black hostility toward whites has deepened because of the heightened awareness of and sensitivity to race exploitations created by the black protest movement.

The intensity and direction of black protest is related to beliefs concerning black people's ability to confront the white society and to produce significant changes in the racial alignment. Thus, on the one hand, during periods in which blacks are frustrated by racial injustice but nonetheless (1) feel that the system is vulnerable to black protest and (2) that the widespread use of pressure tactics will force whites to share the resources they disproportionately control, black hostility will be expressed in both organized and unorganized attacks against the system. On the other hand, during periods of black resignation, despair, and hopelessness—when it is believed that protest or attack against racial subjugation will not generate any meaningful change—black hostility is displayed in racial solidarity movements wherein great stress is placed on developing black cohesiveness, controlling black institutions, establishing viable black communities, and creating a social structure that would decrease contact and interaction with whites.

The first seven years of the turbulent 1960's marked a period of black optimism and active protest against racial injustice. However, the heightened expectations created by the success of the civil rights movement were increasingly frustrated by belligerent white resistance from 1963 to 1965 and were actually lowered in the late 1960's by the rise of a conservative Republican Administration to political power with its "law and order" atmosphere of repression. In response, increasing numbers of blacks have questioned the value of interracial cooperation and the efficacy of violent and nonviolent protests, and have begun to place greater emphasis on racial cohesiveness as the mechanism to promote black advancement. This does not imply, however, that blacks are abandoning their efforts to compete with whites for limited housing, jobs, and other scarce resources, but it does suggest an increasing reliance on the ideology of racial solidarity or black nationalism to achieve a more balanced distribution of resources. J. Herman Blake is essentially correct, therefore, in asserting that: "While nationalism in the nineteenth century was notable for its lack of mass support, and for its lack of intellectual backing, in the mass movement of the twentieth century in recent years, intellectuals and the masses have combined their skills to give new impetus to nationalist movements."

Black college students provide a clear example of this increasing nationalistic mood. Cleveland Donald's essay describes black students' drift toward black solidarity and their increased antipathy toward whites at Cornell University. Indeed, in predominantly white colleges around the country, white administrators, teachers, and students confronted an expanding black student population that exhibited an undisguised antagonism toward whites and an evangelistic fervor for black solidarity. As the sense of nationalism among black students increased, their relationship with whites became more estranged. The mood had set in. Racial solidarity and hostility toward whites precluded cooperation with any whites—even radical students who, as Jan Dizard's essay indicates, were among the most committed to ending racial oppression.

The fact that the theme of racial solidarity has reached unprecedented heights in the black community and has, in effect, transcended social class lines, should not allow us to overlook the variation in black responses to racial oppression, variation that quite closely corresponds to the degree of satisfaction and security blacks feel about their position in society.

The views on race of black immigrants and blacks born in the United States provide an interesting contrast. Although West Indian immigrants contributed several black protest movement leaders in recent years, black immigrants as a whole, according to Roy Bryce-Laporte, tend to be more conservative in their racial outlook than blacks born in the United States. Bryce-Laporte observes that the average immigrant comes to America already deeply committed to the "Protestant Ethic." If he has been able to elevate himself from a subordinate rank to a position of status and respect, as a significant number are able to do within a decade or two, he becomes "a traditionalist in favor of the status quo." He does not blame white society for the black man's plight, rather he feels that United States' born blacks can also improve their lot if they apply themselves. Thus he is unwilling to support any movement for social change which could possibly threaten his newly obtained status or interests. Bryce-Laporte points out, however, that the successful black immigrant's criticism of United States' born blacks fails to consider the latter's different background, experiences, and prerogatives. Indeed, such criticisms often resemble arguments used by white racists to justify the continued subjugation of blacks around the world.

Aside from the contrasting racial views of black immigrants, there is a notable diversity in views concerning race relations matters among blacks born in the United States. For instance, empirical findings reported in Edgar Epps's essay reveal that younger blacks tend to be more separatist in their thinking than older blacks and that nationalistic separation appeals more to blacks at the poverty level than to those whose incomes are higher. If it is correct to assume that separatism has less appeal for blacks in stable and secure socioeconomic positions, then it is understandable that older and higher income blacks are more inclined to support less extreme positions on race distinctions.

However, as Epps notes in his description of accommodationists, assimilationists, and cultural pluralists, there are even some fundamental differences in perceptions of race relations among blacks classified as integrationists. Epps argues that accommodationists accept a gradualist approach to eliminating racial injustice in part because they feel comfortable in those aspects of racial separation that remove them from competition with whites. The accommodationist feels secure in a segregated system and for that reason he is not overly hostile toward whites, nor is he disturbed by society's racial order.

The major difference between the assimilationist and the cultural pluralist (since in Epps's formulation they both accept the ultimate goal of integration), is that the former emphasizes individual mobility while the latter stresses group action to achieve social-economic parity with whites. Accordingly, the cultural pluralist's greater reliance on group strategies is indicative of his beliefs (1) that the outcome of interindividual competition is in large measure negated by racial distinctions and (2) that white racism restricts individual blacks from achieving positions of status and wealth regardless of their capabilities or competence. For this reason he is likely to be more distrustful and hateful of whites than is the assimilationist.

Cultural pluralism, states Epps, is a conservative adaptation of the Black Power ideology; the emphasis is not on separatism (that is, physical separation) or revolution, but on group cohesiveness and cultural distinctiveness. And the more highly educated blacks seem to be those "most likely to be attracted to cultural pluralism."[2] In this connection, Johnetta Cole argues that cultural pluralism (or cultural nationalism in her terminology) provides the black middle class with a mechanism whereby they can "satisfy their own interests (via black capitalism) in the disguise of helping black folks." In other words, during the present period in which racial solidarity has reached unprecedented heights, the black middle class with interests in private business can "perpetuate the interests of corporate capitalism in maintaining control of the American economy, and yet speak to the black masses in nationalistic terms (own black and buy black)."

Although group interests affect perceptions and approaches to race relations in the black community, there are individual differences in views and responses even within certain occupational categories. Sethard Fisher's analysis of black professors provides an interesting case in point. Fisher identifies three major orientations held by black professors—(1) the militant problack with a minimal commitment to the academic community; (2) the traditional academic involved in black affairs; and (3) the traditional academic-scholar with little or no involvement in black affairs.

The black professors representing the third orientation, according to Fisher, tend to be the most secure in their academic positions. They have little regard for black student demands and their ultimate and primary concern is academic excellence. In effect, they "have resolved their preoccupation with race and racial oppression by relying on individual professional prestige." Fisher argues that professors associated with the second orientation experience the greatest difficulty on campus. Neither as involved or committed to students as the militant professors nor as academically secure as the scholar-oriented aloof professors, they are deeply anxious about racial incidents on campus. The militant professors, on the other hand, have the support of black students and, as long as the student support lasts, leverage against white administrators. Their hostility toward whites is likely to be quite keen and derives, in part, from their general approach to race relations—namely that basic institutions of American society are inherently racist and must be changed before meaningful black progress can occur—and, in part, from their own marginal position within the academic community. Accordingly, they are not concerned with promoting academic norms of scholarship but are involved instead in black student demands and grievances.

Up to this point I have attempted to show that even though blacks and whites tend to view American race relations "through different eyes," perceptions within each group vary depending on specific situations and socioeconomic positions. Let me attempt one final application of these arguments by drawing upon the essays in this volume that discuss politicians, police, teachers, prison officials, and welfare workers.

Although the American political institution has played a major role throughout its history in keeping blacks suppressed, in recent years several white politicians, especially those on the national level, have identified with aspects of the black struggle and have pressed for the passage of civil rights legislation and the allocation of antipoverty funds. Certain white politicians have been motivated to work for black equality because the black vote became large enough in certain pivotal regions to decide close elections. It is a known fact that the political survival of many white politicians is very definitely dependent on the support of black voters. When blacks do not have voting power, there is a distinct tendency for politicians to ignore their demands and interests. Moreover, as recent events have shown, even liberal politicians tend to waver in their support for black demands when they sense that their white constituencies are upset because of increasing black competition.

This view is consistent with the arguments expressed in Munger's essay on white politicians. Munger maintains that in explaining a politician's voting behavior on civil rights, one can ignore his personal views on racial justice and concentrate solely on his judgment of constituency opinion. In contradistinction to Andrew Greeley's argument (that the Kennedys "might have very well believed in racial justice before 1960"), Munger maintains that former President John F. Kennedy was emotionally uncommitted to attaining equality for blacks and that his position on civil rights was essentially tactical—based on his desire to win support from black voters.

The efforts of Black Americans to gain more political power, and thus yield greater influence in the political process, is one of the central concerns in Chuck Stone's essay. Stone argues that Black Americans are just beginning to develop the kind of ideological sophistication that white ethnic groups have had throughout their political history: the ability to manipulate the political process to satisfy their own selfish ends "without regard for the best interests of the country." Black Americans are now pursuing a similar course of action, according to Stone, as reflected in their belated use of selective violence and their development of a sense of nationhood. However, Stone believes that the reality of the American political situation dictates that blacks, as did the white ethnic groups before them, use violence selectively, not excessively, relying on its shock value to buttress participation in the political mainstream. He argues that blacks must become more ethnocentric in their politics by placing black interests ahead of the nation's interests. To do this effectively black politics must incorporate the ideology of black solidarity to ultimately triumph in the struggle for power. Stone seems confident that blacks are gradually moving in that direction.

It is true that racial solidarity is becoming a dominant theme among black politicians. I suggested previously that because of the disillusionment and bitterness experienced since the middle sixties, the ideology of racial solidarity is gaining momentum among all segments of the black population. With the increased politicalization of the black masses, particularly the lower classes, black politicians have found it increasingly necessary to openly promote racial solidarity (The 1972 National Black Political Convention in Gary, Indiana provided the clearest example of the black politicians' new profile).

The politicization of the black masses and their heightened sensitivity to racial injustice correspond with an intensified concern about the misuse of police power. Although Rosen is willing to grant that "policemen are somewhat insensitive to the desires and needs of blacks," he also argues that "the black community has tended to be insensitive to the problems of police as well." However, Joyce Ladner, writing "through the eyes" of lower-class blacks, presents a directly opposite view. Ladner states that lower-class blacks view the police with the utmost suspicion because they have often seen them use repression against people who cannot strike back. Nonetheless, it is difficult to assess the degree of hostility in the black community toward the police. Whereas some blacks resent the police and the misuse of police power, others complain of lack of police protection. The ghettoes are very dangerous, states Winston Moore, "not only for white people passing through but especially for the vast majority of law abiding black residents." Moore asserts that "the black community wants law and order because it needs law and order for its own survival." But regardless of black support for law and order, the issue of police insensitivity and brutality in the ghetto still remains. Data reported in Rosen's essay suggest that of the occupational groups servicing the ghetto, the police and merchants were most likely to be disturbed about increased interaction and competition with blacks. Nonetheless, Rosen is reluctant to grant the argument that the police actually treat blacks differently than they do whites.

The only empirical study that sheds light on the issue of police brutality reports no significant difference between the way the police handle white and black suspects. The validity of this study can be questioned, however. Since the trained observers of police behavior rode in squad cars, it is reasonable to argue that they created an "unnatural setting." Police were aware that their behavior was being recorded and under those conditions may have exercised self-restraint.

But the problems (real or perceived) that blacks have with public servants are not restricted to police or to politicians. Winston Moore argues that the racism exhibited among prison officials is more intense and vicious than it is among other segments of the society. Barely two per cent of correctional officials are black or Spanish-speaking despite the fact that the urban nonwhite population constitutes more than 60 per cent of the inmate population in the nation's jails and prisons. Most of the lower-ranking prison officials, such as guards, belong to the social class elements that are most resentful of, and antagonistic toward, blacks, and since the attitude of correction officers is to "lock 'em up and throw away the key," racial bigotry inside the prison is not easily tempered.

Racism in the public school system, however, is more subtle and indirect. Black children continue to be mentally crippled in urban public schools and they continue to be the victims of the recurring power struggles between the teachers' unions and school boards. The mounting problems of the urban school system seem to be related to the fact that the public schools are becoming increasingly black. (In Philadelphia, for example, the black student population has increased to 60 per cent of the total public school enrollment, with a majority of the white pupils attending parochial schools. In Chicago, the white enrollment in the public schools dropped during 1972 from 34.6 per cent to 31 per cent.) As whites withdraw from public schools and increasingly enter private and parochial schools, concern for public education decreases. Urban public schools are therefore neglected; rising operating costs become difficult to meet—including teachers' salaries. The tripartite struggle between the teachers' unions, the school board, and the community creates an atmosphere where, as Lawrence Fink points out, teachers become more concerned about their own welfare than with teaching the students. Under these conditions the most sensitive teachers described in Fink's essay find it difficult to teach effectively.

But, to repeat, black students, and those decreasing numbers of white students still in the public school system, are the ultimate victims of the urban school crisis. Efforts to make teachers more responsive to the needs of students have, by and large, failed. In Washington, D.C., for example, Kenneth Clark's plan to promote teachers not automatically but on their demonstrated performance in the classroom was rejected by the teachers' union.[3] The traditional teachers' prerogatives were threatened by this proposal: and since the teachers' union in Washington is predominantly black, this suggests that the matter cannot be reduced simply to a question of race. The class (or occupational) interests of both black and white teachers help to reinforce the enduring system of institutional racism which originated from beliefs in the biological and cultural inferiority of blacks.

Finally, it is no coincidence that we have a welfare crisis at the very time that the urban public schools are deteriorating. As Zweig points out, "there can be little doubt that the racism so characteristic of all aspects of American life is deeply established within the operational structure of the broad spectrum of organizations known as welfare agencies." Just as the neglect of urban public schools is related to their becoming increasingly black, so is the public hostility to welfare a function of the popular stereotype that it is an institution for blacks. During periods of economic tension, such as experienced in the early 1970's, racial intolerance tends to increase especially among lower-status whites who, because of economic strains, have become more concerned about the way scarce resources are distributed. Accordingly, proposals to increase welfare are severely resisted and efforts to cut back welfare payments are loudly applauded.

The growing public hostility to welfare parallels the emerging militancy of welfare recipients. As one aspect of the black protest movement of the 1960's against racial injustice, welfare clients pressed "for consumer representation on policy making boards throughout a wide spectrum of welfare offices." This not only posed a threat to welfare organizations but, as Zweig emphasizes, also increased welfare workers' ambivalence toward the poor—an ambivalence already generated by a policy constituency more concerned with the enforcement of regulations and cutting of payments rather than with aiding impoverished families.

Thus, we have seen throughout this volume that images of American race relations are influenced and shaped not only by race but also by social, economic, political, and historical situations. Although people tend to view racial problems through particular sociocultural prisms, a common underlying variable ultimately determines whether their racial attitudes will be hostile, friendly, or indifferent—namely, a belief that in-group claims to certain rights and privileges have been (or will be) jeopardized or threatened by the specific actions of outgroup racial members.

A Confusion of Perspectives

STANLEY ROTHMAN

I. Introduction

The essays in this volume differ widely in style and content. Some of the authors have stuck closely to the task of describing the perspective of given segments of the black or white communities. Others have added a touch of polemic to their writing. However "objective" they may have tried to be, almost all of the authors make certain assumptions about the major sources of racial conflict in contemporary America.

As one attempts to analyze these underlying (or between the line) assumptions, one becomes increasingly aware of the wide range of perceptions which even scholars bring to the subject. One also becomes aware that, despite the growing tendency of whites and blacks to view each other in monolithic terms, both communities are quite diverse.

The diversity of views in the white community is developed rather more explicitly by the white contributors than is the diversity of the black community by the black contributors. The white authors, for example, include scholars like Dizard, Wiley, Zweig, and Blauner who tend to see "racism" as embedded in "the system" and who imply at least that only a radical change in the system can bring an end to the oppression of blacks. Other white contributors deny, at least implicitly, that such a transformation is required. Writers such as Fink, Friedman, Welks, and Rosen seem to feel that, over time, reform within the system can improve relations between blacks and whites. Further they clearly do not feel that all the problems which blacks face stem from "institutional racism." Rather they argue that a history of repression has led to the development of a black community which contains a substantial number of disadvantaged, personally disorganized individuals, and that, with the best will in the world, it is difficult to find ways to help such persons, in the short run at least.

Thus, to take Rosen's essay as an example, the hostility between the police and the black community is viewed not simply as the result of contemporary police racism or brutality, but also as reflecting the high crime rates which characterize the ghetto. Similarly, Professor Fink argues that the inability of schools to more effectively aid lower-class black students has much to do with the orientations and skills which these children bring to the school, which are a reflection of their home environment. He tends to feel that teachers have too often been blamed for situations which—given our present knowledge and resources—they could only marginally affect.

The contributions of the black scholars are rather less diverse. Whatever their degree of militancy, all of the authors urge a concept of black identity, even if they reject separatism and the use of violence, and all of those who comment directly see institutional racism as the major source of racial tension and injustice. Only in very rare cases (see, for example, the essay by Winston Moore) will black authors argue that some of the problems of the black community may be causally related to the existence of a large black lower class, but even here the burden of responsibility is placed on the continuing actions of the white community. The major differences among various black contributors are those of style, perceptions of strategy, and depth of rage. Most black authors seem to feel that their task is not merely to describe the world but to change it.

Of course, all of the authors, black and white, agree on one issue. Whether they argue in terms of past actions or in terms of continued racism, the major burden of blame for America's racial tragedy is seen to lie with the white community. The black authors write with the certainty of those sure of their moral position. Most of the white authors are, at the least, somewhat apologetic if, indeed, they do not fully share black criticisms of white society.

Even those who feel that the nature of the black lower class today—rather than present institutional racism—is among the key sources of our problems accept the fact that the existence of this class is a function of past racist attitudes and actions. If there is, as many blacks argue, a "white power structure," its intellectual wing is hopelessly divided against itself.

In examining the contributions, is it possible to get some sense of the range of perspectives in both the black and white communities? The decision to produce this book had its source in our belief that a fuller understanding of such perspectives might lead to a better understanding of the contemporary American racial tragedy and thus (hopefully) contribute to developing better ways of ameliorating it. My colleague, Professor Wilson, has attempted to draw out and integrate some of the sociological generalizations implicit in the book's essays. My own task is the related one of developing a typology of group perceptions and attempting to understand some of their underlying dynamics.

II. A Spectrum of Views

An effort to summarize various perceptions of the racial issue in America today calls for some sort of classification system. I intend to use a fairly simple one. Views on the issue of racial conflict will be examined along a continuum from conservative through liberal-integrationist and radical, with the addition of another dimension which, theoretically at least, cross cuts that classification, namely "nationalist." It should be noted that this classification refers to attitudes as regards racial and ethnic conflict rather than economic or social ideology, although the position taken on both sets of issues often overlap. Since the same position on the scale can involve somewhat different perceptions for whites and blacks, we have eight categories, running from white conservatives through black nationalists, and it is in terms of these categories that my discussion will proceed.

White Conservatives

To a relatively small, and declining—although still probably significant—segment of the white population, the source of our current dilemmas lies in the reforms of the past fifteen years or so. Blacks are considered "inferior" and "animal like" and need to be controlled for their own good as well as that of the larger society. The position need not detain us, for it is a view which, when held, is voiced only in the privacy of the intimate circle. This group can legitimately be described as bigots.

A much more significant segment of "race relations" conservatives is not so easily classified in this way. This segment is made up of many southern whites, northern middle-class Protestants, and significant segments of the working-class ethnic community—people of the type described in the essay by Welks. A good many of the members of this group view the current malaise of the country partly as a function of the behavior of blacks and the support—they would say excessive support—of blacks by the intellectual and media establishment. They see the black community as disorganized and violent. They are not sure why blacks behave the way they view them as behaving, but they fear them. They would claim that they are perfectly willing to grant blacks equal opportunities for jobs, housing, etcetera, but they also feel that blacks are getting much more than their due. Indeed they often seem to feel that they personally are the victims of a kind of reverse discrimination.

To them, many blacks are poor because, for reasons they do not understand, blacks refuse to work hard, to take care of their homes or to raise their children properly. They will admit that blacks have had a raw deal in the past, but so, they say, did they. Since the ethnics are mostly second-generation immigrants (or even first generation) they feel little responsibility for slavery or its aftermath. Many of them had never seen more than a few blacks until a relatively short time ago, and many feel that they themselves lean over backwards to be fair in their personal relations with blacks.

Many of these ethnics see no reason why they should not be left alone in their own neighborhoods with "their own kind," and send their children to neighborhood schools. Many others are willing to live with a few "nice" blacks, or even to have their children attend integrated schools with "well behaved" blacks, but they fear an "inundation" by the black community and the violence they fear will accompany that "inundation." A good many of them have already fled neighborhoods which they felt deteriorated and became more violent as blacks moved in. Since they are convinced that they worked hard to live better and give their children more opportunities than they had, they feel that it is unfair to send their children back into the old neighborhoods, or to be forced to flee again.

Most of them also feel that America was a good society until recently. They are not sure quite what happened, but they think that blacks and the media have so destroyed respect for authority, including that of the police, that the society is rapidly deteriorating. They also feel that they are being made to pay the price for helping blacks while the "rich liberals" cheer from the sidelines.

On economic issues the ethnics are liberal or even radical, but, in their view, many blacks are freeloading on welfare and they are suspicious of the "reform" measures sponsored by "liberal" candidates. It is from this group, then, which Wallace drew a good deal of support in the North by combining populist and anti-black slogans, and it is this group which deserted the Democratic Party in 1972 to vote against McGovern—not really for Nixon—whom they identified with all that was ruining the country. Many of them are now confused and disoriented. They claim that they want to do the "right thing," but they do not know what is right. In many cases they have retreated to personal concerns, and they concentrate on defending themselves and their families against onslaughts from the outside world.

The group as a whole finds few defenders in the intellectual community, although there are some signs of an increasing awareness of their fears and concerns. A special issue of *Dissent*,[1] for example, treated them not unsympathetically, and Michael Novak's book, *The Rise of the Unmeltable Ethnics*,[2] tried to articulate their position. In terms of policy alternatives, the scholar who has come closest to speaking for their view is Edward Banfield, in the *Unheavenly City*,[3] although he sees the issues largely in class terms. Most recently a few black scholars have begun to evince some sympathy for their plight as well as the plight of the "respectable" black working class and lower-middle class, and to criticize some of the same people the ethnics have criticized for ignoring the realities of black lower-class life in formulating policy alternatives.[4]

Black Conservatives

It is hard to specify the perceptions of black conservatives. Their views have received but little attention in the media or in intellectual journals. One suspects that, as a group, they include older blacks who still accept the idea of subordination, but that beyond this the group probably includes some who have made it economically and see no reason why other blacks cannot do the same if they work hard. The middle-class segment of the group undoubtedly accepts many of the dominant myths of middle America, and is as worried as are other middle Americans about such things as bussing and "ghetto violence." Many are undoubtedly torn between their identification with other blacks (and their sense of still being subordinate) and status and/or safety concerns, but the latter outweigh the former in their minds. As the gap between blacks who are making it within the system (roughly half the black community) and those who have not, widens, it is at least possible that increasing numbers of blacks will find that their senses of racial and ethnic identity is counterbalanced by class interests. Indeed, there is good evidence that this is already beginning to occur, as reports mount of black parents in relatively integrated middle-class neighborhoods who do not want their children bussed into ghetto schools, or who, along with white parents, express anxiety about the introduction of low-income housing. Perhaps more indicative is the fact that while over 90 per cent of the black vote in the ghettos was for McGovern, this fell to 80 per cent for those blacks living in nonghetto urban areas and to 67 per cent of those blacks (only about one out of 16) living in the suburbs.[5]

White Liberal-Integrationists

These include a fairly wide spectrum of the white population. Indeed, ideologically at least, this position is probably the dominant one in the white community today, or so various studies of public opinion seem to indicate. Like their black counterparts, to be discussed below, intellectuals adhering to this view range from moderately reformist to democratic socialist. They are included under the rubric liberal primarily because of their commitment to working for reform within the system even if such reform is seen as leading eventually to a fairly radical transformation of its political and economic organization.

In this volume authors like Greeley, Friedman, Rosen, and Fink probably best represent the position, implicitly if not explicitly. Enough has been said about this group to obviate the need for a detailed discussion of their perspectives here. Suffice it to say that, whatever their long-range views of the ideal society, they tend to feel that the problem of racial conflict is not primarily an economic-exploitive issue in the Marxist sense and that it can be solved, or at least partially solved, within the broad framework of contemporary American society, provided one can develop the right kind of programs. However, while their goal remains an integrated society and while many of them look to a coalition of the black and white working class to back such reforms, they are probably less optimistic as regards the possible pace of reform, and the ease with which racial problems can be resolved, than they were even ten years ago.

When the civil rights revolution first began many of them probably felt that the culmination of their efforts was now at hand. The granting of equal rights to blacks with some special assistance would integrate them rapidly into the general population, and the race issue would permanently disappear from American life. The expectation was that blacks would, because of their suffering, adopt the "best" American values and would serve as a reformist leaven in the society. Nevertheless, blacks were "brothers under the skin" who would essentially come to resemble white American Protestants.

The past ten years have not dealt kindly with liberal integrationists, and, indeed, the group has fragmented, segments of it moving to the right or to the left. Many of those who remain faithful to an integrationist ideal now feel that they underestimated the difficulties involved in achieving integration. Most feel that considerable progress has been made, but that (aside from continued prejudice) the personal and social disorganization which characterize segments of the black community call for even greater public efforts to aid both white and black poor.

However, liberals find themselves in an uncomfortable position.

They feel that they understand and sympathize with the anxieties of white ethnics and they are of two minds on such issues as bussing, and scatter-site housing. They find, too, that the dominant black voices today reject their *bonafides* and, indeed, resent them. With an acute sense of their own ambivalence and the "failures" of the liberal effort during the 1960's, they find it harder to whip up enthusiasm for their programs, or even to engage in meaningful dialogue with the new generation of black leadership. They resent (but feel guilty about) black charges that their "new realism" is really subtle racism, an issue which has become quite charged over questions of community control of schools and the establishment of "quotas" in colleges and universities.

Caught between their belief in universalistic standards, and the feeling that blacks must be permitted to define themselves; torn between their commitment to civil liberties and concern for the underdog, and recognition of the reality of urban violence, they have been partially immobilized and partly pushed aside.

The essay by Lewis Killian, although concerned primarily with Southerners, catches the poignancy of the liberal dilemma quite well. He himself now feels, albeit reluctantly, that, given the impossibility of meaningful integration, he must become a white supporter of black nationalist aspirations.

Black Liberal-Integrationists

If white integrationists have had the rug pulled from under them, blacks who support a "liberal-integrationist" point of view have fared even worse. After all, it was only fifteen or twenty years ago that the integrationist position and black leadership were synonymous, and that integrationist leaders could point to the disorganization of the black community as a condemnation of white society. To the younger generation of black militants, however, such positions are a species of "uncle tomism," just as are opposition to separate dormitories, skepticism about black study programs, or a positive view of the language and norms of "white middle class society."

Among our black contributors no author explicitly identifies with the liberal integrationist position, although many are willing to accept the integrity of those holding it, and to recognize their contributions to the black cause. In the black community at large (assuming the public opinion polls are correct) integrationist leaders have rather more support. Indeed, one of the constant complaints of the group has been that white school administrators and whites in control of the media have given the impression that radical nationalists are dominant in the black community when, in fact, they are not. The support of the liberal integrationist position is largely passive, however, and there can be little question but that men like Kenneth Clark, Roy Wilkins, and Bayard Rustin lack the ability to mobilize activist black youth at this point in time.

Black liberal-integrationists have even found it somewhat more difficult to communicate with their white counterparts in the past few years, although contact remains reasonably good. The issues which divide them largely involve differences in the assessment of particular problems and remedies. Black integrationists are likely to place rather more blame for the problems facing the black community on current white practices than are white integrationists, and they are likely to press harder for such policies as bussing and even temporary "quota-like" arrangements than are their white counterparts. They are also less sympathetic to the complaints of white ethnics. Privately, however, and increasingly, publicly, they will tell white colleagues that the personal and social disorganization of segments of the ghetto population is a problem, although, like their white colleagues, they are less sure than they used to be as regards effective remedies.

White and Black Radicals

This group differs from the liberal integrationists not in their commitment to integration as an ultimate ideal, but rather in their analysis as to how it is most likely to be achieved. Their view of America, as expressed on the white side by Dizard, Zweig, and Wiley is that racial problems are secondary to economic and social exploitation and that the elimination of the latter would, more or less, take care of the former. In a sense racism is epiphenomenal in that it derives from—or at least is maintained by—a competitive exploitive society. At best the existing power élite perpetuates racism by its adherence to outmoded values. At worst it uses racism as a mechanism to maintain and exploit its power position.

Discussions of personal or social disorganization within the black community, or discussions of the "culture of poverty" are simply ways of avoiding facing the need for a root change in American society. The hope of white radicals—which rose to a peak in the late 1960's but has since diminished—lies in a counterélite of students and intellectuals who, leading the working class—black and white—could bring about this root change.

As compared to the 1930's when a number of black intellectuals, including such figures as Harold Cruse and Richard Wright, joined the Communist Party, the "radical" position as a pure type does not command much support today within the black community. One wing of the Black Panthers flirted with Marxism and the idea of a united black and white revolutionary working class for a time, but not much is heard of this position today, despite the enthusiasm generated by Angela Davis. The reasons for this probably lie in part with the attitudes of white workers. They also lie at least partly beyond the borders of the United States. In Africa, Asia, and Latin America, the attraction of traditional radical categories (that is, Marxist categories) is far less pronounced than it once was. Marxist theory was always based on the assumption of the dominant revolutionary role of the working class and was Europe centered. Increasingly, however, Third World nations—even when Marxism is paid substantial lip service—are coming to see social conflict as at least partly related to the power of the developed countries, mostly European and white, vis-à-vis the developing countries, whose populations are largely nonwhite.

Black Nationalists and White Sympathizers

It was noted earlier that a concept of black identity ran through all or, at least, almost all, of the black essays in this volume. The "transvaluation of values" implicit in this notion can be traced back to earlier nationalist antecedents in America, but the contemporary version of this attitude finds its origins primarily in the concept of "negritude" which developed among literary figures in the West Indies and was adopted by substantial numbers of African intellectuals in the late 1950's. In the United States "negritude" has become associated with the view that Africans should seek to reclaim their African heritage and, often, the argument that black ghetto styles can be traced back to that heritage. Rhetorically, and sometimes organizationally, it has involved attempts to form coalitions with other groups (Chicanos, Asians, and so forth) in an attempt to develop a coalition of Third World peoples with common concerns and problems.

In general, the stress is upon black or Third World separatism, with the associated argument of the superiority of black or Third World culture, revolving around such conceptions of "soul." The "disorganization" seen as characteristic of some ghetto families by many white and some black sociologists in the past is dismissed, for example, in Joyce Ladner's essay, as essentially white or "Uncle Tom" sociology. What seems to whites to be pathology is, as she argues, a rational response to continued white oppression.

Those most involved in the nationalist movement in its political and social aspects have faced a number of difficulties, not the least of which is that "negritude" as a concept is operating with diminished force in Africa as African nations strive to modernize. Beyond that, few if any, black writers have clarified the unique character of black culture or personality, or indicated in any detailed way what kind of social organization would be associated with it. In the end, for example, Ladner's discussion of black girls in the ghetto leaves one with the feeling that, given reasonable life chances, ghetto blacks would behave very much like anybody else. In short, their underlying values still seem largely white "middle class."

A rather different problem is reflected in Chuck Stone's essay. While he is unsparing in his criticism of "white power structure" and of those black politicians who merely take reformist stances, he is quite clearly ambivalent. At times he writes as if nothing but the destruction of the whole system would satisfy him. However, in the last analysis, he draws back, implies that blacks, like other ethnics, merely want in. Mr. Stone points out in his essay that black politicians must of necessity be rather schizophrenic as regards the black role in America. I suspect that he would be willing to agree that this is true of large numbers of young black intellectuals today. Many of these young people are torn between the desire to establish a black identity and the desire to gain the skills which are required for survival in a modern society. Fighting to achieve leverage in the society by bringing black people together as a unified force, but recognizing that they are still a minority within the society and need white allies, black nationalists have yet to develop an ideological orientation which integrates the complexity of their feelings about America, Africa, and themselves.

Relatively few whites identify wholeheartedly with black nationalism and its associated symbols, although, for a time, in the late 1960's, the nationalist movement drew to it a fringe of white intellectuals and college youth, who agreed with the more militant black nationalists that white culture was sick and acknowledged the superiority of the black alternative. In this volume, Robert Blauner comes closest to such a position. He accepts the nationalist argument that black culture is different from white culture, and that it offers a legitimate alternative to the dominant American ethos. Indeed he implies, and others have stated the position rather more strongly, that if we are to succeed in developing the radical reorientation our culture requires—if a truly humanistic society is to be established—we must learn from the black experience and the black life style. He rejects, as do black nationalists, the idea that American black culture is merely the culture of poverty, and sees taints of continued "institutional" racism in the failure of many of his white colleagues to accept it on its own terms.

III. Toward a Sociology of Knowledge

Ideological positions such as those described in this essay are difficult to evaluate with objectivity—by "turning to the facts." All so called "facts" are embodied in a matrix of beliefs and theories, and what we see is very much colored by our basic assumptions. We all like to believe that we think "rationally" and that our ethical views and policy recommendations are informed by an honest attempt to understand contemporary reality and future possibilities, but few of us, especially in times of crisis, are capable of developing the necessary detachment that enterprise requires, assuming such detachment and "objectivity" are really possible.

At least some social scientists would even argue that it is impossible to develop an integrated and "objective" perspective on race relations in the United States, and imply that there is little to be gained by trying. To this group our understanding of any social issue derives primarily from value commitments which are not subject to empirical confirmation or disconfirmation. Whatever their personal views, their orientation is ultimately highly pessimistic in its consequences, for if we accept it, conflicts between blacks and whites in the United States or Protestants and Catholics in Northern Ireland can only be resolved by force, or by some accommodation based on the threat of force. This is not my view, nor is it, so far as I can determine, the view of the contributors to this volume. All of the authors use essentially the same canons of evidence in attempting to describe things as they are, while aware of the difficulties of doing so. All of them, too, seem committed to the view that an understanding of things as they are and might be can lead to some broader agreement on public policy issues. Indeed, the very nature of the dialogue in this volume would seem to support Charles Taylor's view that whatever the logical status of "facts and values," all of us derive our conceptions of the "good" and our sense of how best to achieve the good from our perceptions of human needs and possibilities.[6] In principle, therefore, it is at least possible to develop some sort of overview which might enable men and women of "reason" to move in the direction of a fuller and more humane understanding of the issues with which we are confronted.

To attempt such a task in an essay of this length would be presumptuous. I can, however, take another tack. The analysis of the underlying, but often unrecognized, sources of ideological perspectives cannot solve concrete problems, for the knowledge of the sources of ideas tells us nothing about their truth value. However, one of the assumptions of all sociologies of knowledge—from Marx to Freud—has been that understanding of this type can often enable us to take one or two steps in the direction of greater objectivity. To this task, then, I shall now turn, offering some suggestions as to the sources of contemporary black responses to white society, as well as comments on possible sources of some of the responses to black demands by segments of the white majority.

. . .

It is perhaps easier to develop a typology of the reactions of the black community to current racial problems than it is to deal with the white majority. Whatever their background, blacks have shared the common experience of extreme oppression. In this sense the white community is a far more diverse group, ranging, for example, from Jews or Italians or Irish who, for varying periods of time, were outsiders to the dominant culture, to those WASPs for whom until recently the American experience was a confirmation, if not of superiority then at least of the rightness of the values by which they lived.

Elsewhere Peter Rose has outlined the possible responses by members of any minority to their marginal and subordinate position in a culture.[7] They can accept the definition of inferiority imposed by dominant segments of the society with all its attendant political and personal consequences. They can also attempt to overcome their "inferiority" in a variety of ways. One possibility is that of "assimilation" or "passing." For Jews or Irish this involved the relatively simple step of abjuring their religious faith and incorporating themselves as part of the majority culture, often by adopting its values in heightened form. In America, this type of response has become less and less necessary. Indeed, it has been possible to retain one's religious identification and to be accepted by the culture, provided one clearly adopted "Protestant-American" values. Hence the phenomenon of the assimilated Jew who attends Ivy League schools and internalizes dominant values, or the lace-curtain Irish whose style and manner differ little from the image traditionally held of the "Philadelphia Gentleman" or "Boston Brahmin." The vigor with which many ethnics have come to the defense of "American" values in the current crisis, and the vigor with which they supported "Americanism" in the 1950's, certainly has had something to do with a desire to belong, and to be accepted. The phenomenon is not confined to the United States by any means. As Robert Haddad has cogently argued, the identification of Arab Christians in the Middle East with the nationalism of secular Arab states can be seen as a mechanism designed to end their inferior status in a predominantly Muslim world. If being a Syrian became more significant than being a Muslim, then the fact that one was a Christian no longer identified one as a marginal person.[8] The same analysis has been applied to the early commitment to nationalism on the part of Nigeria's Ibo population. Hammelstrand has pointed out that the Ibos, as a relatively small minority, had much to gain by substituting national for tribal loyalties.[9] Their effort failed in that it provoked an ethnic reaction which led Ibos to reassert ethnic nationalism themselves, but Hammelstrand's analysis of their initial enthusiasm certainly seems cogent.

The route of assimilation has been taken by some blacks and, historically, attempted by many more. Those who were light enough could hope to "pass," and, among the "black bourgeoisie, as Johnetta Cole points out, there was often a self-conscious effort to copy WASP life styles, and adopt WASP social institutions.

As against white Jews and Catholics, however, blacks faced the obstacle of color. No matter what their manifest behavior their chances of being fully "accepted" (except for the few who passed) was quite small. Indeed a number of commentators have noted that, in its origins at least, the civil rights movement had more to do with the desire for "status" by middle-class blacks, than with a conscious desire to raise the level of the black masses. This changed as the black masses became politicized. It also changed as segments of the black middle class became increasingly convinced that color itself bound their fate inextricably with that of their poorer brethren in ways that were not true for middle-class white ethnics.

Two other routes are available to minority groups seeking to enhance their position and end the ascription of inferiority. The first lies in identifying with some universalistic transcultural standard which denies the relevance of the national or ethnic categories which define them as inferior and, indeed, promises to seriously undermine, if not abolish, these categories and the institutions which have supported them. Thus, the attraction of Marxism to Jews, and later of Soviet communism as an international movement, can be seen as a reflection of their marginal position in Eastern Europe; a marginal position which could not be overcome by appealing to national loyalties in an area of Europe where nationalism and ethnicity went hand in hand. They were joined in this attachment, as Burks points out, by other minority groups (Slovaks and Magyars, for example) who found themselves in a somewhat similar situation.[10] The position of blacks in the United States has certainly been analogous, and the identification of some prominent black intellectuals with communism in the 1930's and even the 1960's can be explained, partially, in these terms.

Finally, one can escape one's minority status by creating a situation in which one's group is the majority, and the majority with power. Jews who embraced this path turned to Zionism, just as Germans in Czechoslovakia turned to pan-Germanism. In the United States of the late 1960's and early 1970's black nationalism probably has similar roots.

Indeed, the attraction of the nationalist alternative, sometimes tied in with a Third World orientation, has, as had been noted, turned out to be far more attractive than traditional Marxism. The reasons are not hard to find. To accept a Marxist position is to continue to subordinate oneself to traditional European categories. Thus, just as China and the Arab nations have developed their own brand of Marxist humanism, so African nations and many American blacks are attempting to develop an ideology which ends their subordination to Europe and emphasizes their unique cultural heritage. As Clement Moore has pointed out, in describing a similar pattern in North Africa, the process is, in some sense, dialectical. Early resistance to European encroachment often involved rebellions in terms of traditional cultural patterns and looked backward to a golden past. This was followed by widespread acceptance of European ideas with an emphasis on assimilation. Today most Third World peoples are trying to integrate the most advanced of European positions (socialism) with a version of their traditional culture that is stripped of its archaic features.[11] The history of blacks in the United States is not all that different.

And the effort does involve a "transvaluation of values." In describing the unique features of black culture, Vernon Dixon emphasizes the (1) emphasis of passion above reason (2) diunital (or dialectical) thinking (3) and communalism as against individualism.[12] The first of these points, at least, takes a character trait which white racists have always ascribed to blacks, and used as a basis for excluding them, and proudly asserts its legitimacy if not superiority to "white" modes of behavior. It is little wonder, then, that at least a few white conservatives have found black nationalism, in some of its aspects, far from unattractive.

The sources of at least some white reactions to the black community and to the civil rights movement have been partially explored earlier in this essay. To ethnics the attack on traditional middle-class American values by blacks and their supporters is probably all the more frightening because they gave up so much (as Michael Novak points out) to be accepted. Beyond these feelings lie perceived conflicts of interest, and, on a deeper level, primordial attitudes as to the nature of whiteness and blackness which are so much a part of our culture and others. Associated with such feelings is, of course, the tendency for many whites to project aggressive and sexual impulses, which are unacceptable to the self, upon blacks. So much has been written by sociologists and psychologists on the dynamics of white prejudice, however, that there is little reason to deal with these issues in any detail. Indeed, despite the complaints of the new generation of black militants there can be little question but that the (white) sociological establishment has, in the past twenty-five years, tended to deal with the race issue either as a symptom of underlying faults in the American economic and social system, or as a reflection of the pathology of prejudiced white individuals.

Far less attention has been paid to the sources of behavior of those upper-middle-class Protestants and Jews who have served, within the white community, as the major supporters of black aspirations, except to comment on the "idealism" of this group. There is some reason to believe, however, that white liberals, radicals, and nationalist sympathizers may, as do others, derive some of their attitudes from sources of which they are not completely aware.

In the case of Jews it seems fairly clear that the support of various universalistic solutions to the problem of black marginality is tied in with their own historical marginality, and the feeling that working toward this end with regard to blacks strengthens their own position. Among those who have chosen a more radical position (or a position sympathetic to black nationalist aspirations) there may be a partly unconscious desire—as some black intellectuals have hinted—to use blacks as a battering ram against a Christian dominated society, toward which they still feel considerable hostility. In this light the recent backing off of many Jews from support of more radical black movements can be seen as a belated recognition on their part that, in the United States at least, they were now willy nilly part of the "white establishment," and that the more militant versions of the black attack on American society might be injurious to their own interests. At least implicitly this is one of the points that Friedman makes in his essay on Jews.

For many upper-middle-class Protestants, identification with the black cause may well have served (at least partially) another function. WASP cultural and political power in the United States has, in fact, been seriously weakened in recent years by the upward movement of second-generation ethnics who have adopted American competitive individualism as their own. What better way to recoup status and to justify inherited wealth (and the loss of a competitive drive) than to attack the ethos which their forebears sired as banal and narrow-minded? After all, aren't we as upper-middle-class liberals, far superior than those narrow-minded bigoted ethnics in their "ticky tacky" houses?

Beyond this, one suspects that blacks have continued to satisfy many of the same projective needs in radicals as they have in reactionaries. By identifying with black "virility" and "power," many an upper-middle-class male has overcome his own feelings of weakness. One can find some of these attitudes expressed, at least indirectly, in the writings of intellectuals who have identified with black causes.

Norman Mailer, for example, in his essay "The White Negro," wrote with some envy of the "instinctual" freedom of blacks.[13] And Dotson Rader describes the excitement he felt when he thought he was going to be attacked by a group of black teenagers, and the disappointment he felt when they did not physically molest him:

> When it was over I was disappointed, for I had expected violence. I thought the living shit would be knocked out of me . . . , I both feared and wanted it to happen, wanted violence that tested a man, brought into the open the ambivalency of feelings I held. . . . I was about fifteen and I suspected that part of the significance of the

black in the white imagination was the potential of their violence. And violence was liberating.[14]

Certainly, some white women ostensibly dedicated to the cause of black liberation have had mixed motives, expecting to find that black men were as virile as racist stereotypes suggested they were. The classic description of the syndrome is to be found in Ralph Ellison's *The Invisible Man.* When the hero (or antihero) becomes involved with the American Communist Party, he discovers that a few of the women are more interested in his supposed sexual virility than they are in his existence as a unique living, breathing human being. To them, too, he is invisible.

. . .

What, if anything, can be said of the future of black-white relations in the United States? There is in this volume as much for the pessimist as the optimist as, indeed, there is on the American scene as a whole. The optimist can point to the fact that a substantial number of scholars have been able to collaborate on a book designed to explore divergencies in perspective, and by so doing have indicated their desire to communicate with each other. The pessimist can note that the perspectives of the authors differ so widely in some cases that the possibility of a common definition of the issues seems quite remote.

The optimist can point to the fact that most of the legal barriers to full black participation in American society have been eliminated, and can add that many middle-class blacks, at least, are making it. The pessimist can argue that the gaps between blacks and whites seem as great as ever, and perhaps, in some ways, greater. In the 1950's, for example, the artistic and intellectual community included many to whom color was less relevant than common professional and intellectual concerns. There may well be fewer people today for whom that is true than there were then. Further, need one point out that within American cities millions of blacks are still living under conditions which have improved very little during the past ten years, and that most programs designed to help them seem to have failed, for whatever reason? In addition the American electorate, if it has not moved to the Right, has certainly shown less sympathy for new programs than it seemed to feel in 1964 and 1965.

The optimist can point to the fact that, all things considered, black-white confrontation has remained relatively nonviolent as compared to events in Northern Ireland, Pakistan, or Nigeria. The pessimist can indicate that we are far from over the hump and that that heightened violence remains a real possibility.

In Western Europe the class issue remained the pivot of politics for at least one hundred and fifty years, and, despite an inordinate amount of violence, it has yet to be fully resolved. Historically, clashes over ethnic and racial issues have proven even more intractable and more dangerous. Thus, it seems quite likely that the issues will be with us for some time to come. Can we develop a genuine dialogue between blacks and whites? Can we restructure our society so as to recognize and encourage black desires for identity and yet permit those to whom this identity is less important than a common humanity, to relate to other individuals on different grounds? The issues involved represent both a threat and an opportunity.

A number of scholars have referred to the United States as the first modern nation, in that it was perhaps the first nation to accept most of the institutions we have come to accept as constituting modernization. Certainly a good many other peoples have seen America as a testing ground for those institutions and an example, for good or evil, of the path that their societies might take.

In the postmodern world Americans are engaged in another experiment, whose results may be equally significant. However great the recent resurgence of ethnic and communal violence has been, it is clear that most of those conflicts are on the decline, with the exception of clashes which involve the issue of color. Indeed, it can be argued that color is among the major sources of fragmentation in the human community today. If Americans can somehow reduce that fragmentation and create a society in which blacks and whites can develop a reasonable accommodation, this could have significant consequences for the community of nations. If they cannot, the results for them as well as for the rest of the world are likely to be disastrous.

NOTES

The Urban Poor
Joyce Ladner

1. Walter Stafford and Joyce Ladner, "Comprehensive Planning and Racism," *Journal of the American Institute of Planning* 35, no. 2, (March 1969): 70.
2. W. E. B. DuBois, *Souls of Black Folk* (New York: Fawcett World Library, 6th Premier printing, August 1968), p. 16.
3. Frantz Fanon, *Black Skins, White Masks* (New York: Grove Press, 1963).
4. Robert Coles, *Children of Crisis* (Boston: Little, Brown, 1964), especially Chapter IX.
5. The following is an adaptation of Chapter III (entitled, "Racial Oppression and the Black Girl") of Joyce A. Ladner, *Tomorrow's Tomorrow* (New York: Doubleday, 1971).

The Black Bourgeoisie
Johnnetta B. Cole

1. For a discussion of stratification in black society using three categories, see Andrew Billingsley, *Black Families in White America* (Englewood Cliffs, N. J.: Prentice-Hall, 1968).
2. Harold Cruse, "Revolutionary Nationalism and the Afro-American," *Studies of the Left* (February 1962): 76–77.
3. J. H. O'Dell, "A Special Variety of Colonialism," *Freedomways*, 7, no. 1 (1967).
4. Robert Allen, *Black Awakening in Capitalist America* (New York: Doubleday, 1970), p. 11.
5. Frantz Fanon, *The Wretched of the Earth* (New York: Grove Press, 1963), p. 34.
6. Ibid., p. 53.
7. Ibid., p. 32.

8. Ibid.
9. Allen, *Black Awakening* . . . pp. 17–20. A very different view of "the new Black middle class" is presented in Sidney Krounus's work, *The Black Middle Class* (Columbus, Ohio, Charles E. Merrill, 1971). Krounus reviews the profile of the black middle class as presented by Frazier and by Hare and compares that profile with the individuals in his sample, all of whom reside in the Chatham community area of Chicago, an all-black residential area on the South Side. He summarizes as follows: ". . . . we argued that the Black middle class is composed predominately of darker, occupationally mobile persons. In terms of life style and consumption patterns, they appear to live within their means, to take life seriously, and to accept their responsibilities to family, work, and community. As a whole, they have minimal desires for the superficial. Their positions in the civil rights movement indicate a positive racial stance. Finally, their disassociation with the Democratic political machine of Chicago supports the idea that they are critical of the white power structure and seek a self-determined role in the advancement of their race" (pp. 38–39).
10. E. Franklin Frazier: *Black Bourgeoisie* (Glencoe, Ill., Free Press, 1957), and Nathan Hare: *Black Anglo-Saxons* (New York: Collier, 1965 edition). In his introduction to *The Black Anglo-Saxons*, Oliver Cox labeled the works of Frazier and Hare as the "Black Bourgeoisie school." Other important works addressing the bougie life-style include John Dollard, *Caste and Class in a Southern Town* (New York: Doubleday, 1957); Gunnar Myrdal, *American Dilemma* (New York: Harper & Row, 1942); Hylan Lewis, *Black Ways of Kent* (Chapel Hill: University of North Carolina Press, 1955); Hortense Powermaker, *After Freedom: A Cultural Study in the Deep South* (New York: Viking, 1939); St. Clair Drake and Horace Clayton; *Black Metropolis: A Study of Negro Life in a Northern City* (New York: Harper & Row, 1962); and Allison Davis's article "The Negro Deserts His People," *Plain Talk*, 1929, pp. 49–54.
11. Hare, *Black Anglo-Saxons*, p. 16.
12. Drake and Clayton, *Black Metropolis* (vol. 2, p. 661).
13. Davis, "The Negro Deserts His People," p. 49.
14. Mao Tse-tung referred to the national bourgeoisie and the middle bourgeoisie as a vacillating class. See "Analysis of the Classes in Chinese Society," *Selected Readings from the Works of Mao Tse-tung* (Peking: Foreign Language Press, 1967), pp. 11–19.
15. Herbert Aptheker, "Afro-American Superiority: A Neglected Theme in Literature" in *Afro-American History: The Modern Era* (New York: Citadel Press), pp. 68–79.
16. Hare, *The Black Anglo-Saxons*, pp. 185–86.
17. Allen, *Black Awakening*, pp. 128–29.
18. Ibid., pp. 142–43.

The Integrationists
Edgar G. Epps

1. J. H. O'Dell, "The Contours of the Black Revolution of the 1970's," *Freedomways* 10 (Second Quarter, 1970), p. 105.
2. James L. Farmer, "Are White Liberals Obsolete in the Black Struggle?" in *Black Viewpoints*, eds. Arthur C. Littleton and Mary W. Burger (New York: New American Library, 1971), p. 86.
3. Whites who favor integration are not treated systematically in this paper.
4. This typology represents a revision of an earlier formulation presented elsewhere (Eric Krystall, Neil Friedman, Glenn Howze, and Edgar G. Epps, "Attitudes Toward Integration and Black Consciousness: Southern Negro High School Students and Their Mothers," *Phylon* 31, 2 (Summer, 1970), 104–13.
5. Martin Luther King, Jr., "The Future of Integration [1968]," in *Black Man in America: Integration and Separation*, ed. James A. Moss (New York: Dell, 1971), p. 41.
6. Whitney M. Young, Jr., *To Be Equal* (New York: McGraw-Hill, 1964).
7. Roy Wilkins, "Integration," *Ebony* (August 1970), 54.
8. Wilkins, "Integration," p. 106.
9. See, for example, Angus Campbell and Howard Schuman, "Racial Attitudes in Fifteen Cities," in *Supplemental Studies for the National Advisory Commission on Civil Disorders* (New York: Praeger, 1968), and William McCord and John Howard, "Negro Opinions," in *Life Styles in the Black Ghetto*, eds. William McCord, John Howard, Bernard Friedberg, and Edwin Harwood (New York: Norton, 1969).
10. Campbell and Schuman, "Racial Attitudes . . ." pp. 5–6.
11. Krystall *et al.*, "Attitudes Toward Integration . . ."; Neil Friedman, Agatha White, and Edgar G. Epps, "Attitudes of Southern Black College Students Toward Black Consciousness and Integration," *Afro-American Studies*, vol. 1 (1971): Glenn Howze, "Attitudes of Adult Black Males in a Southern City: The 1969 Tuskegee Area Study" (unpublished); Edgar G. Epps, "Achievement Orientation and Racial Attitudes Among Urban Black High School Students" (unpublished paper, 1971); and Edgar G. Epps, "Sex Differences in Attitudes Toward Black Consciousness and Integration Among Southern Black College Shudents," in *Race Relations: Current Perspectives*, ed. Edgar G. Epps (Cambridge, Mass: Winthrop Publishers, 1973).
12. Krystall, "Attitudes Toward Integration . . . , p. 112; McCord and Howard, *Life Styles* . . . , p. 95, report that unemployed persons in Houston expressed greater "willingness to use violence in defense of the Negro cause" than did employed persons. Among employed persons, the unskilled expressed greatest willingness to use violence. However, this study also found that college-educated respondents in

Watts were least likely to oppose the use of violence. It is clear that there are situational variations in the way background variables relate to attitudes toward violence.

Black Nationalists
J. Herman Blake

1. Vincent Harding, "The Uses of the Afro-American Past," *Negro Digest*, Vol. 17 (February, 1965), p. 5.
2. E. U. Essien-Udom, *Black Nationalism: A Search for an Identity in America* (Chicago: University of Chicago Press, 1962), chap. ii; and August Meier, "The Emergence of Negro Nationalism," *The Midwest Journal*, Vol. 4 (Winter 1951), pp. 96–104, and *ibid.* (Summer 1952), pp. 95–111.
3. Meier, *op. cit.*
4. *Ibid.*
5. Edmund David Cronon, *Black Moses: The Story of Marcus Garvey and the Universal Negro Improvement Association* (Madison: University of Wisconsin Press, 1955). The UNIA was actually organized in Jamaica in 1914 by Garvey, but he experienced his greatest success in the United States.
6. Cronon, *op. cit.*, pp. 22–27.
7. John Hope Franklin, *From Slavery to Freedom* (New York: Alfred A. Knopf, 1963), p. 483.
8. Cronon, *op. cit.*, chap. iii; Franklin, *op. cit.*, pp. 481–83.
9. Essien-Udom, *op. cit.*; and C. Eric Lincoln, *The Black Muslims in America* (Boston: Beacon Press, 1961).
10. U.S., Department of Commerce, Bureau of the Census, *Current Population Reports*, Series P-20, No. 157, December 16, 1966.
11. Karl E. Taeuber and Alma F. Taeuber, "The Changing Character of Negro Migration," *American Journal of Sociology*, Vol. 70 (January 1965), pp. 429–41.
12. Claude Brown states this issue well by raising the question: "Where does one run to when he's already in the promised land?"—*Manchild in the Promised Land* (New York: The Macmillan Company, 1965), p. 8.
13. This fact has been discovered by white middle-class youth as well, and they now seek to experience the authentic feeling-tone of Afro-American existence. Among black people, this new form of rejection of white America is authenticated by one's possession of that ethereal quality "soul," and is expressed in the "funky" music of black artists.
14. For a particularly profound and moving articulation of such issues, see Vincent Harding, "The Gift of Blackness," *Kattallagete* (Summer 1967), pp. 17–22.
15. J. Herman Blake, "The Black University and Its Community: Social

Change in the Sixties," *Negro Digest*, Vol. 17 (March 1968), pp. 87–90.

16. Stokely Carmichael and Charles V. Hamilton, *Black Power: The Politics of Liberation in America* (New York: Random House, 1967).
17. EDITOR'S NOTE—El-Shabazz is better known to most readers as Malcolm X.
18. Malcolm X, *Autobiography* (New York: Grove Press, 1966); also, the brief movie *Malcolm X: Struggle for Freedom* gives important insights into his post-Nation of Islam ideas, including his expansion of the concept "Afro-American."
19. LeRoi Jones, *Home* (New York: Morrow, 1966), p. 243.
20. Eldridge Cleaver, *Soul on Ice* (New York: McGraw-Hill, 1968), p. 59.
21. See the moving eulogy of El-Hajj Malik El-Shabazz by Ossie Davis in *Liberator*, Vol. 5 (April 1965), p. 7.
22. Stokely Carmichael, "What We Want," *New York Review of Books*, Vol. 7, September 22, 1966, p. 5.
23. For two excellent articulations of this view, see: Carmichael and Hamilton, *op. cit.*, chap. i; and Cleaver, *op. cit.*, pp. 112–37.
24. Jones, *op. cit.*, pp. 244 and 249.
25. See Anthony Oberschall, "The Los Angeles Riot of August, 1965," *Social Problems*, Vol. 15 (Winter 1968), pp. 322–41.
26. I received an excellent personal view of the impact of the new black consciousness on youth while teaching Afro-American history to junior high school youth each summer in a black community near San Francisco. In 1966, I showed the youths a picture of Crispus Attucks, and some exclaimed, "He's sure got a nappy head." In 1967 this same picture was greeted with the comment, "He's got a boss natural." This was the same community and some of the same youth. The only thing that had changed was their consciousness of themselves.

White Southerners

Lewis M. Killian

1. Herbert Blumer, "The Future of the Color Line," in *The South in Continuity and Change*, ed. John C. McKinney and Edgar T. Thompson (Durham, N.C.: Duke University Press, 1965), p. 323.
2. Milton M. Gordon, *Assimilation in American Life* (New York: Oxford University Press, 1964), chap. 3.
3. Blumer, "The Future of the Color Line," pp. 324–25.
4. See Harold U. Faulkner, *Politics, Reform and Expansion* (New York: Harper, 1959), p. 270; and Herbert Shapiro, "The Populists and the Negro: A Reconsideration," in August Meier and Elliott Rudwick, *The Making of Black America* (New York: Atheneum, 1969), Vol. II, pp. 27–36.
5. Ellis G. Arnall, *The Shore Dimly Seen* (New York: Lippincott, 1946).
6. *Ibid.*, p. 99.

7. Lillian Smith, "Addressed to White Liberals," in *Primer for White Folks*, ed. Bucklin Moon (Garden City, N.Y.: Doubleday, 1946), p. 487.
8. Blumer, "The Future of the Color Line," p. 323.
9. *Ibid.*, p. 328.
10. James Baldwin, *Nobody Knows My Name* (New York: Dell, 1961), p. 70.
11. Bertram W. Doyle, *The Etiquette of Race Relations in the South* (Chicago: University of Chicago Press, 1937).
12. Quoted in Doyle, *ibid.*, p. xxi.
13. *Ibid.*, p. xvi.
14. Sarah Patton Boyle, "Inside a Segregationist," in *White on Black*, ed. Era Bell Thompson and Herbert Nipson (Chicago: Johnson Publishing, 1963), p. 48.
15. *Ibid.*, p. 49.
16. *Ibid.*
17. Olive Quinn, "The Transmission of Racial Attitudes Among White Southerners," *Social Forces* 33 (October 1954), 41.
18. *Ibid.*, p. 45.
19. Bobby Seale, *Seize the Time* (New York: Random House, 1968), pp. 88–89.
20. Pierce L. van den Berghe, *Race and Racism* (New York: Wiley, 1967), p. 21.
21. Gunnar Myrdal, *An American Dilemma* (New York: Harper, 1944), p. 470.
22. Will Campbell, "The Faith of a Fatalist," *New South* 23 (Spring 1968): 54.
23. Myrdal, *American Dilemma*, p. 470.
24. Charles J. Levy, *Voluntary Servitude* (New York: Appleton-Century-Crofts, 1968), p. 8.
25. James M. Dabbs, *The Southern Heritage* (New York: Knopf, 1958).
26. "New South Notes," *New South*, 25 (Spring 1970): 1.
27. Frank P. Graham, *A Hundred Years Later* (Atlanta: Southern Regional Council, 1962), pp. 25–26.
28. Leslie W. Dunbar, "Middle-Age Thoughts," *New South* 25 (Spring 1970): 4.
29. *Ibid.*

The Silent Majority
Norbert Wiley

1. Quoted in C. Vann Woodward, *Tom Watson, Agrarian Rebel* (New York: Oxford University Press, 1963), p. 220.
2. Harold M. Baron, "The Web of Urban Racism," in Louis L. Knowles and Kenneth Prewitt (eds.), *Institutional Racism in America* (Englewood Cliffs, N.J.: Prentice-Hall, 1969), pp. 134–76.

The Irish
Andrew M. Greeley

1. Sister Marie Leonore Fell, *The Foundations of Nativism in American Textbooks, 1783–1860* (Washington: Catholic University of America Press, 1941), p. 170. I am grateful to Daniel Patrick Moynihan for bringing this passage to my attention.
2. *Ibid.*, p. 171.
3. Leonard Patrick O'Connor Wibberley, *The Coming of the Green* (New York: Henry Holt, 1958), p. 49.
4. We here follow the conclusion of Professor Philip Converse and his colleagues that John Kennedy lost a net of 5,000,000 votes because of his religion.
5. One of the ironies of the 1970 election in Cook County was that Cicero and Berwyn, the most blatantly white suburbs in the county, are represented in the U.S. Congress by a black representative. Conveniently for the Organization, the gentleman has a name which sounds Irish. There were, you can depend on it, no pictures of him in campaign posters in Cicero or Berwyn.
6. It will be obvious to the reader that in the second half of the article I have been forced to rely almost entirely on impression and instinct. A good social scientist would dearly love to have much more in the way of "hard" data to substantiate his hunches and instincts but, alas, there is little in the way of hard data on any American immigrant group, and there lurks in the depths of my Celtic soul the primordial intuition which says that I'm right even without the data. The reader is, therefore, duly warned.

The Jews
Murray Friedman

1. For information on early Jewish participation in the antislavery movement see the pioneer essay by Maxwell Whiteman in *The Kidnapped and the Ransomed* (Philadelphia: Jewish Publication Society of America, 1970).
2. *New York Times*, January 23, 1969.
3. David W. Abbott, Louis H. Gold, and Edward T. Rogowsky, *Police, Politics and Race: The New York City Referendum on Civilian Review* (A Publication of the American Jewish Committee and The Joint Center for Urban Studies of the Massachusetts Institute of Technology and Harvard University, 1969), pp. 2 and 13.
4. Henry Cohen and Gary Sandrow, *Philadelphia Chooses a Mayor, 1971* (The American Jewish Committee, 1972).
5. Lenora E. Berson, *The Negroes and the Jews* (New York: Random House, 1971), p. 187.

6. As quoted in Harvey Brotz, *The Black Jews of Harlem* (New York: Free Press of Glencoe, 1964).
7. Murray Friedman, "Is White Racism the Problem?" *Commentary*, January 1969, pp. 61–65. See also Ben Halpern, *Jews and Blacks* (New York: Herder and Herder, 1971).
8. Robert Alter, "Israel and the Intellectuals," *Commentary*, October 1967, pp. 46–52. Publication of Arthur Morse's *When Six Million Died*, (New York: Random House, 1968), showing that Franklin D. Roosevelt, a hero to many Jews, procrastinated in using American resources to rescue Jews from the Nazis has also added to the skepticism of some Jews about outsiders as the guardians of Jewish interests.
9. Richard L. Rubenstein, "Jews, Negroes and the New Politics," *Reconstructionist* (November 17, 1967), p. 15. It is, nevertheless, a peculiar sort of conservatism that finds 81 percent of Jews voting for Hubert Humphrey in 1968.
10. Nathan Glazer, "Social Characteristics of American Jews, 1654–1954," *American Jewish Year Book*, Vol. 56, American Jewish Committee and the Jewish Publication Society of America, New York, 1955, pp. 3–36.
11. Stephen Steinberg, "How Jewish Quotas Began" (September 1971); Earl Raab, "Quotas by Any Other Name" (January 1972), and Paul Seabury, "HEW and the Universities" (February 1972).
12. Daniel P. Moynihan, "The New Racialism," *Atlantic* (August 1968): 39.
13. The Black Panther Party—The Anti-Semitic and Anti-Israel Component (prepared by Trends Analysis Division, American Jewish Committee, January 23, 1970).
14. Ultimately, Dr. Arnold H. Einhorn, who had been informed he was being replaced because of a need for a director "of a different ethnic background," was reinstated and later rotated to another hospital. *New York Times* (December 21, 1970).
15. Gary T. Marx, *Protest and Prejudice* (New York: Harper & Row, 1967). A revised edition published by Harper Torchbooks with a 27-page Postscript appeared in 1969. Gertrude J. Selznick and Stephen Steinberg, *The Tenacity of Prejudice: Anti-Semitism in Contemporary America* (New York: Harper & Row, 1969).
16. See *Survey of Jewish Businessmen Operating in Selected Inner City Areas of Philadelphia* (Center For Community Studies of Temple University and Jewish Community Relations Council of Greater Philadelphia), 20 pp. The "typical" Jewish businessman in the nine areas covered in this study has been operating in his location for 23 years and is about 55 years old. Forty per cent are over sixty. Only 25 per cent extend credit. Fifty per cent who responded to the questionnaire said they planned to stay in business in the area, 49 per cent wanted to get out, and 1 per cent was undecided. Twenty-five per cent of the respondents said they

had been held up at least once, one man reported 11 holdups. Fifty-two per cent said their businesses had been vandalized; 52 per cent had been burglarized, and 54 per cent claimed shoplifting was increasing.

17. Milton Himmelfarb, "Negroes, Jews, and Muzhiks," *Commentary* (October 1966): 83.
18. The theologist-social scientist, Richard L. Rubenstein, was one of the first Jewish intellectuals to abandon the Black-Jewish alliance largely because of this fear. "Jews constitute a highly visible minority near the top of the economic ladder without real power," he wrote in 1968. "As such they arouse envy. They are disliked. They can be easily displaced. This has happened elsewhere. It can happen here. Furthermore, the American Jew lacks the disruptive power which makes a measure of violence a real option for the Negro. American Jews are by training and disposition incapable of utilizing violence to attain a social objective. The Negro knows that he has great power to disrupt the normal functioning of American urban society. If he utilizes this capacity intelligently he can extract important concessions from the White community." "The Politics of Powerlessness," *Reconstructionist* (May 17, 1968): 12.
19. Earl Raab, "The Black Revolution and the Jewish Question," *Commentary* (January 1969): p. 30.
20. Review of Proposed Administrators Training Program (undated) (School District of Philadelphia: Office of the Superintendent of Schools).
21. Berson, *The Negroes* . . . , p. 508.
22. Tom Wolfe, "Radical Chic: That Party at Lenny's," *New York* (June 8, 1970): 26–56. Many Jewish scholars and intellectuals have identified also with Blacks in the political positions they take and in their scholarly interests. In a review of recent studies by Gary T. Marx and Gertrude J. Selznick and Stephen Steinberg that deal with Negro anti-Semitism Lucy Dawidowicz has charged they have minimized its current significance. "Can Anti-Semitism Be Measured," *Commentary* (July 1970): 42.
23. Milton Himmelfarb, "Jewish Class Conflict?" *Commentary* (January 1970): 37–42.
24. Samuel Z. Klausner and David P. Varody, "Synagogues Without Ghettos," February 1970, unpublished manuscript (University of Pennsylvania: Center for Research on the Acts of Man), p. 186.
25. Abbott, Gold, and Rogowsky, *Police, Politics and Race*, p. 43.
26. Louis Harris and Associates, Inc., *Sources of Racial and Religious Tensions in New York City*, Study No. 1925 (July 1969): p. 150.
27. Murray Friedman, "Intergroup Relations and Tensions in the United States," *American Jewish Year Book*, 1972, Vol. 72 (New York and Philadelphia: American Jewish Committee and Jewish Publication Society of America).

28. Philip Perlmutter, "Vigilantism in Our Urban Badlands," *Reconstructionist*, 36 (March 27, 1970), p. 17.
29. Friedman, "Intergroup Relations."
30. Haskell L. Lazere, "Haganah W.S.A.?" *Dimensions in American Judaism* 4 (Spring 1970): 10.
31. Perlmutter, "Vigilantism . . . ," p. 22. "Jews in our urban badlands know the dangers, feel them, and live them, just as Blacks know, feel, and live them. It is they who should be listened and responded to—and it is here where the opponents of community defense are at their most irrelevant, for their public condemnations are barren of hope, promise, and remedy, and thereby certain to intensify the helplessness and desperation and militancy of the poor."
32. Dorothy Rabinowitz, *The Other Jews: Portraits in Poverty* (Institute of Human Relations Press of the American Jewish Committee, 1972).
33. One interesting datum reported by Arnold Schwartz is that 15 per cent of Jews in 1967–68 had incomes under $5,000. "Some Recent Reports on The Education, Occupations, and Income of American Jews," *American Jewish Committee Information and Research Services* (October 1969): 4.
34. Arthur Waskow, "A Radical Haggadah for Passover," *Ramparts* (April 1969): 25–33.
35. Nathan Glazer, *Jewish Journal of Sociology* (December 1969): 130.
36. The strongest supporters of Negroes today appear to be nonaffiliated Jews. Asked in the Harris poll whether Blacks in New York are justified in their demands, 60 per cent responded they are, and only 8 per cent said they are not.
37. Berson, *The Negroes* . . . , p. 431.
38. *Survey of Jewish Businessmen*, p. 1. George Sternlieb's study of the economics of New York City's housing found that 52 per cent of all-Black buildings and 20 per cent of the buildings that are mostly Black are owned by Black landlords. See letter of Richard Cohen, Associate Executive Director of the American Jewish Congress to *New York Times* (July 20, 1970).
39. The UFT has also entered into a three-year program with the Board of Education to achieve a more equal ethnic balance in New York's schools. During the first year, recruiters hope to bring at least 1,000 new black and Hispanic teachers into the city system. *The United Teacher* (December 13, 1970).
40. Maurice J. Goldbloom, "Is There a Backlash Vote?" *Commentary* (August 1969): 19.

Black Politicians
Chuck Stone

1. J. C. Harris, "Life of Henry Grady" (New York, 1890).

2. "Report of the National Advisory Commission of Civil Disorders" (March 1968): p. 10.
3. Published in 1965 as an official document of the U.S. Department of Labor, it also became known as "The Moynihan Report." At the 1965 White House Conference on Civil Rights in Washington, D.C., civil rights leaders almost unanimously attacked the report as racist.
4. In the 1968 Presidential election, Nixon received 9 per cent of the Black vote. In his 1972 re-election bid, he received 15 per cent of the Black vote, making Blacks the only significant group in America to vote against Nixon.
5. For a more extensive discussion of the Black vote's historical record in local, state, and national elections and its role as a "balance of power" in such elections, see chapter four, "The Negro Vote: Ceterus Paribus," in *Black Political Power in America* by Chuck Stone (New York: Bobbs-Merrill, 1968).
6. *New York Times Magazine* (September 21, 1958). Quoted in an article by Richard Hughes.
7. P. 13.
8. Frederick Douglass, "My Bondage and My Freedom" (New York, 1855). From a letter written in 1849 to Gerrit Smith, the abolitionist.

White Politicians
Frank Munger

1. (New York: Harcourt, Brace, and World, 1957). John Foster is a pseudonym; the book was in fact written by Governor Foster Furcolo of Massachusetts.
2. From a letter to W. G. McAdoo, quoted in Edmund A. Moore, *A Catholic Runs for President: The Campaign of 1928* (New York: Ronald Press, 1956), p. 114.
3. Quoted in William A. Osborne, *The Segregated Covenant: Race Relations and American Catholics* (New York: Herder and Herder, 1967), p. 124.
4. *Campaign Addresses of Governor Alfred E. Smith, Democratic Candidate for President, 1928* (Washington, D.C.: Democratic National Committee, 1929), p. 25.
5. Norman Hapgood and Henry Moskowitz, *Up from the City Streets: Alfred E. Smith, A Biographical Study in Contemporary Politics* (New York: Harcourt, Brace, 1927), p. 141. See also: Henry F. Pringle, *Alfred E. Smith: A Critical Study* (New York: Macy-Masius, 1927); Alfred E. Smith, *Up to Now: An Autobiography* (New York: Viking, 1929); Emily Smith Warner, *The Happy Warrior: The Story of My Father, Alfred E. Smith* (Garden City, N.Y.: Doubleday, 1956); Oscar Handlin, *Al Smith and His America* (Boston: Little, Brown, 1958); and Robert Moses, *A Tribute to Governor Smith* (New York: Simon and Schuster, 1962).

6. Walter F. White, *A Man Called White* (New York: Viking Press, 1948), pp. 99–101.
7. The state campaign is described in Hugh Dorsey Reagan, "The Presidential Campaign of 1928 in Alabama" (Ph.D diss., University of Texas, 1961).
8. One exception might be said to be David Burner, in *The Politics of Provincialism: The Democratic Party in Transition, 1918–1932* (New York: Knopf, 1968)—he devotes two sentences to the racist campaign for Smith in the South (p. 225). Burner also documents the fact that Smith received substantial black support in his own New York State—though less, apparently, than a majority—but in Chicago polled only traditional, pre-1920 Democratic party support among Negroes.
9. Theodore G. Sorensen, *Kennedy* (New York: Harper & Row, 1965), p. 471.
10. *Ibid.*
11. The evidence for this interpretation of the 1956 and 1960 nominations is presented in greater detail in Frank Munger and James Blackhurst, "Factionalism in the National Conventions, 1940–1964: An Analysis of Ideological Consistency in State Delegation Voting," *Journal of Politics* 27 (1965): 375–94.
12. In all fairness to Sorensen, it should be noted that he argues that Kennedy's experiences as president did make him a confirmed and committed supporter of civil rights, whatever his previous state of mind may have been.
13. Examination of the frankly political memoirs of the Roosevelt period shows an astonishing lack of interest on Roosevelt's part in Negro reactions. Thus, Edward J. Flynn in *You're the Boss* (New York: Viking, 1947) manages to discuss New York City politics without one reference to Adam Clayton Powell or to the beginnings of a black settlement in Flynn's own Bronx. His only reference to blacks in national terms occurs in discussing the 1944 vice-presidential nomination, when he cites, among other reasons for James Byrnes's "unavailability," the fact that "since he came from South Carolina the question of the Negro vote would be raised." He then remarks that Truman, on the other hand, "had never made any 'racial' remarks," and, in an often-quoted comment, "just dropped into the slot" (pp. 180–81). On the all-white politics of the Democratic party in the 1930s, see also James A. Farley, *Jim Farley's Story: The Roosevelt Years* (New York: McGraw-Hill, 1948). Both Flynn and Farley seem to have been far more concerned over the failure of politicians to give due recognition to women than their indifference to blacks. Farley's views on equal rights for women are the subject of a full chapter in John T. Casey and James Bowles, *Farley and Tomorrow* (Chicago: Reilly and Lee, 1937), pp. 216–30.

14. Samuel Lubell, *The Future of American Politics*, 3rd ed. (New York: Harper & Row, 1965), p. 26.
15. The one possible exception to this generalization for the time span referred to may have been Wendell Willkie. There is some evidence to indicate that Willkie held a strong, personal, but largely hidden commitment to racial equality on which he planned to act only after election as president, but the record is too incomplete for certainty. See, however, particularly, Joseph Barnes, *Willkie: The Events He Was Part Of, The Ideas He Fought For* (New York: Simon and Schuster, 1952), but also Mary Earlhart Dillon, *Wendell Willkie* (New York: Lippincott, 1952); Donald B. Johnson, *The Republican Party and Wendell Willkie* (Urbana: University of Illinois Press, 1960); and Ellsworth Barnard, *Wendell Willkie: Fighter for Freedom* (Marquette: Northern Michigan University Press, 1966); as well as Wendell Willkie's own *An American Program* (New York: Simon and Schuster, 1944).
16. These great days in Chicago politics have been vividly described in Lloyd Wendt and Herman Kogan, *Big Bill of Chicago* (Indianapolis: Bobbs-Merrill, 1953).
17. The circumstances of Yorty's first election are described in Charles G. Mayo, "The 1961 Mayoralty Election in Los Angeles: The Political Party in a Nonpartisan Election," *Western Political Quarterly* 17 (1964): 325–37.
18. Martin Meyerson and Edward C. Banfield, *Politics, Planning, and the Public Interest: The Case of Public Housing in Chicago* (Glencoe, Ill.: Free Press, 1955).
19. This is why Mike Royko's account of the Daley political style is so unsatisfactory: he never comes to grips with the question of how the racist monster he describes continues to sweep the black wards of Chicago in election after election. *Boss: Richard J. Daley of Chicago* (New York: New American Library, 1971).
20. The reference is to the distinction drawn by Edward Banfield and James Q. Wilson between public-regardingness and private-regardingness in political culture. For an elaboration of these concepts, see their "Public-Regardingness as a Value Premise in Voting Behavior," *American Political Science Review* 58 (1964): 876–87. A critique of the categorization can be found in Raymond Wolfinger and John Osgood Field, "Political Ethos and the Structure of City Government," *American Political Science Review* 60 (1966): 306–26; with a rebuttal by the authors at 998–1000.
21. Osborne, *Segregated Covenant.*
22. James Q. Wilson, *Negro Politics: The Search for Leadership* (Glencoe, Ill.: Free Press, 1960).
23. Marvin G. Weinbaum, "A Minority's Survival: The Republican Party of New York County, 1897–1960" (Ph.D. diss., Columbia University, 1965).

24. Irish control of Tammany was finally ended by the election of an Italian, Carmine De Sapio, in 1949.
25. John Albert Morsell, "The Political Behavior of Negroes in New York City" (Ph.D. diss., Columbia University, 1950).
26. Theodore J. Lowi, *At the Pleasure of the Mayor: Patronage and Power in New York City, 1898–1958* (Glencoe, Ill.: Free Press, 1964).
27. Morsell, "The Political Behavior. . . ."
28. Brooke's views, expressed at various times, are cited in *The New York Times* (June 28, 1970).
29. Nathan Glazer and Daniel Patrick Moynihan, *Beyond the Melting Pot: The Negroes, Puerto Ricans, Jews, Italians, and Irish of New York City* (Cambridge, Mass.: MIT and Harvard University Presses, 1963), pp. 208–16.
30. The argument makes, of course, the shaky assumption that blacks did not exist before their arrival in Northern cities during the First World War, but the assumption is realistic so long as the viewpoint is that of the city politician.

Policemen
Lawrence Rosen

1. Of course, the prime concern in this paper is the white policeman, and whenever the data allow us to refer to white policemen we will do so. However, in some instances this will be impossible, and in those circumstances any conclusions must be taken to refer to *all* police. In addition, unless otherwise indicated, the reference will be to patrolmen, and not officers or police assigned to special units (detectives, traffic, community relations, and so forth).
2. The *highly prejudiced* remarks referred to were: ". . . Negroes as sub-human, suggested an extreme solution to the 'Negro Problem,' expressed dislike to the point of hatred, or used very pejorative nicknames" (e.g. "These scum aren't people," "Bastard savages", "Filthy pigs"). *Prejudiced* remarks were those that "showed general dislike for Negroes as a group without making 'extreme' statements" (e.g. "Most of these Niggers are too lazy to work for a living"). (Black and Reiss, 1966, p. 133).
3. According to the official arrest statistics for traditional crimes (assault, robbery, theft, etc.), this belief is a "correct" one, even allowing for possible biases in the arrest statistics.
4. Kephart (1957) in the early 1950's found the same tendency among Philadelphia policemen (white) to inflate the black crime rate.
5. Some caution must be exercised in comparing the results in time periods 2 and 3; for it is possible that the attitudes and beliefs of those who left the force in that time period were quite different from those who remained. Therefore, it is difficult to say if any changes (or lack of changes) in the distributions were affected in any appreciable way by

those who were "lost" to the sample. However, there is no problem in using the results of the different time periods to describe "collective" attitudes of the police at the respective time periods, which may be due to persons of certain attitudes leaving the force or any changes (or lack of changes) of those that remain.

6. James Q. Wilson (1968) makes note of the same tendency: ". . . the police officer sees the struggle over police-minority relations primarily as political efforts to challenge the authority of individual police officers and constrain them by threatening their career interests—their salaries, promotion prospects, self-respect, and morale. He sees challenges by Negroes as no different from the challenges of politicians or any other outside group, all of which are equally resented even when they cannot be resisted." (p. 231)
7. This action is not necessarily the same as a formal "arrest," an action which is part of the "booking" procedure at the station. Since the Black and Reiss study dealt primarily with observation of "field actions" it is the decision to "take into custody" that was being researched. It is likely, however, that the majority of such persons were subsequently "arrested."
8. The issue, of course, is more complicated than this statement implies. The thesis of "under arrest" is only for selected types of offenses, and therefore, over-all arrest rates do not constitute an adequate test of the thesis.
9. In slightly less than three-fourths of police encounters involving a criminal suspect, there is also a complainant involved (Black, 1968, pp. 94 and 158).

Bibliography

Bayley, David H., and Harold Mendelsohn. *Minorities and the Police: Confrontation in America* (New York: Free Press, 1969).

Black, Donald J. *Police Encounters and Social Organization: An Observation Study* (University of Michigan: unpublished Ph.D. Dissertation, 1968).

Black, Donald J., and Albert J. Reiss, Jr. "Police and Citizen Behavior in Field Encounters: Some Comparisons According to the Race and Social Class Status of Citizens." Report prepared for the President's Commission on Law Enforcement and the Administration of Justice (1967).

———. "Police Control of Juveniles." *American Sociological Review* 35 (February 1970): 63–77.

Bodine, George E. "Factors Related to Police Dispositions of Juvenile Offender" (Montreal, Canada: American Sociological Association, unpublished paper, August 31, 1964).

Bouma, Donald. *Kids and Cops: A Study in Mutual Hostility* (Grand Rapids, Mich. William B. Eerdmans, 1969).

Ferdinand, Theodore N., and Elmer G. Luchterhand. "Inner-City Youth, the Police, the Juvenile Court, and Justice," *Social Problems* 17 (Spring 1970): 510–27.

Groves, W. Eugene, and Peter H. Rossi. "Police Perceptions of a Hostile Ghetto: Realism or Projection," *American Behavioral Scientist* 13 (May–August 1970): 727–44.

Hohenstein, William H. "Factors Influencing the Police Disposition of Juvenile Offenders," pp. 138–49 in Thorsten Sellin and Marvin E. Wolfgang (eds.), *Delinquency: Selected Studies.* (New York: J. Wiley, 1969).

Kephart, William M. *Racial Factors and Urban Law Enforcement* (Philadelphia: University of Pennsylvania Press, 1957).

Lohman, Joseph D., and Gordon E. Misner. *The Police and the Community: A report to the President's Commission on Law Enforcement and the Administration of Justice* (Washington, D.C.: U.S. Government Printing Office, 1966).

McEachern, A. W., and Riva Bauzer. "Factors Related to Disposition in Juvenile Police Contacts," pp. 148–60 in Malcolm W. Klein (ed.), *Juvenile Gangs in Context* (Englewood Cliffs, N.J.: Prentice-Hall, 1967).

McNamara, John H. "Uncertainties in Police Work: The Relevance of Police Recruits' Backgrounds and Training," pp. 163–252 in David J. Bordua (ed.), *The Police* (New York: J. Wiley, 1967).

Mendelsohn, Robert A. "Police-Community Relations: A Need in Search of Police Support," *American Behavioral Scientist* 13 (May–August 1970): 745–60.

Niederhoffer, Arthur. *Behind the Shield: The Police in Urban Society* (New York: Doubleday, 1967).

Piliavin, Irving, and Scott Briar. "Police Encounters with Juveniles," *American Journal of Sociology* 70 (1964): 206–14.

Reiss, Albert J., Jr. "Police Brutality—Answers to Key Questions." *Transaction* 5 (July/August 1968): 10–19.

———. and David J. Bordua. "Environment and Organization: A Perspective on the Police," pp. 25–55 in David J. Bordua (ed.), *The Police* (New York: J. Wiley, 1967).

Rossi, Peter H., et al. "Between White and Black: The Faces of American Institutions in the Ghetto," pp. 71–215 in *Supplemental Studies for the National Advisory Commission on Civil Disorders* (Washington, D.C.: U.S. Government Printing Office, 1968).

Savitz, Leonard. *Socialization of Police* (Philadelphia: unpublished data, 1971).

Skolnick, Jerome H. *Justice without Trial* (New York: J. Wiley, 1966)

Smith, A. B., B. Locke, and W. F. Walker. "Authoritarianism in Police College Students and Non-Police College Students," *The Journal of Criminal Law, Criminology and Police Science* 59 (September 1968): 440–43.

Terry, Robert M. "Discrimination in the Handling of Juvenile Offenders by Social Control Agencies," *Journal of Research in Crime and Delinquency* (July 1967): 218–30.

Wilson, James Q. "The Police and the Delinquent in Two Cities," pp. 9–30 in Stanton Wheeler (ed.), *Controlling Delinquents* (New York: J. Wiley, 1968).

———. *Varieties of Police Behavior* (Cambridge, Mass.: Harvard University Press, 1968).

White Professors
Robert Blauner

1. As early as 1963 Murray Friedman diagnosed the situation:

> Liberal whites are, consequently, caught in the dilemma of believing in equal rights for Negroes and even of working for them, while at the same time attempting to escape from the real and fancied disadvantages of desegregation. . . . The liberal white is increasingly uneasy about the nature and consequences of the Negro revolt. . . . In the final analysis, a liberal, white, middle-class society wants to have change, but without trouble. . . . In other words, to the Negro demand for "now," to which the deep South has replied "never," many liberal whites are increasingly responding "later." But the Negro will accept nothing short of first-class citizenship, now.

"The White Liberal's Retreat," in Alan Weston, *Freedom Now* (New York: Basic Books, 1964), pp. 320–28. See also Charles Fager, *White Reflections on Black Power* (Grand Rapids, Mich.: Eerdmans, 1967); and Charles Levy, *Voluntary Servitude* (New York: Appleton, 1968).

2. See Harry Edwards, *Black Students* (New York: The Free Press, 1970), pp. 64–65. For two accounts dealing with Berkeley, see J. Herman Blake, "Racism at a Great University: The Agony and the Rage," *Negro Digest 16*, no. 5 (March 1967), 9–15; and George Napper, "The Black Student Movement: Problems of Unity," Doctoral dissertation, School of Criminology, University of California, Berkeley (1970).
3. These estimates are calculated from data in Christopher Jencks and David Riesman, *The Academic Revolution* (Garden City, N.Y.: Doubleday, 1968), p. 440.
4. The National Survey of the Carnegie Commission on Higher Education (in cooperation with the American Council on Education), directed by Clark Kerr and Logan Wilson, is a study of more than 300 colleges and universities that was conducted in 1969. The findings I quote here and later in the paper are preliminary prepublication data tabulated by the Survey Research Center, University of California, Berkeley. I am grateful to Stephen Steinberg for providing me with these statistics.
5. Cf. Paul Lazarsfeld and W. Thielens, *The Academic Mind* (New York: The Free Press, 1958).
6. The liberalism of the university and its professors is stressed by two leading critics of contemporary student movements, Daniel Bell and John Bunzel. See Bell, "Columbia and the New Left" and Bunzel, "Black Studies at San Francisco State." Both appear in *The Public Interest, 13* (Fall 1968). Immanuel Wallerstein and Paul Starr have subtitled vol. 1 of their valuable *The University Crisis Reader*, "The Liberal University Under Attack" (New York: Vintage, 1971).
7. Clark Kerr's analysis of the multiversity, its many publics and constituencies and the mediating role of the university president that follows from them, is also a useful framework for understanding this receptivity of the administrator. C. Kerr, *The Uses of the Multiversity* (Cambridge: Harvard University Press, 1963).
8. On the faculty as a privileged group, see Kerr, *op. cit.*, pp. 42–44,

109–110; James Ridgeway, *The Closed Corporation* (New York: Random House, 1968) concentrates on the professor's special opportunities for lucrative consulting and business operations. See also, Richard Lichtman, "The University: Mask for Privilege?" in Wallerstein and Starr, *op. cit.*, vol. 1, pp. 101–20.

9. Provocative discussions of academic values in the face of campus racial conflict appear in Cushing Strout and David I. Grossvogel, eds., *Divided We Stand: Reflections on the Crisis at Cornell* (Garden City, N.Y.: Doubleday, 1970). See especially the address by George Kahin, "A Personal Narrative of a Rude Awakening" by Cushing Strout and "The University in Transition" by David I. Grossvogel. The latter argues that academic freedom often becomes a shield for privilege and noncommitment.
10. *New York Times* (July 21, 1968).
11. See Wallerstein and Starr, *op. cit.*, vol. 1, pp. 295 ff.
12. *New York Times* (September 18, 1969), 43. For the changes at Harvard see Lawrence E. Eichel, *et al., The Harvard Strike* (Boston: Houghton Mifflin, 1970), p. 15; and for Northwestern, see Wallerstein and Starr, *op. cit.*, p. 300.
13. *Chronicle for Higher Education,* 5 (March 29, 1971).
14. William H. Friedland and Harry Edwards, "Confrontation at Cornell," *Trans-action* (June 1969), 32.
15. *New York Times* (October 14, 1969).
16. Julie Paynter, "Graduate Opportunities for Black Students," unpublished, c/o Julie Paynter, 6753 S. Chappel Ave., Chicago, Illinois 60649.
17. *Chronicle of Higher Education,* 5 (April 12, 1971).
18. Martin Trow, "Reflections on the Transition from Mass to Universal Higher Education," *Daedalus* (Winter 1970).
19. Wallerstein and Starr, *op. cit.*, vol. 1, p. 297.
20. In an article which also identifies universalism as central to the liberal philosophy and discusses its implications for race and ethnicity in education, Lawrence Fein makes a parallel point: "The corollary of the liberal ethic that white people ought not to pay attention to the blackness of Negroes was the proposition that Negroes ought not to pay attention to their own blackness." "The Limits of Liberalism," *Saturday Review of Books* (June 20, 1970), 84.
21. The statement is Peter Winograd's, *New York Times* (October 9, 1969), in the article "More Blacks Turning to the Study of Law," by Lesley Oelsner.
22. Fein, *op. cit.*, p. 96.
23. Eichel, *et al., op. cit.*, p. 279.
24. An extreme statement of this position is found in Seymour Martin Lipset, *Political Man* (Garden City, N.Y.: Doubleday, 1960).
25. Strout and Grossvogel, *op. cit.*, and Friedland and Edwards, *op. cit.*

26. At Cornell it was an economics instructor whose Spring 1968 course on poverty provoked a protest of black students. This proved to be one of the precipitating events that led to the large-scale crisis one year later. See Strout and Grossvogel, *op. cit.*, pp. 5–11.
27. Badi G. Foster, "Toward a Definition of Black Referents" in Vernon J. Dixon and B. Foster, eds., *Beyond Black or White* (Boston: Little, Brown, 1971), esp. pp. 17–19.
28. For example, see Martin Kilson, *et al., Black Studies: Myths and Realities* (New York: A. Philip Randolph Educational Fund, 1969), which includes contributions by Thomas Sowell, Andrew Brimmer, Norman Hill, Martin Kilson, and C. Vann Woodward, as well as Rustin, Clark, and Wilkins.
29. Friedland and Edwards, *op. cit.*, p. 32.
30. George Kahin in Strout and Grossvogel, *op. cit.*, p. 32 ff.
31. Wallerstein and Starr, *op. cit.*, vol. 1, p. 306.
32. For a clear formulation of this position see the policy statement of Northwestern black studenhs in Wallerstein and Starr, *op. cit.*, vol. 1, p. 303.
33. Harold Cruse, *The Crisis of the Negro Intellectual* (New York: Morrow, 1967), p. 365.
34. See for example the remarks of the white participants in the Yale symposium, *Black Studies in the University*, ed. Armstead I. Robinson, *et al.*, (New Haven: Yale University Press, 1969).
35. On the role of the black administrator, see Roosevelt Johnson, "Black Administrators and Higher Education," *Black Scholar, 1*, no. 1 (November 1969), 66–76.

Radical Students
Jan E. Dizard

*Several friends have been invaluable to me in writing this essay. David T. Wellman's sharp criticisms have consistently prodded me to whatever clarity I have been able to achieve here. In addition, Robert Cole and Charles A. Goldsmid have read parts of the article and their suggestions and encouragement are most gratefully acknowledged. Robin Dizard has long suffered my cumbersome writing and has again patiently labored to make my writing readable. Finally, I would like to record my indebtedness to the student radicals I analyze: I trust they will understand the criticisms here as a product of my own involvement with them and as an expression of my optimism.

1. Several excellent studies of the New Left are available that relate in detail these similarities. See Richard Flacks, "The Liberated Generation: An Exploration of the Roots of Student Protest," *Journal of Social Issues* 23 (July 1967): 52–75; Kenneth Keniston, *Young*

Radicals: Notes on Committed Youth (New York: Harcourt, Brace and World, 1968).

2. The following overview is based on the following works: Paul Jacobs and Saul Landau, *The New Radicals* (New York: Random House, 1966); Massimo Teodori, *The New Left: A Documentary History* (Indianapolis: Bobbs-Merrill, 1969); Howard Zinn, *SNCC: The New Abolitionists* (New York: Knopf, 1965); and Terrence Cannon and David Wellman, "No Hiding Place: White Radicals and the Civil Rights Movement," unpublished manuscript, 1967. In addition, after this paper was largely written I had occasion to read three as yet unpublished papers which helped me to clarify certain points. I regret that I was unable to more fully digest and explore the wealth of ideas they raise. See Richard Flacks, "The New Left and American Politics: After Ten Years," paper presented at annual meeting, American Political Science Association, Los Angeles, September, 1970; Flacks, "Beyond Student Protest," paper presented at annual meetings, Society for the Study of Social Problems, Washington, D.C., August, 1970; and Milton Mankoff and Richard Flacks, "The Changing Social Base of the American Student Movement: Its Meaning and Implications," *The Annals*, 395 (May, 1971): 54–67.
3. See "The Port Huron Statement," Students for a Democratic Society (reprinted in Jacobs and Landau, *The New Radicals*, pp. 149–62. Also, Flacks, "The New Left and American Politics: After Ten Years."
4. See Teodori, *The New Left*, pp. 163–82 for a selection from New Left documents that chronicle this transformation.
5. See Zinn, *SNCC*, p. 190 ff. One incident in the March stands out as representative of this split. John Lewis, then chairman of SNCC, was to deliver an address in which he would voice the young radicals' strong criticism of the liberal Kennedy administration. He was prevailed upon by the more moderate forces in the coalition to censor his critical remarks for fear of alienating the liberal politicians.
6. See Todd Gitlin, "The Radical Potential of the Poor," *International Socialist Journal*, 25 (December 1967); and Todd Gitlin and Nanci Hollander, *Uptown* (New York: Harper & Row, 1970), pp. xxi–xxvi.
7. For a brief discussion of this split, see Teodori, *The New Left*, pp. 60–63.
8. I am thinking here especially of the work that provided a fresh look at the class structure of modern America. See Teodori, *The New Left*, pp. 80–83. This discussion was updated by H. Gintis, "The New Working Class and Revolutionary Youth," *Socialist Revolution*, 1, 3 (1970): 13–42.
9. Subsequent events, primarily the mobilizations accompanying the war in Vietnam, have greatly expanded the ranks of student radicals. As a result, serious proposals have been put forward urging that youth, itself, be considered the primary constituency of the new radicals. For

example, see John and Margaret Rowntree, "Youth as a Class," *Our Generation*, 6 (1968): 155–90; and Bruce Franklin, "The Lumpenproletariat and the Revolutionary Youth Movement," *Monthly Review*, 21 (January 1970): 10–25.

10. Personal ambivalences were also involved, and these were not lessened by the fact that SNCC and CORE were the groups most attractive to the young white radicals during the early phase of the Civil Rights Movement. For a discussion of some of the interpersonal dimensions marking the interaction between whites and blacks that created this atmosphere, see Charles J. Levy, *Voluntary Servitude* (New York: Appleton-Century-Crofts, 1968).
11. Actually, each of these three groups engaged in all three strategies. SCLC was the most versatile of the three, and also came closest to meeting the criteria that the student radicals had decided were necessary for the building of an effectual movement. Nevertheless, SCLC and its leader at the time, Martin Luther King, were criticized for their general unwillingness to move beyond episodic demonstrations aimed more at Washington, D.C., than at the masses of black and white people.
12. Each year the statistics on black unemployment, school integration, housing integration, and the like have largely confirmed the apprehensions of the radical whites and the more radical blacks regarding the efficacy of the integrationists' strategy: the large mass of black people have remained poverty-stricken and excluded.
13. In Newark, this interaction was seen as clearly as anywhere. SDS had initiated an organizing project in the black community of Newark in 1964 and had had rough going in spite of the leadership there of Tom Hayden, one of the most able of the new student radicals. Things got considerably worse in the aftermath of the summer uprising in 1967 when LeRoi Jones, who had also based an organization in Newark, oriented around a nationalist and nominally separatist program, denounced the SDS project as having promulgated the riot at the same time that he began appearing at public meetings with leaders of the most reactionary law-and-order factions in Newark.
14. Certain important exceptions can be pointed out, especially the writing of Eugene Genovese and Christopher Lasch. It is important to note, however, that both, while in sympathy with aspects of the student radical movement, were not notably active participants in it. See Eugene Genovese, "The Legacy of Slavery and the Roots of Black Nationalism," *Studies on the Left* 6, 6 (November–December 1966): 3–26; and Christopher Lasch, "The Trouble with Black Power," *The New York Review of Books* (February 29, 1968): 4–13.
15. I am not suggesting here that the growth of nationalism among blacks had no positive effects. I am content, on this matter, to rest with James Boggs's analysis. He writes: "Black Nationalism has created a united

black consciousness, but black consciousness which does not develop into a real and realistic attack on the causes of black oppression can only become false consciousness, in other words, a breeding ground for the cultism, adventurism, and opportunism which are now rampant in the movement." ("The Revolutionary Struggle for Black Power," in Floyd B. Barbour, ed., *The Black 70's* (Boston: Porter Sargent, 1970), p. 40.)

16. A report by Marvin Garson, a participant in the Free Speech Movement and an antiwar activist, discussing a rally held in Oakland, California to celebrate the birthday of Huey Newton, jailed leader of the Black Panthers, is to the point. The rally was also the occasion for announcing the short-lived merger of the Black Panthers and SNCC. Garson wrote (in the *San Francisco Express Times*, February 22, 1968): "Three thousand black people and two thousand whites came to the birthday party for Huey Newton. . . . Black people in the audience understood that they were being asked to join a guerrilla army. White people were wondering where, if at all, they would fit in. They got different answers from the Black Panthers than they did from SNCC. For despite the merger between the two groups, . . . Bobby Seale and Eldridge Cleaver were so far apart from Rap Brown and Stokely Carmichael on the question of white people that it might as well have been a debate." [Seale and Cleaver explicitly rejected antiwhite sentiments; Brown and Carmichael were explicitly antiwhite.] Garson concludes: "White liberation movements looking to form alliances with the black liberation movement would be wise to address themselves to the Panther side of the merger rather than the SNCC side."
17. See Julius Lester's column "Aquarian Notebook" in *Liberation*, 15, 4 (Autumn 1970): 72–74.
18. See Note 1, above.
19. Jerry Farber, *The Student as Nigger* (New York: Simon & Schuster, 1969).
20. 1968 (New York: McGraw-Hill), pp. 82–83.

The Significance of Social and Racial Prisms
William J. Wilson

1. For a more complete discussion of this point, see William J. Wilson, *Power, Racism, and Privilege: Race Relations in Theoretical and Sociohistorical Perspectives* (New York: Macmillan, 1973), Chapters 2–4.
2. Epps was cautious about this generalization, but a recent study found a strong positive relationship between race consciousness, one aspect of cultural pluralism, and education. See William J. Wilson, Castellano B. Turner, and William A. Darity, "Racial Solidarity and Separate Education," *School Review*, in press.

3. Walter Goodman, "Kenneth Clark's Revolutionary Slogan: Just Teach Them to Read!" *New York Times Magazine* (March 18, 1973): 14–15 and 59–65.

A Confusion of Perspectives
Stanley Rothman

1. "The World of the Blue Collar Worker," *Dissent* (Winter 1972).
2. Michael Novak, *The Rise of the Unmeltable Ethnics* (New York: Macmillan, 1971).
3. Edward Banfield, *Unheavenly City* (Boston, 1970).
4. See Winston Moore, Charles P. Livermore, and George F. Galland, Jr., "Woodlawn: The Zone of Destruction," *The Public Interest* (Winter 1972), pp. 42–59.
5. S. M. Lipset and Earl Raab, "The Election and The National Mood." *Commentary* (January 1972), p. 47.
6. Charles Taylor, "Neutrality in Political Science" in Peter Laslett and W. G. Runciman (eds.), *Philosophy, Politics and Society*, third series (Oxford, 1967), pp. 25–57.
7. Peter I. Rose, *They and We* (New York: Random House, 1964).
8. Robert Haddad, *Syrian Christians in Muslim Society* (Princeton, 1970).
9. Ulf Hammelstrand, "Tribalism, Nationalism, Rank Equilibrium and Social Structure," *Journal of Peace Research* (1966), pp. 81–103.
10. R. V. Burks, *The Dynamics of Communism in Eastern Europe* (Princeton, 1961).
11. Clement Henry Moore, *North Africa* (Boston, 1970).
12. Vernon J. Dixon and Badi Foster (eds.), *Beyond Black and White*, (Boston, 1971).
13. Norman Mailer, "The White Negro," *Dissent* (Summer 1957), pp. 276–93.
14. Dotson Rader, *I Ain't Marchin Anymore!* (New York, 1969), p. 6. See also August Meier, "Who Are the True Believers. . . ." in Joseph Gusfield (ed.), *Protest, Reform and Revolt* (New York, 1970), pp. 473–82, and Charles W. Levy, *Voluntary Servitude* (New York, 1968).